Who Would Ever Believe It ?

Allan Lazare

Order this book online at www.trafford.com
or email orders@trafford.com

Most Trafford titles are also available at major online book retailers.

Print information available on the last page.

ISBN: 978-1-6987-0603-0 (sc)
ISBN: 978-1-6987-0601-6 (hc)
ISBN: 978-1-6987-0602-3 (e)

Library of Congress Control Number: 2021903005

Trafford rev. 02/12/2021

www.trafford.com
North America & international
toll-free: 844-688-6899 (USA & Canada)
fax: 812 355 4082

For Arlene, who has shared these experiences with me and is the best partner in life.

And to my greatest achievements, my two children, Marc and Lauren, who make me proud each day.

And to my fabulous grandchildren, Hunter, Sydney, Devin, and Justin, all of whom I love dearly.

Contents

Introduction

This is the story of my unique life and the experiences I have shared with my wife, Arlene. We are two people from Brooklyn who married, moved to Manhattan, and lived a lifestyle that brought us into intimate contact with many of the most famous people in the world. I started out as a dentist in Brooklyn and Arlene as a housewife, raising two children. This book describes my experiences over the last fifty years as I interacted with the most well-known and fascinating personalities in the world. Some of the people involved in the chapters ahead include, in no significant order, Sammy Davis Jr.; Liza Minnelli; Gina Lollobrigida; Paul Simon; Jackie Mason; Farrah Fawcett; Frank Sinatra; Cher; Robert De Niro; Truman Capote; Presidents Clinton, Nixon, Trump, and Reagan; the real housewives of NYC; Steve Rubell; Halston; Don Rickles; Lindsay Wagner; Neil Sedaka; Tony Danza; Michael Feinstein; Jack Haley Jr.; Henry Mancini; Tony Martin; Cyd Charisse; Rocky Graziano; Christopher Reeve; Julie Budd; Lorna Luft; Anthony Quinn; Michael Jackson; Hal David; Joe Pesci; Kate Jackson; Barry Manilow; Leslie Bricusse; Andy Warhol; Madonna; Bette Midler; Jimmy Webb; Elizabeth Taylor; Mike Tyson; Chita Rivera; Robert Goulet; Marvin Hamlisch; Bill Wyman; Sheryl Lee Ralph; Obba Babatundé; Joan Collins; Charlie Sheen; Rhod Gilbert; Alan Cumming; Burt Reynolds; Charles Aznavour; Storm Large; Bill Cosby; Ben Vereen; Howard Stern; Eddie Murphy; Mother Teresa; Martin Scorsese; Federico Fellini; and many more.

Along with the personal interactions with these unique people and nights as regulars at the legendary Studio 54, included is the story of my business adventure, culminating in me inventing a mouthwash and creating a company. It was sold to Pfizer in 1988 in the largest purchase of a private company by Pfizer up to that date.

The following pages chronicle some of my unbelievable experiences. I am not a trained writer nor an English major, so I apologize in advance for my mistakes in grammar, especially in the diary entry chapters. I was always too busy having fun to learn perfect English. This book contains my recollections of encounters and events over many decades. They are not in chronological or any significant order. You will find repetitions of some topics, people, and information in different chapters. Many paragraphs are written in a diary format, even if they are not actual entries; they are my memories that flow from my stream of consciousness and often describe situations that are unrelated and occurring in different periods. I have attempted to write as if I were talking to the reader, and I can go off on tangents as many people do in natural conversations.

CHAPTER

ONE

My Beginning

I grew up in Manhattan Beach in Brooklyn, New York. I was an only child and had two loving parents, named Jack and Helen Lazare. We lived a relatively simple life. We did not travel much, and my parents stayed home most nights. I moved to Manhattan from Brooklyn when I attended Columbia College and New York University (NYU) College of Dentistry. I became a periodontist (a dentist specializing in gum disease) and opened my first office in Brooklyn.

While I was in graduate school, I wrote a textbook called *Periodontal Therapy: A Review*, published by NYU Press. It became standard reading in many dental schools, and my reputation and practice grew quickly. Soon I opened a dental practice in Manhattan, where I lived with my wife, Arlene, and later our two small children, Marc and Lauren.

Arlene and I both loved the nightlife of NYC and all aspects of the entertainment world. That would prove to be a major part of our lives. We had had many memorable, unique experiences and had met and become lifelong friends with people whom we never imagined we would ever know. As I grew older, my desire to explore the world and the people in it increased, and I embraced my gregarious nature. I wanted to make the most out of life and pursue a career, have a family, and enjoy cultural experiences while having fun with friends.

I feel like I have accomplished my goals in life, and they have even exceeded my expectations in all the aspects. As for some of the people I will meet along my journey, all I can say is "Who would ever believe it?"

TWO

Liza Minnelli

We met Liza in 1973. She had just won the Oscar for Best Actress for her role in *Cabaret* the previous year and became an instant superstar. Winning the Oscar, combined with her being the daughter of Judy Garland, made her the darling of international society. Arlene and I were invited to a dinner party at Elaine's, the celebrity NYC restaurant, by Allan Carr. Allan was a legendary agent and producer, a larger-than-life character with an amazing personality. Allan knew everyone, and we had met him through common friends. He had organized a large table of celebrities for a dinner party and, by chance, sat us opposite Liza and her new husband, Jack Haley Jr. We had been friends with Liza's younger sister Lorna Luft, so she was interested in getting to know us.

Liza, Jack, Arlene, and I just hit it off and bonded immediately. We thought, *Why would a superstar, who is jet-setting around the world, be interested in hanging out with a dentist and his wife once this dinner was over?* However, it turned out that Liza was a lovely, warm, wonderful person who really loved having some regular friends who were not in her industry. It was the start of a lifelong friendship, and we have been her closest friends now for forty-seven years. We still talk a few times a week, no matter where any of us are in the world.

A few months ago, we received a full-sized Andy Warhol portrait of Liza from her as a gift. It is an exact copy of the original. Enclosed with it were two notes, one saying on the outside envelope, "To My Hero."

Inside was a note that read, "To my darling Allan with love, light and all the kisses in the world. Love, Liza."

The other outside envelope said, "To Beautiful Arlene."

Inside was a note that read, "To my beautiful Arlene you are the light and joy of my life now and forever, Liza." This sums up the affection we have for each other. On future pages, there will be many recollections of times we have had together.

CHAPTER

THREE

Sammy Davis Jr.

We met Sammy when he was married to Altovise, his last wife. We first met Altovise when we were in LA in the '70s, and Arlene went to a charity luncheon at her home. Arlene and Altovise hit it off at the luncheon. By that time, we had several friends in common, so conversation flowed easily. Arlene told Altovise to call her to meet for lunch the next time she was in NYC and gave Altovise our phone number. We did not really expect her to call, but to our surprise, she did. Both Arlene and I met her in NYC for lunch, and we became instant friends. She was so warm and friendly that we immediately felt like old friends. We told her to please stay with us rather than a hotel when she came to NYC alone, without Sammy. The next time she came to NYC, she did just that; and for the rest of her life, she was a regular houseguest.

She told us that she spoke highly about us to Sammy, and sometime in the future, when they were both in NYC together, he would like to meet us. Few people in the world lived as exciting and public a lifestyle as Sammy. He was considered by many to be the greatest entertainer of his time. He seemed to be someone who spent his time with every famous person in the world, including his best friend, Frank Sinatra. Arlene and I said to ourselves that it was nice for Altovise to say that Sammy wanted to meet us, but it would never happen. Even if it did, what would we have to talk to him about? Well, it turned out that we did all go out together, and it was a friendship connection that would last a lifetime.

Our friendship with Sammy turned out to be one of the most intimate and honest relationships we have had with any person we have known. We spent many days and nights, often until the sun came up the next day, discussing every aspect of our lives and personal feelings. Sammy had no formal education, but no one else had the uncanny ability to be aware of everything happening around him and had the natural intelligence and charm that he possessed. He is another person whose fun times with us will come up frequently in the pages of this book.

CHAPTER

FOUR

Gina Lollobrigida

I knew of Gina as this amazingly beautiful Italian movie star and sex symbol. Growing up, Arlene and I had both seen her movies and her many photos on the covers of magazines. Her English-language films include *Beat the Devil* with Humphrey Bogart, *The World's Most Beautiful Woman*, *Trapeze* with Burt Lancaster and Tony Curtis, *The Hunchback of Notre Dame* with Anthony Quinn, *Never So Few* with Frank Sinatra, *Solomon and Sheba* with Yul Brynner, *Come September* with Rock Hudson, *Woman of Straw* with Sean Connery, *Strange Bedfellows* with Rock Hudson, and *Buona Sera, Mrs. Campbell*.

One night we were having dinner at Elaine's Restaurant in NYC. As we were leaving, we noticed a good friend of ours, Leslie Bricusse, sitting at a table with a beautiful woman. We had been good friends with Leslie and his wife, Evie, for a number of years. Leslie, along with Anthony Newley, has written many of the greatest songs of our generation. "Talk to the Animals" from *Doctor Dolittle*, "The Candy Man," "What Kind of Fool Am I?," "Once in a Lifetime," "Who Can I Turn To?," "My Kind of Girl," "Goldfinger," "You Only Live Twice," "Two for the Road," and "Pure Imagination" are just a few. Some of his musicals are *Stop the World—I Want to Get Off*; *Roar of the Greasepaint*; *Victor/Victoria*; *Jekyll and Hyde*; *Doctor Dolittle*; *Goodbye, Mr. Chips*; *Scrooge*; and *Willy Wonka and the Chocolate Factory*.

Sammy Davis had recorded many of Leslie's songs, so we had friends in common. Leslie and Evie were also good friends of Liza, and we were introduced to them by her. Leslie is quite charming and very social, and we hit it off very well with him and Evie. We have stayed in their home in the south of France, and they have stayed with us at our home in Westhampton.

Evie is a very beautiful woman, and as we started to walk over to say hello, Arlene said to me, "Although the woman with Leslie looks like Evie, it is not her." Then Arlene remarked that she looked like Gina Lollobrigida, the Italian movie star. We walked over to their table and greeted Leslie, who proceeded to introduce us to Gina and invited us to join them for coffee. We were thrilled to meet her as she and Sophia Loren were the two greatest Italian screen legends of our time.

Gina, who we later found out speaks many languages, was amazingly warm and approachable. She was not pretentious and did have a guarded wall that many celebrities put up to fend off interaction with people in social settings. It turned out that Leslie was in NYC for meetings about a new Broadway show he was working on, and Gina was also in NYC for a project. Gina was friends with Leslie and Evie, and Leslie was showing her around NYC for the day. Gina spoke a little broken English at that time. It turned out that when she started making films in America, the studios found her broken English so charming that they did not want her to learn too much English and lose the charm of her accent. So as friendly as Gina was, we found it somewhat difficult to communicate with her. We were just two people brought up in Brooklyn with no knowledge of the Italian language. Gina lived in Rome and, at that period, had little opportunity to come to NYC, so her English was very rusty. Fortunately, Leslie was quite the raconteur, so the conversation was flowing well, and we all hit it off wonderfully. We figured it was a great, once-in-a-lifetime experience to meet Gina, who was going back to Rome in two days.

By chance, the designer Halston had invited Arlene to a fashion show he was having at his studio the next day. We were about to leave, and Gina excused herself to go to the bathroom. I whispered to Arlene, "Why don't you invite Gina to go with you to the fashion show?"

Arlene replied, "I just met her, and how can I even carry on a conversation when she speaks very little English and I speak no Italian?"

I answered, "She seems so pleasant and friendly and does not seem to know many people in NYC. What do you have to lose because we will never see her again?"

Gina came back to the table, and as she and Leslie were about to leave, Arlene asked her. Much to our surprise, she said she would love to go with Arlene to the fashion show. She gave Arlene the name of the hotel where she was staying, and Arlene said she would pick her up the next day. Gina, we found out as we got to know her, always dresses like the elegant movie star she is wherever she goes. Arlene was somewhat intimidated but found Gina to be extremely down to earth and real.

Their time together the next day was very special. They developed a bond that eventually led to Gina being part of our extended family. We have been like family now for forty years, traveling the world together. Gina stays with us in NYC and Westhampton, and we stay with her at her homes in Rome, Switzerland, Pietrasanta, and Monte Carlo.

CHAPTER

FIVE

Lorna Luft

We had been recently married, and although on the surface we seemed like just your regular dentist-and-housewife couple, we both loved the world of show business. One night friends of ours invited us to dinner at their apartment in NYC. They also invited another couple, Ron and Ellen Delsener. Ron was a young promoter who was already quite successful in bringing top acts to Madison Square Garden, Jones Beach, and many other venues around town.

In the middle of our dinner, Ellen suddenly turned to me and said, "I think I went out with you in high school." She was right. I had one date with her years before, but I had forgotten. I remembered when she brought it up. I had driven out to Great Neck, where her parents' home was. When I arrived, the famous comedian Alan King was walking around the house, and I spent some time talking with him. It turned out that he had just bought the home from Ellen's family and was checking it out. Ron and I got along great at dinner, and over the ensuing years, he invited us to many of his concerts. He became the premier entertainment promoter in the United States, eventually selling his business to Live Nation, who today is the top music promoter in the country.

It turned out that Ron was very involved with the Friars Club in NYC, a private club for entertainers. He invited us to a Halloween party that he was throwing for the club. Arlene and I really got into Halloween, and I arrived dressed in a doctor's outfit with fake blood and a very scary mask. We arrived at the party and were dancing up a storm when Arlene noticed a familiar-looking person dancing near us with her date. We were all sort of dancing together as a small group and were having a lot of fun. We introduced ourselves to the young girl who turned out to be Lorna Luft, Judy Garland's youngest daughter, and her date, Noel Craig. Lorna had appeared on some TV shows with her mother, so Arlene must have seen her on one of the shows. (I had not seen her television show because it was on opposite *Bonanza*, which was one of my favorite programs.) I had never seen her perform live and did not have any other exposure to Judy except for seeing *The Wizard of Oz*.

Over the past five decades, Arlene and I have had the very special experience of being best friends with both of Judy Garland's daughters. They each have become family to us, and we cherish the fact that we have been so close with both of these amazing people. We have a unique perspective on their personal lives, interactions, and careers. They have both gone on to be very successful performers in their own right, as well as dynamic and fascinating personalities.

A few other people were dancing near us, and we all just hit it off. Halloween that year fell on a Thursday. We stayed at the Friars Club party until the early morning hours. We then told our new friends that we were invited to some fun Halloween parties on Friday and Saturday and gave them the addresses. We met up with Lorna and Noel both nights.

One other fun girl joined us named Mackenzie Phillips. We later found out she was only fifteen years old and was a very independent, wild child. She was the daughter of John Phillips of the Mamas and the Papas singing group. Mackenzie would go on to star in the TV show *One Day at a Time*, but at that time, she was unknown. We spent time with Mackenzie in LA in future years but stopped seeing her when we realized that she had a substance abuse problem. She eventually sought help in rehab and finally straightened herself out.

We instantly bonded with Lorna and Noel and spent three straight nights with them from 8:00 p.m. to 4:00 a.m. at Halloween parties. Each night I wore the same scary mask. Although we were becoming best friends after spending so much time together until the early morning hours, they had no idea what I looked like. I refused to remove my mask. When we left one another on the third night, now best friends, I said, "Let's have dinner Sunday at Elaine's Restaurant, and I will take off my mask."

We arrived at Elaine's in full Halloween costumes, and I said I would take off the mask for dinner. I had put on a different mask under the scary one I wore, so when I took off the mask, I still had another one on. After a good laugh, I took off the second mask so they would know what I really looked like. (I am happy to report that they did not tell me to put the mask back on.) That was the start of a lifelong friendship of almost fifty years.

Every Halloween no matter where we all are, we call one another. We thought Noel and Lorna were a couple, but it turned out he was a gay actor friend, and we remained friends with Noel until he passed away from AIDS in the '80s. Lorna wrote a best-selling book about her life, called *Me and My Shadows*. She detailed some of our fun times together in her book. She has become part of our extended family, our best friend, and we are godparents to her children.

 CHAPTER

SIX

Improbable Friends

There are many other well-known people who, as improbable as it seems, we have had lifelong friendships with. The singer-songwriter Neil Sedaka has been probably our closest male friend for the longest time. The singers Lorna Luft and Julie Budd have been dear friends for more than forty-five years. We have had very long-term friendships with such diverse people as Truman Capote and Jackie Mason. We have spent a good deal of time with Michael Jackson, Frank Sinatra, Robert De Niro, Andy Warhol, and many other world-famous people. Henry and Ginny Mancini have made us feel part of their family for years. Lindsay Wagner, Tony Danza, Barry Manilow, and Michael Feinstein are some of the people we share a close bond with by staying in either our home or theirs over the years. The following pages will detail some of the memories we have of times with some unique and very special people, none of whom will be thought of as being an intimate part of the life of a dentist, housewife, and their two children.

CHAPTER

SEVEN

Robert Goulet

I first met Arlene at the Concord Hotel in the Catskills. She was in her teens and had been picked up after camp by her parents. They had asked her where she wanted to go before they all returned home, and she said the Concord Hotel. The Concord was a very popular resort, and each weekend they featured many of the top entertainers in the world. Arlene chose the Concord because she was a big fan of the singer Robert Goulet, and he was performing there that weekend. His role on Broadway as Sir Lancelot in the musical *Camelot* (starring opposite Richard Burton and Julie Andrews) made him famous. His great voice and good looks made him one of the most popular entertainers of that time.

I went there the same weekend with a friend to enjoy the food and entertainment but mainly to try to meet girls. Arlene entered and won the bathing beauty contest, and when I saw her, I wanted to meet her. She was with her parents and her younger sister, Susan. I only asked her for her phone number and didn't spend time with her then because she was there with her family. I asked her out when I returned to NYC. We fell in love, married, and in a short time had two young children. We always marveled at the fact that had Arlene not been such a fan of Robert Goulet, we would have never met.

Even in our first few years of marriage, we both loved the entertainment world of nightclubs and shows. One of our friends managed a hotel in NYC that had major performers entertaining in their showroom. One day he told us that Robert Goulet was playing in the showroom for two weeks and asked us if we would like to join him for the opening night. He said after the show that Goulet would do a meet and greet for special guests in the room adjacent to the showroom. We always said to each other how wonderful it was that we met, and it all happened because Arlene liked Robert Goulet.

All during the show, we were filled with excitement at the prospect of meeting him and telling him how important he was to our lives. After the performance, our friend took us to the room where Goulet would greet the opening night special guests. We waited our turn, and our friend introduced us to him. We were so happy to tell him that Arlene was a big fan and went to the Concord Hotel to see him. We proceeded to tell him how, because of that, we met, got married, and had two children, and we owed it all to him. He looked us in the eye and said, "Why are you bothering me with that story?" And he quickly went on to the next person waiting in line. We were both dumbfounded and humiliated. Our fantasy was crushed, and from that night on, we hated him.

We found, however, that life often takes strange twists. As the years went on, we became good friends with many people in the entertainment industry. Leslie Bricusse, who I mentioned earlier as a composer of many musicals, was working on a new musical. It was called *Jekyll and Hyde*, and he invited us to attend a run-through before it started its out-of-town bookings. (Leslie and Evie had stayed at our home in Westhampton while he was working on this show. He had gifted us with a book of his songs, with an inscription thanking us for our hospitality while he worked on this musical, which we cherish.) Leslie is always working on several musical ideas at the same time, and one was a musical about King Henry VIII, which would be starring

Robert Goulet. Leslie invited Robert to the run-through of *Jekyll and Hyde,* and he seated us right next to Robert and his new wife, Vera.

Having no memory of his previous slight to us years before and seeing how close we were with Leslie, they could not have been nicer. We were just gritting our teeth and giving them perfunctory responses to the conversation with them. At intermission, Leslie came over to the four of us and invited us to join him after the show for dinner. The thought of spending any more time with Goulet was odious to us, so we said, "Unfortunately, we made other plans."

Over the next number of years, we were constantly at social events where the Goulets were present. It turned out that we had many common friends. Each time, they could not have been friendlier, but we were unable to get over our original meeting. We subsequently learned that he had some drinking problems when we first met him, which led to mood swings and some unpleasant behavior.

The last time we saw the Goulets was in Las Vegas. We did a lot of traveling with entertainers, like Sammy Davis Jr. and Liza Minnelli, especially to fun places like Las Vegas and Atlantic City. Liza was doing a show at a hotel in Vegas, and we stayed at the same hotel. Each night she had us seated at the table reserved for her friends. That night, we arrived at the show to find that she had seated us with Robert and Vera Goulet. Arlene and I agreed to just get through the small talk at the table and then lose them after the show.

At the end of the show, we rushed out to greet Liza as she was coming off the stage. She was sweating and had a towel around her neck. She informed us that she had to do a fairly long meet and greet with VIPs in a room near her dressing room after she showered and changed. She did not want Robert Goulet to have to wait in a crowded room with all the other people waiting to see her. She arranged for a small room for them to relax in until she finished her greetings. She asked us to keep them company so they didn't have to sit alone. We were led by security to a small room with a bar and some food, and for the next hour, we were alone with them until Liza joined us.

By this time, after all the years of bumping into one another, Vera and Robert were overfriendly. They asked us where we were staying. We replied that we were staying in the hotel that Liza was working in. They both told us that they lived in Las Vegas, and we should never come to Las Vegas and stay in a hotel when they were in town. They proceeded to give us their contact information and insisted that we stay with them the next time we came to Las Vegas. The twists and turns of life are amazing. It turned out to be the last time we saw him because he died a few years later.

CHAPTER

EIGHT

Sammy Davis Jr.

When Altovise told us Sammy Davis wanted to meet us, we figured that it would never happen. Sammy hung out with Frank Sinatra and the Rat Pack, not a dentist and his wife. Boy, were we wrong! From the day we met him to literally the day he died, we were two of his closest and most intimate friends. It turned out that his other closest friends were also two people not in show business.

He had many friends in the entertainment industry, and over the years, we were amazed at the famous faces coming in and out of his home and hotel rooms at all hours of the night. We might be sitting with him in his hotel suite at the Waldorf Astoria, and at two in the morning, we would answer the doorbell, and famous people would enter and join us to hang out for a time. Arlene, who rarely gets flustered, answered the door one night, and a very suave Roger Moore walked in and gallantly kissed her hand. I must say that he was really handsome and charming. She sat opposite him at dinner in Sammy's suite that night and had the best time. Groups of famous comedians loved to hang out at Sammy's suite, trading stories. They would all congregate there after their shows and try to top one another with jokes. One by one, the doorbell would ring, and another great comedian would enter. Each comic was probably auditioning to be his opening act; but regardless of whether they were selected, everyone, including us, always had a great time.

Sammy loved to cook and took along his pots and pans and cooking utensils wherever he traveled in the world. He had a large Louis Vuitton suitcase that opened up vertically. It contained all his cooking utensils, Crock-Pot, and pans. At many of his parties, after the guests left, he would bring us into the kitchen and cook some soul food. At his LA property, he built a small kitchen off his main house. He and Arlene both liked the room temperature to be very warm. He would often be entertaining in the main house, and then quietly, he and Arlene would sneak off to the separate kitchen. There, he could cook for the guests in a place where he kept the temperature very warm, while the guests could remain at a normal temperature at his main house.

Altovise always stayed with us when she came to NYC without Sammy. When Sammy came to NYC, they stayed at the Waldorf. One of our memorable nights with Sammy was a time he came into NYC by himself for a project. He always had fascinating people around him as he loved to entertain guests and be surrounded by a crowd. Usually, when the crowd started leaving at around midnight, he would pull us aside and tell us to wait in the back room until everyone left. Then we would talk until all hours of the night, sometimes just us and occasionally with another friend or two.

On this specific trip to NYC, he took us aside and said that he knew Altovise had gone to Plato's Retreat with someone the last time she came to NYC. He figured it must have been us because she stayed with us, but we insisted that we never went. Plato's Retreat was famous in the early '70s at the start of the sexual revolution. It was a place where couples could go for swinging sex with other couples. It was pictured on the cover of *New York* magazine with a long story about the new sexual freedom. Much of NYC was talking about it and bursting with curiosity about what really went on there. The sexual activity there was not our thing, but we were as curious as the next person after witnessing all the talk and press. However, we never intended to go there as I was a prominent dentist in NYC, and it would be terrible if anybody saw us there.

On this night, Sammy told us to come over to his apartment at the Waldorf and dress up because David Frost was taking us out to dinner. David was a British journalist who became a huge television star interviewing famous people. His interview with Richard Nixon after Watergate was so popular that an Academy Award–nominated film called *Frost/Nixon* was made about it. David had a limo pick the three of us up and take us to meet him and his date at Maxwell's Plum, a very popular restaurant at the time. David was a very gifted raconteur, and we had a stimulating time talking with him. He had been to parties at our apartment, and we loved spending time with him. At the end of the dinner, he told us that the limo was waiting outside to take us home. Sammy told him that we wanted to walk. This was quite unusual for us to hear as Sammy could not walk down a street in NYC without drawing a crowd of people.

Once we were outside, Sammy hailed a taxi. He said to us that, despite our denials, we must have been the ones who took Altovise to Plato's Retreat, and he made arrangements for the three of us to go there after dinner. Sammy was someone who wanted to experience everything life had to offer. We again told him that we had never been there. He uttered that it didn't matter, but we were all going that night. We were torn between not wanting to be seen in a place like that and being curious about it. We felt that being with Sammy, we were safe. Sammy liked being recognized and interacting with people. When our typical NYC taxi driver never turned around to see him, even when he started singing, "Candy Man," Sammy told him that there was a fifty-dollar bill for him if he turned around.

We arrived at Plato's and rang the doorbell, and the man at the door saw the three of us and said, "Sorry, only couples are allowed in." The owner of the place was Larry Levinson. Sammy told the man that Larry had arranged for the three of us to be admitted to the club. The man again said it was a couples-only club and that he was sorry, but we could not come in. Sammy told him to go find Larry. He did, and Larry came to the door and welcomed us in. Sammy and I were dressed in suits and ties and Arlene in cocktail attire. Larry told us to walk around and enjoy ourselves, and he would meet up with us in a short time.

We entered into a large room filled with couples in various sexual embraces, most of them naked, and some were in towels. When some patrons looked up at the new arrivals and saw Sammy Davis, they forgot about the sex they were having and rushed up to get his autograph. To them, sex was an everyday experience, but meeting Sammy Davis was special and exciting. It was before the age of cell phones, so many people cherished autographs. Unfortunately, no one had a piece of paper or a pen because most of them were naked. Along the bar area, there was a buffet set up for the customers to eat when they took a break from their sexual acts. These people stopped what they were doing and ran up to the buffet table to get paper napkins for Sammy to autograph.

Larry soon came over and brought us to another area, which he said was the orgy room. He told us that he would come back in a short time to get us. Arlene and I kept hoping that we did not bump into friends or any of my patients. At the entrance to this room was a bouncer. Sammy, who wanted to witness everything but not participate, asked him to let us in to see it. The man firmly stated that only couples were allowed in. Sammy wanted to see it, and Arlene was the only woman, so I stayed outside while the two of them went in.

Arlene later told me there was one very large mattress covering the floor with couples in various sex groupings fornicating on it. Arlene clung to Sammy's arm as they observed the scene for a few minutes. He just wanted to say that he had been there and then leave. The people there all wanted to have the experience of having Sammy Davis join them. He declined and said, "Hey, man, we are just hanging for a few minutes and not interested in sex." After a few minutes, they both came out of the room, and I joined them with Larry in the next room that had a pool table.

Larry challenged Sammy to a game of pool. While Arlene and I watched their game, a couple in towels walked by us and asked if we wanted to go into the back room with them. We politely declined, and five minutes later, when they again walked by us, this time totally nude, we declined again. Sammy and Larry were down to the last shot for Sammy to make to win the match. All he had to do was sink the ball in the side pocket. Larry called over a very buxom naked girl to bend over the pocket with her breasts hanging over it, so Sammy had to shoot the ball between them to make the shot. He playfully missed the ball completely with the cue stick while watching her breasts.

Larry then invited us into a private back room, where we sat around a circular table with Larry, who was wearing a bathrobe. Sammy, Arlene, and I sat with Larry, who had a few naked girls on either side of him. He had people serve us drinks and passed around a joint, which Arlene and I declined.

As the evening went on, Sammy's demeanor transitioned from casual to proper, and he started speaking with a British accent and fixed his tie and collar to appear more formal. He began to ask Larry questions about how he developed the concept to start the club. As Larry was answering Sammy's business questions, one of the girls next to Larry bent down, untied his bathrobe, and started performing oral sex on him while he was conversing with Sammy. His answers were punctuated with oohs and aahs as the girl got more and more aggressive. Sammy, sitting opposite him, got more and more serious in his questions.

Finally, Sammy had enough. He had seen Plato's Retreat, and now his wife could not say that she had been there and he had not. We took Sammy home by taxi, saw him upstairs, and went home. We thankfully never bumped into anyone we knew and were relieved that we were able to see the place that everyone talked about without being seen by anyone.

About six months later, Sammy was in NYC again without Altovise before he was scheduled to meet her and us in Atlantic City. He had one of his fabulous parties in his suite at the Waldorf. The party started to break up, and as we were leaving, he told us to wait in the back room until all the guests left. He let them all out and then came back to talk to us. We commented on how interesting it was to have seen Plato's and how glad we were able to do so without bumping into anyone we knew. He then said, "Guess what, we are going back tonight." We were dumbfounded as we felt that we escaped being seen the other time and had no desire to go back. Sammy told us that he promised Larry he would stop by one more time just to say hello. Arlene and I had seen it once and had no reason to wander around and take a chance at being seen by a friend or a patient. We decided that we would walk in, let Sammy hang with Larry for a while, and find a corner to hide in until we all left.

Sammy had ordered a limo to take us there and instructed the driver to stay until he wanted to leave. The three of us walked in, and while Larry greeted Sammy, we found a spot in a corner to wait.

Larry then came over to us with Sammy and declared that he wanted Sammy to come because it was their once-a-month amateur night. We figured that we could just hide in the back until it was over and then leave before anyone recognized us.

They set up chairs for the people, who were mostly naked or in towels, to sit on while they watched the show. There was a large spotlight on a small stage that was set up. Larry informed us that he had a special bench for Sammy and us to watch the show. He then put a bench right on the stage and sat only the three of us on it. We were now on the stage with the various naked performers for the remainder of the show and were now more visible for everyone to see. Thank goodness no one did, and we escaped our second and last experience at Plato's Retreat.

We got even with Sammy for dragging us back to Plato's Retreat a second time. Six months later, when he came back to NYC with Altovise, we decided to include her in our scheme. Sammy had bad hips from years of dancing. He was trying to avoid hip surgery as long as possible. He had a female physical therapist come in three times a week to his suite at the Waldorf. Sammy loved to watch the daytime soap operas every day. He always had a TV turned on to his favorite soaps while the therapist worked on him. We arranged for Altovise to tell Sammy that the therapist could not make her Wednesday appointment, but her colleague would be able to come in a day earlier, on Tuesday. Arlene and I hired a stripper to come in for the hour and pretend to be a physical therapist.

On the day of the appointment, Sammy was in the small extra bedroom, watching his soaps on TV. The stripper was dressed as a nurse, and when she entered the room, she told Sammy that she did her therapy with soft music in the background. He was reluctant to turn off the TV, but she insisted. As the music began playing, she gently began a light massage. Sammy, as I mentioned earlier, liked the room temperature hot. She announced that she was dressed too warm and proceeded to remove her nurse's uniform. Altovise, Arlene, and I were listening to everything right outside the door. She was now in her bra and panties and started to move sensually to the music. Sammy, rarely at a loss for words, said, "What's going on here?" She proceeded to get into the bed with him, and that was when we opened the door, and the flashbulb from our camera went off, leaving us all in hysterics.

He said, "You guys really got me." Needless to say, we destroyed the photo.

Sammy never went to school as he was on the road at age five with his father and uncle, entertaining. He was educated by watching movies and theater. He was extremely intelligent and absorbed everything he read and saw. He loved Shakespeare, and every time he came to NYC, if a Shakespearean play was running there, he would take us. In those days, there were frequent productions of Shakespeare, so we went a number of times with him. We found Shakespeare hard to follow, and after the first embarrassing time with Sammy, when he wanted to discuss the play at his apartment afterward, we realized what to do. As soon as we learned which play we were going to see with him, we would go to the bookstore and buy the CliffsNotes that students used to study Shakespeare. That way, we could discuss the plays with him after seeing them.

In 1979, Sammy took us to see Al Pacino on Broadway in *Richard III*. After the intense play, the three of us went backstage to see Pacino. Usually, guests of the performers have to wait for a while until the performer can shower and change clothing before greeting his guests. I guess because it was Sammy Davis, they immediately opened the dressing room door to let us in. Pacino was lying down on a small couch in his dressing room. He was almost in a trance, slowly coming out of his character, when Sammy said, "Great show, man." Pacino, still in character, lifted one hand and extended it to Sammy to kiss the ornate ring on his hand. It was method acting on display. In a few minutes, he became Al Pacino again, and we all had a lively discussion of the play.

We never knew what to expect with Sammy. One night he asked us if we had ever been to a house of prostitution in NYC. When we answered no, he proceeded to take us to a very fancy Upper East Side apartment. We had drinks with the madam while the girls wandered about. Sammy told her we were not interested in the women but just wanted to come up and have a drink. When we left, he told us that he wanted us to see what went on in NYC. He only wanted to let us know that he was the hippest guy in town.

One time when we were with him in Florida, he picked us up in a car to go to dinner. When we entered the vehicle, there was a woman already seated in the back, so we sat beside her. Sammy told us that she was a friend of his, and she would be joining us for dinner. She seemed very sweet, and the reason it is memorable is that her name was Linda Lovelace. Her movie *Deep Throat* was the talk of the town. It was hard for Arlene and me to try to make casual conversation with her. We had many questions that we really wanted to ask but refrained from doing so, and contrary to what one might expect, she seemed shy and demure. Sammy just loved to shock and surprise us.

Sammy always wanted to have the best of everything. If any new technology equipment came out, he would be the first person to have it. Sammy had the first video recorder before it had even reached the marketplace and the first to have every video game system before it reached the general public. He was always one step ahead of everyone else, but everything he had he wanted to share with his friends. He would be like a ringmaster at his parties, making sure that everyone was happy.

One day he was raving to us about how terrific amyl nitrite was for sex. We had no idea what he was talking about. He gave us a few capsules and told us to try it at home the next time we had sex. He explained that when you break the vial and inhale, it gives you a rush of energy. He said that it greatly heightens sexual arousal. Later that night, when we got home, we decided to try it. We got into bed, and we each broke a vial of amyl nitrite. We didn't realize that we were only supposed to take one breath of it. We each inhaled several deep breaths. We both immediately felt our hearts racing wildly and our heads pounding. Rather than being sexually aroused, we both felt like we were dying. We each went to opposite parts of the bed and nervously waited for the pulsations to stop. Our desire for sex was gone. We were just happy to be alive.

Sammy was one of the most generous people we ever met. When we traveled with him to Vegas, Atlantic City, and tours all over the world, he would rent out multiple suites for everyone traveling with him. If you admired his coat, he would take it off and give it to you. He had a six-gun collection, and he loved to show off his handling of the guns. He would put on his holster and quick draw like in the Westerns and spin the guns around his fingers. He had a fabulous collection of decorative canes. He would go out for the evening dressed beautifully, carrying one of his canes, first for effect and eventually for help when his hips started bothering him. He had one expectation from his very close friends. When Arlene and I would leave, he would always kiss us on the lips. For me, this was unusual; but for Sammy, this was how close friends said goodbye for the day.

Sammy always performed on the Jerry Lewis muscular dystrophy telethon. One particular year, he gave a very touching speech, and we saw in his expression a sad emotion that we never noticed before. As we knew his feelings so well, we contacted Altovise, who told us that he had throat cancer and chose not to operate as he would lose his ability to speak. Ironically, we had just returned from a trip to Indonesia. While there, we visited the island of Sulawesi. The burial tradition there is most unique. They do not bury people in the ground. When someone dies, they are buried on a hilltop or mountain. Instead of a tombstone, a wood carving of them is made. This small figure is placed high on the mountain, and one can look up and see all the figures representing the deceased. In time, some of the carved figures are taken down and sold as souvenirs to tourists. We saw in a gift shop a figure that looked remarkably like Sammy. It had his chin and nose and even had a piece of cloth on its head, which resembled the do-rag that Sammy wore to bed. We bought it intending to bring it back as a gift for Sammy. Even though it was originally meant to represent the deceased, the figures were now sold as artwork. We debated about giving it to him when we got home because of what it represented. When we found out that he was dying, we, of course, never gave it to him. We keep it today in our home, and each day when we walk by it, we think of him.

The next time we were in LA, we went to his home as we always did the day after we arrived. Sammy always ran the latest movie, which he received from the studios, at his home on Sunday nights. His guests were a mixture of the major movie and entertainment stars of the time, all wanting to participate in Sunday night at Sammy's.

After everyone left, we went into a small room off his kitchen for a light bite. We sat around a table, just the three of us. Arlene and I knew he was dying and did not know what to say. It was a rare time in our conversation with Sammy that it was just an evening of small nonsense talk around a table. We just could not bring ourselves to express how we felt about him. We felt so bad about not being able to tell him our feelings that, when we returned home to NYC, we wrote him a letter. We explained how we felt and what his friendship meant to us. Needless to say, we had tears in our eyes.

In his last days, we flew to LA and was at his home every day. Altovise hosted a few other people and us each day. She would say each time that he was resting and was not ready to see anyone, but he was doing better. Finally, we had to go back home to NYC. When our plane landed in NYC, we saw on the news that he had passed away that night.

As with many entertainers who are focused on their careers and not their finances, sadly, he was taken advantage of by his financial advisers. They stole his money, taking for themselves money that was meant for the IRS. When he died, the IRS took everything he had left, even plastic cups from his guest bathroom with his name on them. When he knew he was dying, he left wonderful gifts for his friends, knowing the IRS would take everything. I had always admired the gold and diamond watch he wore, and when by chance it fit my wrist perfectly, it was mine.

NINE

Frank Sinatra

We had many experiences with Frank Sinatra. We witnessed his multiple different moods. His longtime manager, Eliot Weisman, was a good friend of ours. We spent a lot of time with Eliot when he was Liza's road manager and eventually her manager, traveling all over the world with him. Eliot became Sinatra's manager and, later on, also managed Steve Lawrence and Eydie Gormé and Don Rickles. Over the years, whenever any of these entertainers appeared in NYC, Florida, Las Vegas, or Atlantic City, we would be invited to the shows and dinner with them afterward.

Steve and Eydie were great fun along with their assistant, Judy Tannen, who brought female profanity to a new level. Steve Lawrence was one of the most naturally funny and witty people we have met. He and Eydie were wonderful to be around, full of great stories about their experiences. We always had terrific dinners with them and Eliot whenever they played in Florida, where Eliot lived.

One time we were with them after a show and a fan involved in Eydie's fan club came back to see her in the dressing room. The person gushed over Eydie and told her that he was such a big fan that he bought her name on the internet so he could run his fan page. Eydie told him that she wondered why she could not get her own name for a web page. She asked him if he would give her back her name, but we never found out if he complied.

We spent much time with Tony O, who worked for Eliot. Tony was Sinatra's main assistant until Frank retired and then became Don Rickles's main assistant. Rickles's insult comedy was world famous, but offstage, he was one of the nicest people we ever met. Don started out as a comedian working in the lounge in Las Vegas. He became the favorite performer for all the famous Las Vegas names due to his brilliant brand of insult comedy. People loved to come to his shows and listen to him make fun of everyone because they realized that he was just doing his act, and his razor-sharp wit was brilliant. Frank Sinatra loved bringing friends to Rickles's shows, and they became friends.

A good example of Don's humor is the night he was at a restaurant in Las Vegas with a date, and Sinatra was at the other end of the same restaurant with some friends. Don excused himself to go to make a phone call and went over to Sinatra's table. Sinatra was the most famous entertainer in the world and king of Las Vegas. Don begged Frank to please do him a favor. Don explained that he wanted to impress his date with the fact that he was friends with Sinatra and asked Frank if he would come over to Don's table to say hello during the dinner. A short time later, Sinatra got up, walked over to Don's table, and gave him a friendly greeting. Don sternly looked at Sinatra and said, "Frank, would you please stop bothering me? My date and I are trying to have a nice dinner and don't want people coming over and disturbing us." Don never changed expression, and Sinatra, realizing he had been pranked, walked away and waited until he returned to his table to laugh hysterically.

Dinners with Don were some of the most entertaining we ever had, and his humor and stories dominated the conversation. Every time we would see him, either before or after his show in his dressing room or at dinner, he never failed to say something personal to Arlene, me, and each person in the party. Every time he saw me, he would point to his teeth and laugh. When we went out with him and his lovely wife, Barbara, without Eliot, Don would overorder at the restaurant. He wanted his guests to try everything. After charming us with his witty comments and tales of show business, he always insisted on picking up the check. In his later years, he performed with various physical problems but never lost his amazing sense of humor. (The younger members of our family know Don as the voice of Mr. Potato Head in the *Toy Story* movies.)

Frank Sinatra was the most unusual person to be around as you never knew which Sinatra was showing up. He could be moody, charming, curt, and funny all in the same evening. People working for him were always tense. They were often overprotective of him, so before or after a show, people were nervous, trying to not get in his way. However, in social settings with his friends, it was a different story. Everyone was more relaxed but always gave the respect due to the "Chairman of the Board."

One night we were with him on his birthday, and after the show, he made a small private party outdoors. That night, the regular comedian who usually opened for him, Pat Henry, was not on the bill and was replaced by another whose name I forgot. Frank and his friends were doing some serious drinking and were in great spirits. They made this comedian sit down on a chair at the end of the room, and they each took turns throwing pies at him to see who could hit him in the face. We were so embarrassed for this poor guy, who had to endure this humiliation to keep his job. Frank and his friends were hysterical each time the pies landed, but we stood there mortified.

One night in LA, Sammy Davis invited us and our young children, who were with us on that trip, to his home for a party. Sinatra came in and walked right over to us. He took the hand of our daughter, Lauren, and told her how beautiful she was. To this day, she never forgot how lovely he was to her. She had seen him perform onstage multiple times with Liza and Sammy, but it was really special for her to have met him because, even at that young age, she appreciated the talent that we exposed her to.

Sinatra, along with Sammy Davis Jr. and Liza Minnelli, went on a world tour playing arenas under the name "The Main Event." Frank really set this tour up to help Sammy Davis pay off his IRS bills. Originally, Dean Martin was the third performer along with Frank and Sammy; but when he backed out after a few weeks, Liza took his place. One night onstage, Frank made a comment about Dean that he did not like, so Dean just walked off the stage and the tour. Dean did not need the money, and he was not the same fun guy since the death of his son in a plane crash.

Liza rescued the tour by stepping in to take Dean's place. They arranged to fly in a world-famous photographer and his crew from England to take new publicity pictures. The promoters took a suite at the Waldorf for the weekend and set up equipment and lighting. We were going out for dinner with Liza and Sammy that evening, so they invited us to meet them for the shoot. Sammy, Liza, Arlene, and I—along with the large film crew, PR people, and various assistants— were all there. Everything was ready for the shoot, except there was no Sinatra. After a few hours, Sinatra finally walked in, looked around, and announced, "Okay, you have five minutes, and then I'm gone." The photographer and his crew, who had flown in expecting to take many various shots over a period, were in shock. The three stars posed for a few quick pictures, and true to his word, in five minutes, Sinatra was gone. He knew his power and used it often.

Sinatra's friendship with Sammy was a strange one. Early in Sammy's career, Frank treated him like a younger brother. His support for Sammy was important in opening up the racial barriers of the day. Frank used his power and influence to make sure Sammy was treated well. As Sammy's career took off, things started to change. There was a subtle tension as Sinatra wanted to make sure he was the main man. There were a few years that the friendship was strained, but overall, it was a strong and long-lasting one.

One night we were at Sammy's suite at the Waldorf with him, and he was cooking for us. Sammy took all his cooking gear wherever he went and loved to cook. Sinatra was also in town and staying in a suite at the Waldorf as well. Frank's assistant called Sammy's room and invited the three of us to his suite, where he was having a party. Sammy was comfortable relaxing and cooking in his suite but told us that we all have to go up and pay our respects. We were happy to go as a Frank Sinatra party was usually exciting. Sammy told us, as we were heading to the party, that he just wanted to stay for a short time. Sammy explained that he would greet Frank and his guests, and then we could go back to Sammy's and relax.

When we arrived, Frank was a wonderful, pleasant host. He had arranged for many assorted boxes of pizza to be sent to his suite. Sammy told Frank that we could only stay for a short time and, after mingling for a while, told us it was time to leave. We were having a great time but were ready to leave whenever Sammy wanted to go. Frank came over to Sammy with one of his assistants and told the three of us to take some pizza back to Sammy's room because we did not eat at the party. Sammy said "no thanks" because he was cooking, but Frank insisted. Frank started to pile up boxes of pizzas for Sammy to hold. After a minute, we could not see Sammy's face anymore because he was holding so many boxes of pizza. As soon as Sinatra walked away, I immediately took the boxes from Sammy so he would not have to endure the embarrassment of walking to the door carrying all those boxes of pizza. I interpreted that as an attempt by Sinatra to show that he was the boss. When we got to Sammy's suite, we dumped all the pizza, and Sammy cooked dinner for us.

When Sinatra wanted to be charming, he could be wonderful. One time when Gina Lollobrigida was staying with us in NYC, she was doing a series of celebrity interviews for Italian media. She had starred in a movie with Sinatra called *Never So Few*. He invited her to go to Atlantic City, where he was performing, to film an interview with her for RAI. Arlene went with Gina to Atlantic City and told me that Sinatra could not have been nicer to both of them. They sat with his wife Barbara at the show. Arlene liked her very much and enjoyed her company.

One very rainy night, we were driving to New Jersey for a sold-out concert of "The Main Event." As we were pulling up to the arena, Liza called us on the phone in our car to tell us not to bother to park as Sinatra's teleprompter displaying his lyrics never arrived. He canceled the sold-out concert, giving no notice to the fans who were entering. She and Sammy told him that they would cover for him and that he would be doing songs that he had been singing for decades. He simply said, "I'm out of here." And he left. However, he went out on this tour to earn money for Sammy to pay off his debts, so who am I to criticize?

CHAPTER

TEN

Robert De Niro

I was a periodontist for many years, and I developed a large celebrity clientele. A number of our famous friends came to see me if they had dental issues. Most of my patients were referred by general dentists when they felt a specialist was needed to save their teeth. Robert De Niro was a close friend of Liza, and when his dentist told him that he had some gum problems, Liza referred him to me. He was a delight to treat, and I found him extremely bright, although soft spoken and quiet. He had one tooth that was in very bad shape, and I explained that there was a new bone-grafting procedure that was just developed but had no long-term studies. He said that he would think about it and call me back. Two weeks later, he called and proceeded to discuss this complicated technical procedure with the knowledge of a specialist. He had researched it to such a degree that I felt as though I was conversing with an expert.

Although he was not a very talkative person in the office, there was another time when I was working on him that he was particularly insightful. I told him how much I admired the fact that his professional work is so long lasting. I marveled that his movies will remain for many years after he is gone and how satisfying it must be to realize that. I commented that most people's work is forgotten as soon as they stop. He did not respond for a while (which could have been because I had a sharp tool in his mouth). However, when he did, he remarked to me that his movies would eventually fade in time. "One thing," he said, "that lasts for centuries are mummies. When we dig them up or find remains of human skeletons, the only thing still intact are the teeth." So he told me that my work as a periodontist saving teeth would long outlive his movies. What a wonderful thing to say to me, and such a brilliant observation!

We have not spent much time with him over the years as he is a very private person, but he has always been very friendly whenever we see him. He is one of those men who, if we see him in a restaurant or theater, always stand up to say hello to us rather than remain in his seat.

One time when Gina Lollobrigida was staying with us, she wanted to discuss a possible project with De Niro. Most Italians have a fascination with Gina, and it turned out he wanted to meet with her as well. She asked me if I would contact him, and I did. He was busy working for the first time as a film director on the movie *A Bronx Tale*. All phone contact with him was through his assistant as there were no cell phones at that time. We invited him for dinner at our apartment. Arlene had no idea what to serve him, so I went to several specialty places in the neighborhood and gathered an assortment of Italian dishes and healthy salads. He came to our apartment on time, and dinner turned out great. He and Gina hit it off wonderfully, and although he was very reserved, Gina was in great conversational form, and we all had a fantastic evening. It was one thing for me to treat De Niro as a dental patient but really special to have him over my apartment for a casual dinner.

Another memorable evening with him was in 1983 when the legendary Italian film director Sergio Leone, famous for his "spaghetti Westerns" starring Clint Eastwood, planned to make his first film in the USA. The film was titled *Once upon a Time in America* and would star Robert De Niro. It was the most anticipated film of the year, and every major Hollywood actress was desperately trying to get cast in the movie. Liza was no exception, and she had the advantage of being friends with De Niro, but the casting was up to Leone. He had flown in from Italy to cast the movie.

One scene in the movie was to take place in the famous nightclub El Morocco. Liza felt that if Leone could see her chemistry with De Niro in the setting of El Morocco, he would see how perfect she would be for the part. The original nightclub had closed down, but a close friend of mine, named Albie, had bought it to use for private events. He also converted part of it into a restaurant. Liza asked me if I could ask Albie to let us use the place for a private dinner. She suggested that we all meet at five o'clock before the public arrived at eight at the nightclub.

Albie was a former patient who was so thankful to me for saving his teeth that he was amazingly generous to me in many ways. He was quite a character. He spoke in a gruff, gravelly voice and looked and acted like a gangster character out of central casting. Everything he did was over the top, but being in show business had little appeal for him. However, an evening with Liza and De Niro seemed fun for him, and he said that he would set up the dinner. He would cater a fabulous private meal and close the place while we were there. He asked if he could join us for dinner, and I said, "Of course."

The night of the dinner, Leone arrived with his interpreter as he did not speak English. Liza sat next to De Niro, with us opposite them. Leone, his interpreter, and Albie joined us at the large round table. Liza, as always, was charming and full of conversation. Albie, when asked about El Morocco, answered in his gravelly manner, and Leone seemed to be fascinated by him. Albie liked to bring his own guitar player with him whenever he went out to dinner. I have been with him when he had the man play for us while we were in the men's room, washing up before eating. On this night, he had the guitar player come over near the end of the meal and ask De Niro for a request. He chose the song "Fascination."

At the conclusion of the dinner, everyone left quite happy. It turned out that Liza was never offered the part. A few days later, I got a call from De Niro's assistant asking me to have Albie call his office. It seemed that Leone was completely taken with him and wanted to offer him a part in the film as the head gangster. Every actor in Hollywood was trying every possible way to try to get a part in this movie. Ironically, Albie—with no acting experience—was offered a leading role in this film. I called him up with this exciting news, and in a gruff voice, he said, "I have no interest in being in any f——ing movie." The next year when we saw the movie, the main gangster role was played by an actor looking and sounding just like Albie.

❦{ CHAPTER }❦

ELEVEN

Andy Warhol

In 1979, Andy Warhol published a very popular book called *Andy Warhol's Exposures*. He detailed his life in words and pictures. The following are his words about time spent with me and others at Studio 54: "I see a lot of Diana Ross since she's moved to New York because she likes to go out. Especially to Studio 54. I see Cher there whenever she's in town. Cher and Diana Ross love to dance together. Studio 54 is where I see Liza, too, and Lorna, and Lorna's husband Jake Hooker, and Lorna's dentist, Allan Lazare, and Lorna's dentist's wife, Arlene, who looks like Liza. They're all singing and dancing."

We knew Andy Warhol quite well through our common friends and time spent with him at Studio 54. He was very quiet and a keen observer of life around him. We often went downtown to the Factory, his studio, where he held court among a diverse group of people. He offered us the opportunity to have our portraits painted by him. The cost to us as friends would have been $25,000. We thought that it was too much to spend on his work, which we did not consider real art. That was a big financial mistake because his work sells in the many millions today.

Part of our decision that his work was not so great was influenced by an experience one day at the Factory. He was entertaining a group of us there, and I excused myself to go to the bathroom. I headed into the back room area, and instead of making a right to the bathroom, I mistakenly made a left. I walked into a room where a short male was painting typical Warhol paintings on several canvases. I recognized him as Rupert, whom I knew as Andy's assistant and friend. He often hung out with all of us at Studio 54. So that day, I saw Andy in the main room entertaining his guests, while Rupert painted away in the studio.

Wherever we went with Andy, he always traveled with a small tape recorder. He would quietly set it down on the table and then record all the gossip and conversations. He published a magazine called *Interview* in which every word in each article could not be denied. They just published the printed words directly from the recordings Andy made. Andy hired Bob Colacello, who was a patient of mine, to put out the magazine each week. When Studio 54 reopened after Steve Rubell, the co-owner, was released from jail for white-collar crimes, Bob put my picture jumping up with my hands in the air in his lead article. It said, "Studio 54 had its grand reopening today, and everyone was there from Halston to my dentist!" After that article, my friends started calling me the "Disco Dentist."

Andy was very subtle when he put his small tape recorder down at social gatherings, and people forgot that it was recording while they told their secrets to him. One night we went out for dinner with Andy, Liza Minnelli, and Sammy and Altovise Davis. After dinner, we all came back to our apartment and had drinks around our dining room table. Andy loved to hear stories and was terrific at getting people to talk to him. He started asking Sammy about what it was like in the old days in Havana, Cuba. Sammy related how he was paid huge amounts of money to entertain and was also asked by the mob people to bring suitcases full of cash back home into the United States. All of us were fascinated by the stories of those days in Cuba until Altovise suddenly realized that the tape recorder was running. She immediately told Andy to shut it off, or the evening would be over because she wanted no record of those conversations.

However, I still have fond memories of the stories traded that night among Liza, Sammy, Altovise, and Andy as we all talked into the early morning hours at our apartment. Andy was a unique character and unfortunately died in the prime of his life. His death was caused by the mistreatment of a gallbladder problem; it was massaged instead of being treated properly. The night before I went in for removal of my gallbladder in 1987, I received a call from Liza to make sure that what happened to Andy was not going to happen to me.

TWELVE

Halston

One of the most exciting periods of our lives revolved around Studio 54, the legendary discotheque. We were recently interviewed and filmed for several hours for a movie about it, and we are in the screen credits. We have been interviewed on Sirius 54 radio several times because we have a unique perspective on it. Myra Scheer, who handled all the celebrity contacts in those days, has a radio show along with the former doorman, Marc Benecke. They had us tell our stories, and at our last appearance, we had Neil Sedaka join us for our interview.

Studio 54 had the most difficult door policy of any club in the country. When it first opened, we gained entry by going with celebrities, who were whisked right in. We wound up going three to four nights a week for the entire time it was open. The eclectic crowd was amazing, and during those years, we hung out with people from all backgrounds, including many of the most famous people in the world. Arlene, who looks like Liza, was often mistaken for her by the press. Liza had stated that she was blamed for staying out many nights when it was really Arlene. Arlene would go each night in very dramatic outfits, some of which we have saved for Halloween parties decades later.

For the entire length of its run, we were always waved in, never paid for admission or drinks, and were treated wonderfully. We had a large group of friends whom we saw almost every time we were there. However, with all the noise and dancing, we really didn't know much about one another's real lives. We, of course, recognized the celebrities who were well known. We became very close with the regulars like Truman Capote, Halston, Andy Warhol, Bianca Jagger, and Liza. We would sit on the few couches reserved for VIPs. After being waved in past the enormous crowds by either Steve Rubell or Marc Benecke, we were usually let into the club by a small Asian girl named Yeh Jong. She never had me pay and gave us free drink tickets for our guests and us.

When the club finally closed, I remarked to Arlene that Yeh Jong was always so nice and never charged us. I suggested that we take her out for dinner as a small token of our appreciation. We met her at Elaine's Restaurant, and as the drinks arrived, she expressed what a nice gesture it was for us to take her out. I explained to her that it was the least we could do because she always was so wonderful to us. I told her that we were just a dentist and his wife. "And you never charged me during all those years."

She looked at us in astonishment and said, "You're a dentist? I thought you were a PR person." She had assumed I was in PR because we often walked in with Liza, Liza's sister Lorna, Truman Capote, or other celebrity regulars. I wonder now if she still would have given us free drinks and admission had she known I was a dentist at that time.

The main person holding court every night was the famous designer Halston. Halston's designs using cashmere or Ultrasuede redefined American fashion in the 1970s. *Newsweek* called him "the premier fashion designer of all America." His fame started when he designed the pillbox hat for Jacqueline Kennedy for the inauguration of John F. Kennedy in 1961. Halston was extremely close to Liza, and she was his muse and best friend. Halston was very elegant and somewhat aloof as he sat with a cigarette holder in his hand, keeping people he didn't know well at a distance.

Liza had shown us the book he made for her, depicting each outfit he designed for her. He detailed exactly what accessories she should wear with each outfit when she went out. We were always invited with her to the elegant parties he would host at his apartment. Everyone famous in NYC was there, along with many avant-garde types. Liza told us that Studio 54 became popular as a celebrity hangout when Halston became close friends with Steve Rubell. It was hard to get people to leave Halston's parties at his town house, so Halston would say to his guests, "Let's all go now to Studio 54, where there is a great after-party." It was then that Studio 54 got its reputation as a place where celebrities go late at night.

Halston's elegance contrasted with the man he lived with, named Victor Hugo. Victor was a totally insane, charming character. We had seen him take off his shoes, put them in purple paint, and paint footprints on the walls. Victor, in time, became a patient of mine, and Halston paid all his bills. Although we had spent a good deal of time with Halston, he looked on us as these two crazy friends of Liza, one who wore wild outfits (Arlene) and danced all night. We loved to dance, and Studio 54 and its great music became a wonderful party for us each night.

During the Studio 54 years, I changed my office schedule so that I could start work later. I would come home from the office and have an early dinner with our two young children. When they went to bed, I took a nap until midnight. We were fortunate to have live-in help. We would then dress up and go to the corner coffee shop, and I would get two large coffee containers. One I would drink there and one in the taxi to the club. While people were spending their money on cocaine, I spent mine on two dollars' worth of coffee, which gave me great energy.

I was still running a very busy practice but cut down on my hours without losing income. Most of my patients were referred to me for periodontal treatment by their dentists. One day I arrived at my office and saw on the schedule that Halston was coming in for a consultation. I knew that he had no idea what I did for a living but viewed me as this crazy friend of Liza who danced around all night at Studio 54. I have found that no matter how elegant and sure of yourself you are, when you walk into a dentist's office to find out whether you need surgery on your gums, you are apprehensive. From a distance, I could see Halston looking nervous as he awaited the specialist who would be doing gum surgery on him. My nurse went into the room, with me following her, and told him, "Here's Dr. Lazare."

Halston let out a scream, his legs jumped up in the air, and he yelled out, "You!" It was his worst nightmare as he envisioned this crazy Studio 54 party guy operating on him. I quickly calmed him down by explaining that I am a very serious professional during the day, just like him. I reminded him that he also was at Studio 54 at night, but during the day, he produced his world-class designs.

That day, our relationship changed. He let down the wall he put up to people, and we became good friends. In fact, I was one of the first people to find out that he had AIDS. His medical doctor informed me because he became a regular patient. As hard as it was, I never told Liza due to doctor-patient confidentiality and privacy, even though she wondered why he had to cancel some evenings with her. When she eventually found out about his condition, she respected the fact that I kept his information private until he told her himself. Tragically, Halston died in 1990 at the age of fifty-seven.

CHAPTER

THIRTEEN

Studio 54–Café Central

People like Cher, Diana Ross, and Michael Jackson were regulars at Studio 54. Michael loved to hang out in the DJ booth. It was before the days of cell phones, so celebrities like Cher, Diana, Michael, Rod Stewart, Bianca, and Mick Jagger could dance while freely mixing with the crowd. There were no paparazzi in the club, and no one had cameras. On any night, Stevie Wonder would sing; and Elton John, Chuck Berry, and Keith Richards would be hanging out on the dance floor. Donna Summer, "the Queen of Disco," entertained at the club's second anniversary party. We would often find ourselves sitting on the couch with Alana and Rod Stewart, Tina Turner, and Cher as the partygoers danced around us. Diana Ross loved to come in jeans and dance wildly with everyone on the dance floor.

Bianca Jagger was there most nights, sometimes with Mick. Besides being beautiful, she was married to a legendary rock star, and

49

Bianca became the "it girl" of the moment. The widely circulated photo on May 2, 1977, of Bianca riding into Studio 54 on a white horse for her birthday became world famous. We were often in her company, along with an actress friend of hers named Laurie Bird. (Laurie unfortunately committed suicide in Art Garfunkel's apartment at age twenty-six.) Bianca was one of the few people we found not to be unduly congenial. After our fifth evening out with her, common friends told us that she was just shy. We accepted the fact that we were just having fun and not trying to make lifelong friends with everyone.

We felt lucky to be part of this amazing time in NYC. David Bowie, Woody Allen, Sylvester Stallone, Warren Beatty, Gregory Peck, Sidney Poitier, Mikhail Baryshnikov, Muhammad Ali, Bruce Springsteen, Barbra Streisand, Chevy Chase, Jack Lemmon, John Belushi, James Brown, Bob Fosse, Tennessee Williams, Magic Johnson, Joe Namath, Bruce Jenner, O. J. Simpson, Rudolf Nureyev, Vladimir Horowitz, Leonard Bernstein, Paloma Picasso, Jacqueline Kennedy, John F. Kennedy Jr., Calvin Klein, Brooke Shields, Bette Midler, Ali MacGraw, Salvador Dalí, Richard Gere, Valentino, Yves Saint Laurent, Givenchy, Donna Karan, Dolly Parton, Richard Pryor, Omar Sharif, Jon Voight, Tony Curtis, Rob Reiner, Alice Cooper, Clive Davis, Lily Tomlin, and Suzanne Somers were just some of the famous faces I remember dancing around us on these nights. To meet any of these people in person usually is unique, but to be around all of them in a space of a few years is special, more so because they were all having a good time in a relaxed atmosphere and not working or making a paid appearance.

In the late seventies and early eighties, there were a number of other clubs to go to after leaving Studio 54 that first started their activities after two o'clock. There were also a few great hangouts for food and drinks that catered to a select small group of show people. We spent many nights in these places as well, either before, after, or as an alternative to Studio 54.

Café Central was a small place on the Upper West Side with almost no decor. However, each night, its few tables were filled with performers who either were famous or would later become famous. The two hosts at the door were Paul Herman and Sheila Jaffe. It was like a club where everyone knew everyone. Paul Herman was good friends with De Niro, Pesci, and Scorsese; and when he wasn't running the restaurant, he would have small roles in most of their movies as he is a very fine actor. Sheila Jaffe went on to become one of the top casting agents in Hollywood. Along with our friend Georgianne Walken, the wife of actor Christopher Walken, Sheila has been the casting director for more than eighty television shows and movies, including *The Sopranos* and *Entourage*. Many of the regulars would become big stars, and they mingled nightly with those who already were famous or were just starting to be recognized.

Bruce Willis was the bartender at Café Central, and Danny Aiello helped out as a host. Bruce, of course, would go on to star in the TV series *Moonlighting* and then become a major movie star in films like the *Die Hard* franchise and numerous others. Danny would also go on to become a major movie star in such films as *The Godfather Part II*, *The Purple Rose of Cairo*, *Moonstruck*, *Harlem Nights*, and *Do the Right Thing*, where he was nominated for an Academy Award for this Spike Lee film.

Café Central was a very animated scene, with people table-hopping in various states of inebriation. A young Robin Williams, just starting out, would go from table to table most nights, greeting everyone with unbelievable energy and comic wit. His frantic, nonstop comedy was on display all night, long before he was well known. He would later become famous for playing the alien Mork in the TV hit series *Mork and Mindy* before becoming a major motion picture star. He has won Oscar, Emmy, Grammy, and Golden Globe Awards in his long career. Sadly, he committed suicide by hanging at sixty-three years of age. I still remember the young Robin as the extremely jovial life of the party who was so much fun to be around.

When Café Central closed, Paul and Sheila moved to a new restaurant on Columbus Avenue, named Columbus, and the party continued. Several famous people like Regis Philbin, Mikhail Baryshnikov, and Neil Sedaka became investors in Columbus. One night when our daughter, Lauren, was in high school, Madonna came into Columbus while we were there. We knew Lauren liked her, and we called home and told Lauren to immediately jump into a taxi and join us. Lauren walked in the door and observed Billy Joel, Penny Marshall, Jon Lovitz, and Billy Crystal sitting at the table next to us. Lauren sat down with us, and when Madonna got up from her table and headed to the ladies' room, Lauren followed her in. Lauren told Madonna how much she liked her music and tried to chat with her. The last thing Madonna wanted to do was to have a conversation in the ladies' room with a teenager. Even so, Lauren had the best time that evening, watching some of her favorite performers interact with one another.

The other restaurant we frequented regularly was Elaine's. Elaine Kaufman was the most well-known restaurant owner of the time, and she ran her restaurant on Second Avenue and East Eighty-Eighth Street with a firm hand. She personally chose where every customer would be seated. She fiercely protected the celebrities from the people who attempted to approach them. She had a VIP area of tables set aside for them. No restaurant of its time came close to having the mixture of celebrities who ate there, despite the mediocre food.

CHAPTER

FOURTEEN

Truman Capote

One of our favorite people was Truman Capote, whom we met at Studio 54. Truman was one of the mainstays of NY society. His books included *Breakfast at Tiffany's* and *In Cold Blood*. He became the darling of NY society when, in 1966, he threw the most famous party in NYC history. It was a masquerade party called the Black and White Ball. Every celebrity and socialite attended, and from then on, he was in constant demand at every future society event.

He knew or made up everything about everyone. He was a great storyteller and often appeared on major TV talk shows. He was a regular at Studio 54 and held court there on the main couches along with Halston, Andy, Liza, Bianca, and Steve Rubell. Being privileged to sit in that area, we got to know him quite well. He loved to dance with Arlene, and when Studio 54 eventually closed its doors, he gave Arlene the plaid cap he wore most nights as a gift.

When he found out I was a periodontist, he asked if I would treat him. He was about to cap all his teeth, and his dentist told him that he needed to have periodontal work on his gums first. Truman was the most interesting patient I ever had. My nurses would gather around him while he sat in the chair, telling fascinating stories and gossiping about the rich and famous. The truth was that he was fearful of gum surgery, so he would stall by telling stories. We then all realized that only ten minutes were left of his one-hour appointment, so we had to reschedule.

We became great friends out of my office and at Studio 54. He loved to invite us up to his apartment in the UN Plaza and tell us his stories. He had a devilish sense of humor. While we sat in his living room, he would call up one of his society friends and start telling them a fabulous tale of gossip. Then just at the punch line, he pretended that something happened with the phone connection and hung up. He knew that they were dying to hear the ending, and they would immediately call him back. After hanging up, he would take his phone off the hook. (Those were the days before cell phones.) He would then giggle to us about their frustration in not being able to reach him.

Truman unfortunately had drug and alcohol problems that led to his early death. He had a long-term partner, Jack Dunphy, with whom he had a tumultuous relationship. We often met him at his place at UN Plaza, and he would take us to his favorite nearby restaurant, La Petite Marmite. He would be very animated and tell story after story. By the middle of the meal, his voice began to get softer and softer as whatever drugs he was taking started to kick in. When he reached the end of a juicy piece of gossip, we had to lean over very close to him because we could hardly hear the ending. By dessert, it would be almost impossible to understand what he was saying; his voice was barely a whisper. At that point, his assistant—who usually knew how long Truman could last— would magically show up and help Truman stagger back to his apartment.

At one of our last dinners with him in 1982, he gave us a book he wrote about muses. He told us stories about him and an ex-lover in Switzerland. Truman said he had sold his house for $800,000 and wanted to avoid taxes, so he sold it for cash and had his lover bring the money back to the United States. The lover told Truman that he was robbed at the airport, and they took the cash along with some Cartier watches of Truman's. Truman did not believe him, and they broke up. We, of course, never knew if any of these stories were true, but we didn't care because he told them with such flair.

CHAPTER

FIFTEEN

Sammy Davis Jr.

We had a live-in housekeeper to stay with our children while we were out at night. Her name was Melrose, and she was born in Africa. When one night we told her that Sammy Davis Jr. was coming over to our place for the evening, she asked if she could make dinner for him. She told us that he was her idol, and she wanted to cook him a special African meal. Sammy arrived, thanked her profusely for the wonderful meal, and then took us aside and told us that he hated African food. He suggested we go back to his hotel suite, where he had some real soul food ready to cook.

Another memorable time with Sammy Davis at our apartment happened one December night before he was about to go to the Bahamas for a vacation. He stopped in NYC for a few days. He had rented a yacht in the Bahamas that would take him and some friends out for a week and then end up in Miami. He liked to take trips with his own group of friends and each year would rent a boat for a small number of people. He was very close to Liza's ex-husband, Jack Haley Jr. Both of them knew the most minute details about every movie made and tried to top each other with their knowledge of every aspect of film. Jack was staying with us at our apartment for a few days before he and Sammy were leaving for the Bahamas.

They were at our apartment one night with Sammy's assistant, David Steinberg. David was more than just Sammy's assistant; he was a good friend. He had the same name as the comedian, and all his life, people would confuse them. David was a fun guy who, when he found out that Arlene was a housewife with young children mingling with world-famous celebrities, made up a box of personalized calling cards for her. They listed her as "vice president of creative affairs," along with a list of other made-up titles for her to give out to people.

Our phone rang, and when Arlene answered, she told me that it was our neighbor, Gail. She lived in the apartment building across the street from us and wanted to talk to me. Gail had a daughter the same age as our son Marc, about seven, and they had playdates together. Arlene would walk Marc across the street when he played at Gail's apartment, but she never met Gail because only the nanny greeted Arlene at the door. The nanny would also drop Gail's daughter at our place for playdates. Gail was an extremely wealthy, divorced woman whose father was one of the richest and notorious businessmen in the country. Gail had no desire to meet, much less socialize, with a dentist and his wife.

When I picked up the phone to talk to Gail, she told me that while she was flossing her teeth, a piece of floss broke and was wedged between two teeth. She knew that I was a dentist and asked me to come right over to her place and help her. I explained that I had company and could not leave, but she was welcome to come over to my apartment. After she told me what a problem it would be to get dressed and walk across the street, she reluctantly agreed. I knew what a snob she was and told my guests about her background.

When she rang the bell, Sammy decided that he would answer the door. When he did, she was shocked. She expected a common dentist to open the door, not a world-famous superstar. What I didn't know at the time was that Gail always wanted to be an actress. She was very attractive and very, very rich. David, who was divorced and not financially well off, immediately showed her considerable attention. I took care of her floss problem in my bathroom, and instead of leaving, she wanted to stay. She really wanted to hang out when she heard that Jack Haley produced the Academy Awards, and he too was in our apartment with Sammy. We were having dinner the next night with Sammy, Jack, and David before they were to leave for their vacation. David, seeing a possible chance of marrying a wealthy, beautiful woman and retiring early, asked Sammy if he could invite Gail for dinner. Gail was excited about being around these famous Hollywood people and told us that she would meet us at the restaurant. She called us the next morning to confirm and acted like our best friend.

When we met at the restaurant, Gail was the last to arrive. She walked into the restaurant wearing a very sheer, see-through top, which left little to the imagination. She walked over and sat down next to Sammy on his left. Sammy (who lost his left eye in an auto accident at age twenty-nine), without missing a beat, told her to please sit on his right side as he wanted to enjoy the scenery. The next day, Sammy and friends left for the boat trip in the Bahamas.

When we returned home from dinner that night, our phone rang. It was a call from our new best friend, Gail. She excitedly suggested that we all go to Florida with our children and then meet Sammy and the group when they returned from their boat trip. It was Christmastime, and the kids were off from school. We had decided that year to spend Christmas in NYC instead of traveling. We told Gail that, on such short notice, we would never find hotel rooms for the family and us. She explained that we would not have to worry about that because she owned two large homes right next to each other on an exclusive private island in Miami. Her father also had an estate there where he lived and worked. She had not been to Florida in eight years but told us that she kept a full-time staff there in case she ever decided to go. She said that she would need a few days to get herself packed, but we could leave immediately. She would have her driver pick us up at the airport, and her staff would take care of us at one of her two homes.

After checking with Sammy that, indeed, he, Jack, and David were planning to spend time in Miami after they docked, we decided to book a flight and go. We landed, were picked up by her limo driver, and arrived at a mansion. The staff was there to greet us, and for three days, our family had a great time in the marble baths, giant playrooms, and wonderful grounds. Each day as the staff waited on us, they told us that Gail would arrive soon. When she finally arrived, four days later, to stay in the huge house next door to us, she found that it was not ready for her to occupy. The two homes had not been lived in for seven years, the water was rusty, and the air-conditioning needed repair. Gail announced that she would sleep in our home until the other house was ready.

The next morning, Arlene and I were having breakfast while Gail was still asleep. There was a large sliding glass door facing the bay in the back of the home. I saw two men with guns by their side and a man in a black bathrobe knocking on the glass door. I nervously opened it, and the man said, "I'm Gail's father." And he walked in, with two other men following him. The four bodyguards sat down in the back of the room while her father introduced himself. He explained that he wanted to meet Gail's guests, told us to tell Gail when she woke up that he was here, and invited all of us to dinner that night.

He sat down, picked up a phone, and started to give orders to the person on the other end of the phone. He wanted to sell thousands of shares of this stock and thousands of shares of that stock. He was, for some reason, trying to impress us and did. I told him that I was nervous just buying a few hundred shares of stock and then asked him what business he was in. He told me that he had businesses in every state in the United States, except two, and in most countries around the world. After a few more phone calls, he had his first two bodyguards open the glass door. He followed them out, trailed by the other two bodyguards. I watched them all get into a long black cigarette boat and speed off. That night, we had dinner with Gail and her father as the four bodyguards ate at an adjoining table in the restaurant.

When Sammy returned to Florida from the trip, he invited us all to join him on the boat for the day. Gail told him that the next time he came to Florida, he should not rent a boat because her father had a much bigger one that she can use. Sammy was not happy with her remark because he did not want to be upstaged by this rich, showy woman. Then next night, Sammy invited us all to see the movie *Superman*, which had just been released. It was playing at a local theater. Sammy rented out the entire theater, so it was just us and our families would have a private evening there.

Gail did not tell any of us that she had a serious boyfriend. When her boyfriend found out that Gail was going to Florida, he flew down to be with her. Gail, however, wanted to be with our group, and she could not have her boyfriend in the same room as David. Each day Gail gave the boyfriend a different excuse to ditch him until he finally flew back home. Gail told us that it had been the best time of her life, and she was going to stay a little longer while we made our plans to return home. She vowed to call us when she got back to New York; however, she enjoyed Florida so much that she remained there, never to return to NYC. It was the last time we ever saw her.

David Steinberg never saw her again either. He eventually left Sammy and went out on his own. He became the very successful manager of such talents as Billy Crystal and Robin Williams and was instrumental in guiding their careers.

CHAPTER

SIXTEEN

Kate Jackson

On Saturday, May 1, 1982, we were in Westhampton with Liza Minnelli and Mark Gero. I played tennis with Mark, and then we all went to see *Victor/Victoria* at the local movie theater. We had a wonderful weekend, and Liza told us about her desire to play Mama Rose in *Gypsy*. We watched her ex-husband Jack Haley's TV show *Ripley's Believe or Not!*

Mark got a call that night from his best friend, Waldo, who was going to marry Kate Jackson. Kate was a major celebrity starring in *Charlie's Angels* on TV and was on hiatus in NYC, visiting with Liza, and met Waldo. Mark Gero had a group of close friends who were not in show business. Waldo was his closest friend, and when Mark married Liza, Waldo got a taste of being around a celebrity. When he met Kate, he got his chance. It was a strange pairing because he lived and worked in the family business in NY, while Kate lived and worked in LA. On Friday, May 14, 1982, Kate Jackson flew into NYC after her week shooting *Charlie's Angels* ended. She and Waldo got married and were driving out to Westhampton to honeymoon at our home. I drove out later, and the next day, Gina Lollobrigida was flying in from Rome to spend a week with us in Westhampton.

Gina is a fabulous photographer and took dozens of pictures of the two of them. Waldo and Kate were hot and heavy to the point of embarrassment. They would periodically interrupt the photo session to retire to their bedroom, where we soon heard the vibrations. They would emerge, take some more pictures, and go back to the room. We all went to our local pizza restaurant, Baby Moon, for dinner. Kate and Waldo held up slices of pizza while they embraced, and Gina took photos. We then put candles on a large cheesecake and took more pictures for their honeymoon album.

The only tense moment was when a local person tried to take a picture, and Kate exploded and demanded the film from her. (Those were the days when cameras had film.) After an uncomfortable altercation, the woman gave Kate the film to destroy. The next day, the honeymooners left to visit Waldo's family. The following Monday, Kate flew back to LA to resume shooting on *Charlie's Angels*, and Waldo returned to his work in NY. They both soon realized how foolish they were to get married. They hardly saw each other again and, within a short time, got divorced.

Arlene and I have always maintained a close and strong family bond. Even during the crazy Studio 54 days, we had dinner with the children every night, tucked them into bed, took a nap, and then went out at midnight to Studio 54. On late nights, I would get home from Studio 54 by six o'clock, shower, wake the kids for school and breakfast, and go back to sleep for a few hours before leaving for my office. My working hours started later on the days after my Studio 54 evenings. Our children were used to coming with us when our entertainer friends performed locally, or many times, we traveled with the children to see our performer friends.

When our daughter, Lauren, was seven years old, we took her with us to see Lena Horne's wonderful one-woman show on Broadway called *The Lady and Her Music*. When we asked Lauren after the show how she liked it, she told us that she enjoyed it but said, "I'd rather see someone I know." She was used to going out to see a show and knowing the performer, and she also enjoyed going backstage.

We have a large circle of friends who are not in the entertainment industry who have also fulfilled our lives. They have mixed together at our parties with our family and friends in the entertainment world. That has made our family weddings and bar mitzvahs quite unique.

SEVENTEEN

Bar Mitzvah and Weddings

In 1983, our son, Marc, had his bar mitzvah party at our friend Albie's El Morocco nightclub. One of the reasons we love Liza and think of her as part of the family is her reaction to this event. She was at the height of her fame and touring all over the world. We were walking with her in NYC one day and told her that Marc would be having a bar mitzvah. She said to us, "That's an important occasion to you, right?"

When we said yes, she walked into the nearest telephone booth and called her manager. She told him the date and said, "No matter what comes up, do not book me on that date."

One of our friends, Nikki Haskell, had a local weekly television show that highlighted the top entertainment events in the city. She asked if she could film our party for her show, and then she would give us all the footage for ourselves. We told her that we would only allow it if her cameras would film our guests in a respectful, unobtrusive manner. We wanted our guests to have privacy and enjoy the evening, and she promised that she would. A few months after the event, our party was seen on her show and advertised as "the jet-set bar mitzvah." Her show had two parts, our bar mitzvah and the opening that week of Trump Tower. When our family members were called up to light honorary candles for our son, Marc, Liza and Mark were one of the couples, along with Julie Budd. The whole group from Café Central came, including the owner Peter Herrero. Paul Herman, Joe Pesci, Liza Minnelli, Gina Lollobrigida, Obba Babatundé, Prince Egon Von Furstenberg, William B. Williams, Georgianne Walken, and even Steve Rubell. Steve was in a great mood and danced with everyone. In all our many nights at Studio 54, we never remembered him dancing there.

A few weeks before the bar mitzvah, we were at Café Central. One of our new favorite people whom we met there was an actor named Jimmy Hayden. He was starring on Broadway with Al Pacino in the critically acclaimed play *American Buffalo*. He had just finished filming a major role in the soon-to-be-released movie *Once upon a Time in America*. He was on his way to becoming a major star on Broadway, as well as Hollywood. We found him to be one of the most upbeat and friendliest people we have ever met. Only Robin Williams, bouncing around from table to table each night at the restaurant, could match Jimmy's energy and enthusiasm.

Jimmy came over to our table and remarked that everyone he knew at the restaurant was talking about going to our son's bar mitzvah. He asked us what takes place at a bar mitzvah because he had never attended one. When he walked away from the table, Arlene and I decided that since all his friends were coming, we would include Jimmy. We told him the details and invited him with a date. He showed up and expressed to us, on the way out of our party, what a wonderful time he had.

The day after the bar mitzvah, we saw the *New York Post* front-page headline: "Jimmy Hayden found dead in Harlem street from a heroin overdose." On the cover was a full-page photo of Jimmy and his date, taken at our bar mitzvah celebration. We had hired a photographer to take pictures at the party; he obviously heard the news and quickly sold his photo to the paper. It was the last picture taken of Jimmy alive.

The next day at my office, I received a call from the *New York Post* saying they were trying to find the mystery woman last seen with Jimmy. I had no desire to be involved in this story and told them that I had no idea of her name and to please leave me out of it. The reporter asked me how I could not know the names of all the people in attendance at my event. I replied that my invitation was to Jimmy Hayden and guest. That was one sad memory from an otherwise happy occasion in my life.

Our daughter Lauren's bat mitzvah was also not your typical one. At the morning temple service, the rabbi asked us to choose two people to have the honor of opening and closing the arc when the Torah was taken out. That morning, the temple congregation, the children, our friends, and relatives watched as Gina Lollobrigida opened the arc. Then at the end, Lindsay Wagner, whom everyone knew as "the Bionic Woman," closed the arc. We met Lindsay when she was dating Jack Haley Jr. She is a very spiritual person and is the person our children, Arlene, and I go to for guidance in many things.

The party was at Windows on the World on the 101st floor of the World Trade Center. It was a very windy, stormy day. We feared that many people would not show up because the weather was frightening. Luckily, everyone came, and we were so thankful to have our friends and relatives with us for that joyous celebration. The towers were swaying back and forth from the high winds, and it really was a "rockin' party." Our friend Sheryl Lee Ralph, at one point, gathered all the children together to hold hands, and she led them in singing the Whitney Houston song "The Greatest Love of All."

When our son, Marc, had his bar mitzvah, Gina flew in from Italy. She had never been to a bar mitzvah before, but she knew it was a birthday celebration. She bought him an expensive cashmere sweater. She later realized how important this event was for a thirteen-year-old. A few years later when she attended Lauren's bat mitzvah, she decided to get her a more significant gift. She flew to Switzerland and bought Lauren a $10,000 gold and diamond Omega watch inscribed "To Lauren, Love Auntie Gina." Lauren was thrilled, but Marc felt gypped. He said that was the disadvantage of being the elder sibling.

Our son Marc's wedding was at the Saint Regis Hotel, and Lauren's was at the Pierre Hotel. We mixed in family speeches, speeches of our children's friends, and dancing with entertainment by some of our friends. Marc had booked the Saint Regis date before proposing to his wife, Amanda. He knew that she always wanted to be married at the Saint Regis roof. He was and still is a romantic. Our guests told us afterward that it was the greatest wedding party they had ever attended. Julie Budd, whose voice is often mistaken for Barbra Streisand, sang to a standing ovation. Liza Minnelli spoke emotionally about knowing our children since they were babies and sang to another standing ovation. Gina Lollobrigida congratulated the newlyweds. Neil Sedaka performed some of his amazing songs.

Neil was the person Lauren chose to sign the ketubah (the Jewish marriage contract) at her wedding because she felt very close to him. He wrote a romantic brand-new song for her and her husband at the time, Illya Shell, called "I Fell in Love with a Dream," which he sang for the very first time at their wedding. (The marriage turned out to be not such a good dream, and eventually, they divorced.) Neil and our friend Denise Rich also wrote a special song for Lauren and performed it together at the wedding.

When Lauren was an infant, her baby nurse would bathe her while singing the Hal David song "Raindrops Keep Fallin' on My Head." We were close friends with Hal David and his wife, Eunice, and have spent great times with them in NY, LA, and Europe. Hal wrote the lyrics and Burt Bacharach the music for many of the greatest songs of our generation—"Walk on By," "Close to You," "One Less Bell to Answer," "Wishin' and Hopin'," "What the World Needs Now Is Love," "I Say a Little Prayer," "Anyone Who Had a Heart," "Message to Michael," "Do You Know the Way to San Jose?," "I'll Never Fall in Love Again," "The Look of Love," "Alfie," "Broken Hearted Melody," "A House Is Not a Home," "Promises, Promises," "This Guy's in Love with You," "What's New Pussycat?," and countless others. After I told the guests about the significance of Hal's song to Lauren, he got up and sang it. We had let the band take a short break, and when we realized Hal did not play the piano, Neil Sedaka saved the day by playing it for Hal.

The week of Lauren's wedding, Liza's husband and manager, David Gest, had her booked for two weeks at the Palace. When she realized Lauren's wedding was on a Saturday night during her run, she had David make the unheard-of request of scheduling her Saturday night show at five o'clock instead of eight. Arlene was in the ladies' room during our cocktail party. She overheard three of the guests of Lauren's in-laws saying that they were told that Liza was supposed to sing at the wedding, but that was ridiculous because she was appearing on Broadway. People were shocked when Liza and David entered dressed in their formal attire as the newlyweds were about to begin their first dance. Julie Budd shared fond memories and said some lovely things about Lauren and, as always, sang wonderfully. Liza gave an emotional speech about Lauren and sang beautifully and dramatically. She then announced to our guests that Luigi, Arlene, and Liza's legendary dance teacher would lead them all onto the dance floor doing the "Luigi walk." We actually didn't have time for all the friends who wanted to entertain because we did not want to take time away from traditional wedding speeches and dancing.

The wonderful singer Freda Payne was a guest. She brought with her the orchestral arrangements for her hit song "Band of Gold." Sammy Davis had passed away years before, and Altovise attended with a date. He looked and acted like Sammy. She told us that he was a great singer and asked if he could sing at the wedding. They all understood our time limitations and were happy to just enjoy the evening without having to sing. I did make a speech thanking everyone for coming. I mentioned that many people had been asking me how I felt after throwing such a magnificent party. I confessed, "To be honest, I feel a lot poorer."

CHAPTER

EIGHTEEN

Tony Martin–Cyd Charisse

We have had some wonderful parties throughout our lives. We had our thirtieth wedding anniversary at the Rainbow Room in Rockefeller Center. We included our family and a very small group of friends consisting of Julie Budd and her fiancé, John Wagner; Neil and Leba Sedaka; Ginny and Henry Mancini; and Tony Martin and Cyd Charisse. Arlene and I were great admirers of Cyd as she starred and danced in those great MGM musicals such as *Singin' in the Rain*, *The Band Wagon*, *Brigadoon*, and *Silk Stockings*. She and Tony were close friends of Ginny, and when Ginny introduced us to them, we instantly hit it off. Cyd was very soft spoken and lovely.

Tony was charming and wonderful to be around. He was a favorite of Arlene's mother, and we had always enjoyed watching his movies when they were shown on TV, especially *Ziegfeld Girl* and *Casbah*. In 1958, Tony Martin became the highest-paid performer in Las

Vegas with a five-year deal at the Desert Inn. We traveled with them to Florida and Atlantic City, where Tony performed. Tony sang at Feinstein's nightclub at the Regency Hotel in NYC when he was in his midnineties and was amazing. One weekend we went with Cyd, Tony, and Ginny to Atlantic City to hear Tony perform. Arlene sat with Cyd at a table in the nightclub while Tony sang. Arlene could not get over how great he sounded. When Arlene told this to Cyd, she simply said with pride, "Of course. Don't you know he's the best?"

When Tony was in his nineties, he was booked in Florida at senior citizen resorts, and he would do a few venues each night. He invited us to travel with him while Cyd was in LA. We watched the residents scalping tickets outside as they piled in to see him. Often, there were no seats left for us, and Tony would have the stagehands place two chairs for us on the side of the stage behind the curtain to watch the show.

Ginny Mancini was a backup singer for Mel Tormé when she met Henry, who was the rehearsal pianist. After both Henry and Cyd passed away, Ginny remained close friends with Tony Martin until he died. We still remember one of the last times we saw Tony; he was ninety-eight years old. Together with Ginny, we picked him up for dinner; and before dropping him off at the end of the evening, Ginny put on a CD in her car. They both sang along beautifully to it. It was a song that he had recorded seventy years earlier, and she was one of the backup singers. It brought tears to our eyes watching and listening to them.

The last time we saw him in LA, Ginny brought us over to his apartment. He was ninety-nine years old, wearing a baseball cap, and barely able to talk or even look up. Ginny put on some music and suggested that he sing along with it. He immediately came to life and sang each lyric in perfect tune. The wonder of music! At our anniversary party, both Neil Sedaka and I got the rare opportunity to dance with Cyd. Neil afterward told me that dancing with her was one of his great thrills as he admired her so much in those wonderful MGM musicals.

{CHAPTER}

NINETEEN

Jack Haley Jr.—The Oscars

When Liza and Jack Haley divorced, he converted Liza's large closet area into a guest room. We remained very close friends with Jack and stayed with him in that room whenever we came to LA. It was a large room, but it had no windows. When he arose in the morning to have breakfast with us, he would come to the door and bellow out, "Good morning, cave people!" In time, he would expand out the room, and our guest room then had large windows with wonderful views of the mountains.

Jack was a brilliant filmmaker. He was Liza's second husband, after Peter Allen. Even after they divorced, they still remained friends. Jack directed the films *That's Entertainment!* and *That's Dancing!*, among others. He created the TV show *Entertainment Tonight* and received a royalty check from it until the day he died. He was also responsible for the successful TV show *Ripley's Believe It or Not!*

Jack produced the Academy Awards shows a few times and invited us to it each time. It was very exciting for us to attend the Oscars with the producer. We sat in the producers' seats, and that had the famous actors sitting near us wonder what films we were in. Everyone sitting around us were major stars nominated for Oscars that year. On one of the occasions, we met at Jack's house for drinks before heading over to the award show with Sammy Davis and Altovise; Lorna Luft and her husband, Jake; and Jack's date for the evening, Kim Novak. Jack had arranged for Kim to be honored at the Oscars that year.

Sammy Davis and Kim had a personal relationship years before, and it was fun to see Sammy and Jack compete for her attention, although Altovise was not very happy. Kim Novak was becoming a major star in Hollywood when she started dating Sammy Davis. In 1957, Sammy Davis Jr. was considered the world's greatest entertainer. He was performing at Chicago's most famous nightclub, Chez Paree. He was singing to his date, Kim Novak, who was seated ringside. Kim had just finished filming Alfred Hitchcock's film *Vertigo*. The role would make her a superstar. (Her films include *Picnic*, *The Man with the Golden Arm*, *Pal Joey*, and *Bell, Book, and Candle*. In 1966 and only in her midthirties, she withdrew from acting.)

Harry Cohn, who ran Columbia Pictures, was the toughest and meanest mogul in Hollywood. He did not want his star to be seen in public with a black man because he felt that it would ruin her career. He got word to Kim that if she continued to date Sammy, he would make sure that Sammy would lose his other eye. That evening became the last time they were seen together in public.

Jack loved the idea of having Kim as his Oscar date, partly to enjoy Sammy and Altovise's reaction. Jack had a devilish side to him. Sammy was his closest friend, and he understood Jack well. There was a little friendly competition that night for Kim's attention, and Altovise kept her feelings quiet.

Kim turned out to be a very lovely woman, and we got along very well with her. She told us that she decided to leave Hollywood early in her career to live in the country. She was very happy with her horses and animals and only came that evening because she was being honored. She seemed very happy with her life away from Hollywood.

After the Oscar broadcast and the parties, many people continued the celebration at Jack's home. It was fun casually hanging out with stars like Clint Eastwood, Jack Palance, and Charles Bronson in Jack's living room. One year when Jack produced the Oscars, he had a segment honoring *The Wizard of Oz*. We went in his limo with him to pick up his father, Jack Haley Sr., and Ray Bolger. As we arrived at the homes of the former Tin Man and Scarecrow, each of them very slowly limped their way into the limo. They both could hardly walk, and we wondered how they would be able to walk out for their bows. Later, we sat in our seats while their entrance was announced and observed each of them enthusiastically bounce onto the stage as if they were "off to see the wizard." Turn the spotlight on an entertainer, and they come to life.

Years later, we were in LA and were invited to an annual event held at a high school honoring people in LA who originally came from Brooklyn. As we were seated, we saw two people help the legendary comedian Sid Caesar into a chair right behind us. Sid was best known for two pioneering 1950s live television series, *Your Show of Shows* and *Caesar's Hour*, which were watched weekly by sixty million people, and he was also the coach in both *Grease* movies. He could barely move and seemed to be almost in a vegetative state. Well-known people from Brooklyn were introduced to the audience to say some words or perform. When Sid's name was called, we turned to see his seatmate help him to his feet. He suddenly managed to not only get up but also ad-lib joke after joke until he sat back down to cheers from the crowd. Show business folks are a special breed when a spotlight is on them. (Fortunately, no one was interested in honoring a successful dentist, so I didn't have to get up and speak.)

TWENTY

Michael Jackson

The year Jack honored *The Wizard of Oz* at the Academy Awards show, he had Liza and Lorna there to represent Judy Garland. Liza and Michael Jackson performed on the telecast. After the broadcast, I had a great time dancing with Liza at the Governors Ball with a band led by Max Weinberg, the drummer from Bruce Springsteen's E Street Band. (I managed to keep up with Liza on the dance floor, although upon reflection she may have held back a bit to make me feel good.)

Arlene and I later went back to Jack's house, where he had a party for some of the movie stars and friends involved in the Oscars show. When they left, Jack said good night and went to sleep after his long day producing the event. We retired to our room, removed our formal attire, and got ready for bed when we heard the doorbell ring. We opened the door to find Liza and Michael Jackson. They had come to pay their respects to Jack after going to one of the after-parties.

Michael had a huge limo parked in the driveway waiting for them, and we invited them in. When we told Liza that Jack was asleep, she asked if it was okay for her and Michael to hang out for a while. We had met Michael a few times but hadn't spent long periods with him before. Once while getting off the elevator at the Waldorf to visit Sammy, we rang the wrong doorbell. It was answered by a sleepy Michael Jackson, informing us that Sammy's room was down the hall.

We were amazed at how shy Michael was. He spoke with a very high-pitched voice and was very polite but was not much of a conversationalist. As quiet as he was, Liza was the opposite. She was animated and in great spirits. She kept the conversation going nonstop with Michael, asking him all sorts of questions about his music. He had just released the song "Billy Jean," and it was a big hit. Liza kept asking him about the meaning of the lyrics. Liza also had Michael show her his dance steps, and we loved watching them dance together. It was a treat to see them both dancing away to his music.

Liza had come in wearing a tuxedo suit and carrying a big bag. She excused herself to go into our room to change and soon came out wearing a casual top and comfortable black pants. Left alone talking to Michael while she changed was not easy for us as he spoke so low, but we found him extremely warm and friendly. We were able to exchange stories about Sammy Davis, whom he greatly admired. The four of us stayed up talking and trading stories until we noticed that the sun was coming up. We looked at the clock and noticed that it was eight o'clock. Michael's limo and the driver were still parked in the driveway. Although none of us wanted to leave, we had a noon flight to NYC, and Liza had a late afternoon flight.

Liza went into our room, grabbed her tuxedo suit, stuffed it into her large bag, and got into the limo with Michael, who drove her to her hotel. Liza was married to Mark Gero at the time, but Mark did not come out for the Oscars. We were exhausted but managed to pack up and make our plane. We liked all of Liza's husbands, including Peter Allen, Jack, and Mark. The other husbands were more show business, and Mark was more macho Italian but very nice.

We had a formal event the next day in NYC. When we arrived back home, I immediately unpacked and hung up my tuxedo. Something was wrong; the pants did not match the jacket. I suddenly realized that when I had taken off my tuxedo, I left it on the bed when the doorbell rang. When Liza went into our room to change, she left her tuxedo suit on our bed as well. When she went back to get it, she took my pants by mistake instead of hers. She was flying back that night with my pants while I had hers. I needed to get my pants back for the formal that I had the next day. *How do I go over to her apartment and explain to her husband that, while he was not with her in LA, we somehow switched pants?* It did not look good as some of her past relationships ended when she had a flirtation with someone else.

First thing in the morning, I called her assistant, who worked out of an office in Liza's apartment. I explained the mix-up as best as I could and told her to find my pants in Liza's suitcase and to call me when Mark left to exercise. A few hours later, she called, saying that Mark went out, and Liza was still asleep. I rushed over to the apartment with her pants and met her assistant at the door, and we quickly exchanged pants.

⊰[CHAPTER]⊱

TWENTY-ONE

Jack Haley Jr.—Special Party

Jack Haley always stayed with us when he visited NY. Every summer he flew to NY to spend the Fourth of July in Southampton with his friend Jamie Niven, the son of actor David Niven. Jack would stay with us for a few days, and then we would drive him out to Niven's home in Southampton. One year the Fourth was on a Wednesday, and we mixed up the weekend that Jack was to go to Southampton. He came to NYC one week earlier than we assumed, and we were away. My mother, who loved Jack, told us that she would be glad to look after him while he stayed at our apartment. She enjoyed feeding people and checked in with him every day to see what he needed.

Jack had one major vice; he was an alcoholic. Each day for four days, my mother would stop by and ask Jack what he wanted to eat. Each time, he declined food but asked her to get him a liter of vodka. After four days, my mother called me, saying that the local liquor store owner was giving her funny looks because she came in each day to purchase a liter of vodka. She got a kick out of our show business friends but was sometimes wary of their personal habits.

One time during the run of Studio 54, we told her we would take her to witness the scene. She was overwhelmed by the energy and atmosphere. The next day at her beauty parlor appointment, she gushed to her hairdresser about spending an evening at Studio 54. He asked her how she reacted to seeing all the poppers there. (Poppers were vials of amyl nitrite passed around on the dance floor for the people to sniff to get an immediate rush of energy.) My mother, upon hearing his question about all the poppers at the club, simply answered, "No, there weren't papas. It was a young crowd."

When Jack was in town, he brought us to many interesting events. At the opening night party for the first show of his new TV concept called *Entertainment Tonight*, Robin Leach was the host. Every celebrity in NYC was there, and it was a great start to what would become a popular TV staple. Today there are many versions of Jack's original idea of presenting programs with multiple celebrity interviews and stories. We got to know Robin and his many girlfriends well over the years. His popular show *Lifestyles of the Rich and Famous* made him rich and famous. When he moved to Las Vegas, he would arrange for us to see all the best shows when we came to town.

One day when Jack was staying with us, we made him a birthday party at our apartment. We had just finished redecorating, and the decorators persuaded us to make a step-up platform to add more visual interest to the apartment when entering it. When we mentioned that we were afraid someone would trip and fall, they told us that it was ridiculous to think a person would not see this one step when walking in. The first guest to arrive at our party was the famed musician Mitch Miller, known at the time for his very popular TV show *Sing along With Mitch*. We had never met him. We opened the door and greeted him with a warm hello. He promptly stepped forward, tripped on the platform, and fell down face forward on our carpet.

An amazing group of guests continued to arrive. Steve Rubell came early and bonded with Mitch Miller, David Frost, and Peter Boyle. Peter played the comical monster in the Mel Brooks film spoof *Young Frankenstein* and would later star in the TV show *Everybody Loves Raymond*. He was best friends with John Lennon, who was the best man at Peter's wedding.

Jack was going to produce a TV special with the rock group Kiss; therefore, Gene Simmons and Paul Stanley were invited to the party. Kiss was extremely popular at that time. The only request they had was that no pictures be taken of them because no one knew what they looked like without their makeup. Gene Simmons had a wild reputation in the media, so we did not know what to expect. (Gene was known as "the Demon" and "the God of Thunder" but was born Chaim Witz. He had had live-in relationships with Cher and Diana Ross and is currently married to former *Playboy* playmate Shannon Tweed.) We were shocked when it turned out that Gene came to our party with his mother, Flora, who asked us if we had some milk and cookies for her son. A year later, Jack invited us and our children to a rock concert Kiss was doing at Madison Square Garden. Jack was filming it for his TV special. Arlene, who hates loud music, put in her earplugs and dozed off. She abruptly awoke at the finale only because giant flames in the background on the stage gave off so much heat that she felt it.

Our party had a great crowd, including Liza Minnelli and Lorna Luft. I was walking around, making sure that everyone had enough food and drinks, and then the doorbell rang, and I answered it. It was Debbie Harry, the lead singer of Blondie, one of the most popular rock groups of that day. (Blondie, with such major hits as "The Tide Is High" and "Heart of Glass," was inducted into the Rock and Roll Hall of Fame in 2006.) I tried to act like the hip host and asked her what she would like. She looked me in the eye and asked, "Got any smack?"

I answered, "No, but we have some mini-hot-dogs." I think she was disappointed, but she turned out to be a lovely guest. I have several pictures of me sitting in the living room next to her while eating dinner. We recently saw her in Southampton, where she participated in our friend Eugene Pack's *Celebrity Autobiography* show. (The show consists of celebrities reading from other celebrities' autobiographies, and it is a lot of fun.) She could not have been nicer, and we laughed about that night at our party.

Chita Rivera, one of our favorite people whom we have been friends with for years, was also at the party. (Chita is known for originating roles in Broadway musicals, including *West Side Story*, *Chicago*, *Bye Bye Birdie*, *The Rink*, *The Visit*, and *Kiss of the Spider Woman*. One other time, Chita came to our apartment when Gina

Lollobrigida was staying with us because Chita was looking into doing *The Rose Tattoo*. She wanted to talk to Gina about it, and Chita came over to chat with her. They got along wonderfully, but nothing happened with that project.

Arlene and I were friendly with Chita's limousine driver, Gail, because Gail drove for many celebrities. I still remember the shock in 1986 when their car got hit by a speeding taxi while making a U-turn on West Eighty-Sixth Street in Manhattan. Chita had multiple injuries, including breaking her left leg in twelve places. Fortunately, by 1988, Chita was mended after rehabilitation and was able to perform again, continuing to win awards for her work.

During the party, our son, Marc, was in his bedroom working on a fourth-grade project for school. His assignment was to interview an immigrant on their experience in coming to the United States. Chita had asked to see Marc to say hello, and we mentioned the project that he was working on. She told us that she would be happy to have him interview her and went into his bedroom, where it was quiet. When she rejoined the party, she told us she really enjoyed spending time with him and helping him with his project. She also remarked that, just between us, she was born in the United States. Chita wanted Marc to have an interesting interview and changed a few facts for his assignment.

Geoffrey Holder, a well-known dancer and actor who was in the movie *Annie* and a famous 7 Up commercial, was also at the party. He, too, agreed to be interviewed by Marc, and he was really born in Trinidad. At the end of the party, Steve Rubell invited us all to Studio 54 to continue the celebration.

TWENTY-TWO

Richard Nixon–Ronald Reagan–White House Dinner

When I first met Arlene, I was living in Manhattan, and she was living in Brooklyn with her parents. She had just enrolled in Finch, a small women's college. She was very close friends with Tricia Nixon and would sometimes sleep over at the Nixon apartment in Manhattan when we went out on late-night dates. Nixon was not yet president, but Arlene remembered seeing the book *The Making of the President* in his home library. We went to her end-of-school event, the Finch Ball, with Tricia and her boyfriend, Ed Cox. We sat with them at the affair, and they were a cute couple. They eventually married, and we lost contact with them after Nixon resigned. Tricia stopped seeing her old friends from school after Watergate.

During the Nixon presidency, he invited all the graduates of Finch to the White House for an event. It was my first private visit to the White House, and he was a charming host. One unfortunate moment occurred when Grace Slick, the lead singer of the popular group Jefferson Airplane, who had attended Finch for one year, managed to snare an invitation. (Jefferson Airplane were headliners at the Monterey Jazz Festival, Woodstock, and Altamont Free Concert. Their songs "Somebody to Love" and "White Rabbit" are considered two of the top rock and roll songs of all time by *Rolling Stone* magazine.) Grace brought as her date Abbie Hoffman, a revolutionary social activist, to the event. The FBI had them both barred from the event when it was discovered that they planned to spike the punch bowl with hallucinogenic drugs.

Up to that White House visit, my closest experience with a head of state was when I treated VP Nelson Rockefeller in my office. That morning, secret service agents arrived early to check out every corner of my dental office and stayed during his treatment. I was extracareful not to hurt him.

Arlene was taught impeccable table manners by her mother. When I first came into her life, she would occasionally correct me on how I held my fork and how to place down my silverware when I finished my meal. I would tell her to leave me alone and let me enjoy my meal. She would reply, "What if you are invited to dine at the White House and people noticed you eating like that?"

I looked at her and answered, "Seriously, when am I ever going to be invited to the White House for dinner?"

On March 19, 1985, I was invited by Gina Lollobrigida to be her escort at a White House dinner given by Pres. Ronald Reagan for the president of Argentina. Arlene traveled with us to Washington, but she had to remain at the hotel during the dinner. At nine thirty in the morning, I accompanied Gina to a welcoming ceremony at the White House for the Argentinian president. A young Arnold Schwarzenegger also attended with his mother as did golf legend Lee Trevino, tennis great Guillermo Vilas, Irene Cara, and a few other celebrities and foreign dignitaries. The formal dinner that night was for 109 people, divided into tables of eight. Gina was seated with Secretary of State George Schultz, and I was at another table. My mother had always instructed me to learn how to eat with proper table manners because "you never know if you might be invited for dinner one day at the White House." I thought of those words as I nervously sat down. Everyone there was notable, and I actually felt sorry for my table companions who drew me as their seatmate in this room full of luminaries.

Secretary Schultz had the first dance with Gina when the music started. Our entry into the main ballroom was very exciting. When they announced, "Presenting Dr. Allan Lazare and Miss Gina Lollobrigida," we entered, escorted by marines. It was one of the most exciting evenings of my life. I spent a good deal of time chatting with Nancy Reagan. When she heard that I lived in NYC, she told me how much she missed her friends there. I felt that this was a woman who would love spending time gossiping about various people and events in NYC because she seemed so anxious to talk.

After all the guests arrived in the main room, we lined up to take private pictures with the Reagans and the Argentinian president as they greeted us and shook our hands. I decided that I would also like a private picture with President Reagan. I asked the White House photographer where the best place to take a photo would be, and he pointed to a portrait of one of the presidents in the adjacent room. I walked up to President Reagan, who was having a conversation with Secretary of State Schultz, and requested a private photo with him. He looked somewhat dazed and asked me where we should take it. I took him under the arm and walked him into the next room. I then positioned him in the best place under the portrait and signaled to the photographer to snap a photo of us. President Reagan walked away from the conversation with George Schultz and followed me so obediently that I wondered about how easily he was led. I thought about that night years later when rumors surfaced about his possible periods of dementia in the final days of his presidency.

A few weeks after I returned home, I received photos from the evening. I sent back the private one with President Reagan and asked if he would please sign it and return it to me, and he did. As I was leaving the dinner and the waiters started to clear the tables, I went over to the president's table; and as a souvenir, I took President and Mrs. Reagan's place cards, my place card, the engraved White House matchbooks, the menu, and my invitation. After all, when was I going to be invited again?

As it turned out, I was invited again by Gina to escort her to an event at the White House honoring Italian Americans. Our close friends Ginny and Henry Mancini were also invited. It was a wonderful time. Many well-known Italians were there. I enjoyed spending time with Phil Rizzuto, Danny DeVito, and Nancy Pelosi, among others. This time, I was able to bring Arlene along with us. Nancy took pictures with Arlene and Phil, and Danny took pictures with me. It was a very intimate event, and everyone was very friendly to us. We have found that any Italians we have met all love and admire Gina.

❧{CHAPTER}❧

TWENTY-THREE

Bill and Hillary Clinton

Our last encounter at the White House occurred when a friend of ours invited us to donate $1,000 to attend a meet and greet at his home with Hillary Clinton. Her husband, Bill, was running for the presidency. We found her to be charming and very personable. We have been in her presence over the years since that time and found her always to be warm and attentive to everyone she comes in contact with. In person, she is quite different from the public image of sometimes appearing cold and artificial.

At the event, we met a couple who were close supporters of the Clintons. They lived in Washington, DC, and told us to please give them a call if we ever visit Washington. Bill Clinton became president, and one year we decided to spend a few days in Washington. We found their number and called them. We were surprised that they remembered us, and we met them in DC and had a lovely dinner.

At dinner, they asked us if we would like a private visit to the White House; and when we said yes, they set it up. When we arrived at the visitors' entrance, we showed our ID and were greeted warmly. A woman introduced herself as an assistant to the Clintons and expressed their regrets that they were out of town. She informed us that she had instructions to give us a private tour. She took us into all the rooms, and we even took pictures outside the Oval Office with the Clintons' cat, Socks. She brought us into the area where the president conducted his press conferences and photographed me behind the podium. It was a very special experience, and we later received a letter from the Clintons thanking us for being there. We wondered, *If contributing $1,000 brought us this degree of access to the White House, what perks do large contributors get?*

Years later, while vacationing at the Boca Raton Hotel in Florida, I was taking a walk on the grounds when I saw former president Clinton with a few people. It was before the days of cell phones, so I called up to my room and told Arlene to meet me downstairs with a camera. We did not get a chance to meet him at the White House, but here was an opportunity to take a picture with him. Arlene met me, and I told her to go over to him while he stopped to talk to the people with him. Arlene had met him once before at an event, but no pictures were taken. She had mentioned to me at that time that his piercing eyes looked directly at her, and she felt that he seemed to really focus on her.

Arlene went over the camera with me, focused it, and had me do a test picture of Clinton with the people he was talking to. She then went over to him and said, "I am sorry to bother you, but would you mind taking a photo with me?" She mentioned the name of our friends from DC, and he could not have been nicer. He posed with her for a photo as I pointed the camera and snapped. The shutter didn't click, and I tried again. Arlene, seeing my frustration, told Bill that she was sorry that the camera didn't work, but that she would fix it and return. She came over to me, surprised that I did not know how to take a simple picture. When she tried to press and snap, we discovered that I was not at fault. For the only time in all the years we owned the camera, the battery had died. The test picture of the group before had come out fine, but the battery died on my attempted photo of Arlene with Clinton. Our rare opportunity to take a picture with the former president was gone.

A few years later, we returned to the Boca Hotel for one night during our stay in Florida for a nostalgic visit. Just as we were joking about how years before we had missed the chance to take a picture with Bill Clinton, a group of people walked toward us. By the strangest of coincidences, it turned out that he was invited back to the hotel to speak at a convention. By this time, the iPhone had been invented. We went over to him and mentioned the problem with our camera years before, and he gladly took wonderful pictures with us both.

CHAPTER

TWENTY-FOUR

Lorna Luft

When we met Lorna Luft, she was twenty years old. We have been with her through all her personal relationships. She has been our dearest and closest friend now for forty-eight years. She is an intimate part of our family, and both of our children love and admire her. She is close with our grandchildren as well and even helped Lauren's son, Justin, get over his fear of dogs when she brought a potential Seeing Eye dog she was training to our house in the Hamptons. We often talk for hours about every aspect of our lives. She has been a constant presence in our world, and it has been a great joy having her in our lives. She has had some health issues with cancer over the past number of years, and the way she has handled it is an inspiration to many. She has helped so many others with her advice and actions, and we feel blessed to know her. She also has a fantastic personality and is always fun to be with. We only have to call and say hello and then find that, two hours later, we are still talking to one of the most interesting people we have known.

At one time, Lorna had a boyfriend who looked just like the famous nine-time Olympic swimming champion Mark Spitz. Whenever we were all out together, people would come over to him for his autograph. He had to disappoint them by explaining that he only looked like Spitz. After Lorna and he broke up and we had not seen him in a while, we suddenly bumped into him at a restaurant. We walked over and told him that we missed the fun times we had with him. He looked at us like we were crazy. To our embarrassment, we realized that we mistakenly walked over to the real Mark Spitz.

When Lorna's sister, Liza, was filming a movie in Mexico with Gene Hackman and Burt Reynolds, she invited Lorna to fly down to spend time with her on the set. Lorna and Burt had a fling in Mexico and dated for a time after they returned, but it did not last long. Unfortunately for Liza at the time, the paparazzi seeing the three of them out for dinner in Mexico led to stories of Liza and Burt having an affair. These false reports did not make Liza's husband, Jack Haley, too happy. No one knew that the relationship was really between Lorna and Burt. We always told Lorna that we looked forward to her settling down and that we would be at her wedding.

One day Lorna announced to us that she was indeed getting married, and we could finally go to her wedding. However, it was not in the USA but in England. She had met a rock star named Jake Hooker, who was in an English band called the Arrows. Jake had cowritten a song titled "I Love Rock and Roll," which became a huge hit, and his group was getting well known in England. We did not expect to have to fly to England for a wedding but were very happy to celebrate with her. After the wedding, they planned to live together in NYC. She was now going to be the wife of a rock star. She decided to keep her own name because taking his name would make her Mrs. Hooker.

It was 1977, and the British rock groups were very popular. When we arrived, Lorna told us the wedding events that were planned. On the day of the wedding, we were killing time at the bar of our hotel before driving to the church for the ceremony. We were dressed and ready early, and it seemed that time was moving very slowly. Suddenly, I looked at my watch and realized the time hadn't changed. After flying into London all the way from NYC, I thought we were going to miss the wedding because my watch battery had stopped. We raced out to hail a taxi, and fortunately, the wedding started late. Apparently, rock and roll people are not always on time.

A stag night for the men and a hen party for the women were planned for the night before the wedding. The women's night out looked fabulous. They were riding in stretch limousines to all the exclusive private clubs. At 5:00 a.m., the men and women were planning to meet up at a very hip, casual soul restaurant that served all night. The ladies all were dressed up in cocktail attire for their evening. I had bought a guidebook to London and read up on where to go. I read warnings about never getting into a car with strangers offering you private tours due to the criminal element in certain parts of town. I felt relief when Lorna told me that the small group of Jake's friends knew where to go. When I heard they were members of the most popular rock and roll groups, like the Rolling Stones, I felt that I was in for a special experience.

As I watched Arlene get into her limo with the other girls, I asked Jake what our evening plans were. He told me that we were meeting everyone, including Bill Wyman of the Rolling Stones, who was organizing the evening. We arrived at a street corner and met with a small group of rock and roll types. They were members of various popular rock groups of the day, along with a fellow named Dreyfus, from the famous banking family. I was looking forward to seeing the highlights of the London nightlife with these rock stars. I asked Bill where the limo was, and he replied they did not order one. They all started to ask one another, "Where should we go?" I suddenly realized that they had made no plans. We were now standing on some street corner in a bad section of London.

Just then, a man stepped out of a parked car and asked us if we were looking for a fun place to go. He told us that he would be happy to take us to a great location for a good time. Much to my fear and amazement, Bill said it seemed like a great idea. We all piled into the stranger's car. Soon we arrived at a sleazy-looking dive, and our driver said that we were at our destination. We were seated at tables and served cheap-tasting wine. A short time later, a show began featuring a broken-down group of strippers. A huge lady appeared in a clown suit and peeled off her clothing, only to reveal that, naked, she was still enormously fat. Mercifully, we didn't stay long.

Our new guide to London nightlife brought us to a few more places, one worse than the other. All the food was unappetizing, so we arrived at the hip soul food restaurant at four o'clock, one hour earlier than we were due to meet Lorna and the girls. It was a place where you had to knock on a small opening in the door so they could see you and then let you in. They took one look at our now worn-out and hungry-looking group, and they turned us away. It was only when we knocked again and the guys showed them their IDs with the names of famous rock stars that we were let in. We were starving and woofed down greasy portions of bacon and eggs. At five o'clock, our ladies arrived dressed in their cocktail finery, with stories about their time at Annabel's, Tramp, and the other prestigious private clubs where they wined and dined.

We grew to know Bill Wyman well over the years, and he always was wonderful company. He invited us to Rolling Stones concerts and dinners with him; his girlfriend, Astrid; and Lorna. He did have a passion for photography and kept a photo travelogue of the Rolling Stones tours. He also liked to take pictures of any attractive women he met along the way, and his photo collection was large. When he wanted to take a sexy picture of Arlene with his Polaroid camera, she was flattered but declined. When Gina Lollobrigida stayed with us one year, he invited us to hang out backstage with the group before they went onstage at Madison Square Garden. It was not just a favor to us but the group also wanted to meet Gina. We had a memorable time with them that night. There is a special high in hanging out with the Stones. (Note to my family: the high I mean is not from drugs ingested with them but the exciting energy of being around them.)

When Lorna and Jake returned to NYC to live, we were proud to be godparents to their first child, Jesse. (Jesse, I am happy to report, has grown up to be a fantastic young man with a wonderful family of his own.)

Lorna Luft and her husband at the time, Jake Hooker, lived two blocks from us on the Upper East Side. We loved to go to Studio 54 together, especially for the many special events. One winter night, there was to be a party for Cary Grant and Farrah Fawcett thrown by Faberge at Studio 54. It promised to be a fabulous party; however, on that day, there was a massive snowstorm in NYC that totally crippled the city. I thought about the old joke that "it was storming so hard I saw Superman getting into a cab." First Avenue outside our home was almost impassable, with snow piled up high, leaving just one lane for emergency traffic. We all made the same decision. "Let's try to go." We had no idea if Studio 54 would even be open, but Lorna and Jake trudged over to our building on the corner of First Avenue. We met them on the corner but saw no traffic and no way to get to the nightclub. The snow was piled up high in the street, and an attempted walk to the subway was out of the question.

As we looked down the deserted street, we noticed a lone taxi approaching with its off-duty light on. I said to Lorna that I'd handle this, and I promptly lay down in the street across the one remaining traffic lane. It was one of the dumbest things I ever did because the taxi would either stop or run me over. Fortunately, he stopped, and I made him a financial offer he couldn't refuse, and he drove us to Studio 54. Lorna wrote about this night in a chapter in her best-selling book about her life and her relationship with her mother, Judy Garland, and sister, Liza Minnelli, titled *Me and My Shadows*.

Off we went to Studio 54 in a blizzard, not knowing if it would even be open. When we arrived, we walked in and found three thousand people jammed into the place to party with Cary and Farrah. When we went to leave at four o'clock, we realized there was no way we could get home. Lorna spotted Huntington Hartford, a very wealthy elderly playboy, leaving with some young women. Lorna charmed him into taking us all home in his limo. Lorna told us after we got home that Huntington fell sound asleep on her shoulder, and she thought he died.

After Lorna and Jake divorced, we flew to London to join her on a tour that she was doing in various cities in England. She was touring with the legendary British dancer and choreographer Wayne Sleep. He was the person that Princess Diana chose to dance with when she performed at the Royal Opera House in 1985. (This dance was recently featured on the TV series *The Crown*.) We rode on the bus with Lorna and the band and noticed that she was spending a lot of time with her piano player and conductor. His name was Colin Freeman, and he was from England. Colin had a dry British wit and was very easy to get along with. We kept teasing her that we didn't want to fly over to England again for another wedding.

It turned out that she did marry Colin, and they had a magnificent wedding in England. It was at Highclere Castle, otherwise known as Downton Abbey. We weren't able to attend that wedding, but we have been best friends with them both now for many years. Colin is an extremely talented arranger, pianist, and conductor. They are a great couple and very supportive of each other. At her concerts when she introduces him, she describes Colin as the half that makes her whole.

CHAPTER

TWENTY-FIVE

Plax Mouthwash

When Studio 54 finally closed its doors in the early '80s, I suddenly found that I had time on my hands. I had shortened my office hours and realized that I was still earning the same income working fewer hours. For someone who was always busy either working or socializing with friends and family, I still had moments where I felt I could do more. This all changed after a trip to LA.

We always stayed with Jack Haley in LA. The day after arriving, we would go over to Sammy's home to say hello and plan our week. Every Sunday night Sammy would obtain from the studios the latest movie and run it in his living room for friends. This was before cable TV, and Sunday night at Sammy's home was a popular event. It drew many celebrities and interesting people.

There was one woman there who had a similar look to Arlene, and she came over to introduce herself. Her name was Beverly Sassoon, the wife of the famous hairstylist Vidal Sassoon. When the movie screening ended, people started to leave. Sunday night in LA was not a late light. We mentioned to Beverly that we just came in from NYC and were used to late nights and asked her if she knew of anything going on that night in town. She invited us to go back to her house, have some drinks, and hang out there because nothing was happening on Sunday night in LA.

She drove a two-seater sports car and told Arlene to come with her, while Jack Haley and I followed in Jack's car. We arrived at a gate, which opened, revealing a small home. We drove by this home, which turned out to be a guesthouse, and parked outside a huge mansion. We had been to many beautiful homes in LA, but this was spectacular. There were amazing grounds with two tennis courts. She invited us in and gave us a tour. Jack had his dog with him, which had a bowel movement accident in the hall during our tour. The home was very impressive, and she led us into a den for drinks and put on some music.

Soon a very upset man dressed in a bathrobe walked in and told her that the music system was also playing in his bedroom and woke him up. It was Vidal Sassoon. She told us after he left that they were going through a divorce but still living in different quarters in the same home. When Arlene and I returned to Jack's home later that night, we wondered how a hairdresser could afford such a magnificent mansion. We knew he was famous, but how much could he charge for a haircut and styling? We decided that there must be inherited money in the family.

When we returned home to NYC the following week, by chance, we saw that David Susskind—who had a popular weekly Sunday night TV interview show—had Vidal Sassoon as his guest. We were anxious to tune in and discover more about this man and how he earned all that money enabling him to live so well. Susskind asked Vidal the very questions we were wondering about. Vidal told him that while he had a very famous clientele and a great reputation, he realized that he could just charge so much for a styling. He decided that he needed to have a product that he could sell. By using his name and the fame of his clients, he could sell products to a mass market. He found an investor who believed in him, formed a company, and made his fortune.

As I watched this program, a light went off in my brain. I saw a parallel situation that I had with him. I was, at that time, very well known in the dental world. I had written a textbook used in many dental schools and had given talks in large hotel venues in NYC where dentists came from all over the country to sign up for my courses. I had a celebrity clientele, including Liza Minnelli, Farrah Fawcett, Ryan O'Neal, Robert De Niro, Halston, Truman Capote, and Gina Lollobrigida, to name a few. After the program ended at two o'clock, I took out pen and paper and stayed up all night making a list of possible dental products. In the early 1980s, many of the products we now have did not exist. Many things on the list that I made that night eventually came to market, like whitening agents. I decided to pick one product to start with and concentrate on that. I decided to develop a mouthwash.

At the time, there was no product that mentioned dental plaque. As a periodontist, I realized that the main cause of most dental diseases was the film of germs on teeth and gums called plaque. There was not a single product on the market addressing that problem. Toothpaste and mouthwash products advertised their ability to treat bad breath or tooth decay. Listerine and Scope were the leaders in helping people deal with bad breath. I immersed myself in research for the next few weeks and put together a mixture of substances to create a mouthwash to eliminate plaque. I wanted to change home dental care by developing a mouthwash that would allow the patient to remove plaque efficiently. People occasionally rinsed with mouthwash and then spat it out, intending to improve their breath after eating things like garlic. My concept was to have a mouthwash that, besides killing germs, acted as a soap to loosen the plaque clinging to teeth, allowing the toothbrush to remove it more easily. It would be a prebrushing rinse, designed to be used before every brushing. Every few weeks, there would be a need to buy a new bottle.

I hired a chemist to put the necessary ingredients together and tried it out on my patients. I had Farrah Fawcett try out the solution before it was a legitimate product. I realized that with her famous smile, she would be a good judge of how it worked. She wrote me a letter saying how much she liked it and told me how much it also helped her boyfriend and my patient, Ryan O'Neal.

I had an older distant relative who, after trying his hand in advertising, was involved with a few inventors raising money for their product ideas. He approached me about investing in his latest product, which was a miniature cigarette lighter small enough to fit in the outer sleeve of a pack of cigarettes. I did not feel that smoking products were the future and declined to invest. I told him about my mouthwash idea. He liked it and said that he would love to work on it with me because he knew about the ins and outs of registering and bringing products to market. An attractive container was developed, and we named the product Plax.

I did several presentations to major mouthwash companies like Warner-Lambert, who made Listerine. My goal was to sell it to them and receive a royalty. After each presentation, I received the same reaction. The company executives loved it, but the lawyers advised them that they could not make a claim to remove plaque. Plaque, they advised, was a film of germs, and people would not be able to buy Plax over the counter. They would need a prescription, greatly limiting their sales. They decided that there was no possibility of bringing Plax to the mass marketplace. I put the product on my shelf and stopped thinking about it, until a year later when I saw an ad for Listerine on TV. Instead of their usual claim about killing the germs causing bad breath, they were now advertising it as removing plaque. Their lawyers finally realized that I was right in believing that a plaque claim can be made without a prescription. Rather than buying my product, they just changed their advertising claims. When I look around today and see almost every dental product making claims about reducing plaque, I am proud to be the first person to recognize the importance of a plaque-reducing product.

In a short time, I found investment capital and became a private company called Oral Research Laboratories, manufacturing Plax in a New Jersey plant. The original red color was expanded to other colors to get more shelf space. The details of what followed are too numerous to elaborate on here as my experience in the business world could fill another book. There was intrigue and drama different from anything I had ever experienced. I spoke at dental conventions and did a good deal of media to help promote Plax. After a year, this one product company, formed in 1986, was doing a fabulous business. I was looking for a corporate big brother to invest in and increase our sales force. It was a private company, so no one knew how much we were earning. When we approached Pfizer and they saw the numbers, they agreed to invest $20 million for 20 percent of the company. This gave the company a value of $100 million. All the money stayed in the company, and my income was still mostly from my dental practice, which I did not want to close just yet. I felt most new companies fail in time, and I wanted to make sure that I still had my practice.

We earned more than $100 million that first year, and Plax was named one of the ten best new products of the year in *Fortune* magazine. They featured me in their article as did other financial publications. We were courted by many firms to go public, and we chose Alex Brown. Everything was ready to go when the stock market crashed in 1987, and that was the end of our public offering. However, after much drama that traumatized me from ever going back into business, I continued to forge ahead and find another solution. In one year, we had become a very large company, with our main offices taking up an entire floor in the Chrysler building on Forty-Second Street.

Despite considerable arguments among our board of directors, the company was sold. We had a one-day bidding war between Pfizer and Colgate, which Pfizer won. The final price was $265 million, an enormous price for a one-product company in 1989. Pfizer already owned 20 percent of the company, and after giving percentage ownership to some people running the day-to-day operations instead of salary and with other investors added along the way to help finance rapid expansion, my ownership percentage had decreased considerably. I still was left with enough to allow me to retire, close my dental practice in 1988, and pursue other interests.

When I had first discussed my concept of a mouthwash with Sammy Davis, he immediately offered to invest if I needed money. At that time, I never expected the idea to actually succeed and rejected the offer because I didn't want to lose his friendship if it failed. Years later, after I sold it, I had an uncomfortable night with him when he seriously berated me for not letting him invest and make money with it.

CHAPTER

TWENTY-SIX

Doing Media

A year after selling the company to Pfizer, they contacted me to ask if I would be interested in introducing Plax to other countries all over the world. Although I no longer had a financial interest in Plax, I was proud to do it. They offered to pay me one hundred thousand dollars a year if I would give them six days a year of my time. I figured one hundred thousand dollars in 1989 for six days of media work sounded like a pretty appealing deal, certainly easier than doing gum surgery. I could choose any days I liked, and they agreed to fly Arlene and me first class. They would pay my expenses for any length of time I wanted, and we could stay in any hotels I chose.

They booked me as a celebrity dentist from NYC and had me do media in each country, promoting Plax. For a few years, we flew all over the world, were put up in the finest resorts, and had a car and driver at our disposal. I appeared on TV and radio shows while enjoying the benefits of a vacation. We introduced Plax in England first, where I toured around from city to city, judging the "brightest smile in Britain" contest in each city. (Dental care is not good in England, and it was not easy finding great smiles in each city.) In the last interview before I left, the reporter asked me to judge the smiles of the royal family. I gave my opinion of each member, and when reading the newspaper on the plane the day I departed, I was shocked to see a large article about me. It described me as a famous dentist from the USA who criticized the royals. I was happy to be leaving the country that day.

I did several popular television shows in England. One was a number-one live TV show whose guests for the day were me as the celebrity dentist from the United States and a well-known author. He had just published a controversial book about the long-term sexual affair between Danny Kaye, the famous American actor, and Sir Lawrence Olivier, the celebrated British actor. Both of them were married, and this book was quite the topic of conversation. I was called out first and had organized in my mind how I would talk about my famous patients and how they used Plax. The first question she asked me was "Tell me about the sexual habits of Danny Kaye and Lawrence Olivier." I was stunned, to say the least. She had mixed up her two guests, and when I informed her that I was there to talk about teeth and not sex, we had a good laugh.

The next night, I was scheduled to do a live interview with Jonathan Ross, the top-rated interviewer feared by everyone. He was often compared to David Letterman but had the reputation for being nasty. I had never seen his show, so I tuned in the day before at my hotel. He had two guests on that night. The first was the renowned singer Sarah Brightman, who was married to Andrew Lloyd Webber and starred in many of his shows. The first question he asked her was "Do people tell you that you look like a chipmunk?" It went downhill from there.

The next guest was a popular and beloved actor-comedian who Jonathan implied was sympathetic to the Nazis. I was in a panic at the thought that, the next day, he would tear into me, a dentist from the States, and say disparaging things about Plax and ruin our campaign. The night of the appearance, I decided that I would not let him attack me. I sat down, and before he could ask me a question, I said to him, "You should be glad that I am on your show because I observed your teeth, and you need a lot of dental care. I can tell you how to improve your smile, and you really need my advice." He looked shocked, but that started an interesting conversation, and he turned out to be very nice to me.

I think many powerful people are intimidated by dentists. Years before, I had a patient who was very fearful when he sat down in my chair, almost shaking with fear. One day when Arlene and I were on a cruise that had gambling, we noticed a lot of activity at the dice table. A high roller was playing, and the crowd was cheering him on as he forcefully rolled the dice with authority. I told Arlene that I thought he might be a patient of mine, but I wasn't sure because my image of him was much different. I walked over to him, he took one look at me, and his body slumped down. He went from a "king of the world" demeanor to a meek, shy person in a few seconds. That's the effect a dentist can have on some people. If you have ever seen Lawrence Olivier in the *Marathon Man* movie or the dentist in *Little Shop of Horrors*, you will know what I mean.

After introducing Plax into England, we spent a few years traveling all over the world, introducing Plax into different countries. I turned my few hours of media in each country into a long vacation. Pfizer flew us to Japan to bolster their introduction, which got off to a bad start when they didn't realize the TV commercial showing the whole family rinsing and brushing together in the bathroom was offensive to their culture. We were treated wonderfully in Japan.

The only uncomfortable moment was when, on the way to the airport, our guide stopped to take us to a temple site. Our luggage was piled up in his car. He couldn't close the trunk, so he used a rope to keep it secure enough to prevent the luggage from falling out when he drove. However, our luggage in the half-open trunk was exposed to anyone who wanted to simply walk over and take what they wanted. When he told us not to worry because no one stole anything in Japan, we reluctantly agreed as we didn't want to insult him. We were so nervous about losing everything, but sure enough, nothing was missing when we returned.

I introduced Plax into Rio de Janeiro, Brazil; Malaysia; Indonesia; Singapore; France; Germany; Wales; and other locations all over the world. It was the perfect thing to keep me occupied, and we could travel the world. When I was asked to introduce Plax in France, I told Pfizer that I could not fit it into my schedule because it was my daughter's school break from school. They said that was no problem and booked all of us round-trip flights on the Concord. The Concord was a supersonic plane that could fly passengers to Europe in three hours and was extremely expensive, about ten thousand dollars per person. Unfortunately, it only lasted for a few years due to sonic boom noise and costs. So flying the three of us back and forth that week would have been a huge personal expense for me but not a problem for a company like Pfizer.

Pfizer timed my media appearances to introduce Plax into Brazil to coincide with the annual dental meeting of the Brazilian Dental Society. They had a large exhibit set up at the convention center and had me there to demonstrate the effects of Plax mouthwash and answer questions. The woman who was my interpreter walked over to Arlene and me and asked if we would go with her to the other end of the exhibit hall. She led us through a doorway that opened into a large auditorium, seating a few thousand people. She had two chairs by the doorway for us to sit and observe what was taking place. I speak a little Spanish but no Portuguese, so I had no idea what was going on.

There was a large stage with two giant screens, and two people were speaking in Portuguese to the audience. I did not know who this audience was and what topics were being discussed. The people could have been reporters or dentists or tourists, and I witnessed two lecturers onstage speaking to them. As I was about to ask my interpreter what was going on, I heard mixed in with the Portuguese words the sounds "Dr. Lazare." The interpreter turned to me and exclaimed that they wanted me to go up on the stage. I had no idea why, and despite my hesitancy, she led me up to the stage. There were two chairs at the center of the stage, and when I approached that area, a third chair was placed for me. My interpreter sat next to me, and I frantically asked her why I was brought up on the stage. I again heard my name mentioned by the speaker, and my interpreter informed me that they wanted me to say something. I desperately tried to ask her who the people in the audience were as I had no idea what they expected me to talk about. She then told me that they wanted me to speak for about twenty to thirty minutes.

The speaker motioned for me to come up to the microphone as I heard him introduce me to much applause. I was now about to speak to a group of people, and I had no idea who they were or what they expected to hear. I also had to speak with nothing prepared and no concept of a topic for a minimum of twenty minutes. It was the most uncomfortable thirty minutes I have ever experienced. I was hesitant to discuss dentistry because I did not know if the audience were dentists. For the next twenty or thirty minutes, I just spoke. I mentioned how nice the weather was in Brazil, how beautiful the beaches were, how important it is to have a good smile, the need to floss every day, and who knows what else. It was thirty minutes of verbal tap-dancing until I finished by thanking them for inviting me.

Thankfully, when I finished, the interpreter led me off the stage and out of the auditorium. To this day, I have no idea what I said and what group of people I spoke to. I was in too much shock to find out. I later heard that the introduction of Plax in Brazil was a huge success.

A memorable experience was the introduction of Plax into Germany. The German representative flew into NYC for a day to plan the event with me. He told me exactly how much time I was to speak at the event. I replied that I usually did not plan an exact talk, but he gave me details on how the event would run minute by minute. Instead of introducing Plax to the press in Germany, they would fly the press to Paris for a weekend. They planned a dinner at the famous restaurant La Tour d'Argent the first night, followed by the press event on the next day. I told him that I would book myself at the Ritz Hotel because I always chose my own hotels on these trips. He advised me that, for this introduction, he was booking Le Meurice Hotel for everyone because he had very good connections there, and I would be treated very well.

Arlene and I decided to begin our trip in Normandy, because we had never been there, and then proceed to Paris. While in Normandy, we visited a museum that displayed a book about the Nazi occupation of Paris. On the cover was a picture of the Nazi headquarters, clearly showing it to be at the Le Meurice Hotel. After seeing that, we were not too thrilled at the thought of staying there. When we arrived in Paris and told the front desk at Le Meurice about the reservation under our host's name, we were treated like royalty. Even so, we never felt comfortable there, knowing that it was the former Nazi headquarters.

(I brought home a souvenir of an inactive grenade from Normandy for my son, Marc, and forgot when I was leaving Paris that it was in my carry-on bag. I meant to tell them at the airport and show them it was not able to be detonated. There was massive security at the airport checking every passenger. They even made Arlene put her camera through the X-ray machine, which she unsuccessfully argued would ruin her film. Amazingly, my carry-on with the grenade passed through security. That did not make me feel so secure flying Air France knowing that a grenade got through so easily. It made for a somewhat more apprehensive flight home.)

I had a wonderful rapport with one of the German reporters, and at the end of the weekend, he gave us his contact information. He told us to call him if we were ever in Munich, where he lived. On a spring break vacation in Europe with our sixteen-year-old daughter, Lauren, a few years later, we decided to make Munich one of our stops. We tried to make the trip interesting for her, and aside from museums and tours, we felt it was important for all of us to see the former concentration camp Dachau while in Munich.

I called my reporter friend, and he arranged to meet us for dinner with his wife and son. We arrived at the restaurant first, and shortly after, he walked in with his wife and seventeen-year-old son who looked like a movie star. Lauren's face lit up; she was obviously very happy to spend time with this handsome young man after a week of traveling with her parents. Our reporter friend told us at dinner that, although he was working the next day, his son would pick us up and show us around Munich. Lauren was thrilled; her vacation was turning more pleasant. I told him that we wanted to visit Dachau, but he quickly dismissed it, saying that there were many more interesting things in town to see, like the English Garden.

The next day when his son came to pick us up for the city tour of the gardens and local sights, we informed him that we wanted to visit Dachau. He had lived nearby and had never been there. He ended up seeing it with us for the first time and was overwhelmed by what he saw, and he began crying and apologizing. We all found it to be a unique experience, and when he drove us back to the hotel, we felt that we did a good deed. We showed him a part of history that he was unaware of as his family and school never informed him of the atrocities that occurred practically in his backyard. I never heard from his father again.

After a few years, I had introduced Plax into most of the major countries of the world. Pfizer then asked me if I was interested in doing media for them in the United States. That was not as appealing as my trips throughout the world, and I ended my contract with them. Arlene had an idea for a toothbrush design that was unique, and I presented it to Pfizer. They declined as they did not seem interested in more dental products because that was not their core business. A year after I told the few people in the meeting about the toothbrush, I saw in a supermarket an exact copy of my toothbrush design made by a large foreign company. Despite having signed papers from Pfizer protecting me from them copying my product, someone apparently left that meeting and pitched it to another company. My lawyers advised me that if I tried to sue to find out who the person was, my legal fees would be huge. I realized that it was not worth it.

I later developed a vitamin for dental health. I was granted a patent for it, and an investor spent a million dollars to become my partner. We began the process of test-marketing the product. However, I lost the fire in my belly needed to get involved in all the work necessary to be in the vitamin business when I realized that my partner was not capable of handling a business of this magnitude. It required a great deal of time and effort on my part, and I would have had to give up the wonderful life that I was enjoying.

![CHAPTER]

TWENTY-SEVEN

Jackie Mason–Howard Stern

In 1988, Jackie Mason opened on Broadway with his one-man comedy show, *The World According to Me.* It was a huge hit, and the popular longtime comedian became the talk of NYC. We saw the show and thought Jackie was hilarious. Jackie was a single man who loved the ladies. When we met him that year at a party, he immediately asked Arlene if she was single and, if not, if she want to fool around. He could say anything with that accent and delivery and get away with it. When she told him that she was married to a dentist, he was curious to talk to me because he had some dental problems. I told him that I loved his show and admired him so much that he was welcome to come to my office for an examination at no charge. My office was across the street from his apartment on West Fifty-Seventh Street, so he took me up on my offer.

I found him to be extremely smart and well read, and we hit it off immediately. He enjoyed walking around town with a friend in hopes of meeting some available women. He also liked to stay up late, hanging out at coffee shops, chatting with people. His hours fit in perfectly with mine, and Arlene and I became fast friends with him. Arlene and I have always kept late hours. When the clock approaches three o'clock, we sometimes look at each other in bed and sing together, "It's quarter to three," from the Johnny Mercer song "One for My Baby." Jackie was the perfect friend to fit in with our social schedule.

Arlene, who doesn't care for most comedians' humor, found him clever and funny. Soon we were meeting him after his show because he was looking for friends to spend time with at night. He loved to pick our brains about our way of life. He was single and loved telling jokes about how couples act, and our lives became a great source of comedy material for him. We fit in with many of the stereotypes that Jackie loved to make fun of. We were a couple who used our exercise equipment for a place to hang our clothes. We were a couple who wanted the most comfortable seats with the best location at a restaurant but did not want a draft blowing in our direction. We were a couple who declined dessert but devoured every bite when the owner sent over desserts on the house. We were a couple who would rave about how blue the water was on vacation in Saint Bart's. Jackie would state the fact that the color of the water is blue, whether one is in Saint Bart's or New Jersey. We were a couple who would go to a show, count the number of seats in the theater, and wonder to each other how much the performer must be making. People had always told me how funny I was (you might not see it when reading this book, but hey, it's an autobiography, not a comedy book), and in Jackie's company, my ideas blossomed as he wove my thoughts into his material. Soon we found ourselves creating comedy concepts and routines.

Celebrities loved his humor and enjoyed being in his company. Howard Stern rated Jackie as one of his favorite comedians and invited him to be on his show twice in 1989. In those days, Howard could be really tough on people, and I loved listening to him. When Jackie invited me to accompany him to the studio on the days of his appearances, I jumped at the chance to meet Howard.

The second time we went, I was sitting in the guest dressing room, listening to the interview. I heard Howard asking Jackie who his friends were. At that moment, Howard's producer, Gary, told Howard on the air that Jackie was here with his friend who was waiting in a back room. I heard Howard say to Jackie that he was curious to meet one of the people who benefited from Jackie's generosity. I heard Jackie inform Howard that his friend was actually a very important person whom Jackie was honored to have as a friend. Howard then announced on the air, "I want to meet this person." I started to panic because this was the final week of the due diligence that the Pfizer lawyers were doing before final approval of the financial deal for buying my company. I was fearful that I would be interviewed by Howard about my company and that something might be said that would harm the deal. I also loved the show, and the prospect of being on it was also appealing.

I stood in the doorway of the studio rather than take a seat as Howard started to interview me. When I declined Gary's offer to sit down in the studio, he brought out a microphone to me. Fortunately, it went well, and I was able to dodge any questions about my business venture. I was amazed after the show how personable Howard was off the air when he came out to say goodbye. He has mellowed quite a bit since those early days, but at that time, he was intimidating. (Over the years, Arlene and I have attended events in the Hamptons and Manhattan where Howard's wife, Beth, was present. Many of these events supported animal rights, and her care for cats and other creatures is commendable. We have spoken with her briefly several times and found her extremely lovely. I think she has been a positive influence in Howard's life, and his anger on air has diminished considerably.) When I returned home after being on the show, people whom I had not spoken to in years called to say they heard me on *Howard Stern*. A few months later, with the Pfizer sale completed, I found myself with time to spare, and my days with Jackie expanded.

Jackie liked my ideas, and Arlene often accompanied me while we filled Jackie in on the funny aspects of a Jewish couple living in NYC. We started to meet every day. I would call Jackie at eleven o'clock when he was waking up and then meet him at a restaurant or coffee shop each day at one o'clock. Every morning I read the newspapers to keep up with current stories and politics. We spent hours writing comedy material, bouncing ideas off each other. Arlene or I might have a clever thought, but Jackie had a talent for comedic timing and inflection that made his comedy brilliant.

In addition to our afternoon sessions, we met with Jackie many nights after whatever other plans we had. I worked with Jackie on his Broadway shows almost every day. We started working on a new show as soon as the last one had closed. He was a huge success on Broadway. I didn't know him when he had his first show, but I worked with him from his second show on, for the next eight years. I did not get paid for my work. I just loved the pure enjoyment of working with him and filling my time. We traveled all over together, spending time in Florida in the winter while he tried out new material in comedy clubs in preparation for the next Broadway show. I learned to appreciate how hard it is to write great comedy. So much time can be spent on each line to make sure it is perfect.

When all Jackie's preparation and tryouts were done, it was back to Broadway. His sharp humor and witty comments thrilled the celebrities and made them laugh. I was spending fun times with many people whom I admired and read about. Each night backstage after the show, the rich and famous came to see Jackie. Arlene and I had many enjoyable moments observing Jackie playfully insult each person while they rolled in laughter.

I was around Jackie so much that I started to sound like him at times. I began calling women "yentas" instead of ladies. *Yenta* is a Jewish word for a Jewish woman who is a gossip. When Jackie used the word, it was funny; when I used it, I sounded ridiculous. People loved it when a husband introduced Jackie to their wife and Jackie would say, "So sorry for you." When I did the same at a party, all I received were dirty looks. When Jackie would meet someone and say, "Happy to meet me," it came off adorable. When I tried it, I received blank stares. Who says "happy to meet me" without people looking at them strangely? Jackie had a charm and personality that almost everything he said with his timing and inflection came off funny.

We did develop a close bond. When our son, Marc, proposed to his future wife, Amanda, he called us with the news. We were with Jackie at a restaurant, and Jackie told them to meet us. When they arrived, Jackie ordered champagne, and we celebrated their engagement. Jackie was raised to be a cantor and told me that he felt so close to us that he wanted to marry the couple. He said we could use our regular rabbi, and Jackie would take part in the ceremony. I was very touched by that gesture. Unfortunately, it turned out that Jackie had been booked in Boston on the wedding date and could not change it.

One day Jackie told me to meet him for lunch with Dustin Hoffman, who took us to Barney Greenglass for fabulous Jewish food. He was a wonderful host, and he ordered almost everything on the menu for us to try. We had a stimulating conversation, and I enjoyed his company. I reminded him that Arlene and I had last seen him when Arlene was pregnant and we were taking a Lamaze class for couples. Dustin was in our class with his first wife and participated along with us each week in the procedures.

Another time, Arlene and I went to the Carnegie Deli with Jackie, and we had a great meeting with Steven Tyler of Aerosmith. He loved Jackie, and we had a lot of laughs. The only sour note was when I told him that my close friend from college managed Aerosmith for many years. Steven let me know how this person stole money from them until they eventually sued him.

One time we were having lunch with Jackie at the Russian Tea Room, and the well-known comedian Alan King walked over to our table. Jackie told Alan that he was flying to London the following week to do a Royal Command Performance for the queen. Alan explained to Jackie that the British would not understand the way Jackie spoke and advised Jackie to speak more slowly and adjust his timing for the British audience. Jackie thanked him, and when Alan walked away, Jackie said to us, "That bastard, he's trying to get me to change my act and manner of speech so I will fail." When the NY Friars Club asked Jackie to be the Man of the Year at their next event, Alan King found out and persuaded them to give the honor to Alan instead. Jackie immediately quit the club, never to return.

Michael Caine loved spending time with Jackie, and we had many laughs with him; his wife, Shakira; and Jackie, at a restaurant Michael owned in South Beach. Michael was very close to our friend Leslie Bricusse, so we had many stories to share. When Michael Caine found out that Jackie was in town, he invited us all to his restaurant. Michael is ranked number twenty on the list of highest-grossing movie box office stars. Why Michael Caine wanted to own a restaurant in South Beach I have no idea, but he treated us wonderfully.

Jackie spent time in Florida in the winter when he was in between shows. One time Arlene and I checked into the Eden Roc Hotel for a week so we could work with Jackie on new material. He then would try it out at a local comedy club. When any of the new material didn't go over well, Jackie would say to the audience, "What do you expect for a twenty-dollar cover charge?"

Jackie loved women, and he would wander around NYC looking to meet them. He was so well known from his string of successful Broadway shows that he managed to meet quite a few. After a six o'clock dinner with his manager, Jyll, and some other friends, he would schedule dates with multiple women each night. At eight, he would meet one date in a deli; and then at ten thirty, he would have another date waiting in a coffee shop. If Arlene and I were having dinner with him at six, he would have us make up an excuse to leave, and then we would go to keep his eight o'clock date company until he was able to get there. Then at ten, we would make an excuse to leave and go over to meet up with his ten thirty date until he arrived. This went on almost every night.

We were friendly with the supermodel Beverly Johnson and brought her to see his show one night. Beverly was the first African American model to appear on the cover of American *Vogue* magazine. The *NY Times* named her as one of the most influential people in fashion. She was also one of the women who recently claimed to have been sexually assaulted by Bill Cosby. When we brought Beverly backstage to meet Jackie after the show, he immediately asked her out. Much to our surprise, she accepted, and they actually dated a few times. It shows what the power of fame can do when a short chubby comedian can date a beautiful tall black supermodel.

Jackie's closest friend was the world-famous divorce lawyer Raoul Felder. Raoul would join Jackie and Jyll almost every night for an early dinner. Rudy Giuliani was one of his clients and friends, so Jackie and I spent time with Rudy when he was free from his busy schedule. Raoul's clients include Elizabeth Taylor, Liza Minnelli, Martin Scorsese, Johnnie Cochran, Mike Tyson, Tom Clancy, Al Roker, Mick Jagger, Sean Combs, Peter O'Toole, Tom Jones, David Merrick, Anthony Quinn, and Carol Channing or the spouses of the aforementioned people, to name a few. Raoul and Jyll were always up to date on the latest gossip and politics, and Arlene and I loved our many dinners with them. Raoul's wife, Myrna, was also a brilliant lawyer and the backbone of his law firm. However, Raoul was the famous name in the firm. The door of his office lists only Raoul's name, followed by names of fictional detectives like Sam Spade, Philip Marlowe, and Perry Mason.

Raoul's elder brother was Doc Pomus, who is in the Songwriters Hall of Fame and the Rock and Roll Hall of Fame. My childhood friend Mort Shulman was his songwriting partner. They composed many of the greatest songs of the early rock and roll years. Raoul's first major case was Mort Shulman's divorce. When Felder discovered that Mort's wife was having an affair with the best man at their wedding, the newspaper headlines made Raoul famous overnight.

One show I really enjoyed working on with Jackie was called *Politically Incorrect*. When Bill Maher gave his TV show the same name, Jackie threatened to sue him. Jackie wound up not suing but was very upset about Bill using his title. Jackie loved politics and, one year, told me that he wanted to run for NYC public advocate. Although I warned him that it was a mistake, off he went on the campaign trail. The same jokes that thrilled his audience did not go over as well with the political press. When he held a press conference and described NYC mayor David Dinkins as "a fancy *shvartza* [Jewish slang for black] with a mustache," his campaign was all but over. The jokes that went over so well at his shows did not sound right at a political forum.

After a string of Broadway shows, Jackie started to run out of new ideas. Brought up in a family of rabbis, Jackie as a young man was training to become a cantor. That ended when he found himself looking at the women in the temple instead of thinking about the prayers. Periodically throughout his comedy routines, he would take a break and chant a Jewish song. When he decided that his next show would be a musical with him singing, I decided that my time working with him was over. Needless to say, the musical flopped, and it was his last show on Broadway.

A woman in Florida named Ginger claimed that she had a baby and that Jackie was the father. She told the press that she took tests that showed with 99 percent certainty that he was the father. Jackie denied everything and refused to have any contact with her. I don't know what happened after she made those claims. As the baby grew up into a young girl, Ginger started to perform in venues with her young child. The girl, named Sheba, would walk out onstage and act like a mini-Jackie with all his mannerisms. Ginger wrote a musical about her life with Jackie. She named it *702 Punchlines and Pregnant: The Jackie Mason Musical*. She said the 702 title was for the number of times that she was with Jackie. There is a real twist in this production. Sheba (the daughter whom she claims she had with Jackie) played her mother, Ginger, in the show. I actually saw it out of curiosity, and I knew it was not going to win a Tony on Broadway. Songs included "I Never Met This Yenta" and "Ode to the Early Bird Special."

I still run into Jackie on occasion in NYC or Florida. I don't know Jackie's real age, but he always has amazing energy. At one time, he met with a ghostwriter about doing his autobiography, and I was at the meeting. The ghostwriter vented his frustration about this project to Jackie. He explained that it was hard for him to move the date of World War II by ten years to justify Jackie's chosen age.

CHAPTER

TWENTY-EIGHT

Donald Trump

Donald Trump loved to be with Jackie Mason. Donald invited Jackie and me up to his apartment in Trump Tower a few times. He proudly showed us all around the very ornate home. The furnishings were magnificent, with gold everywhere, including chandeliers, ornaments, and fixtures. He was married to Marla Maples at the time. There was a stack of magazines on the desk featuring Marla on the cover. He gave me one, stating, "Look what I did for her." He had a large ego, and he loved to have people write about him.

Jackie, due to his hit Broadway shows, was also constantly in the papers. When Donald gave Marla an engagement ring, the *New York Post* had their picture on the front cover displaying the ring. Jackie's manager, Jyll, commented to us that the ring was surprisingly small. She convinced Jackie that if they told the *New York Post* that Jackie proposed to Jyll with a larger ring, he would be on the front page of the *Post*. They would show up Trump, and Jackie would get great press. When they did so, the *New York Post* did not put their picture on the front page. The paper merely ran a small mention of it in their page 6 column. To this day, I don't know if they really went through with the marriage. It backfired on Jackie because many women he tried to pick up told him that they did not want to go out with a married man.

Donald Trump likes to win, and when he opened Mar-a-Lago, he always chose the best player in each sport to be his partner in tournaments. The golfers would talk behind his back, telling stories about him cheating, but I didn't play golf, so I have no firsthand knowledge of that. Our good friend Moira, whom we often stayed with in Palm Beach, was the best female tennis player at the club. Whenever there was a mixed doubles tournament, she would receive a call from Donald asking her to be his partner.

He was always very nice to the entertainers appearing at his resorts and clubs. When Liza was hired to entertain, he arranged for her to stay in a beautiful cottage on the grounds. We were with her when she was having trouble with the large TV in her room, and he came over himself to help fix it. He also drove her around in his golf cart to tour the grounds.

Mar-a-Lago is adjacent to one of the restricted beach clubs in Palm Beach. Many Jewish people who were denied membership in Palm Beach clubs joined Mar-a-Lago when it opened. We were on the beach one day when his wife Marla tried to arrange a beach volleyball game. There were not enough people on the beach, so she walked along the sand and asked people on the beach to join her game. We watched as they totally ignored her. She had walked onto a restricted club's beach, and they wanted no part of the people at Mar-a-Lago.

A few years later, when Donald was with Melania, Arlene, Lauren, and I were invited to Mar-a-Lago by friends, and Gina Lollobrigida was with us. They both were very wonderful hosts to Gina and us. Little did we realize then that he would become president, and the entertainment community he loved to mingle with would almost all turn against him. We have been friends with Donald's sister, Elizabeth, and her husband, Jim, for many years. They lived near us in Westhampton, and we also saw them in Palm Beach, where they have a home. Elizabeth is completely opposite in personality from Donald. You would never imagine that they were in the same family. Elizabeth is very soft spoken and shy. She is a lovely person, and we always find her to be very warm and cordial. She is Donald's elder sister and has worked as an administrative assistant at Chase Bank before retiring to Florida.

We have many friends who are members of Mar-a-Lago, Donald Trump's private club. In past years when we were in Florida and invited there for dinner or lunch, we were always impressed seeing Donald walk from table to table, asking how people were enjoying their food. There were mixed feelings among our friends about whether he was being a great host or constantly needed to hear how terrific everything was at his club.

After Donald became president, having lunch or dinner at Mar-a-Lago meant going through rigorous security. It was frustrating dealing with multiple checkpoints to have dinner there but exciting at the same time being at the residence of the president. Shortly after Donald became president, we were invited for lunch at Mar-a-Lago by friends. It was during one of Trump's first crisis situations with North Korea, and we had read that he and some members of his cabinet were hosting some world leaders at Mar-a-Lago. While we were having lunch outdoors, we suddenly noticed Donald Trump walking near us with several dignitaries and secret servicemen. As he passed by, he stopped at our table to inquire how we liked our lunch. He didn't know us, but even as a president handling a world crisis, he wanted to make sure we loved the food at his club. We told him that everything was wonderful, and a smiling Trump rejoined his cabinet and dignitaries to prevent a nuclear war with North Korea.

After Donald Trump became president, we had dinner at Mar-a-Lago a few times while he was residing there. Each time, we would observe him walking through the dining room, greeting each table. He and Melania would often sit together at a small table either by themselves or with a few family members or friends. Occasionally, the secret service men around their table would allow someone to talk with them.

One night last year, our friends Sher and Don Kasun invited us after dinner to go to Mar-a-Lago for a disco night. When we arrived there, we passed the dining room on the way to the disco room. Donald and Melania were having dinner there after attending an earlier event. Our disco evening started at ten o'clock in a small room downstairs at the club. While we were dancing, we observed a few secret service men entering the room, followed by Donald and Melania. We were surprised to see them because they had a long day of events before their dinner at Mar-a-Lago. The two of them were standing near us, watching people dancing and listening to music. Donald shook hands with everyone, and we figured he was doing a quick walk-through.

Thirty minutes later, a small love seat was brought in for the two of them because there was no seating in the room. We were tired and ready to leave but thought it was proper to wait until the president and the First Lady left. However, even though it was getting late, they seemed to be enjoying themselves so much that we finally decided that we could go. We wondered if this man ever slept.

On the way out, Arlene snapped a cell phone picture of them. I posted the picture on my Facebook page with a silly comment about never knowing whom you would bump into at a disco. An article had been written that week claiming that Donald and Melania were not happy together. Newspapers had printed a picture of her seemingly refusing to hold his hand, and speculation arose that their marriage was in trouble. By chance, just at the moment, Arlene was taking their picture as we were leaving, Melania's hand was on Donald's arm, and she was smiling at him. Two days later, I observed Arlene's photo of them making the front pages of many publications. A reporter, who obviously saw my posting on Facebook, wrote an exclusive story using the photo as his own. The story expanded to many major news services all over the world, with multiple articles about this photo proving how affectionate they were to each other. I have no idea if I helped stop the negative rumors and saved Donald's marriage. Every day for the past four years, there have been controversial articles about him, so this was just one of many.

{CHAPTER}

TWENTY-NINE

Elaine's Restaurant

Both of our children attended a private school in Manhattan named the Dalton School. We made wonderful friendships with some of the parents of our children's friends. Our son, Marc, had a classmate whose parents seemed very nice, and we made dinner plans one evening to get to know them. We enjoyed going to Elaine's Restaurant because it was casual and attracted an interesting crowd.

When Elaine Kaufman took over the space on the Upper East Side, it quickly became a popular spot for writers and artists. She loved those people and fed them for free when they were not working. In time, it became the most popular celebrity restaurant in the world. There were more famous people eating there every night than any other place in town. Elaine ruled with an iron hand, protecting her celebrities from being bothered by fans or paparazzi.

We sat down for dinner with our new friends and were having a nice time. The wife suddenly remarked to us that one of her favorite actors, Ben Gazzara, was sitting a few tables away. Ben was a major star on Broadway, in films, and on television. We asked her if she knew him. She said she did not but informed us that she caught his eye and was going to go over to his table to meet him. She got up, went over to where he was sitting with two other people, sat down, and never returned to our table. When we finished dessert and paid the check, I asked the husband what we should do. He informed us that they had an open marriage, and he would be leaving alone. We waved goodbye to his wife and Ben, left the restaurant, and watched as the husband hailed a taxi to go home by himself. That was the last time we saw that couple socially.

We did have many positive experiences meeting the parents of our children. Our daughter was a classmate and cocaptain of the tennis team with Dylan Lauren, the daughter of Ralph Lauren. Dylan is one of the most unspoiled people we have ever met. Each time we see her parents in a social setting, we never fail to tell them what a wonderful job they did in bringing her up with great values. I did remind Ralph that I remembered him and his brother because they were counselors at Camp Roosevelt when I was a camper, but at that time, they were known as the Lifshitz brothers.

Our son, Marc, was in the same class as Amy Redford, Robert Redford's daughter. To raise money for the school charity, Redford held a screening of his new film *The Great Waldo Pepper*. After the screening, we went into a small room with a few couples for the after-party. Dustin Hoffman and his wife were there, along with the Redford family. When Arlene spoke with Redford up close, it was one of the few times in her life she looked flushed because he was so good looking in person. I teased her about it, and years later, when I made her a surprise birthday party, I remembered that evening spending time with Redford. The party theme was to come as your favorite fantasy. I had a cake made with an image of Robert Redford and Arlene embracing. The cake was inscribed with the words "So glad you could come!"

Elaine's Restaurant was one of our favorite haunts. She was quite a character and fortunately liked us. She was a very large woman and was there every night. People always criticized her food, but we found things we liked and enjoyed eating there. Everyone was afraid to return any dish they didn't like and risk incurring the wrath of Elaine. Arlene enjoyed the veal chop there and always recommended it to our friends.

One night something in the kitchen went wrong, and it came out tasting somewhat rancid. We were afraid to return it and tried to quietly ask the waiter to exchange it. In a few minutes, Elaine came over to our table, pulled up a chair, took a knife and fork, and ate the entire chop. She let us know that it tasted fine to her, so we were happy to pay for it to avoid being thrown out. We knew what we had to do to continue to remain on her good side.

Ron Galella, the famous photographer who stalked Jackie Kennedy, among others, loved to stay outside of the restaurant and photograph the celebrities coming in and out of Elaine's. We were there at a window table the night she went outside and chased him away from the sidewalk. He came back in his car and parked in front of the restaurant, taking pictures from his open car window. Elaine walked outside, picked up a garbage can, and emptied it into the open window of his car.

Another time, we were sitting at a table near the bar when a young girl, fueled by a few drinks, started to walk over to a well-known celebrity. Elaine intercepted her and slapped her across the face. The astonished, somewhat inebriated young lady looked at us stunned and said to us, "Did you see what she just did?" We looked at her blankly and told her that we saw nothing. Elaine came over to us later and said, "Her parents should have done that to her a long time ago."

For years, Woody Allen ate at Elaine's almost every night. He sat at the same table, the most prominent one in the restaurant. He chose the table that everyone had to pass on their way to the back tables and the restroom. Even if we were there with people who worked with him in his movies, he would rarely look up when introduced. Arlene and I could never understand why such a shy person would want to sit at the most notable table in the place.

Elaine's thirtieth anniversary party drew quite a crowd. Every major NYC writer was there, along with any celebrity in town that day. We sat at a table with Liza and Katie Holmes, whom we hadn't met before, and found her to be lovely company.

We became so close with Elaine over the years that when our son, Marc, became a dentist, she went to him for partial dentures. Unfortunately, she died just before he was able to insert them, and he had no choice but to throw them out. Some people suggested that he display Elaine's partial dentures on his desk as a tribute to his work on celebrities, but understandably, that did not sound appealing to him.

 CHAPTER

THIRTY

Tony Danza–Paul Simon

We used to go to Elaine's often with our close friend Tony Danza. He is one of our favorite people. He is unbelievably smart and a great conversationalist. He is a fabulous cook, and Sunday dinners at his apartment are a treat. We love it when he comes to our home in Westhampton and brings his ukulele. Listening to him sing and play the ukulele outside on the deck after a traditional home-cooked Italian meal is paradise. Tony also is a terrific singer and tap dancer and performs all over the country to sold-out audiences. Tony is very recognizable after starring in two hit TV shows, *Taxi* and *Who's the Boss?* Each show ran for many years.

One night we brought a female friend of ours named Maude to Elaine's for dinner. She was a very attractive, witty, and bright young lady. She, however, knew nothing about show business. While we were sitting there, Tony walked in by himself and came over to our table to say hello. When he saw this attractive girl, he sat down to join us. She had no idea who he was. He realized that and found it very refreshing and charming. People kept stopping by our table to say hello to him all night. After dinner, Tony told us that he would take Maude home because they got along very well. The next day, she called us to tell us how much she enjoyed her evening with Tony. The only thing she could not figure out was why this taxi driver was so popular with everyone in the restaurant. She kept hearing people tell him how much they enjoyed him in *Taxi*, and she assumed he was a taxi driver.

The following week, Tony was singing at Michael Feinstein's nightclub in the Regency Hotel. When we told Tony that Maude thought he was a taxi driver, he invited us to bring her to hear him perform at Feinstein's so she would see what he really does. We called Maude to tell her about the invitation Tony extended to her to come to see him at Feinstein's. She wanted to know why he was inviting her to meet his relatives, the Feinsteins. We informed her of his background and explained that Feinstein's was a popular nightclub run by the singer Michael Feinstein. She was embarrassed that she had no idea who Tony was. Tony did get a kick out of it, and they went out a few times, but it was not meant to be.

One of our friends was dating a beautiful young girl named Melonie. She was very sexy and longed to be a star. She would ask Arlene and me to take her to Elaine's in the hope of meeting someone in the business. She was with us one night when Paul Simon was sitting at a nearby table. Melonie related to us that she had once met Art Garfunkel at a party and tried to figure out how she could meet Paul. She had long blond hair down to her waist and a great body. She walked by his table, and when she saw his eyes following her, she went over and sat down.

After a while, she came back to our table and asked us if she could invite Paul back to our apartment with her. Our children were away at camp for the summer, and Melonie asked if she and Paul could go into a private area of the apartment. She explained that she did not want to have sex with him but just tease him enough to make the contact. When we all arrived at our apartment, she whispered to us that she had given Paul a quaalude to relax him. We told her that we were going to sleep and that she was welcome to entertain him as she wished.

In a little while, she knocked on our bedroom door. Melonie told us the pill had caused Paul to fall asleep on our son's bed and that she was going home. We got into our bed and were almost asleep when there was a knock on our bedroom door. It was a very groggy Paul Simon asking, "Where is the party?" I answered that there was no party, the girl left, and we were going to sleep. I put on a robe, walked a wobbly Paul Simon to the elevator, and put him in it. That was my last encounter with him. For years, whenever we saw him at an event, we would walk the other way. However, I doubt that he had any recollection of the evening because who knows what pill she gave him that night?

Ironically, Melonie eventually appeared in a top-rated TV show called *Welcome Back, Kotter*, starring John Travolta in his first major role. She went to Hollywood and camped out on the lawn at the home of the creator of the show until he noticed her, let her in, and cast her as the first female Sweathog. The truth of how she landed that role I will never know. She was not much of an actress, and her role was cut at the end of the season. She also appeared in an issue of *Playboy* magazine one year.

Since Melonie had moved to California, we contacted her when we were in LA. She invited us to visit Hugh Hefner's Playboy Mansion. The goings-on there were legendary, and people were fascinated by Hefner's home. She told us that Hefner only invited a few male celebrities to the parties, which featured many very beautiful women. She explained that it was no problem for her to bring an attractive girlfriend with her but not a male friend. We were curious to see what went on there, so I volunteered to be the limo driver taking her and Arlene to the party. I pulled up to the gate, dropped them both off, and drove back to our hotel to wait for Arlene to call me to pick them up. Arlene got a chance to see the mansion and the grottoes, so at least one of us had the experience.

We lost track of Melonie over time. Several years later, she became the focus of a major criminal case. She was featured in headline stories in *New York* magazine and on the front pages of all the major newspapers. When her acting career stalled, she went to a party at the Southampton home of a famous producer. After attending his party, she was found unconscious and bloodied on the Long Island Rail Road. She claimed that she was given drugs and raped at the party, and a guest there was later convicted and incarcerated.

 CHAPTER

THIRTY-ONE

Eddie Murphy–Julie Budd

Another parent of one of our children's schoolmates was Bob Wachs. Bob was an entertainment lawyer who had a great eye for talent. He signed up some very talented people, but they all eventually left him as they became popular to sign with a larger agency. Bob decided, along with two partners, to open up a comedy club in NYC. The other two men would handle the bar and food, and Bob would book the talent. They called it the Comic Strip. The week before it opened, I used the club for a surprise birthday party for Arlene. Bob booked new young comics to come in and do their routines.

One day Bob told me that he saw a terrific unknown young comic perform, and he and one of the other partners decided to manage him. The third partner was not interested in managing but only wanted to handle food at the club. Bob invited Arlene and me to join him for dinner with his new client, and that was how we met Eddie Murphy.

He was a very charming and polite young man. We remember the dinner because our friend Obba Babatundé was in town, and we invited him and his date, Tamar, to join us. Eddie, although quiet at dinner, paid a lot of attention to Tamar. Obba told me later that Eddie obtained her phone number and took her out a few times. Bob was a smart entertainment lawyer, and this time, his client stayed with him. Eddie soon became a very big star. When he expanded into film, Bob became the producer of each movie.

Eddie's close friend Arsenio Hall also became a client of Bob. Within a short time, Arsenio had his own very popular talk show on television. Bob was now a powerful figure in the entertainment business, handling these top movie and TV stars. In 1988, he invited us to the Los Angeles premiere of Eddie's latest film *Coming to America*. Arsenio costarred in the movie. A few days before the opening, Bob brought us to the studio lot to show us around. Our fourteen-year-old daughter, Lauren, was with us in LA for the movie opening. While we were walking around the lot, she wanted to use a bathroom, and Arsenio told her to use the one in his trailer. When she didn't come out quickly, Arsenio went in and heard her banging on the door. She was stuck inside in the bathroom because the lock was jammed. Arsenio eventually managed to help her get the door open and let her out.

While Bob was busy producing Eddie's films, he was going through a messy divorce. When his wife demanded to see all of Eddie Murphy's financial records to show how much Bob earned from his percentage, Eddie was not too happy. After a streak of top box office hits, one of Eddie's movies did not do well. After that, Bob's relationship with Eddie started going downhill, and he lost both Eddie and Arsenio as clients. Although he still had the black Rolls-Royce Eddie gifted him as a thank-you, Bob went back to square one.

Bob did introduce us to someone who became one of our best friends. He took us one night to hear a very young singer named Julie Budd. We had seen her perform on TV as a young girl on shows like *The Tonight Show, Ed Sullivan Show, Carol Burnett Show,* and others. At age thirteen, she had a voice that reminded people of Barbra Streisand. Merv Griffin, who had a very popular daily TV talk show, had Julie on many times. He even brought his television cameras to Julie's school to film the thirteen-year-old singing live at her school. In her teens, she opened in Las Vegas for the top headliners of the time, such as Frank Sinatra, Jimmy Durante, George Burns, Bob Hope, and Liberace.

We hit it off immediately with Julie and her manager-conductor, Herb Bernstein. Herb started out teaching basketball at a Brooklyn high school. Herb eventually became a top music arranger and producer. He has been responsible for many hit records, such as "See You in September," "Go away Little Girl," "Knock Three Times," "Leaving on a Jet Plane," and "I Can't Make It Without You." His second wife was Anne Roselli, the daughter of the famous singer Jimmy Roselli. Jimmy Roselli was a fabulous singer and a very tough guy. For years, he was the highest-paid entertainer in Atlantic City because of his popularity with Italians. We had some fun times with Julie, Herb, and Anne when Jimmy played there.

We have remained close, lifelong friends with Julie Budd all these years. Our parents and Julie's also became very close, and she has become part of our extended family. We have had wonderful times traveling with her on the road and at our homes.

I am a lightweight when it comes to drinking. Julie never forgets the time she came to stay with us in Westhampton at our new home some forty years ago. I had two glasses of wine and fell asleep at the table with my head on my plate. She has never stopped teasing me about it.

We enjoyed spending five days with her in Atlantic City while she was appearing with the comedian David Brenner. Julie was terrific, and I marveled how Brenner was able to do a new show with completely different material every night. We saw him perform a few years ago right before he died, and he was still as sharp as ever.

Julie comes each summer to spend time with us in Westhampton, and her generous house gifts over the past forty-five years have decorated our home. She has been engaged for many years to Dr. John Wagner, who is an amazing person, as well as a fabulous doctor. He is the head of a large hospital in Brooklyn and has become one of our closest friends. One summer weekend that stands out was when we had both Julie and Liza Minnelli staying with us. We put on some music while Julie sang and Liza danced in the living room.

One weekend Julie was booked to perform at a large nightclub on Fire Island. We had not been there, so she invited us to join her for the weekend. We booked a hotel in the Cherry Grove area near the venue and joined Julie and her manager/conductor, Herb Bernstein. Julie's show was on a Sunday night, and the four of us wandered around the area during the day. We walked into one store and found that, in addition to clothing, there was a large section with various sex toys. We were joking to one another about some of the items we saw when a very strange-looking man approached us. He gave us an extremely menacing look and informed us that those were not items to be made fun of. Julie, sensing that there was something not right about this man, said to us that we should leave the store. His eyes followed us out of the store, and when we turned around, we could still see him staring at us. We were afraid that he would follow us, so we walked away quickly.

Julie had a rehearsal scheduled a few hours before the actual show, and we accompanied her and Herb to the club. When they finished the rehearsal, Julie went to change her clothes for the performance. We were about to look around to secure good seats before the crowds entered when we noticed the strange man from the afternoon standing off to one side. His eyes were following Julie as she left the stage, heading to her dressing room. He was fixated on her, and we felt uneasy about his presence in the club.

When the show went on, we kept our eyes on him during her performance. While the audience went wild, cheering her show, he just stood there coldly. When we told Julie after the show about this man coming into the club, she felt that we should all go back to our rooms and lock the doors. There was a group of tough-looking leather-clad men staying in our hotel, so staying in our rooms did sound like a good idea. As we left the next morning for the ferry back to NY, the hotel manager told us that a few hours after Julie's show at the nightclub, it burned down. Arson was suspected, and it would be the end of that iconic Fire Island landmark nightclub. To this day, we all feel that it was that deranged character who burned down the club.

Julie starred in the 1981 Disney film *The Devil and Max Devlin*, along with Elliott Gould and Bill Cosby. Marvin Hamlisch wrote the music, and Julie became his lifelong friend. Julie sang a song of Marvin's in the movie, called "Roses and Rainbows," which is a favorite of mine. Marvin invited Julie very often to perform as his special guest in symphony concerts. Marvin was one of the few people to win an Emmy, Grammy, Oscar, and Tony. The collection of all four is known as an EGOT. His adaptations of ragtime music for the motion picture *The Sting* was number one on Billboard, and he won an Academy Award for it. That same year in 1973, he also won two Academy Awards for the title song and the score for the motion picture

The Way We Were. He won a Tony Award in 1975 for his Broadway musical *A Chorus Line.* In 1978, his hit musical *They're Playing Our Song,* loosely based on his relationship with songwriter Carole Bayer Sager, was another major success. He received two Emmys for his work as musical director and arranger on the television special "Barbra Streisand: The Concert."

Marvin had a home near us in Westhampton. When his friend Liza or Julie stayed with us, he would occasionally pop over. He would watch a Yankee game (he was a big Yankee fan), and when the game ended, he would just say goodbye and leave. He could be very abrupt, but he was so interesting that the time spent with him was always worthwhile. Marvin had a fabulous wit and could be quite good humored but also moody.

We were invited to his memorial after his passing, and Barbra Streisand arranged a wonderful tribute to him. She organized it along with his wife, Terre. Terre was a very amiable person, and we always enjoyed spending time with her. We have a local performing arts center three minutes from my home in Westhampton, and Marvin was a major reason for its success. He donated his talent and prestige in the early days to make it successful.

Julie is very sharp, remembers every detail from any place she has ever been, and misses nothing. When we were in London for Lorna Luft's first wedding, the one guy I met who was not a rock and roll performer was from the Dreyfus financial family. He was married to a beautiful, elegant black lady named Jewel. One day a year later, she contacted us to say that she was in NYC for a few days and would love to see us. Julie Budd was singing at one of our favorite nightclubs called the Grand Finale. We invited Jewel to join us for the show.

After the show, we brought her backstage to meet Julie. Julie pulled us aside and asked who this person was. We explained that we had met her in London and did not really know anything about her. Julie then told us that, while she was singing, she noticed that the girl was wearing a coke spoon necklace around her neck. Julie, who as I said before does not miss anything, was able to observe Jewel trying to contact two men in the audience. She would tap on her necklace and smile at them in an attempt to score some cocaine. How Julie was able to see all this while doing her show amazed me. After Julie told us this, we politely told Jewel that we were busy the rest of the week and never saw her again. We later heard that she divorced the Dreyfus heir.

THIRTY-TWO

Anthony Quinn— Hirschfeld—De Kooning

We have many personal mementos that we cherish. Gina Lollobrigida is a fabulous artist, photographer, and sculptor. Hanging in our living room is a wonderful portrait that she did of Arlene. It is featured in her published book of art. She also photographed our children, our dog, and our nephew and included them in her best-selling book of special photographs. Her drawings of our grandchildren hang in our bedroom. She also did a portrait of me, which is hanging in my living room. Her award-winning photographs are on many walls of our homes. A huge sculpture of a dolphin and a boy stands in our living room in Westhampton. Gina shipped the heavy sculpture to us from Italy, and we needed our son, Marc, and three of his friends to get it into our home when it arrived.

Gina and Anthony Quinn were great friends, and she introduced us to him. We developed a close friendship with him and his wife Jolanda. Besides being a fabulous actor, Anthony was a well-known and respected artist whose paintings were featured in many galleries. One evening Arlene and I were having dinner with Anthony and Jolanda at Felidia, a favorite Italian restaurant of theirs in NYC. Arlene was wearing a very dramatic hat, and Anthony took out a pen and started to sketch a drawing of her on the tablecloth. Jolanda chided him, asking him how come he never drew her. He answered that he was always with her, but Arlene had a very interesting look, and he wanted to paint her. He asked if Arlene could come to his studio so his assistant could take some photos of her in the same outfit that she wore at dinner. He then had Arlene return wearing the same outfit to pose for him while he painted her. He promised that he would give us a serigraph of the painting as a gift when it was finished.

A few weeks after Arlene posed for the painting, she called Jolanda to set up a dinner date. Jolanda was very curt on the phone and hung up on Arlene. When I called Anthony to find out what happened, he explained that he was having an affair with one of his assistants, and he and Jolanda were having problems. She knew he was cheating on her but didn't know with whom and thought it might be Arlene. When she discovered a few months later that his affair was with one of his assistants, whom he impregnated, she called Arlene to apologize.

Over the next few years, we kept calling Anthony to ask him about seeing the painting and inquired when we were getting our serigraph. He replied that his painting called "The Arlene" was to be a major work, and he still had not finished it to his satisfaction. He sent us a wonderful note, telling Arlene that he was working hard to "paint you as beautiful as you are." We finally gave up asking.

A few years later, we were in Hawaii on vacation when we saw a flyer in our hotel lobby advertising a showing of paintings by Anthony Quinn. There was a giant picture of Quinn kneeling, surrounded by many of his paintings. Directly over his head was the most prominent one. It was a large painting of Arlene, wearing the hat and outfit from our dinner. We never received our serigraph, but we do have the flyer showing "The Arlene" painting, hanging on our wall.

Arlene always wanted to have a Hirschfeld drawing of us. Al Hirschfeld was the famed caricaturist who drew famous people and all the Broadway opening night casts for the *New York Times*. Every major star wanted to have him do a caricature of them, and his works were sold in many art galleries. When I read that he had just celebrated his ninety-ninth birthday, I figured it was my last chance to commission him. His wife had a gallery selling his works on Madison Avenue in NYC. We went to see her, and although it was expensive, we decided to have him do one caricature drawing of both of us together. We were somewhat apprehensive about how it would turn out because many of his caricature drawings highlighted features that were not always flattering to the person, like a large nose or strange expression. He had done three of Liza over the years for the opening nights of her shows. She advised us to ask him to personally sign his work on the back when he finished. He usually didn't, but doing so would make it more valuable.

Hirschfeld worked out of his four-story townhouse, and we went there to meet him. He took pictures of us in different poses. We were interviewed about our hobbies and activities. We told him that we like to dance, my background with Plax, and Arlene's love of fashion. His studio was on the fourth floor of his town house. He had a chairlift to bring him up the four flights of steps. Unfortunately, when we arrived, he had to walk up all four flights because it was out of order. We went back the next week after he developed the photos, posing for him so he could sketch us. The chairlift was still out of order, and all of us again had to walk up the four flights of steps. We felt bad for him at age ninety-nine having to do this, but his energy was quite good.

We left for vacation in Florida and periodically called his wife to see if our work was completed. He was about to celebrate his one-hundredth birthday, and we wanted to make sure he was able to finish it. Finally, she called to say it was done, and we were anxious to see the completed work. We were committed to buying it whether we liked it or not. We had seen some of Hirschfeld's caricatures of well-known people where their worst characteristics were on display. When we finally saw ours, we loved it. The original one is hanging in our apartment in the city, and a duplicate drawing, which we also purchased from him, is hanging in our Westhampton home. We use the caricature on calling cards that we hand out to people who ask for our contact information. We reminded him to sign the back of it, and thankfully, he did.

He died two weeks after the day we picked it up from him. We were the last people to have a Hirschfeld drawing made of them. If we were more famous, it would be very valuable because it was his last work of art. I still have occasional pangs of guilt when I look at it and wonder if I hastened his passing by having him walk up all those steps each time I saw him.

I had another experience with a personal work of art that did not go as well. Elaine de Kooning, the wife of the famous artist Willem de Kooning, was a well-known artist in her own right. She had done many portraits, including one of JFK. She was referred to me for periodontal treatment by her dentist. She had neglected her teeth for many years due to a fear of dentists, which led her to avoid seeing one. I made a barter arrangement with her. I would do her periodontal treatment in exchange for a painting. I could either choose one of her existing paintings or have her do my portrait. I decided on the portrait because I felt that it would be more personal.

She lived with Willem in East Hampton, a forty-five-minute drive from my Westhampton home. Each weekend I drove to her home and sat on a wooden chair in her studio while she painted. Her method of portrait painting was to work on two canvases at the same time. They would be side by side, and she would alternate between the painting of each. If she noticed something was needed on the one to the left, she would try it out on the one to the right. Each week I posed with a big smile as she worked. I had hoped to meet Willem and have him as a patient with the same barter arrangement, but that didn't happen. She never showed me what she was doing each week, explaining that I would see it when she finished. I could then pick whichever one I wanted.

After weeks of smiling for her as I sat in the chair in her studio, she informed me that the two portraits were finished. When I finally saw the result of her work, I was stunned. Each one had my face twisted with a horrible scowl. Instead of seeing my smiling face, all she saw was this frightening-looking dentist. I picked one at random. She also gave me one of her ink drawings of athletes (which she was famous for) as an extra gift. I drove home and showed it to a shocked Arlene. We immediately discarded the portrait in the trash, and my only souvenir of that experience is the framed ink drawing of basketball players hanging today on my wall. I guess some people really don't like dentists, or I'm just not as handsome as I think I am.

❧ CHAPTER ❧

THIRTY-THREE

Liza Minnelli–David Gest

I thought I looked quite handsome all dressed up in the tuxedo I wore to Liza's wedding when she married Mark Gero. (The advantage of writing my book is I can say things like that and leave out any remarks to the contrary.) After a church wedding, we all went to a lovely reception, which was actually a quiet event. Elizabeth Taylor was there with her husband, Sen. John Warner. We were all in formal wear, but surprisingly, Elizabeth was very casual, wearing little, tiny round pearl earrings. Andy Warhol, Halston, and a small group of friends were also there. Elizabeth was very friendly and displayed a good sense of humor. John Warner, on the other hand, was not impressive and seemed somewhat stiff. I thought that he and Elizabeth were a poorly matched couple.

Liza's next wedding, when she married David Gest, was a sharp contrast to the wedding of her and Mark. Before meeting David Gest, Liza had gained a lot of weight after suffering from some medical problems, and it was a quiet time in her career. Michael Jackson was headlining a show at Madison Square Garden, celebrating the thirtieth anniversary of the Jacksons, and he invited her to perform. His entertainers included the Jackson brothers, Marlon Brando, Usher, Britney Spears, and others. The promoter of the event was David Gest. Liza asked us to accompany her to the evening as her guests and included tickets for our children.

After the show, we joined Liza, along with the other entertainers, backstage for a small after-party hosted by Gest. I did get a kick out of meeting Marlon Brando, who was one of my favorite actors. It was our first meeting with David Gest. He immediately focused his attention on Liza. It was the first night of what would be a personal and professional relationship.

It was September 10, 2001. I remember the date because Arlene and I were originally booked on an early morning flight to LA the next day, and I changed it to a late morning flight because we figured that it would be a long night on the tenth. The next morning as we were walking out of our apartment to head to the airport, we were watching TV and saw the planes fly into the World Trade Center. Friends and family, who knew we were going to LA, were calling us all day, worried that we were on one of the doomed LA flights. We were so thankful that we had changed our flights and will always remember that day.

Liza was not in the best shape health-wise when she met David. He quickly overwhelmed her with promises of restoring her career, along with telling her how smitten he was with her. In a short time, he had taken over her life. He told her that he wanted to marry her, buy her a villa in Europe, and adopt children. In no time, he had moved into her apartment and was now running her career. He quickly barred everyone, both personally and professionally, from Liza's life. The only people he kept in her life were us. We were wary of him, but she was so controlled by him that we felt it best to befriend him rather than confront him. In that way, we would be there to protect her. He called us Fred and Ethel, after the best friends on the TV show *I Love Lucy*. David, of course, nicknamed himself and Liza "Lucy and Desi."

Their wedding, on March 16, 2002, was unbelievable. Eight hundred and fifty guests filled the Regent Hotel in Downtown Manhattan. Michael Jackson was the best man and Elizabeth Taylor the maid of honor. Arlene was a bridesmaid, along with a unique group of women, including Gina Lollobrigida and Cindy Adams. I was a groomsman, along with Robert Wagner, Tito Jackson, and others.

David and Liza assigned me the additional groomsman role of ushering people to their seats as they arrived for the ceremony. It was a star-studded wedding like no other in New York—Diana Ross, Donald and Melania Trump, Chita Rivera, Michael Feinstein, Lauren Bacall, Elton John, Rosie O'Donnell, Joy Behar, Carol Channing, Janet Leigh, Marisa Berenson, Jill St. John, Brian May of Queen, Bob Mackie, Mickey Rooney, Barbara Walters, the Doobie Brothers, Joan Collins, Mia Farrow, Anthony Hopkins, Petula Clark, David Hasselhoff, Arlene Dahl, and many others, including our children, Marc and Lauren. Lauren related to me that the dance floor was so packed with celebrities that it was hard to move. (Lauren still remembers literally bumping into a very tall David Hasselhoff, who was dancing right next to her. Marc was surprised to see that same tall person next to him at the urinal in the men's room and, thankfully, did not have Lauren's experience of literally bumping into David at his encounter. David set a Guinness World Record as the most-watched man on TV. *The Young and The Restless*, *Knight Rider*, and *Baywatch* all made him quite recognizable.)

Lauren was also impressed that the singer Mya had recognized her at the wedding and approached her after spending time together at a party for Liza at Tavern on the Green before the wedding. She gravitated toward Lauren because she was the only person close to her age at both events. (That same year, Mya had won her first Grammy Award for Best Pop Collaboration with Vocals for her rendition of "Lady Marmalade" along with Christina Aguilera, P!nk, and Lil' Kim.) At the party after the ceremony, there was entertainment by every major singing star who was in town. Natalie Cole sang "Unforgettable" as the newlyweds walked down the aisle. The very long, lingering kiss between Liza and David made the cover of every newspaper in the world.

As each person entered, they expected to be seated in a prime seat. I tried to place them as best as I could. Most were very pleasant, but some, like Joy Behar, just pushed past me to get to a front seat. Cameras were not allowed, but Rosie O'Donnell sat right in front of me, and she apparently snuck her camera in and was taking snapshots. She told me that she just had to have some personal photos.

After people were seated, I went back to the wedding party. There was a problem; Elizabeth Taylor had come in house slippers intending to change at the venue and forgot her shoes. She had to be driven back to her hotel to retrieve them while the celebrity crowd was becoming impatient. Michael Jackson sat very quietly in the corner, and I made some small talk with him as we all waited for Elizabeth to return. I found Robert Wagner to be very friendly, and Tito Jackson displayed a great personality. Finally, the ceremony was able to begin; it was beautiful, and the party was amazing. Unfortunately, the marriage was not as beautiful and amazing and only lasted sixteen months.

David Gest was a very strange and unique person. He was extremely hyperactive and could be very rude to people. He sensed that we were Liza's closest friends, so he always went out of his way to be nice to us. He was a germophobe and would have housekeepers cleaning even late at night. He would have them change the sheets five times a day. For fun, I loved to buy artificial rubber bugs at novelty stores and drop them around their apartment to drive him nuts.

Liza had not been working for a while, and David decided he was going to take over her career. He wanted to use the publicity from the wedding to begin his goal. He booked her for ten nights at the Beacon Theater in NYC. He was going to revamp her act and decided that she should update her show to include different material. She always liked to rehearse a lot when doing a new act, but David believed in not spending money on that much rehearsal time. Her show at the Beacon was all new. David eliminated all the musicians that Liza had worked with over the years and replaced them with his own band. He would not allow Liza's close friend and longtime pianist and arranger, Billy Stritch, to even attend the opening night of her show. Liza gave me two tickets for the opening night, and I arranged to meet Billy on a street corner near the theater to give them to him without David knowing about it.

David decided that some of the songs Liza was famous for needed to be updated. He wanted her to do her song "Liza with a Z" with a rap artist. He hired a rapper to appear in the show with Liza. David only booked the rehearsal hall for one week. On the first day of rehearsal, the rapper's relative died, and he told David that he couldn't make it the first day but would be back on the second day. David got upset and fired him.

David had a housekeeper and her son working for him who he embarrassingly named Big Negretta and Little Leroy. How they accepted that I never knew. Arlene and I were at the apartment with

Liza when David informed her that he fired the rapper and would replace him with Little Leroy. Leroy had no singing talent but helped his mother do the housework. Liza was extremely upset with the prospect of going onstage at her major comeback concert singing "Liza with a Z" with the untrained person who cleaned her bathroom. We took her for a walk to calm her down, and I told her that this was just David's strange personality. He loved to put people on and lied about almost everything. I told Liza that I would call him to assure her that he was just teasing.

When I called, he told me that he was not kidding because he believed "anyone can do rap." The opening night at the Beacon was amazing. Liza tore down the house, and there were standing ovations after every song. The critics raved, and she was back at the top of her profession. She even got through the new rap version of "Liza with a Z," leading Leroy by the hand through the song. Our children attended the opening and told us how much they loved it. The only thing they could not figure out was why, with so many talented rap artists, she picked such a weak one. They recognized good rap, but most of the audience could not tell the difference.

After the successful nights at the Beacon Theater, David booked Liza for two weeks in London at the Royal Albert Hall. He told the British promoters that Arlene and I were the bodyguard and hairdresser for Liza and succeeded in getting us a free trip. We were joined by the famous actress Jane Russell because she was a friend of David's. David asked us to take care of her while they were doing interviews and other meetings. We knew Jane as an old-time Hollywood sex symbol, but in reality, she was a very religious, lovely lady, and we spent a significant amount of enjoyable time with her. (Jane was considered Hollywood's leading sex symbol in the 1940s and 1950s from her roles in Howard Hughes's film *The Outlaw* and *Gentleman Prefer Blondes* with Marilyn Monroe. When *The Outlaw* was completed in 1941, censorship over the display of her ample cleavage stopped its release. It took two years for the film to finally be shown, and Jane became famous from all the publicity. The eccentric producer, Howard Hughes, personally designed a special underwire bra for Jane to wear during the filming. I was quite surprised to discover her to be a refined woman who enjoyed reading the Bible.)

Liza's return to London was triumphant. At the curtain call, the entire audience stomped their feet so hard that the theater shook.

The renowned actress Vanessa Redgrave walked up to the stage at the curtain call and bowed down on her hands and knees to Liza. The crowds were waiting to cheer for Liza outside the hall. After she changed her clothes, we left the theater with her and David. We were meeting Joan Collins; her husband, Percy; and the British star Elaine Paige at a restaurant for a celebration dinner. Outside the theater, Liza waved to the crowd. The only problem was that David forgot to arrange for a car, so we had to duck back into the theater while he ran through the streets, trying to find a cab.

David pulled me aside after dinner and told me that Joan Collins made a pass at him. I knew that he would be the last person on the earth that Joan would ever be interested in and disregarded his comment. Through all the time we have known them, Joan and Percy are like lovebirds. David always made up stories about how every woman wanted him. Nothing he ever said was the truth.

After he and Liza broke up, he told us that his next plan was to marry either Diana Ross or Elaine Paige. Elaine was a major theater star in England at that time and was considered the "First Lady of British musical theater." She won the British Laurence Olivier Award (the British equivalent to our Tonys) for Best Actress in a Musical for her role in the musical *Evita*. Elaine also originated the role of Grizabella in *Cats* and had a hit song with her version of "Memory" from the show. When she came to Broadway to star in the musical *Sunset Boulevard*, we spent time with her after her performance. We warned her that David had set his sights on marrying her after his divorce from Liza was finalized. She told us not to worry as she had absolutely no interest in him.

Liza was now looking and feeling great. She was beginning to see how strange David was, and the marriage started to go downhill. David was a control freak and was making a lot of enemies with his business dealings and his rude treatment of people. He walked around with dark sunglasses on and wore two very large crosses around his neck, which was fine except for the fact that he was Jewish. He loved to be in the spotlight.

Arlene, over the years, has often been told that she looks like Liza. The short dark hair, along with her long eyelashes and attractive look, does resemble Liza. One will not necessarily think that if they are both wearing makeup and sitting next to each other. Since Arlene and Liza look somewhat alike, there have been numerous times that

Arlene will be mistaken for Liza. When Liza is offstage, she will rather not wear makeup when possible. We have had many moments leaving the theater after her performances where Liza was without her stage makeup. Often, people think that Arlene, wearing full makeup and eyelashes, is Liza. When she appeared at Carnegie Hall, Arlene and I would exit the stage door after the show to meet Liza at a restaurant. We have had times when fans chased us down the street, and a few minutes later, Liza, dressed very casually, would leave and slip into her car while the fans were chasing us.

One time when we went to hear Liza sing in Atlantic City, she asked us after the show to go with her to see friends of hers appearing at a late show in the lounge. Liza had no makeup on and was dressed very casually in a black top and pants. Arlene was all made up and was wearing a striking outfit because we had just attended Liza's show. The maître d' had set aside three seats for us. When we walked in, there was a buzz in the crowd that Liza was in the audience. As we sat down, with Liza on my left and Arlene on my right, a line of people started to form wanting her autograph. The problem was that they were lined up by Arlene, and Liza was ignored. They assumed Arlene, who was dressed more like the image they had of Liza, was Liza.

One day Liza called a shoe store to ask about a particular shoe and told them she would be there soon. Arlene went with her, and the salesman spent a lot of time fitting shoes on Liza. The salesman walked over to Arlene and presented her with the bill, thinking that she was Liza. Liza, smiling, handed Arlene her credit card to give to the salesperson. He never realized that Arlene wasn't Liza. David Gest, realizing the resemblance from a distance, would ask Arlene to hold his arm when we were out walking if Liza wasn't with us. He loved to be recognized, and if Liza was not around, then Arlene would do as a substitute.

David decided that he wanted to put cameras in their apartment and film their life as a reality show. Liza, who loves her privacy, was not happy and very reluctantly succumbed. David was getting more and more controlling and strange, and she did not want to anger him. David decided to try out the reality show concept by filming a sit-down dinner at their home with some famous friends (as if that was how they normally ate at home). He then told the network that the pilot would be filmed in their apartment on Halloween. They would invite a group of famous people to come in beautiful costumes for the cameras to capture. David told us to be there early to help greet the guests and asked us to rent elegant costumes. Liza was quite unhappy with the idea of living with TV cameras in her home for the next six months. I told her that I would help her out in stopping this.

The night of the party, Arlene and I were there early with the camera crew to help greet the guests. I was wearing a brown raincoat and told David that my costume was underneath. My actual costume was that of a flasher. Arlene stuffed one leg of pantyhose with bubble wrap to make the shape of a huge penis, the size of a baseball bat. The other leg of the pantyhose would wrap around my waist. When I opened my raincoat, an enormous penis would spring up. When the cameras started rolling, and the guests started to arrive. I opened my raincoat to greet everyone. The elegant atmosphere changed as people rushed to take photos with me and my enormous penis. It was the first and only episode filmed for David and Liza's reality show and never aired on TV.

The marriage was falling apart fast and ended very abruptly when Liza returned to NYC after a two-week tour. She was shocked and called us to come over to her apartment. The large, multiroom apartment was empty; David had taken every piece of furniture. The only thing remaining was a bed and one lamp in her bedroom. He had moved to Hawaii and had all the furniture taken out and put in storage at an unknown location.

After the divorce, David used the fact that he had been married to Liza to get himself on an English reality television show in 2006 called *I'm a Celebrity . . . Get Me out of Here!* In 2016, he took a group of odd entertainers, including little people dressed up like Liza, to join him while he sang. He planned to tour with them in England. Ironically, another celebrity named David, from the *I'm a Celebrity* reality show in 2006, had died. Headlines in England mistakenly thought it was David Gest who passed away. When David saw the articles, he let everyone know that the David who died was not him. He decided to use that publicity to help sell tickets for his upcoming tour. He renamed his tour "David Gest Is Not Dead but Touring." When he did not show up for the first show of the tour, someone went to his hotel room in London. They ironically found him dead on the bathroom floor from an apparent stroke. The title of his tour proved to be a poor choice.

CHAPTER

THIRTY-FOUR

Sol Kerzner

While Arlene and I were in London with Liza and David, we met a fascinating person named Sol Kerzner. Sol was born in South Africa and was famous for building Sun City, the most famous resort and entertainment project in Africa. In the United States, he opened the Mohegan Sun Gambling and Entertainment complex. In the Bahamas, he developed the Atlantis Resorts. He also had many other resorts all over the world. We had some wonderful times with Sol and his wife, Heather, in London. He loved being with Liza, and we all became good friends. He was an amazing sport, and everything he did was first class.

He invited Liza and us to Monte Carlo as his guests, where he threw a three-day birthday party for himself. His home was situated on a large hill and included multiple giant villas on every level where he housed his guests. Dame Shirley Bassey and Liza both entertained one night, followed by fireworks that would make Macy's proud. A few days before the celebrations, he flew us to Monte Carlo. He put Liza and us up in rooms at the Hôtel de Paris. As a host, he had no equal and spoiled all his guests.

When Sol expanded the Atlantis hotel in the Bahamas to include the Reef and the Cove, he flew us there for the opening celebration, along with a large group of celebrities. We spent three amazing days mingling with his guests. Michael Jordan, Patrick Ewing, Jules (Dr. J.) Irving, and Magic Johnson were some of the sports stars. Spending three days at lunches, dinners, and entertainment events with these basketball heroes of mine was terrific. Even Arlene, who doesn't care for sports, knew who they were. My biggest problem was always looking up and straining my neck to talk to them. When Arlene took some pictures with Michael Jordan, she found it hard to pose with him alone because there were always women surrounding him. Magic was easier to talk with because he was extremely sociable.

John Travolta and Kelly Preston; Sean Connery and his wife, Micheline; Kelsey Grammer; Robin Thicke; Usher; Gloria Estefan; Bo Derek; Lindsay Lohan; and Steven Tyler were some of the exciting guests. There were three days of events, and by the third day, we were all like old friends. Sean Connery's wife, Micheline, was very short, so they made an odd-looking couple. We had this image of him as James Bond escorting beautiful tall women all over the world. However, they seemed very happy together and were quite nice to us.

Arlene brought a number of her fun wigs to wear in the humid weather, so she did not have to worry about how her hair looked. She took great pictures in her silver wig with Kelsey Grammer and in her blond wig sitting on Steven Tyler's lap. Steven Tyler was fun spending time with, and he always had a smile on his face. He loved Arlene in her blond wig and got a kick out of her changing her look every day with different wigs. Lindsay Lohan did not partake in most of the festivities and spent the majority of the time in her cabana with a few friends. The great American band Earth, Wind, and Fire entertained one night and were fabulous.

When Sol renovated the Mohegan Sun resort in Connecticut, he and Heather invited us for the celebration. The guys from NSYNC and Al Roker joined several other celebrities at the events. Al Roker didn't mingle much, but the guys from NSYNC were very friendly, and we had fun hanging out with them over the few days. Cher performed the first evening, and the next night, Rosie O'Donnell and Cyndi Lauper entertained. Cher put on a big production, but much of it was prerecorded. She even jokingly remarked to us that the show would be just as enjoyable for us if she was seated in the audience. However, it was very entertaining and was the basis for the tours that she is still doing this very day. Rosie O'Donnell did a comedy show that did not go over well. She did not seem to be in a good mood and didn't mingle with the people afterward. She was a good friend of Liza's, and we had spent some time with her in the past, so we were disappointed that we did not see her again after her performance.

We have had terrific dinners in NYC with Sol and Heather. One memorable evening at Elaine's Restaurant was with Stevie Wonder. We sat at a round table, but we did not get much of a chance to speak with him. He had two friends dominating much of the conversation. He is a talent that we greatly respect, so we enjoyed just being in his presence. Sol kept a suite at the Saint Regis Hotel for his use while he stayed in NYC.

Every year when Liza was in NY, we spent part of Thanksgiving with her. She loves Arlene's turkey and looks forward to it. Arlene doesn't cook the turkey from scratch but orders it in. She then heats it in our oven and makes all the side dishes for the dinner. Liza was so impressed with Arlene's supposed skill of preparing the turkey and so thankful that she makes it for her each year that Arlene never had the heart to tell her that she orders it in. One year Liza informed us that the Kerzners were in NYC over Thanksgiving, and she told them all about Arlene's amazing turkey. They would be in their suite at the Saint Regis Hotel and wanted to invite all of us for Thanksgiving at their place. They had a chef who would carve, serve, and provide the extras. Arlene decided to fake it again and ordered a large turkey.

On the day of the dinner, we brought it over to their suite at the hotel. Liza told us to dress very casually so we could just have a cozy Thanksgiving dinner with Heather and Sol. We arrived at the Saint Regis before Liza and rang up the Kerzner suite. When the doorman saw us dressed casually and delivering a large turkey, he had us come up the back service entrance to their suite. He thought we were a delivery service, and we were greeted by the Kerzners' housekeeper, who thanked us for delivering the turkey. We explained that we were their guests, and soon an embarrassed Sol came and fetched us. We had a lot of laughs about it with Liza all night.

The Kerzners had an impressive-looking chef with a large hat, and we were all served a wonderful dinner. Everyone loved Arlene's turkey, and Heather asked for the recipe, which Arlene promised to give her at another time. We had lost contact with Sol over the past few years. (And it was not because Arlene was afraid to call, fearing she would be asked for the recipe to the turkey she did not actually cook.) Sol and Heather later divorced, but Heather recently called us to ask if Liza would give her a quote for a tribute they were having for Sol because he was dying. We contacted Liza and gave Heather the quote. It was sad to learn that Sol passed away on March 21, 2020, in South Africa.

1— Liza Minnelli and my grandson, Devin, by the Christmas tree in her apartment. My daughter, Lauren, and her fiance, Seth, and their children. Arlene and Liza in the bedroom at her home in LA. Liza Minnelli hugging our daughter, Lauren, by the Christmas tree in her apartment thirty years before the picture with Devin.

2– At our home in Westhampton with Barry Manilow and his dogs, Garry Kief, Lorna Luft, Colin Freeman, and me. Anthony Quinn in his studio with his painting of "The Arlene" above his head.

3– Our son, Marc's, Bar Mitzvah with Liza Minnelli, Marge Cowan, Joe Pesci, Prince Egon von Furstenberg, Gina Lollobrigida, Barbara Luna, and Jimmy Hayden. (The day after this photograph the front-page story in the New York Post was the death of actor Jimmy Hayden later that night on a street corner in Harlem of a drug overdose.)

4– Our invitation to the Inauguration of President Clinton. Arlene and President Bill Clinton. Arlene with Henry and Ginny Mancini. Henry Mancini and me.

5– Haley Swindal and our family in the Owner's Box at Yankee Stadium. Arlene, Lorna Luft, and Francesco Scavullo at lunch. Arlene and Joan Collins. Our daughter, Lauren, at her wedding with Liza Minnelli.

6– Our son Marc, Arlene, and Sonja Morgan of the Real Housewives of New York television show. Bill Clinton and me in Florida. Our son, Marc, with Jill Zarin of the Real Housewives of New York television show. Arlene, Cassandra Seidenfeld, and Ramona Singer of the Real Housewives of New York television show.

7– Elizabeth Taylor and me at Liza's wedding to Mark Gero. Andy Warhol and me. Me dancing with Cyd Charisse at my anniversary party. Liza Minnelli with Michael Feinstein and me.

8– My son, Marc, and I with Sammy Davis Jr. on his yacht in Florida.

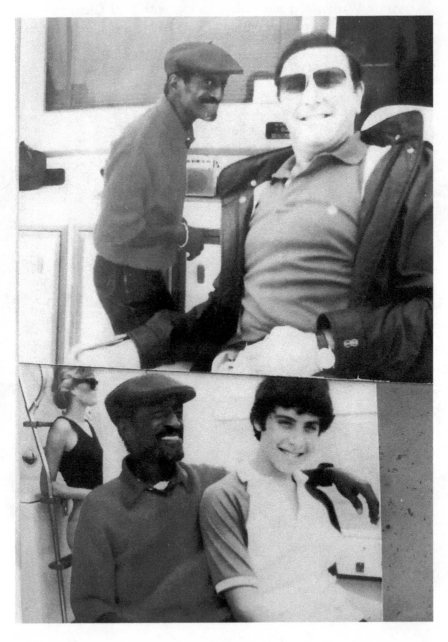

9— Heading out to the Academy Awards with Jack Haley Jr., Kim Novack, Lorna Luft, Jake Hooker, and me. Jackie Mason having coffee cake with Arlene at our home in Westhampton. Our children, Marc and Lauren, Gina Lollobrigida, Leslie and Evie Bricusse, and Liza Minnelli at our apartment.

10– Our children, Lauren and Marc with Christopher Reeve after he just starred in the movie, "Superman." Arlene and Nancy Pelosi at the White House. My dinner menu at President Ronald Reagan's White House Dinner for the President of Argentina. Our children, Lauren and Marc, sitting on ex-middleweight champion Rocky Graziano's lap.

Dinner

Honoring
His Excellency
The President of the Argentine Republic
and Mrs. Alfonsín

Smoked Salmon Cornets
Sesame Seed Twists

Crown of Veal Médaillon
Basil Sauce
Spinach Timbale of Gruyère Soufflé

Radicchio Blossom Salad
Honey Vinaigrette
Port-du-Salut Cheese

Coconut Bombe

11– Neil Sedaka at the piano with our daughter, Lauren, in our home in Westhampton. Henry Mancini giving our son, Marc, a piano lesson at our home in Westhampton.

12– Storm Large and me. Charles Aznavour and Arlene in Paris. Arlene in her silver wig sitting on Steven Tyler's lap. Liza Minnelli and me.

13— Farrah Fawcett sent me her picture and a note thanking me for my dental care and for giving her my mouthwash, Plax, to use.

Dear Arlene and Allan:

Thank you for sending us the Plax.
I can't tell you how faithfully we
use it. It is always nice to hear
from you and we look forward to
seeing you sometime in the near
future.

    With fond regards,

14– Arlene, Liza Minnelli, and me celebrating my birthday after Liza's show in San Francisco. Gina Lollobrigida and me. Ginny Mancini, Julie Budd, and me.

15– My grandson Hunter, my son Marc, Adam Sandler, and Reggie Jackson at Yankee Stadium in the owner's box. Luigi, Arlene, Liza Minnelli, and me dancing at my daughter Lauren's wedding.

16– Sammy and Altovise Davis at their home. Terrence Flannery, Michael Feinstein, Liza Minnelli, Lorna Luft, and us at our apartment.

17– Lindsay Wagner washing her young baby in our sink at home. Billie Jean King and me on the tennis court. Me at the reopening of Studio 54. Liza Minnelli, Ginny Mancini, and me.

18– Mike Tadross and Georgia Witkin, Arlene with Obba Babatunde at our apartment. Liza Minnelli, Luigi, and Arlene.

19– Arlene dancing with Tony Martin at our anniversary dinner. Liza Minnelli, us, and our kids around her Christmas tree. Neil Sedaka, Michael Feinstein, and me at the piano in my Westhampton home.

20– Gina's portrait of Arlene hanging in our apartment. Arlene with friends including Jacqueline Murphy, Sheryl Lee Ralph, Pamela Morgan, Ramona Singer at Sheryl Lee Ralph's Show. Arlene with a group of her girlfriends.

21– Dinner at Elaine's restaurant with Stevie Wonder, a sleepy Sol Kerzner, and us. Lorna Luft, Colin Freeman, and me having Stone Crabs at our apartment. Arlene with Sean Connery.

22– Arlene in a blond wig with John Travolta and Kelly Preston at the Atlantis Resort. Barry Manilow and us after his show. Arlene with Rudy Giuliani when he was Mayor of NYC.

23– Neil Sedaka, Terrence Flannery, Michael Feinstein, and me at our home in Westhampton. Me at the press podium in the White House during my visit when Bill Clinton was president. Arlene and me standing with Gine Lollobrigida at her Studio in Pietrasanta, Italy next to two of her giant sculptures.

24– Martha Graham event with Halston, Martha Graham, Betty Ford, Truman Capote, Elizabeth Taylor, Liza Minnelli, Mark Gero, and us.

Halston, Betty Ford and Martha Graham

Frank Gero and Liza Minnelli

Dr. and Mrs. Allan Lazar

The third annual **Martha Graham Award** was presented to **Halston** by **Mrs. Gerald Ford** in Halston's showrooms. Later, the Halston "crowd" celebrated at **Studio 54** where 2000 or so disco-ers paid $25 each — the proceeds going to the **Martha Graham Foundation.**

Truman Capote

Kurt Meyer and fashion designer Constance

Elizabeth Taylor

30

Visitors East

25– Gina Lollobrigida and me at a White House dinner for the president of Argentina, with Ronald Reagan.

26– Debbie Harry, of Blondie, at our apartment for a party. Our daughter, Lauren, with Debbie Harry 35 years later.

27— Liza Minnelli, Mark Gero, Lorna Luft, and us around the piano in our apartment. Waldo, Kate Jackson, Gina Lollobrigida, and us at Waldo and Kate's honeymoon celebration in Westhampton.

28– Notes from Liza Minnelli to us.

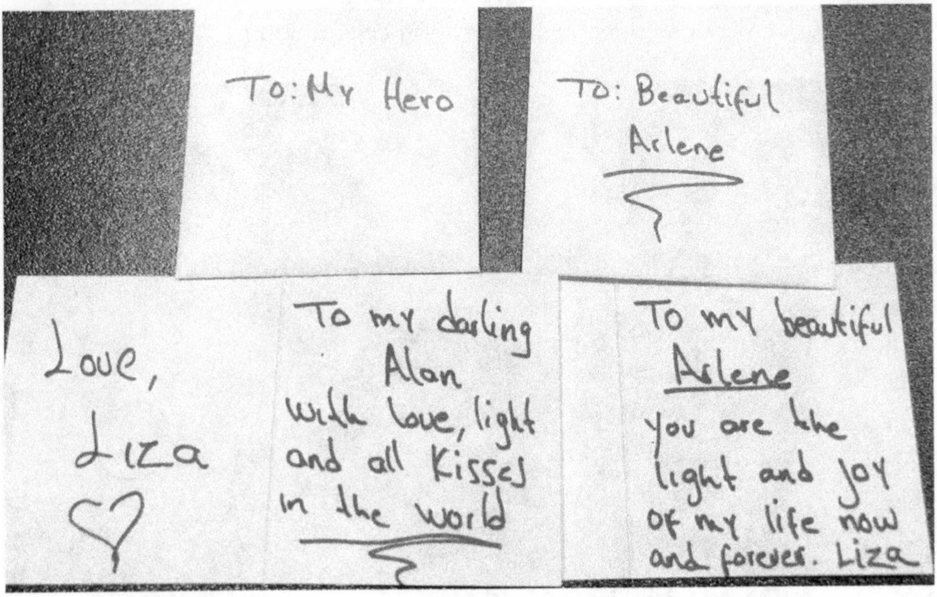

To: My Hero

To: Beautiful
Arlene

Love,

Liza

To my darling
Alan
with love, light
and all Kisses
in the world

To my beautiful
Arlene
you are the
light and joy
of my life now
and forever. Liza

29– Liza Minnelli, David Gest, Gina Lollobrigida, and us at Liza's apartment. Liza Minnelli, Mark Gero, Lorna Luft, and us at Liza's apartment.

30– Halston and I. Ralph Lauren, Dylan Lauren, and my daughter Lauren. My daughter, Lauren, Arlene, and Regis Philbin. Arlene and Ben Vereen.

31– Rod and Judy Gilbert and us. Drag film star, Devine, a friend, and I at Studio 54. Arlene and Tricia Nixon.

Uncategorized | June 15, 2019

The club rarely had a liquor license

32– Rita Cosby, Tomaczek Bednarek, and us. Shelley Goldberg and
Leba Sedaka at our apartment. John Wagner and Julie Budd at
our Westhampton home. Bryant and Lillian Schiller and us.

33– Tony Danza and Arlene on our deck in Westhampton. Hal David, Neil and Leba Sedaka, and us in Europe.

34– Mitch Miller, Jack Haley Jr., and I at our apartment for a party.
Arlene and Mike Tyson. Russell Brand and I on the set of the
remake of the movie, "Arthur." Arlene and I feeding grapes to
Neil and Leba Sedaka.

35– Our son, Marc, with Robert DeNiro. Arlene with Al Pacino.
Our son, Marc, with Lindsay Wagner in his dental office.

36– At Sammy Davis Jr.'s home with Jack Haley Jr.and our children, Steve Tyrell and us, Arlene and her sister Susan, Hillary Clinton and us.

37– Chita Rivera and Arlene. An evening in Florida, as Darren Criss sings, and Michael Feinstein and Alan Cumming play the piano. Magic Johnson and me at the Atlantis Resort. Ann Hampton Callaway and me..

38– Truman Capote and Arlene. Chita Rivera and our son, Marc, in his bedroom at our apartment.

39– Out for dinner with Liza Minnelli and Robert DeNiro. David Gest and Liza Minnelli. (David wrote on the photo, "From Lucy and Desi to Fred and Ethel" to signify our close friendship.)

40– My grandchildren Hunter and Sydney. My son Marc. Barry Manilow, Marc Hulett, me, Jim Caruso, Arlene, Mickey Conlon, Tom Postilio, and Erich Bergen.

41– Our son, Marc, with Bill and Hillary Clinton. Our daughter, Lauren, with Donald Trump and Gina Lollobrigida at Mar a Lago.

42– Our daughter, Lauren, at her wedding with Liza Minnelli, Luigi, and Arlene. Arlene with Tony Martin. Cyd Charisse and me.

43– Neil Sedaka and Denise Rich singing at our daughter Lauren's wedding. Ted Kennedy, his sister Eunice Shriver, and us. Arlene with Michael Jordan and friends. Arlene with Valerie Harper at Luigi studio.

44– Kelsey Grammar and Arlene. Bo Derek and me. Usher and Arlene. Robin Thicke and Arlene. (All at the Atlantis Resort.)

45– Jules "Dr. J" Irving and me. Patrick Ewing and Arlene. Gloria
Estefan and me. (At the Atlantis Resort) Liza Minnelli, Susan
Lucci, and us in Westhampton.

46– Neil Sedaka and Arlene with Siegfried and Roy in Las Vegas. Gina Lollobrigida, Danny DeVito, and I at the White House.

47– Bill Clinton and Arlene. David Raksin (the composer of "Laura"), Liza Minnelli, Billy Stritch, and us in Gstaad, Switzerland. Arlene and Gina Lollobrigida under Gina's photo. Me feeding a tiger in Florida.

48– Arlene with Matthew McConaughey. Arlene with Jim Caruso. Arlene with Natalie Cole. Entertainment lawyer, Allen Grubman, at our home in Westhampton with Steve and Robbie Marks.

49– Tony Danza and Sebastian Maniscalco at our home in Westhampton. Tony cooking dinner for our family before Sebastian's performance at our local theater. Us with Hugh Jackman at Madison Square Garden before his show. Steve Rubell and Mitch Miller at our home in NYC.

50– Liza Minnelli and me on her bed with her dogs. With Regis Philbin, Lorraine Bracco, Paulie Herman, Leba Sedaka, Christopher Walken, Mikhail Baryshnikov, and Peter Max, at Columbus restaurant. At the White house with President Nixon and me. Sheryl Lee Ralph and me.

CHAPTER

THIRTY-FIVE

Christopher Reeve–Rocky Graziano–Chicago–Tom Hanks–Steven Spielberg

Lorna Luft had introduced us to a very nice young actor, Christopher Reeve, and his girlfriend, Gae Exton. Chris had just finished starring as Superman in his first major role. I found him very personable and a bit of a daredevil. He loved to fly and was always asking me to join him on a small plane that he piloted. I have a fear of flying (even though I do apprehensively fly), so I never took him up on his offer in a tiny plane.

I did ask him for a favor though. The *Superman* movie had just come out, and my eight-year-old son, Marc, loved it. Superman was his hero. Marc had a playroom area in our apartment with an air hockey table. I had Chris ring the doorbell of our apartment one day, and I told Marc to answer it. Marc opened the door to find Superman standing right in front of him. When Superman challenged Marc to a game of air hockey and lost, Marc was in shock.

When Christopher was thrown from a horse during an equestrian competition, he was left a quadriplegic. His foundation for people with spinal cord injuries helped many people. We were quite sad when he died in 2004 at only fifty-two years old. We had some wonderful times with him and his girlfriend. He and Gae never married, and we lost contact with her. She did have a daughter with Chris named Alexandra. Christopher married Dana in 1992, and sadly, she died two years after him in 2006 at only forty-four years of age.

Growing up, our children had many interactions with celebrities. Our son, Marc, was with us at a restaurant one time when he was seventeen. We had met Jaid Barrymore several times at different parties. Jaid was at the restaurant that night with her thirteen-year-old daughter, Drew, and tried to fix her up with Marc. We informed Marc about how old Drew Barrymore was, and he told Jaid that he was not available. Marc had known her as a young girl in the movie *ET* and *Irreconcilable Differences* so was still flattered. (Drew later starred in many popular movies including *The Wedding Singer*, *Fifty First Dates*, and *Blended* with Adam Sandler and *Never Been Kissed* and *Charlie's Angels*.) Jaid used to bring her well-known actress daughter to clubs all over NYC, exposing her to an atmosphere not suitable for her age. Fortunately, Drew freed herself from that influence and became an outstanding person.

Around that time, Gina Lollobrigida came to stay with us for a few days. She brought along a nineteen-year-old girl named Juncal Rivero, a beautiful Spanish model who was Miss Spain in 1985 and Miss Europe for 1985–1987. Marc was smitten and immediately lied about his age. Arlene was not too happy to have a son who was suddenly three years older. No romance occurred on that trip, but something good did happen. Marc, thinking of traveling to Spain to see Juncal in the future, started to really concentrate on learning Spanish and became very proficient in the language. He also translated the Bangles' song "Eternal Flame" into Spanish and handed it to Juncal as a love letter to impress her, never telling her that the words were not his own.

Although Studio 54 was the main disco in NYC, another club called Xenon was also popular. They decided to have one event for the children of the regulars, so we brought our kids. They had people dressed as various Disney characters mingling with the children. When our very young daughter, Lauren, saw Mickey Mouse, she was stunned. She kept yelling, "Mickey! Mickey!" She was meeting her favorite superstar and was thrilled.

Our friend Albie was best friends with the ex-world-middleweight-champion Rocky Graziano. We spent many nights with Rocky and his wife, Norma. Rocky loved kids, and we have great pictures of him holding Marc and Lauren in his arms. Rocky had a great time at Marc's bar mitzvah, and everyone wanted to meet him and shake his hand. Rocky gave Lauren a necklace with a gold boxing glove pendant as a gift when he attended her bat mitzvah. When Paul Newman starred as Rocky in the autobiographical film of his life, *Somebody up There Likes Me*, Rocky became a major celebrity. People loved to come up to him and yell, "Rocky!" He certainly inspired Sylvester Stallone when he wrote his Rocky films. Arlene and I had many fun times with Rocky. He could be a tough guy, but his wife, Norma, was tougher, and she called all the shots on everything we did. Rocky was "guest of the world" wherever we went, and people loved to pick up his check. Rocky and Norma loved that too.

The musical *Chicago* has been running in NYC for years now. The original opened on Broadway, with music by Fred Ebb and John Kander. We have known them both for many years because they were a major part of Liza's and Chita's lives. Fred had a sense of humor that was unreal. Much of the wonderful lines sung by Liza and Chita were written by Fred. He was one of the most nervous people I have ever met, and how he functioned in life I don't know. John is, in contrast, a quiet, steady man. Together, they created many of the great musicals of the world, including *Cabaret* and *Chicago*.

Chicago opened in 1975 with Gwen Verdon and Chita Rivera as the stars. When Gwen had to drop out for a few weeks, Liza filled in for her. We had plenty of laughs with Liza and Chita while they were enjoying the moments they performed together. The show was not a success financially and closed after a relatively short run, although we loved it.

In 1995, City Center did a five-day encore performance of *Chicago*. They eliminated the scenery changes and presented a cut-down version of the musical. We are good friends with Fran Weissler, who along with her husband, Barry, is one of the most successful producers on Broadway. Fran told me that on the last night of the encore's run, a friend was unable to use his tickets and gave them to the Weisslers. At that time, they had taken part in producing a few minor shows and were relatively new in the business. When they saw *Chicago*, they were blown away and asked the people who owned the rights to the show if there was any way for them to be able to invest in it. They had hoped as a favor to be allowed to put in a small amount, although they were sure that it wouldn't be available. To their surprise, they were told that no one was interested in investing in it and that if they wanted to see the show run on Broadway, they would have to be the sole investors. The usual rule for producers is to never put your own money in a show but find other people to invest. They decided to mortgage their home and put all their savings into being the sole owner of the production of *Chicago*. It opened in 1996 to rave reviews and has become the longest-running musical in Broadway history. When Fran Weissler invited Arlene and me up to her huge vacation home upstate, she called it the "home that *Chicago* built." They have made many millions from that show and have become legends in the world of Broadway.

A few years ago, our friend Obba Babatundé was cast in the role of the lawyer in *Chicago* for six months. We had met him when he was a backup dancer for Liza and have remained close ever since. When Liza heard that he was in the show, she arranged for us to go with her to see him in it. After the show, we went back to his dressing room to congratulate him, and then we planned to go out to dinner.

Rita Wilson, Tom Hanks's wife, was starring in one of the lead roles, and Liza told us that she wanted to stop by her dressing room to say hello. While Obba was changing, we went with Liza to Rita's room. She had a friend named Kate with her and told us that they were also going out for dinner and asked us to join them. They had reservations at BLT, a popular restaurant on Fifty-Seventh Street. Rita suggested that we go ahead, and she and her friend would meet us there.

Liza, Obba, Arlene and I went to the restaurant and waited for them to meet us. When they arrived, we ordered drinks and some appetizers. We were having a great time with Rita and her friend when I noticed a man dressed in a T-shirt and baseball cap heading toward Liza. I am used to fans coming up to her in restaurants trying to hug her or take a picture, so I immediately jumped up to intercept him. As I moved toward him, I saw Liza hug him and then realized that it was Tom Hanks. Tom joined us at dinner, and the conversations we had that evening were terrific. He was charming and so nice that we felt like he was a lifelong friend.

As we were about to order our meal, the maître d' came over to the table to tell us that Kate's husband was coming into the restaurant and wanted to join us. I moved my chair to the left to make room for him as he walked in. Kate, I suddenly realized, was Kate Capshaw when her husband, Steven Spielberg, walked over and sat down next to me. The evening was really getting interesting. The stories flowed among Steven, Tom, Liza, Obba, and us. I found Steven to be a wonderful conversationalist and loved talking to him. I told him how his movie *Schindler's List* inspired me to take my daughter and Arlene to Kraków, Poland.

He quietly told the waiter to bring a selection of all the appetizers and also ordered some wonderful wines. Soon large platters of seafood and assorted dishes were brought out. Spielberg and Hanks were extremely nice, and we were all having a wonderful time. Steven, at one point, suggested that we take a group picture. I jokingly told him that if he didn't know how to take a good picture, I'd be happy to help him. Tom said he had a camera and handed it to the waiter to take our photo. He promised us all that he would send us copies.

Main dishes of every type were brought out, along with fine wines, and dinner was exceptional. While I was sitting next to Steven, his driver came over to talk to him, and I overheard the conversation. Steven then relayed what was told and how his driver just explained that they had to leave immediately. The helicopter flying him to his home in East Hampton had to depart soon, and if Steven was not on it, he would have to wait until the next morning. He reluctantly said goodbye.

By this time, the restaurant was clearing out, and we were one of the few remaining tables. We were all having so much fun, and desserts of every kind were being brought out, so the conversations continued. Arlene and I were having a great time with this wonderful company, but to Liza, hanging with Spielberg and Hanks was not that unusual.

It was a long night, and she started signaling me to get the check so we could leave. I kept trying to ignore her because the check at this very expensive restaurant was going to be enormous; Steven had ordered bottles of very fine wines, along with a massive amount of lobsters and steaks, and then had to leave. I expected a huge bill. I had no idea how to ask Tom and Obba to share it, and the more I ignored Liza, the more she kept signaling me to get the check so that we could go home. I figured I just better do it. It was a very exciting evening and worth whatever the cost. As I was about to ask for the check, Tom yelled out to the waiter to please give him the check because he wanted to take everyone out as his guests. The waiter then told Tom that Steven had given his credit card information when he left with instructions to pay the entire bill.

We went outside, and I put Liza in a taxi because she was tired and ready for bed. Arlene and I thought that we would walk home. Tom asked us where we lived, and when we told him First Avenue and Seventy-Sixth Street, he responded that his jeep was parked in front of the restaurant and that he would give us a lift home. The apartment where he was residing in NYC was a few blocks away on Fifth Avenue; the opposite direction from our place. We explained that there was no need for him to drive us all the way to First Avenue at this hour and then drive back to Fifth Avenue. He insisted, however, on giving us a ride in his jeep.

We sat in the back seat, and he and Rita drove us home. There is a reason why everyone in Hollywood speaks so highly of him. Even though Obba appeared each night in the show with Rita, unfortunately, we never received the picture taken of the group at the dinner. We saw Rita six months later at a nightclub and, after saying hello, reminded her about the photo. She promised that she would check her camera when she returned to LA, but we never received it. I assume that it must have been buried somewhere in her photos.

THIRTY-SIX

Ginny and Henry Mancini

Ginny and Henry Mancini have been an important part of our lives since the 1970s. Arlene and I initially met them at a party at their home in LA while staying with Jack Haley. During a whirlwind few days in LA, we went to a party at the Mancini home on Baroda Drive. When I first was introduced to Ginny, I hugged her and instantly felt the warmth of friendship.

There was a series of parties that we were all going to, including an engagement party for Rod and Alana Stewart. We didn't know them, but attending the party with Jack and the Mancinis helped make us accepted guests. We did get a kick out of spending time with Rod Stewart because he was one of our favorite performers. Alana has always been amiable over the years, except for one night at Studio 54 when she told me to give up my seat on the couch in the VIP area when Rod arrived. She was completely right in requesting that as he really belonged in that area. I handled it by just sitting on the floor, and Arlene and I were able to remain in the prime spot.

There was another party at the home of David Janssen, who was starring in the popular TV series *The Fugitive*. His wife, Dani, was a popular hostess in LA. After the Academy Awards each year, all the biggest stars stopped by her home after attending the traditional parties that followed the show. They came to mingle and eat her famous "monkey bread." It appeared to me that David may have enjoyed various stimulants, but regardless, he and Dani were a fun couple.

When we returned to NYC and the new club scene, consisting of Studio 54 and other venues like P. T. Barnum, we often bumped into Ginny and Henry. We were quite surprised as our image of the great Henry Mancini was that of a very serious person, not someone partying at these crazy clubs. We did not know at the time that Ginny was telling her family how she and Henry kept running into this couple whom they met in LA whenever they were in NY at a disco. One night the Mancini family were all in NYC at a restaurant that had just opened, and they were talking about us at the very moment we were walking into the same restaurant. When we came over to say hello, Ginny told us that our friendship was meant to be and that we had to exchange numbers and get together.

Ginny invited us to an evening at the NY Friars Club where Henry was being honored not too long after we exchanged numbers. Marvin Hamlisch was one of the performers, and we were happy to see him. Marvin had a great sense of humor, and we always found him stimulating to be around. He and Liza had been friends since their teens, and we all had some great times together, occasionally with Marvin at the piano and Liza singing. We were going out with Henry and Ginny after the event, and we were looking forward to Marvin joining us. When we all looked for him at the end of the evening, we realized that he had just left without saying anything. As I mentioned in a previous chapter, he occasionally had what I considered mood swings, but Ginny didn't seem to mind. Marvin was so talented and witty that friends overlooked his sometimes antisocial behavior. When he performed that night at the Friars, he honored Henry without a fee.

We told Ginny that we were planning on coming to LA and would call her before we arrived to make plans to see her. She replied that she would see us at Jack Haley's home because she knew that we always stayed there. We informed her that Jack was redecorating his home, so this trip, we were staying at the Beverly Hills Hotel. She told us that she would love to have us stay with her and Henry at their home and to call her if we decided to take her up on her offer. When Arlene and I arrived home that night, Arlene expressed how nice it was for Ginny to invite us, but she felt that we did not know them well enough to stay at their home. Arlene felt uncomfortable calling Ginny to take her up on her offer. The thought of staying at their home was somewhat intimidating because we heard what a fabulous home they had. I assured Arlene that Ginny was just being polite, and if we didn't call her back, she would probably forget about it. The next day, Ginny called us and, reading our minds, told us that she really meant what she said. We answered that we would look forward to being with her and canceled the hotel.

When we arrived in LA, Ginny and Henry greeted us with open arms and gave us a tour of their magnificent house. They showed us the guest bathroom that Ginny had decorated, with wallpaper made up of sheet music of every Mancini song. When we first entered the home, we noticed twenty Grammys on the shelves in the den. He had won many Oscars as well. He has written *The Pink Panther* theme, "Moon River," the theme from *Peter Gunn*, the theme from *Mr. Lucky*, "Days of Wine and Roses," "Charade," "Dear Heart," "Two for the Road," "Le Jazz Hot," along with musical scores for countless movies and TV shows. We understood that it was impossible to fit them all on the wall of one bathroom when Henry playfully pointed out to Ginny a song that she missed putting on the wallpaper. We immediately realized that he had a devilish sense of humor.

The parties at Ginny and Henry's home attracted many A-list celebrities because the Mancinis were Hollywood royalty and very special people. They were warm, gracious, and fun to be around. We have been privileged to be included in many of their events. When the United States Post Office honored Henry by putting his picture on a stamp, we were invited to fly out for the ceremony. It was very exciting, and Ginny threw a fabulous party after the event. I remember it well because it was the first time I tasted LA's famous Pink's hot dogs when Ginny handed them out after the ceremony. We still treasure our first-edition Henry Mancini stamps given out that day. It is hard for me to remember all the famous people we encountered at the Mancini home.

An example of one of the Mancini parties during those days is described in Henry Bushkin's recent book about his time as the lawyer for Johnny Carson. He was at the Mancini party with Johnny and Joanne Carson. The other guests were Lalo Schifrin (the composer of the *Mission: Impossible* theme), Jack Lemmon, Walter Matthau, Gene Kelly, Roger Moore, Sean Connery, Michael Caine, Jimmy Stewart, Cary Grant, Tony Curtis, Sammy Cahn, the director Richard Brooks, the producer Ray Stark, André Previn, George Shearing, Michel Legrand, Barron Hilton, Freddy de Cordova (the *Tonight Show* producer), and Suzanne Pleshette. Ginny knew how to throw a party, and when she did, everyone in Hollywood wanted to attend.

We had the most wonderful time staying with Ginny and Hank, as he was often called by those close to him. The only problem we had was with their alarm system; we were afraid of setting it off by mistake. Fortunately, that never happened, and we became comfortable with their hospitality.

We observed Henry's witty and playful personality. One night he drove us to a party at Sammy Davis's home. At the gate, there was an intercom so that people could announce their arrival. Hank pushed the button, and instead of giving his name, he hummed the theme to his famous movie *The Pink Panther*. The gate immediately opened.

Henry was a connoisseur of wine. He knew how to pick a really fine wine for a good price when going to a restaurant. One time when he was alone in NYC for a concert he was doing, we took him out for dinner. We went to Sette Mezzo, a very good Italian restaurant with delicious food that we felt he would like. The one problem was that they were one of the few restaurants in NYC that didn't take credit cards. I was aware of this and made sure to bring enough cash. I always let Henry choose the wines because he knew how to order a good wine. When he scanned the wine list and picked out an excellent wine for about $50, the waiter complimented him on choosing such a fine wine at a reasonable price.

The waiter then told Henry that he noticed his appreciation for wine and said that the owner just acquired six bottles of the most amazing wine. He was sure that a wine connoisseur like Henry would find it a treat but remarked that it was expensive. Henry responded to the waiter that he was not paying the bill and suggested the waiter whisper the price to me. When he quoted a price of $300, I had to make a quick decision. The SOB waiter put me in the uncomfortable position of looking cheap if I didn't order it after hearing the price. I was not as upset with having my $250 dinner turned into a $550 dinner as I was with the fact that I might not have enough cash with me.

When the bill arrived, I emptied my wallet and signaled Arlene to try to find any cash that she might have in her purse. Hank asked if he could help pay the bill as he watched us searching for cash, but I was able to find just enough to cover it. Fortunately, we lived close enough to the restaurant to walk home because I had nothing left for a taxi.

One summer Henry was our houseguest in Westhampton. He was doing a concert on Long Island and was in NY by himself. Our son, Marc, was a teenager, and we had a piano in our home. Marc took some piano lessons when he was younger, but he was not too interested in playing the piano in general. Hank offered to give him a lesson and sat down alongside Marc at the piano. We were thrilled that our son might be inspired as Hank started to give him pointers on how he constructs a melody. In the middle of the lesson, one of Marc's friends knocked on the door and asked Marc to come out and play. Marc abandoned the lesson and left with his friend. He was one of the few people in the world who would run out in the middle of a piano lesson from Henry Mancini.

In 1993, while we were in Florida, Ginny and Henry were invited on the yacht of Ted and Lin Arison, the owners of the Carnival Cruise Line. We were asked to join the two couples for cocktails on the boat before they set sail for a short vacation. We had spent time with the Arisons in the past and always found them to be lovely people. The Arisons were terrific hosts, serving us cocktails and showing us around the magnificent yacht. As they were giving us the tour, Henry mentioned that he was experiencing some back pain and planned on seeing his doctor when he returned to LA. The boat was very special, and the Arisons treated us to a wonderful afternoon of drinks and sumptuous food.

Each year Lin chaired a charity event in Florida, and Ginny always invited us to join her at the benefit. Arlene's parents, who were living in Florida, were invited as well. Quincy Jones was a dear friend of Ginny and usually attended. We loved spending time with Quincy, and he gave us his fantastic autobiography, Q, to read. We always enjoyed hearing his stories, and when we read his book, we understood why everyone respected him so much. Sharon Stone was also a guest at our table one year at the Arisons' event. She could not have been nicer and was interesting to talk to.

When Ginny and Henry returned from this vacation, they flew home to LA. It was there that they learned that Henry's back pain was from pancreatic cancer. Over the next year, we would see them often as they tried different remedies. It was hard to watch Henry experiencing the effects of the disease. For his birthday, we bought him a beautiful, expensive sweater. We knew that he would never get a chance to wear it, but we wanted him to feel like we had confidence in the treatments. They tried many types of therapy, but Henry passed away the following year.

After Henry's death, Ginny sold the Baroda home and moved into a beautiful penthouse duplex apartment in Beverly Hills. We have been staying there whenever we go to LA ever since Jack Haley died. Ginny also has a lovely home on the ocean in Malibu, which she has opened up to our children as well. Our former daughter-in-law, Amanda, who loved being in California and occasionally seeing movie stars, stayed there with us one year. She was quite thrilled to see Leonardo DiCaprio sitting on the deck of the home next to Ginny's house.

We have many wonderful memories of times with Ginny, Henry, and the Mancini family. For a big anniversary, Ginny and Hank rented the Positano home of Franco Zeffirelli (the famous Italian film director) for a month. Each week they invited a different group of friends to visit and stay with them in this idyllic setting. There were a number of villas on the mountain with a long stairway leading down to the beach. Zeffirelli's chef prepared delicious meals each day. It was the best seven days of food and wine that I have ever experienced. This chef should have had his own three-star Michelin restaurant.

Our group included our friends Leslie and Evie Bricusse and George and Jolene Schlatter. Leslie spent part of the vacation time working on one of his Broadway musicals. One year when he and Evie stayed at our home in Westhampton, he also spent part of the time writing his musical *Jekyll and Hyde*. He gifted us with his songbooks, with an inscription thanking us for creating the perfect atmosphere for him to write his show. George Schlatter was the creator of Rowan and Martin's TV show *Laugh-In* and founder of the American Comedy Awards. George was great to spend time with and, most days, would take us out on the water in a boat he rented. I brought along my movie camera, and finally, I learned from George how to take good movie pictures.

One night we met up with Cary Grant's last wife, Barbara Harris, at the San Pietro Hotel in Positano. She was quite nice and shared some interesting stories about her life. We had previously stayed at the hotel with Gina Lollobrigida and remembered the fabulous room that Gina stayed in. It included a very large bath with a full-sized statue of a man with a huge penis that served as the water faucet for the tub.

Barbara told us that she and her last husband, Richard Cohen, had stayed in that same room. She let us know that Richard was not thrilled to have to stand next to this figure with the huge penis whenever he stepped out of the tub. Richard sadly died at an early age during a dinner party after he started to choke on a piece of steak. A very prominent doctor happened to be at his table, and after performing the Heimlich maneuver and mouth-to-mouth resuscitation, Richard started to breathe. Unfortunately, Richard had a severe peanut allergy, and the doctor had eaten peanuts that night. Richard was rushed to the hospital but died from an allergic reaction to peanuts.

Over the years, we have enjoyed memorable days and nights with Henry and Ginny and many of their friends. Norman Lear; John Glenn and his wife, Annie; Buzz Aldrin and his wife, Lois; Tony Bennett; James Galway; Quincy Jones; Polly Bergen; and Julie Andrews were some of their accomplished friends whom we were lucky enough to have had the pleasure of spending time with. We had a wonderful evening out with John and Annie Glenn and had the opportunity to ask him about his experiences. He had an amazing life with a well-known highlight since he was the first American to orbit the earth, circling it three times in 1962. He served as a senator from Ohio from 1974 to 1999 and then returned to his passion in 1998 and flew into space again at age seventy-seven.

Our daughter, Lauren, was with us one time at Harry Cipriani Restaurant in NYC when Buzz and Lois Aldrin were there. Astronauts Buzz Aldrin and Neil Armstrong were the first two humans to land on the moon in 1969 on the Apollo 11 mission. Lauren was happy when we introduced her to Buzz, and he could not have been nicer. He took a photo with her, which she was very excited about, and she showed the photo to her children, Devin and Justin, years later because they were big fans of the movie *Toy Story*. (Justin loved to run around in a Buzz Lightyear costume, which was very adorable, and we would tell him that we knew the real Buzz.)

We had spent several nights with the Aldrins and Ginny over the years. Buzz is quite a charming character, and Lois is lovely. He does have an eye for the ladies, and he did look quite good when we saw him at the restaurant, after excellent plastic surgery in my opinion. Buzz and Lois divorced in 2012, and we have lost contact with him.

When Henry and Leslie Bricusse wrote the musical *Victor/Victoria*, it starred their good friend Julie Andrews. We always admired her from her starring roles on Broadway in *My Fair Lady* and *Camelot* and movies like *Mary Poppins* and *The Sound of Music*. We luckily had the opportunity to spend time with her and always found Julie to be very sweet. She was quite active in helping our local Hampton theater in Sag Harbor.

One day we went with Ginny and Julie to see the apartment Julie and her husband, director Blake Edwards, rented for them to stay in while she was performing in the show in NYC. It was a duplex with a large living room area downstairs and a quaint winding stairway leading upstairs to the bedroom. Unfortunately, Blake's back went out, and he had to sleep in the living room to avoid the steps.

The music in the show was wonderful but very demanding for a singer. During the run, Julie lost her voice. Liza, being a good friend, stepped in to replace her. Soon Liza lost her voice as well because the range of the musical score proved to be very difficult on the vocal cords.

We also spent a lot of time with Ginny's friends Corky and Mike Stoller. Mike and his writing partner, Jerry Leiber, were songwriting and record-producing partners. Some of their songs were "Kansas City"; the Coasters hits like "Young Blood," "Yakety Yak," and "Searching'"; the Drifters hit "There Goes My Baby"; Elvis Presley hits including "Love Me," "Hound Dog," "Jailhouse Rock," and "Don't Be Cruel"; Ben E. King's "Stand by Me," "Young Blood," and "Spanish Harlem"; and many more. Mike was always very friendly, and we enjoyed his company. There was one problem with being his friend. His wife, Corky, was a singer; and since Mike was very supportive of her singing career, every time she booked herself into a club, he brought his friends to the show. The unfortunate truth was that she was not a great singer. She was fun to hang out with, but hearing her perform was a different story.

One year Ginny and Henry invited us to join them and another couple on a jazz cruise on the *Norway*. The other couple was Pat and Larry Gelbart. Larry was one of the lead comedy writers on *Saturday Night Live* and *Caesar's Hour*. He was the creator of the TV show *M*A*S*H* and the writer of such shows as *A Funny Thing Happened on the Way to the Forum* and *City of Angels*. He is considered by many to be the best comedy writer of our generation. Spending a week with him was a treat. He had the quickest mind I have ever encountered. When Larry, who cowrote the film *Tootsie*, was having "creative differences" with its star, Dustin Hoffman, he said, "Never work with an Oscar winner who is shorter than the statue."

We had a table for six on the ship, and there was no loss of stimulating conversation. We all got along very well, except for one minor problem. It seemed that, years before, Pat had caught Larry cheating. Pat possessed a very strong personality, and apparently, since that time, Larry had been at her beck and call. On the boat, we noticed that he was extremely attentive to her. He would move Pat's chair in for her when she sat and wait on her hand and foot. He was one of the nicest and considerate people we have ever met. We noticed at each meal Pat would arrange the seating so Larry and Arlene never sat next to each other. Ginny disclosed to us that since Larry's indiscretion, Pat had become jealous of any female he came in contact with. Arlene, being an attractive younger woman at his table every day, was someone to be watched, although Larry was not interested in playing around since that lapse years ago.

We lost contact with Larry, and he passed away in 2009. A few years before his death, a false rumor went around that he had a stroke and died. Larry then sent an email to his friends that asked, "Does that mean I can stop exercising?"

The ship was amazing and made even better by the various musical talents who played on it. The Count Basie band with Joe Williams was part of the entertainment on this cruise. Joe was a friend of the Mancinis, and we spent a good deal of time with him and his wife, Jillean. We always admired his singing and loved getting to know them as a couple. Many of the top jazz performers of the time were booked to entertain, and every day was filled with great music. Many of the passengers were also musicians. On nights when the different band members would take a break, volunteers among the passengers would come up, pick out an instrument, and join the orchestra. Henry was one of the passengers who joined in on the piano a few nights. Onboard were many jazz legends, and we had a ball hearing their stories and watching them jam each day.

When our daughter, Lauren, was on her March school break from high school one year, Ginny and Henry invited us to their winter place in Vail. It was my first time skiing, and I went each day with the beginners group to learn. Lauren already knew how to ski, so each day she and Henry went skiing together, along with a private ski instructor whom he hired. The Mancini family also had their other friends Bobbi and Jack Elliott join them in Vail.

One evening we all watched the Academy Awards together. Ginny had sheets made out with all the nominees for the Oscars, and each of us filled out our choices. The Mancini family had great knowledge of filmmaking, with Henry winning multiple Oscars. Jack Elliott, besides conducting the orchestra for the Grammys for thirty straight years, also had been the musical director on many Academy Awards shows. It would be a fierce competition to see who would guess the most award winners. Even though Lauren had only seen one of the films nominated, Ginny gave her a ballot to fill out as well. At the end of the evening, when all the results were tabulated to see which of our Hollywood experts picked the most winners, there was a surprise champion. Lauren, who simply guessed every category, was the winner. I don't recall if there was a prize, but in later years, whenever the Grammys were in NYC, Jack provided tickets for Lauren and a date.

CHAPTER

THIRTY-SEVEN

Ginny Mancini

In 1984, Ginny formed the Society of Singers, a charity to help professional singers who were down and out and needed assistance. She established the Ella Award, named after its first recipient in1989, Ella Fitzgerald. Frank Sinatra, Tony Martin, Peggy Lee, Steve Lawrence and Eydie Gormé, Lena Horne, Rosemary Clooney, Joe Williams, Tony Bennett, Julie Andrews, Plácido Domingo, Barry Manilow, Celine Dion, Elton John, Johnny Mathis, Gladys Knight, Andy Williams, Herb Alpert, Natalie Cole, Smokey Robinson, and Mike Love of the Beach Boys have all been recipients. We have been fortunate to have been able to attend almost every event.

It was wonderful meeting and spending time with Ella Fitzgerald. She seemed very frail when we spoke to her, but then the spotlight shone on her at the end of the evening. When she began singing at the close of the show, magically, she became the Ella of old and tore down the house. She had always been one of our favorite singers, and spending time with her was very special.

At each event, additional singers performed along with the honoree. When Sinatra was honored, Harry Connick Jr. sat with us at our table with his wife, Jill. He told us how nervous he was to have to sing in front of his idol, Frank Sinatra. When he was called up to sing, he did freeze at one point. He stopped momentarily and then had the orchestra start the music again for his song. Arlene and I thought he did well, but when he came back to our table, he was very upset with his performance. He took his wife by the hand and left the room, never to return.

I especially enjoyed spending time with Lena Horne the night she was honored. When I told her that I had a crush on her when I was a young man and went to see her many times on Broadway in the musical *Jamaica*, she was very flattered. When Celine Dion was honored, we flew to Las Vegas for her award. While spending time with her after the event, we found her to be extremely emotional in a positive way, quite talkative, and very warm. We spoke with her for a long time and marveled at her enthusiastic personality.

We had the opportunity to spend time each year with the honorees because we were seated with Ginny. We were given the chance to join Ginny with each year's honorees not only at the benefit but also at the private parties and dinners. Each of the events held memorable times for us, and Ginny raised a lot of money to help singers everywhere. It finally disbanded in 2017, unfortunately, when Ginny turned ninety-three years old.

Ginny is one of the most active and outstanding people we have ever met. She started out as a backup singer for Mel Tormé as a member of the Mel-Tones. She met Henry when he was the rehearsal pianist. They fell in love, got married, and were together until his passing. He went from a struggling piano player to a world-famous composer, and their marriage was terrific.

To celebrate one of her major birthdays, she took over the Golden Door Spa for a week. Ginny invited her closest friends as her guests. She told Arlene that her roommate at the spa for the week would be Cyd Charisse because Cyd liked Arlene, and they always got along very well. Arlene loved watching Cyd dance in those great MGM musicals, and we really enjoyed being with her and her husband, Tony Martin. However, Arlene would not allow anyone, not even

Cyd, to see her for a week without makeup and eyelashes. Arlene had to explain to Ginny the reason she was turning down the trip, and although she thought Arlene was crazy, she understood. My wife is one of the only people I know that will turn down the opportunity to spend a week with Cyd Charisse as her roommate at a spa. I guess most people have insecurities, but Arlene looks great without her makeup and really had no need to turn the invitation down.

Tony Martin's hearing was bad in his later years, and Cyd spoke very softly. It was comical at that time to go out with them and listen to him say every few sentences, "What did you say?" I don't find it as funny today because I suffer from hearing loss, and I often find myself asking the same question to Arlene.

When Ginny turned ninety, she invited all her good friends to Vail, where she has a home. She put everyone up at a hotel in Vail, and we had a wonderful three days. Michael Feinstein is a close friend of ours and Ginny's, and he sang as well as organized the entertainment. Ginny and the other ladies of the Mel-Tones had not sung together for seventy years. Two women from the original group flew to Vail for her birthday. With Michael Feinstein at the piano, they all sang together that night. The fourth lady in the group had unfortunately died, so Ginny's great friend Mitch Moore dressed in drag and filled in to restore the quartet. Ginny's twin daughters, Monica and Felice, and her son, Chris, all sang as well. We have known most of Ginny's friends and family over the years and loved celebrating with everyone.

Sherry Lansing and her husband, William Friedkin, were two of the guests. She is the former CEO of Paramount Pictures. When she became president of production at Twentieth Century Fox, she was the first woman to head a Hollywood movie studio. We had met her over the years but hadn't spent much time with her. When she heard that one of my best friends was Michael Tadross, who worked with her at Paramount, she had me contact him to reconnect with her. Her husband, William Friedkin, was a director, producer, and screenwriter. He is best known for directing the films *The French Connection* and *The Exorcist*. We spent three memorable days celebrating with Ginny, her family, and all her guests.

After Henry's death, Ginny would often travel to NY and stay with us either in our apartment in NYC or in Westhampton. She enjoyed NY so much that she decided to buy an apartment. She commissioned a broker to find a suitable apartment for her. He found an apartment and informed Ginny that a decision had to be made immediately. She asked us to look at it and let her know if we thought that she should take it. It was a huge responsibility, but we liked the apartment and felt that it would be perfect for her. She bought it and furnished it beautifully.

Ginny loved to be in Manhattan and enjoyed the pace of our city. I have escorted her often whenever she wanted someone to accompany her to an event. I recently accompanied her when Tony Bennett was honored at the opening of the Frank Sinatra School of the Arts, which Tony founded. I sat with Ginny and the great singer k.d. lang, whom I found to be extremely cordial and delightful.

I was somewhat embarrassed one evening when Ginny introduced me to the songwriter Arthur Hamilton. He wrote the song "Cry Me a River," made famous by Julie London. There was an awkward silence when I told him that it was one of my favorite songs and how much I loved Roberta Sherwood's recording of it. When he walked away, Ginny politely let me know that the Roberta Sherwood song I was referring to was "Up a Lazy River" and not "Cry Me a River." (So much for an ex-dentist trying to show off my knowledge of music to a real professional songwriter.)

We have had many memorable evenings with Ginny. One time she took us to see Mel Tormé entertain at a club in NYC. She was close with him for many decades because, as I mentioned previously, she was one of his original backup singers in the Mel-Tones. She arranged with Mel to meet him backstage after his performance and then go to dinner. Mel sang two songs, and then a drunken heckler in the crowd started to talk out loud. A few songs later, when management didn't act to remove the unruly patron, Mel announced that he was leaving and stormed off the stage. After I paid the check for the shortened show, we went backstage, only to find that Mel left the building. The three of us ended up going to dinner by ourselves. Arlene and I concluded that Mel must not be such an easygoing person because he just walked out without a call or message to Ginny.

For many years after I retired, we spent much of our winters at the Boca Raton Resort and Club in Florida. Arlene's parents lived nearby, and she was able to spend time with them in their later years. We knew many people who lived in Palm Beach, not too far away from Boca. Palm Beach is a beautiful gem of a place, but I am sad to report that it has several restricted clubs. Ginny flew to Florida every year to attend the Arison Arts Foundation charity event in Miami, but she had never been to Palm Beach.

One year Ginny informed us that she met a new couple at an event who invited her to come to their beach club in Palm Beach the next time she was in Florida. She planned to drive from Miami to Palm Beach, we could join her, and all of us would spend the day at the private club. When Ginny mentioned the name, we knew that it was a restricted club that did not allow Jews. We didn't want to tell her not to go, and we were curious to see what went on at one of these places. She was invited to their Sunday buffet, and we agreed to go with her. Fortunately, I knew the location of the club because they had no sign outside. Only members, I realized, would know where the entrance was.

I drove in, and the couple greeted Ginny and us warmly. Arlene and I felt strange from the minute we entered. Everyone wore similar-looking outfits and straw hats. Arlene warned me not to overfill my plate at the buffet due to the stereotype of a Jew overeating. There were about a dozen people at our table. Ginny was seated at one end with our hostess while we were at the other end of the table with her husband.

When they heard we were from NY, the questions began. They mentioned a well-known restricted club in Southampton as their favorite and asked which clubs we were members of in the Hamptons. They inquired about what restaurants and clubs we frequented in NYC. They asked if the name Lazare was Italian or French. The group spoke about a show they had been to the previous night starring the Temptations. One woman remarked how amazing it was that her husband actually got onstage with black people when some audience members were called up to sing with the group.

When our hostess invited me to join her at the buffet, Arlene reminded me to not pile up food on my plate. The rest of the group seemed content to drink, and no one else rushed to the food area. I was starving, and when I saw a magnificent buffet with giant lobsters and steaks in front of me, I began salivating. Rather than take a large plate, I picked up a small dish. I told the server behind the buffet table that I would just have a salad. My hostess implored me to have more food, but I explained that I didn't like to eat much at buffets. Arlene was smiling when I returned to the table with my tiny dish of salad. We started to sense that they suspected that we might possibly be Jews from NYC when they never invited Ginny or us to tour around the club or beach area.

As we were walking out to our car, Ginny ran into a producer friend of hers from LA. She asked him if he was a member of the club, and he replied that he was just a guest for that day. He told Ginny that he would never join a restricted club like the one we were at. Ginny was shocked and asked me if I knew. I explained to her that we did know but didn't feel that it was our place to suggest canceling after she had accepted their invitation. She never contacted them again.

❧ CHAPTER ☙

THIRTY-EIGHT

Gina Lollobrigida

One of our most improbable long-term relationships is with Gina Lollobrigida. Considered one of the most beautiful women in the world, along with Sophia Loren, Gina is the most famous female Italian movie star. Even though Gina lives in Rome and our Italian is nonexistent, we have been like family for forty years.

Arlene and I and our children have stayed at her villa in Rome many times. Her villa is like a museum. Sculptures, paintings, and antiques fill the enormous home and grounds. She has published many best-selling books of her photography, paintings, and sculptures. She has a large studio in Pietrasanta, Tuscany, on the coast of northern Italy. Gina works and lives there when she is creating her massive sculptures, and many of her works are stored in the giant studio. We have stayed with her in Rome and Pietrasanta, as well as in her homes in Switzerland and Monte Carlo. One can spend hours walking through the five floors of her home in Rome.

When the three Apollo 11 astronauts visited Rome after their space trip, Gina made a party in her home for them. In those days, everyone wanted to meet this Italian sex symbol, and they were no exception. Gina showed us a pillow in her den that the three of them signed.

Gina dresses like a real movie star wherever she goes and is always glamorous. However, she is wonderfully down to earth. When she comes to stay with us in NYC or Westhampton, she loves to cook. She taught Arlene how to make her tasty spaghetti carbonara. She also enjoys making her own gowns and jewelry. She created a spectacular dress for Arlene for our son Marc's bar mitzvah and has gifted Arlene with some beautiful jewelry that she made.

She has starred in movies with Rock Hudson, Frank Sinatra, Humphrey Bogart, Tyrone Power, Yul Brynner, Anthony Quinn, Tony Curtis, Burt Lancaster, Errol Flynn, Yves Montand, Sean Connery, Alec Guinness, Bob Hope, and David Niven, among others. Howard Hughes brought her to Hollywood in 1950. He delayed her career due to his obsession with her. He gave her a contract that did not allow her to work for any other producer and then kept her virtually imprisoned in a Los Angeles hotel room. He begged her for years to marry him, but finally, she was able to break free and begin her Hollywood career.

Gina has told us about her relationships with her costars and the many famous people whom she had dated. Her affair with the famous heart transplant pioneer Christiaan Barnard was well known. She discussed with us time spent with Ted Kennedy, Tom Jones, Rudolf Nureyev, Cary Grant, Orson Welles, Bulgari, and many world leaders and monarchs.

Gina was close friends with the legendary Italian film director Franco Zeffirelli. One night in 1969, Franco was driving Gina home in her Rolls-Royce. He skidded off the road, and the car crash almost killed them both. Gina was badly injured but fortunately had a full recovery. Franco has been quoted as saying that he found God that night when he survived the crash. The Rolls was completely demolished, and Gina turned the twisted remains of the car into a sculpture that is displayed on her grounds.

While making the movie *Come September* with the handsome Rock Hudson, she told us that, off camera, she "tried but couldn't change his sexual orientation."

Gina was invited to Cuba by Fidel Castro, who personally took her around for a week. She filmed a wonderful and informative documentary about Cuba, showing the personal side of Castro. Castro was flirtatious, and she was able to portray many facets of his life. She was also invited by President Marcos to photograph the Philippines and published a beautiful and well-received book. She included never-before-seen photographs of the primitive Tasaday cave people. She loved the Philippines, but it was not the most comfortable experience for her due to Marcos's very jealous wife, Imelda. Gina and Imelda clashed often.

We have accompanied Gina on many memorable evenings. We had several dinners with Salvador Dalí, and we found him to be a fascinating and very strange man. (I had hoped that he had some dental problems so I could offer to trade my treatments for one of his works of art but no such luck.)

Many times when Gina visited us in NYC, we would get together with Anthony Quinn. He was another larger-than-life personality, and he knew how to charm the ladies. He had a charisma and magnetism that was rare.

We spent some evenings with Andrea Bocelli and his wife. He was close to Gina and invited us all to his concert. We were able to spend time with him and his wife backstage afterward. Gina sculpted a wonderful bust of him in marble and presented it to him as a gift to celebrate their friendship.

When Julio Iglesias was on his first American tour, we went backstage with Gina after his performance at Radio City Music Hall. She advised him that if he wanted to make it big in America, he should learn to improve his English. He was very charming and flirty with Gina, and we enjoyed meeting him. When Gina told him to contact her if he needed anything while he was in NYC, he answered with two gestures. He asked which way he should contact her, first making a gesture of holding a telephone to his ear and then making a gesture suggesting an embrace.

Gina loved Mother Teresa and the charitable work that she did. Gina sculpted a few gold medals of Mother Teresa as awards. Gina gave us one that we cherish. When Mother Teresa was honored in Rome and asked Gina to appear with her, we happened to be staying with her. After reading so much about Mother Teresa, it was memorable to spend time with her in person. When the event ended and they were taking their bows, we walked up onstage to escort Gina and Mother Teresa off. The press began taking some pictures. We started to guide Gina and Mother Teresa down the stairs to a back exit when we heard Mother Teresa say to her, "Let's go this way because that's where the cameras will be." Arlene and I remarked quietly to each other that Mother Teresa certainly had good instincts on how to get maximum press exposure. She did wonderful things in her life and certainly understood how to get media attention.

Many important people wanted to spend time with Gina. Henry Kissinger tried to see her whenever she was in NY. Whenever we were with them, we always felt that he had a crush on her, but he was married, so they just remained friends. One night he called our home while we were out for dinner with Gina. My mother was there with our children and answered the phone. He asked to speak with Gina, and when told that she was out, he asked my mother to tell her Henry Kissinger called. My mother said that she would write down the message and then asked him to please spell his name. He yelled out, "Tell her it's Kissinger, Henry Kissinger!" And he slammed the phone down.

We recently met Gina in LA when she flew there to be honored at a film festival. We enjoyed a memorable day when they honored Gina with a star on the Hollywood Walk of Fame. Fans lined the street, bringing magazines with Gina's picture on the cover for her to autograph. We had VIP seats next to her and watched as dignitaries and celebrities paid homage to Gina.

There was also a night honoring her where two of her movies were being shown. The opening night of the festival featured the movie *All the President's Men*, the 1976 movie starring Robert Redford and Dustin Hoffman. It was the story of the reporters Bob Woodward and Carl Bernstein and Watergate. After the screening of the film, there was an opening night party with Carl Bernstein as the guest of honor. We were invited with Gina to attend. Carl Bernstein walked into the event with the host in charge. Instead of greeting the press and the other guests, Carl walked directly over to where Gina, Arlene, and I were sitting on a couch. He wanted to meet Gina and sat down next to her. They had a very animated conversation for twenty minutes until the host finally pulled him away. He explained to Carl that he had to mingle with the guests and press and not just talk with Gina. We were sitting on Gina's side all this time, and we didn't want to interrupt because it looked like they were old friends.

As soon as he left, Gina turned to us and said, "Who was that man?" Despite her problems with the English language, she was able to have a long conversation with someone, even though she had no idea who he was or what he did. Carl thought he was winning over Gina with his stories about his role in Watergate and his portrayal in the movie. She thought he was a nice stranger who sat down to talk with her.

We had dinner in NYC one night with Gina and Maria Bartiromo after an Italian event. She is famously known as "the Money Honey" because of her good looks and expertise as a financial reporter on Fox News. Her short hair and beautiful big eyes are very distinctive. Gina had no idea who Maria was but complimented her looks. Gina loved her features and told Maria that she would look even better with longer hair. Maria, like most Italians, was thrilled to meet Gina. Maria was bright and fascinating, and we had a lovely evening.

A few months later, while watching her on TV, Arlene and I almost didn't recognize her. Her signature short hair look had changed. She was now growing her hair long, and it has remained so to this day. She took Gina's advice and changed her hairstyle (although we liked the original look).

One night Gina was invited to see the Broadway show *Private Lives*, starring Elizabeth Taylor and Richard Burton. She took us with her, and we all thought that Elizabeth was not good in the role. We went backstage after the performance with Gina, and the three of us tried to be as enthusiastic as we could. Gina did a wonderful acting job, telling Elizabeth how much she enjoyed her performance. Arlene and I did a pretty good job as well in finding something about her performance that we could compliment. We did enjoy talking to Richard Burton just to hear his magnificent voice.

Another special night for us was having dinner in 1986 with Federico Fellini and his wife, Giulietta Masina. We first went with them and Gina to see his film *Ginger and Fred*. It starred Fellini's wife and Marcello Mastroianni. Despite our problems with the Italian language, we found it exciting to be in Fellini's company. Growing up in Brooklyn, I never expected to have dinner with Federico Fellini.

It was the opening night film at the Berlin Film Festival. Gina was the jury president and invited us to the event in Berlin. We spent a lot of time with Francis Ford Coppola's brother, August, who was a member of the jury. It was quite a week there, full of drama, not all on the screen. There was a controversial film about the trial of the Baader-Meinhof gang that upset a German radical group. They set off stink bombs in the theater before the screening. After that incident, each night when we entered the theater, we witnessed police with German shepherds going up and down the aisles, checking for stink bombs.

Our most unforgettable day in Berlin was when I told Arlene that I wanted to visit East Berlin. The wall was still up between East and West Berlin. Visitors could book a tour and visit East Berlin for the day. We were not allowed to bring in West German money but, before entering, had to buy fifty East German marks per person to spend there. Our car and driver was allowed through the gate after every part of the car was thoroughly searched. The guards lifted seat covers and went over every area of the vehicle.

When we drove into East Berlin, the contrast to West Berlin was striking. Everything was gray and desolate. West Berlin was a vibrant city, lit up, and full of life. East Berlin was depressing. We went into a few shops but found that we could not spend our East German marks because there was nothing to buy. Arlene did not want to go in the first place due to fear of entering East Germany. I reasoned that we were in Berlin, and it was a part of history to see the wall and East Berlin. After a short time, we told the driver that we had seen enough and wished to return.

As he was driving back on the road toward the gate, the long-flashing yellow traffic light at the intersection turned red while he was driving through it. We heard police sirens and were pulled over to the side of the road. There were about fifteen cars lined up, apparently stopped as well. It was an obvious speed trap. The police could then write tickets for traffic violations to get money for East Berlin. We saw what looked like a Nazi storm trooper left over from World War II march up to our car. Our driver opened the window, and they both started shouting at each other in German, scaring the daylights out of Arlene and me.

The policeman demanded that our driver get out of the car. When he returned a few minutes later, he explained that he was being issued a ticket for going through a red light. The cop demanded that he either instantly pay one hundred marks to him at that moment, or the driver, and the car with us in it, would be taken immediately to the courthouse for trial. Arlene kept reminding me, as they were arguing, that she never wanted to go in the first place, and she feared that we might never get out of East Berlin. I told the driver that I was obligated to buy one hundred East German marks upon entering East Berlin, and I would give it to him to pay off the ticket.

He stepped out of the car, and we heard more yelling back and forth in German. When our driver got back in the car, he informed us that the cop would only accept one hundred marks in West German money. We were in East Germany, where only East German marks were used, yet this cop wanted West German marks. I was warned at the border that we were not allowed to bring West German marks into East Germany. Either the policeman was shaking us down for West German money for himself, or he was trying to trap me into giving him West German money so he could arrest me for bringing it in. We were in a panic and had to make a decision. If I gave him the West German money, I could be arrested. If I didn't, we would be heading to the police station in East Berlin.

I made a choice and told my driver that I had one hundred West German marks with me and that he could have it to give to the policeman. This he did, and after some hesitation, the policeman let us go. When we passed through the gate into West Berlin, I was extremely happy to be back. I had to live with the "I told you we shouldn't have gone to East Berlin" comments from Arlene the entire night.

Gina has achieved many accomplishments throughout her life. She sang opera so well that when the Hilton International Hotel opened in Las Vegas in 1969, they approached Gina to be the opening performer. She did not want to become a singer, so she turned them down. They replaced her with Barbra Streisand. It was quite a compliment to Gina to have Streisand as the second choice.

In her later years, Gina starred in *Falcon Crest* on TV. She was nominated for a Golden Globe Award for her role in that show. When she made the movie *Trapeze* with Tony Curtis and Burt Lancaster, Gina did some of her own stunts on the trapeze. Arlene and I saw the sculptures Gina did that are in the famous Pushkin Museum when we were in Moscow.

In her later years, she was offered the starring role on Broadway in Tennessee Williams's play *The Rose Tattoo*. Two of our friends Joe Pesci and Danny Aiello implored us to tell her that they each wanted to play the role of Mangiacavallo in the production. Gina temporarily moved to NY and stayed with us while she worked hard, learning the part made famous in the movie by the great Italian actress Anna Magnani. Right before production was to begin, the producer suddenly died, and that was the end of that project. John Tillinger was to be the director. When he observed Gina's rehearsal at the theater, he was stunned. When the production was canceled, he remarked, "The world will never know what a great Broadway actress she could have been."

In 1985, an Italian television network, RAI, hired Gina to do a series of interviews with celebrities in America. Arlene flew with her to LA when she interviewed Sammy Davis Jr. and Burt Reynolds and Loni Anderson in their homes. Arlene also went to Atlantic City with Gina to interview Frank Sinatra while he was performing there. (Gina and Frank worked together in the film *Never So Few*.) Frank and his wife Barbara were both very hospitable, and Arlene and Gina had a great time with them in their suite and later as their guests at Frank's show.

One time when Gina was staying in NY with us, she came to my dental office for a cleaning. I shared office space on the floor with a young root canal specialist. When he saw Gina leaving my office, he told me that as a young teenager he fantasized about being with her. We were taking her to dinner that night at Elaine's Restaurant. I offered him the opportunity to join us as her date. I asked Gina if it was okay to have this nice-looking young man come with us as her escort for the evening, and she agreed.

Gina dressed beautifully for dinner as she always does. When the young man came to our apartment and walked in wearing jeans and a casual shirt, it was an awkward moment. He and Gina were a mismatched pair, but off we went to Elaine's. He was excited to be with Gina and was trying to make conversation when the actor George Hamilton walked over to our table. We had often spent time with George in LA with Liza because they were old friends. George has a long career as a movie and TV star. George, who is known as one of the great ladies' men of the world, apparently also knew Gina. He was dressed elegantly and took Gina's hand and kissed it. He pulled up a chair for a few minutes and monopolized the conversation. After George left, it was becoming obvious to my friend that his fantasy of being with Gina was not working out well. After dessert, he thanked me and went home alone.

Gina has a history with Prince Rainier, and we had a wonderful day at the palace in Monaco with her. He could not have been more gracious, giving us a personal tour of the palace. That far surpassed our first experience at the palace years before on a group tour. (I must admit that I got a kick out of it when people asked me how I liked visiting the palace while I was in Monaco, and I casually answered, "The prince was a good tour guide.") Rainier was somewhat formal but all smiles around Gina. Gina has a residence in Monaco, and we have enjoyed staying there in the past. Her residence there is small because land in Monaco is very precious.

When Gina was invited to be the guest of honor at an Easter Monday celebration in Sardinia by a wealthy royal, she invited us to join her. He flew us there in his plane and put us up in a beautiful hotel. They roasted a pig on the spit, and it was a very festive day. They served it in a specially treated bark of a cork tree that was cut to form a large platter. That type of platter preserves the taste of the meat, and we were given it as a gift to take home. We still have it in our home and use it when serving barbecued meats.

All our travels throughout Italy with Gina have been memorable. She is such a legend there, so it is hard for her to go out by herself. When Gina visits NY, she has more freedom and is more relaxed. In Capri, they closed stores to the public when we walked in with her. One time crowds of people in Capri started chasing us down the street, yelling her nickname "Lollo." It was like a scene in a movie. We were almost out of breath when a taxi thankfully appeared, and we were able to escape. Our stay with her in Positano, at the magnificent Hotel San Pietro, was a delight. It is a spectacular resort, and they treated Gina and us royally.

While traveling with her through Italy one year, we stopped in Bologna because the city had named a street after Gina, and she wanted to see the sign. When she was told that the sign was not put up, we followed her into the mayor's office. When we barged in, it was once again like a scene out of one of her movies. Gina berated the mayor for not putting up her sign, and then we all stormed out. We are always looking for cultural information about the places we visited so we asked Gina about Bologna. Gina told us that the city of Bologna was famous in Italy for oral sex, not the deli product. That was not the information we were expecting to hear.

Gina was born in a town outside Rome called Subiaco. Her birthday is on July 4. One time when we were in Italy, Gina was being honored on her birthday in Subiaco. We drove there with Gina, and literally, the entire town came out to greet her. It was quite a sight.

Another time, Gina raved about the wonderful antiques in the town of Fuiggi. That weekend, they were having a giant antique auction, and we drove there to attend. Before the auction, the person in charge took Gina and us on a tour of the large building housing all the items. It was huge, filled with hundreds of antiques. Gina loves to buy valuable carpets and has many in her home. As we walked with our host, we asked him about objects that caught our eye. We noticed a number of interesting antiques and wondered how they selected the items for auction because there were so many.

We were ushered inside into a large room filled with people waiting for the auction to begin. Everyone was speaking Italian. We asked Gina how we could bid on items when we didn't understand what they were saying. She told us that she would let us know when to raise our hands if we said to her that we liked something.

As the items were brought out, we noticed that all the things Gina and I had admired while walking with the man were the ones displayed for auction. We figured that he was doing this out of respect for Gina. People started yelling out in Italian, and we asked Gina how much the bids were. Gina said the prices were good and just to raise our hand if we saw something we wanted. I noticed that no one else in the large crowd was bidding, but people were doing a lot of yelling. After an hour, the auction ended, and we went to the office to give our credit card information and pick up our items. We were the only people there, and it seemed that we were the only ones who bought anything.

The large crowd was still in the main room, and we later found out why. To attract people to the auction, they advertised a strip show at the end of the event. The crowd had been yelling for the show to begin, not yelling out bids. They just wanted the auction to end so they could enjoy what they really came for, the strip show.

My favorite item that I bid on was a beautiful large antique silver tray and decorative serving piece for our dining room table. After our impulsive purchase, we realized that it was too large to carry home, and the duty would be quite high. Gina felt responsible and told us not to worry. She offered to bring it with her the next time she came to NY, and she did.

One Christmas, we took our young children, who were at the time ten and fourteen years old, to Gina's winter vacation home in Crans-sur-Sierre, Switzerland, because they loved to ski. It was a beautiful chalet near the top of the mountain, right on the ski slope. The kids could walk out, ski down, and take the lift back to the house. We had taken them to Gina's home in Crans-sur-Sierre the prior year, and that was where and when they first learned to ski, and they wanted to go back. Since they were familiar with the mountain and the slopes, we allowed them to go skiing by themselves because all they had to do was walk out the door of the chalet, and they would be right on the ski trail.

On New Year's Eve, they went out to ski in the afternoon. After a couple of hours of skiing, they noticed, while halfway down the mountain, that the slopes were almost empty, and the chair lift had stopped running. Lauren suggested that they walk home up the mountain. Marc thought that it was crazy to think that they could walk up the mountain, especially in heavy ski boots, carrying skis and poles. They saw one man skiing down, so they followed his route, thinking that the lift was just temporarily suspended. It turned out that he lived at the bottom of the mountain, and he was going home. The ski lift had stopped operating because, as we found out later, it was New Year's Eve, and the slopes closed early. They were unable to read the signs posted on the slopes because they were not in English. The kids could not call us or anyone for help because it was back in the days before cell phones.

We were hysterical for several hours because our two young children were missing. They had no choice but to walk all the way up the mountain to Gina's home. It took them five hours, and by the time they got back to the house, it was starting to get dark. When they walked in and then collapsed in bed for the night, we opened two bottles of rare red wine. Gina had a collection of rare wines, and we had the treat of tasting them during our stay. We celebrated both the new year and their return.

A few years ago, we flew to Rome for Gina's ninetieth birthday. The city went all out to celebrate and honor her. Via Condotti is the most fashionable and busiest street in Rome. It is the center of shopping, and tourists and locals crowd the street. It is like Fifth Avenue in NYC. It runs from the Spanish Steps all the way to the other end of Rome. For Gina's birthday, the entire street was closed to traffic, and a giant red carpet was rolled out down the entire length of the street. As thousands of people lined the sidewalks, Gina traveled down the street in an open Rolls-Royce, waving to them. When the car arrived at the Spanish Steps, Gina stepped out. A giant ten-foot cake was held up in the air, and everyone sang "Happy Birthday" to her. It was thrilling to watch.

We met her at the steps and walked with her a few blocks down the street to a large nineteenth-century palazzo. It was set up for an elegant dinner party, attended by the most important people in Rome. It was a spectacular evening, and Gina looked fabulous. Later, a few of us went back to her villa on the Via Appia Antica for fireworks on her grounds.

Not all the events in Gina's life have been pleasant ones. A charming forty-five-year-old man from Barcelona named Javier had met Gina at a party. He accompanied her to various events in Monte Carlo and other places when she needed someone to escort her. When Gina came into NYC for her eightieth birthday, she told us that he wanted to marry her. Javier tried to convince her that she would always have him to take her to events and that he would look after her in her old age. After she told us about his proposal, I went to my computer and looked him up. He had a shady history of duping rich widows out of their money, with some mysteriously dying. Fortunately, I was able to persuade Gina to turn down his proposal, but that did not stop him.

The following year, Gina's assistant saw an article about a deal that Gina's new husband was proposing to some investors. When he looked into it, he found that Javier was claiming to be Gina's husband. When Gina's lawyers demanded that Javier stop presenting himself as her husband, he made a crazy reply to the media. Javier announced that he and Gina were married in a ceremony in Barcelona. Her lawyers confronted him with proof showing that, on the date of the alleged marriage, her passport confirmed that she was in Rome. He then changed his story. He stated that Gina gave her approval to have a woman stand in for her at the ceremony because Gina was not able to travel to Spain. Photos showed a woman with a cape over her head exchanging vows with Javier. Javier told the press that Gina loved him and wanted to marry him but has dementia. Despite all these crazy statements by Javier, the legal case lasted for years. There was much corruption in Spain, and Javier was able to pay off witnesses to confirm the marriage.

Finally, after years of legal fights, it was settled when the pope himself stated that there was no proof that Gina married Javier. Gina had to go through interviews with multiple psychiatrists assigned by the courts to check her mental capacity. There is no one sharper than Gina, and passing those tests were easy but time consuming. If a sham marriage using a woman dressed up to pretend to be a movie star was in a movie script, no one would believe it. This story made headlines all over Europe.

Another crazy experience happened while Gina was staying with us in NYC. She met a lawyer who told her he had many contacts that he could use to help Gina in advertising her artwork and other business ventures she was involved with. He claimed to be a former judge and wanted to represent her. He arranged a meeting with Gina and gave her several papers to sign. He had her send him all the projects that she was working on for him to evaluate. When she studied the contracts, she noticed that he wanted her to sign papers giving him a large percentage of anything that she does for the rest of her life. When she didn't sign, he made all sorts of threats. He also refused to return the files she had given to him.

His twenty-one-year-old nephew had come in from Rome to stay with him and help him translate while he was negotiating with Gina. The nephew realized how unfair his uncle was, and he removed Gina's papers from his uncle's home and brought them to Gina. When the man saw that Gina's files were missing, he called his nephew and threatened to call the police. The nephew removed his belongings from his uncle's apartment and moved in temporarily with us. The lawyer threatened to have Gina arrested and his nephew deported.

The next few days were like one of Gina's comedy movies. Gina told the super in our apartment building that if the police came looking for her, to tell them she was not there. Whenever our doorbell rang, Gina and the nephew hid in a back room. Finally, Gina went to the Italian Embassy in New York. The Italian ambassador called the lawyer, demanding that he withdraw his threats.

It was a very crazy week because, aside from Gina and the man's nephew, we also had another houseguest staying with us in another guest room. The daughter of one of our closest friends, Moira Fiore, had also come to stay with us for a few days that week. Her name is Brooke, and she was married to Charlie Sheen. Charlie has starred in many movies, and his success in the TV series *Two and a Half Men* made him world famous. His personal life has made headlines for years with reports of alcohol and drug abuse. They were going through a messy breakup, and Charlie was in the middle of a nationwide tour. It was the biggest news story in the country. It was 2011, and Charlie decided to go on tour that he called "My Violent Tornado of Truth/ Defeat Is Not an Option." The tour broke a Ticketmaster record and sold out everywhere. He was playing Radio City Music Hall that week, and Brooke and her lawyers did not want him to be trashing her at the event. There was a lot of press seeking interviews with her, and our apartment was a better place for her to stay in than a hotel.

We had met Charlie with Brooke in the past and found him actually quite interesting. He believed in a lot of conspiracy theories and had some strange ideas but otherwise very nice. One time, I gave him a book on conspiracy theories concerning September 11, and he was fascinated with it. At this time in his life, he seemed out of control, and the public was loving it but not Brooke.

Brooke and Gina were both living with us that week, but neither knew anything about the other. We put them up in opposite areas of our apartment, and they met for quick meals in between each of their respective dramas. Brooke would be in one room on the phone with her lawyers and Gina in the other room with her lawyers. We alternated going from room to room to calm each one down.

CHAPTER

THIRTY-NINE

Liza Minnelli

Over the past forty-five years, Liza Minnelli has become part of our family. Liza lived near us in NYC, and for years until she recently moved to LA, we were over at each other's apartments all the time. Arlene cooking tacos at our place, Liza making her pot roast and piña coladas in our Hamptons home, or us bringing over Kentucky Fried Chicken was some of the low-key fun times.

Liza would also have the best parties in NYC at her home, and very talented and interesting people would attend. After dinner, everyone would gather around the piano, and people would take turns singing. Wonderful pianists like Billy Stritch and Michael Feinstein would play, and friends got up to sing. One memorable night Liza and Lorna sang a duet of "If Mama Was Married" from *Gypsy*. Tony Bennett was often there, and when Liza and Mark got engaged, he sang "The Best Is Yet to Come" for them at the party. Tony Bennett and his wife, Susan, were always very nice and affable. I would see him often playing tennis on the court next to me in NYC. He hit a few times a week with a friend of mine at the same place on the Upper East Side where I played. He wore glasses when he played because he was once hit in the eye with a tennis ball, so he wanted to protect his eyes.

Paul Shaffer was often at Liza's parties playing the piano while others were singing. One of the nights he was there, our daughter, Lauren, was with us as well. She was excited to see him because she enjoyed watching *Late Show with David Letterman*, where Paul conducted the orchestra. Lauren had met him on a few occasions before, including the time she went with us to see Gina when she appeared on the Letterman show. However, she commented on how amazing it was to be in such an intimate atmosphere with all these people as she sat on the couch next to Rosie O'Donnell. Lauren was always a huge fan of Rosie's comedy ever since Rosie was on *Stand-Up Spotlight*. Rosie was very friendly to Lauren on the couch that night and always said hello to her after that, such as when Lauren saw her backstage at one of Liza's shows.

At one of Liza's parties, Michael Feinstein had arrived early to spend some time with Jule Styne. Jule Styne wrote the music for *Gypsy*, *Gentlemen Prefer Blondes*, *Funny Girl*, and other popular musicals. We were at Liza's apartment early to help her light the candles and organize. At one point, Michael sat down at the piano to play one of Jule's songs from an album Michael had released featuring the songs of Styne. Jule ordered Michael to get up, and then Jule sat down at the piano. He said to Michael, "This is the way it should be played." Jule then played the entire song for us all so we could observe the way he wanted it to be done. He had a strong personality, and we laughed about it after he walked away. (When I took a course one year on learning to program a computer, Jule's wife, Margaret, was in my group. We met each week at the class, and I found her to be very nice.)

One year right after the movie *Flashdance* opened, Liza had a large party. There were many major stars at her apartment. However, with all the famous people there, I stopped Jennifer Beals to tell her how excited I was to meet her. She was the star of the movie, and I adored her in it. She was so happy when I told her that, among all the celebrities at the party, she was the one I was most thrilled to talk to.

Arlene and I spotted our friend and my patient Jimmy Russo walking into that same party with a date. Jimmy was a talented actor and had appeared in many shows on and off Broadway. He starred opposite Farrah Fawcett in the off-Broadway show *Extremities*. Farrah broke her arm during the run of that show. She started coming to my office for dental cleanings because she was having trouble brushing and flossing her teeth. Jimmy also became a patient and a friend. He then moved to LA to pursue a movie career. We hadn't seen him for a few years, so Arlene and I rushed up to hug him. We proceeded to ask him all sorts of questions about how he was doing. I realized that in our excitement to see him, we had ignored introducing ourselves to his date. I apologized for not paying attention to her while we spoke to Jimmy and asked her what her name was. When she said, "Madonna," we did a double take. Madonna was dressed very simply, far from the exotic image that we had of her. She had just published a controversial book titled *Sex* with very provocative photographs. All I could think of to say, while apologizing for not recognizing her was, "I loved your book."

Arlene and I had observed a hippie-looking young Madonna before she was famous at many of the underground clubs in NY. She was trying to get noticed by some of our friends in the music business. Madonna managed to get herself on the stage to sing at Studio 54 one night before she was known. Even though she was not yet a star, she acted like one and drove Steve Rubell somewhat crazy with her demands.

These days, we often go to the Birdland nightclub in NYC. Jim Caruso does a weekly Cast Party, where entertainers get up to sing a song with the trio playing there. This concept really grew out of those parties at Liza's place. When people finished cocktails and dinner, they would gather around her piano, and every singer in the room would do a song or two. Jim has created that atmosphere at Cast Party.

Arlene and I have spent a lot of time sitting around the table in Liza's kitchen. Whenever Liza and we have private things to say to each other that we know none of us will ever repeat, we use the term "kitchen table" to suggest that whatever we are now saying is private. We have fond memories of occasions spent in the kitchen with some interesting people. We spent time there with the actor Jeff Goldblum, famous for such films as *Jurassic Park*, *Independence Day*, and *The Fly*, and a very young girlfriend of his. Jeff was a wonderful storyteller and quite an interesting guy. Jeff also played the piano and sang for us.

Another memorable time was hanging in the kitchen with Patrick Swayze, his mother, and his wife, Lisa. They were so nice to be with, and we were very upset when he died so young. He was a great talent, and we still think of him whenever the movies *Ghost* and *Dirty Dancing* are shown on TV.

One day we were in the kitchen waiting for Liza while she was getting dressed, and a handsome young man strolled in wearing only a white bathrobe. We didn't know what to say because Liza was married to Mark Gero at the time. He introduced himself to us as Michael Feinstein. We later found out that Michael was not her lover but a new friend whom Liza had met, and he was staying in her guest room. Liza always had an instinct for talent, and she immediately saw in Michael a unique musical ability. She had heard him play and sing in a club in LA and set up an evening of entertainment in NYC. She invited all the important people of that time to hear him perform. That day in the kitchen was the first time we met Michael, and we have become very close friends with him over all these years. We consider him and his husband, Terrence, to be part of our extended family as well.

Ben Vereen is another person we met through Liza. They have had a close bond between them for many years. Ben is a great singer and dancer and also very spiritual. He has starred in many Broadway shows, including *Pippin* and *Jesus Christ Superstar*; films such as *Sweet Charity*; and the TV miniseries *Roots*, playing Chicken George. He often wears a cap that says "Spiritual Advisor." Several years ago, he was hit by a car while walking along a road in Malibu. In a strange twist of fate, the driver of the vehicle was the famous music composer and producer David Foster. Ben's injuries have impaired his dancing. He regularly goes to Luigi's dance class when he is in NYC. Arlene goes there almost every day, so she has seen him regularly over the years, and we have had many wonderful times with Ben.

A few years ago, we drove four hours each way with Liza to see Ben perform in a venue outside LA. In his dressing room after the show, he showed us all the areas of his body where the years of dancing, combined with his accident, had left him with physical problems. He recently invited us to see him entertain in NYC, and he was wonderful. Even with his physical limitations, he put on a mesmerizing performance.

One funny incident that occurred many years ago was when a Palm Beach charity organization hired Ben Vereen as their featured performer at their annual formal benefit. Ben knew we were in Florida and invited us to attend the event. The organization did not have many Jewish members, similar to a number of the clubs in Palm Beach. Ben was fabulous that night, and the audience was very generous with their applause. After finishing his show to a standing ovation, Ben returned for an encore to do one last song. He had no idea about the composition of his audience, but he knew Florida was where many Jewish people spend the winter. However, this was not Miami Beach but Palm Beach. When Ben began singing the Jewish song "Hava Nagila," enthusiastically encouraging the audience to sing along with him and clap their hands, there was silence. He finished the song with a mild scattering of applause and walked off the stage dumbfounded. He could not figure out why, after such a great reception, his closing song bombed. When we saw him after the performance and explained that many in his audience were not familiar with "Hava Nagila," we all had a good laugh. He overlooked the important rule in show business to always know who your audience is.

Luigi Faccuito was one of the major figures in the world of dance. When he was a young dancer, he was in an automobile accident that almost killed him. After many weeks in a coma, he was told that he would never walk again. He was determined to not only walk but also continue to dance. He developed a workout technique that restored his ability to walk and dance. People from all over came to his classes to learn the Luigi technique. Liza introduced Arlene to him, and she would pick up Liza every morning, and they would go to the class together. The class has a mixture of professional and amateur dancers.

In 2007, Liza was suffering from a number of physical problems, making even walking difficult. We invited Luigi and Liza to our apartment because she was physically unable to go to classes with Arlene. When Luigi saw Liza barely able to walk, he started to cry. He told her that he could help her and proceeded to give her personal workouts. The following year in 2008, Liza was singing and dancing at the Palace Theater on Broadway. She won a Tony Award for this stunning tribute to her godmother, Kay Thompson.

She later filmed the show in Las Vegas for a special. We were with her for the shows in Vegas. There was some drama the day of the filming when the director, Ron Lewis, had an argument with someone on the film crew. He stormed off the set and went home. Despite that, the filming turned out wonderful.

Arlene and I have created many special memories over the years with Liza. One was spending time with Aretha Franklin after her show in Las Vegas. Liza brought us to Aretha's show, and we all went to her dressing room afterward. Aretha was very pleasant and affable. She told us all about her fear of flying and how she arranged her schedule to avoid getting on an airplane.

We have spent interesting evenings with Liza with fashion icons Donna Karan, Elsa Peretti, and Kevyn Aucoin. Liza always wore Elsa's jewelry and helped make Elsa a famous designer. At the height of her fame, Elsa decided that she had enough and moved to a small village in Catalonia, Spain. Liza still cherishes the jewelry she has of Elsa's, and it is her favorite thing to put on when she goes out.

Kevyn Aucoin was the top makeup artist to celebrities like Cher, Madonna, Janet Jackson, Tina Turner, Cindy Crawford, and Naomi Campbell. His products and book on makeup techniques made him the top makeup person in the country. He would come to Liza's apartment to do her makeup for special occasions and was a very sweet man and a friend. We would spend many hours with him there, watching and discussing his makeup tricks. He was a gracious and charming person to be around. Ironically, this beauty expert suffered from the disfiguring disease of acromegaly. The pain from this disease forced him to take many types of painkillers, and he died at age forty from acetaminophen toxicity.

Liza was very close to the amazing dancer Mikhail Baryshnikov, and we were with them for many wonderful personal and professional times together. His TV special in 1980 called *Baryshnikov on Broadway* featured him and Liza dancing together. He was a great ballet dancer but not used to dancing to Broadway tunes. Liza was very helpful in turning him into a terrific interpreter of Broadway dance. Our friend Obba Babatundé was also on that show, and it won four Emmys.

In 1981, Liza appeared in the hit movie *Arthur* with Dudley Moore and John Gielgud. We had fun times on the set of *Arthur* with Dudley Moore when they filmed the luxury car scenes in NYC. Dudley Moore had a great personality, and he and Liza were great friends off camera. Dudley played such a convincing drunk in *Arthur* that people thought he was an alcoholic. In his later years, he developed a terminal degenerative brain disorder. His often strange behavior caused by it led people to believe that he was often drunk. Its early symptoms were very similar to intoxication, and the tabloids misrepresented his behavior. Liza assured us that reports of his alcoholism were far from the truth, and sadly, he died at age sixty-six. Friends of ours were in the business of supplying old luxury cars for movie sets. They worked on this film, and we got a chance to see all the beautiful old cars.

When Liza turned fifty, we flew with her to Paris to celebrate. Charles Aznavour, her mentor and friend, organized a wonderful party for her at Fouquet's on the Champs-Élysées. Charles wrote and recorded over one thousand songs and sold two hundred million records. He is one of the best-selling music artists of all time and was dubbed France's Frank Sinatra. In 1998, Charles was named Entertainer of the Century by CNN. We got to know Charles and his music, which was quite important to Liza and eventually to myself. We found him to be a very sweet man, and his relationship with Liza was very special to them both. We always loved being in Paris, but with Charles as our host, that visit was extraspecial. We had the unique opportunity to celebrate Liza's birthday with Charles over a few days, filled with exciting events. We could not ask for a better person to show us the wonders of Paris than Charles Aznavour. I just wished that I spoke French and that Arlene's memory of her French from high school was better. However, they were all kind enough to speak in the universal language of broken English as much as possible.

A few years into my friendship with Liza, she asked me what she could do for her bleeding gums. I told her that I would be glad to bring her to my office and give her a gum treatment at no charge. She had a real fear of dentistry and tried every excuse to avoid dental treatment. Finally, I persuaded her to come to my office. I offered to bring her in at night, and Arlene would come along to assist me. My office at that time was at 745 Fifth Avenue, on the thirtieth floor. We picked Liza up at her apartment, and we took a taxi to my office. The building was empty, except for maintenance staff. Liza took a large boombox so she could play her favorite music while I did my work. We also carried with us a large bottle of Grand Marnier. We took the elevator up to my office. Finally, she was out of excuses, and I would be able to work on her.

We each had some alcohol, only a tiny sip for me because I was going to work on her. Arlene, who filled in for me at the office when a nurse was out for the day, set out the instruments. Liza began to stall by playing songs for us and singing along. Finally, she ran out of options; and after one more sip of brandy, she was ready. Arlene and I heard sirens coming from the street but ignored them. Liza heard them as well, and we assured her it was just NYC noise. Suddenly, pulsating loud sirens rang out in the building. Loudspeakers on the floor announced that there was a fire in the building, and everyone should evacuate immediately. I looked outside the window and saw multiple fire trucks in the streets below.

A fire alarm announcement implored everyone to use the stairs because no elevators were running. I grabbed the boombox and Grand Marnier, and the three of us went out into the hall. The only way out was down thirty flights of stairs, with me carrying the boombox and alcohol. Liza, who was used to people coming over to her when she is in public, was completely ignored by the maintenance help, who were all running down the stairs. It was an atmosphere of everyone for themselves as we all rushed to safety. When we finally got down the thirty flights into the lobby, we heard an all-clear announcement. It was a false alarm. When I tried to talk Liza into going back up, she smartly refused. We were all exhausted. It would be a year later when I finally persuaded her to come back to my office for treatment.

We have had many great times with Liza at our home in Westhampton. I keep a boat there, but I am a terrible boater. Liza's husband Mark had the nickname "Mark the Shark." For his birthday, I took them, our friend Waldo, and our young children on my boat. I made arrangements to go to a restaurant on the water for a dinner of freshly caught shark. We gave everyone sailor caps and brought along some wine for the short, forty-five-minute trip, and off we went.

I unfortunately have minimal boating skills. I soon found myself in very shallow water on the bay with the motor stuck in the sand. I had drifted from the deepwater path into a very shallow area. A smart boater would have simply stepped out of the boat into the shallow water, lifted the boat out of the sand, and pushed it into deeper water. I was used to driving a car and a little buzzed from a glass of wine, so I chose to get us out of this situation by gunning the motor. That immediately broke the motor, and we were then stranded.

We left in the late afternoon, planning on an early dinner, so we could return before dark. I could see boats going by us in the deeper water. We started yelling for help, but no one wanted to come into the shallow water and risk getting stuck. We were getting desperate. My passengers had already lost confidence in me and realized I obviously was not capable of handling this situation. Trying to get help, Liza stood up and started singing "Life Is a Cabaret," hoping a fan would recognize her and come to her rescue. It was starting to get dark, and we were hungry and shivering. This was before the advent of cell phones, and I had no emergency radio on the boat.

Finally, one boat headed toward us to help. They asked me to throw a line to them and informed our group that they would tow us to the nearest place onshore. They pulled my boat out of the shallow water to a dock on the bay outside a home. We tied up the boat, and our disheveled group got out and walked toward the random house. I wanted to explain that we had our boat tied to their dock and that we would have the boat service we use pick it up the next day. We also needed to use their phone to call a car service to take us home. We hoped to use the bathroom as well. I decided that our best bet for a friendly reception would be if Liza would ring the bell and be seen first and make the request. She was at the height of her fame, and we figured most people would recognize her and not treat us as trespassers.

The occupant answered the door and was very helpful, especially when he saw two shivering small children. He explained that he worked for the famous designer Arnold Scaasi, we arrived at the servants' quarters, and Arnold's huge home was next door. When we eventually got back to our home in Westhampton, the telephone was ringing. It was Arnold Scaasi. When he heard that Liza was part of the group docked at his home, he obtained our phone number from his staff. Arnold told me that he was having an elegant dinner party that evening, and we were all invited. Liza very politely told him that we had other plans. A fancy dinner party was the last thing on our minds.

One summer Liza decided that she would try to lose weight while staying at our home in Westhampton. She got out on the tennis court to play, wrapped completely in Saran Wrap like homemade mozzarella. Liza wanted to sweat away the pounds while she played. In a short time, we were unwrapping her because she started to feel faint from this foolish idea. She did look funny, and we all had some laughs when we showed her the pictures we had taken of her all wrapped up.

One weekend she and Mark had an argument while staying with us. Our home is on the bay, and in those days, there were fewer homes built in our area, and seaplanes could land in the bay. They would pick up and drop off people traveling between NYC and the Hamptons. We had driven into town with Mark to do some shopping. As we drove up to our home, we arrived just in time to see Liza stepping into a seaplane. She had called the company, packed her bag, climbed down the stairs leading onto the bay, and was being picked up in a dinghy to row her out to the plane, waiting in the bay in the back of our home. They made up the next week, but we still had Mark as our guest for the rest of that weekend. I was the big loser that weekend as Mark took out his aggressions on me, trouncing me in tennis.

We have a wonderful performing arts center in town. One weekend they booked Lorna Luft to perform. Liza came out for the weekend to stay with us and see her show. Susan Lucci, who has a home near us, also came to the performance. We all spent time together after the show. It was great fun having both sisters stay with us that weekend. They both have magnetic personalities, and it was a treat being with both of them in our home. There were many laughs and fascinating stories.

We also always enjoy being with Susan and her husband, Helmut. Susan consistently looks beautiful with perfect makeup and style. She is very sweet and lovely, a far cry from her soap opera character. Susan is best known for playing Erica Kane on the ABC daytime drama *All My Children* for its entire run from 1970 to 2011. She attracted a great deal of media attention for being nominated eighteen times for the Daytime Emmy Award for Outstanding Leading Actress and never winning until she finally did in 1999.

Susan is another person whom people occasionally say Arlene resembles. There was a very popular new restaurant in town that was hard to get into when it first opened. When Arlene and I went for the first time alone, we were immediately seated at the best table. They offered drinks on the house, and we remarked to ourselves how wonderfully they treat new customers. The owner came over and told us how happy he was to have Susan Lucci there, and we didn't immediately correct him. We did let him know on the way out that it was Arlene and not Susan that he had welcomed. (Notice I said "on the way out" as we weren't going to return the free drinks that were offered.) We were sure Susan would soon be a customer because she lived in town. The next time we saw Susan, we related that experience to her, explaining how flattered Arlene was by the mistaken identification.

Bob Fosse also lived in town, and Liza visited with him while she was with us. He was a major influence on her career. He directed Liza in *Cabaret*, *Chicago*, and the award-winning TV special *Liza with a Z*. We enjoyed spending time with Fosse but never socialized with him in Westhampton on our own.

Liza loved to have friends in the audience when she performed. It was comforting for her to see familiar faces. She strategically arranged seats where she could spot us from the stage. She liked the idea of singing to friends. One year Liza was performing in Miami, and my mother was living there. I bought an extra ticket to the show for her. When we arrived at the theater, I had my mother sit with Arlene in the seats Liza chose for us, and I took my mother's seat. After the overture, Liza walked out on the large stage to cheers. She looked around to catch our eye and called out to Arlene, "Where's Allan?" She didn't see me and was worried that something happened. The audience couldn't figure out why Liza called that out.

When Arlene responded, "He's here but in a different seat," Liza continued her show with the first song.

In 1981, Arlene's sister, Susan, was getting married in Florida. Their parents were making the wedding at their clubhouse. The night before the wedding we had a rehearsal dinner for the family. As we were leaving, Arlene's mother told us to get a good night's sleep so we would look our best for the wedding the following afternoon. There was one problem. Liza was appearing in Florida and asked us to meet her after her show. We waved goodbye to Arlene's folks, but instead of heading back to our hotel for a good night's sleep, we drove to meet Liza. She was in wonderful spirits, and before we knew it, the sun was coming up the next morning. We had been up all night, first hanging out with the band and then with just Liza.

Arlene told Liza that she did not know how she would be able to walk down the aisle as the matron of honor because she was so exhausted. Liza then instructed Arlene on how to walk because walking normally down the aisle would run the risk of staggering from being overtired. Liza advised Arlene to take one step, stop, and then take the next step. That way, she could slowly and steadily go down the aisle without swaying as she walked. Arlene then looked in the mirror as we were leaving and worried that she would show up at the wedding with telltale bloodshot eyes. Liza told her to say that it was so emotional for Arlene to see her sister getting married that she had been crying tears of happiness.

The next afternoon, we arrived at the wedding, and everyone told us how good we looked. We were still happy from the fun night we had, and our exhaustion didn't show. After the wedding, which was beautiful and where Arlene actually did shed some happy tears, we managed to drive home and collapse in bed. To this day, no one in our family had any idea about our night before the wedding, until now. (Sorry, Susan.)

That New Year's Eve, Liza performed at the Diplomat Hotel in Florida. We went to the show with our friend Rock Brynner and his father, Yul Brynner. Liza had been close friends for many years with the owners of the Diplomat, Irving and Marge Cowan. They loved hiring top stars to perform at their hotel, and we have spent several New Years watching Liza and Sammy Davis perform together.

The Cowans were unique people. The parties at their home were beyond description. They would invite every major star in town to their lavish parties. However, there were areas in their home with drug paraphernalia, as well as a dungeon room. A well-known male entertainer friend of ours told me about a party he attended at their home. He wandered into a room where a woman was sitting on a high stool in a dominatrix outfit. She had on high leather boots and a studded bustier bra and was holding a bullwhip. The room was lit in red, and people were embracing one another. When he opened the door and the dominatrix saw him, she motioned for him to come in. The woman told him, "Come in. We've been waiting for you."

He answered, "I'll be right back." He told me that he closed the door and took off running.

The Cowans were very socially prominent but strange. One night a few days after we had spent an evening there with Liza and various stars, including Olivia Newton-John, we saw Olivia shopping at a store in Florida. When we went over to remind her that we met her at the Cowans' residence, she remarked that it was the craziest party she had ever been to.

One night we went with Liza to see Melissa Manchester perform, and we were all invited after her show to a party at the Cowans' home. Melissa told us the next time we saw her that, after being up all night at the Cowans' home, it took her a week to recover. Melissa is one of the nicest people in the business, as well as a marvelous talent. She has written and performed classic songs such as "Through the Eyes of Love," "Don't Cry out Loud," "Midnight Blue," "Come in from the Rain," and "You Should Hear How She Talks about You." We recently spent time with her and Michael Feinstein after her show at his NYC club, Feinstein's/54 Below, and she was still terrific.

One year the Cowans wanted to try their hand at producing a Broadway show. They were friendly with Peggy Lee and developed a show around her called *Peg*. They invited Liza and us to the opening night. The show consisted of an empty stage with two couches. Peggy Lee starred as herself in this one-woman show. She would sit on one couch, talk a bit, and then sing a song. She would then get up, walk over to the other couch, sit down, talk a little more, and sing another song. Peggy had a long and successful recording career for many decades with songs like "Mañana," "Fever," and "Is That All There Is?" However, as a Broadway show, there was no drama and not much of a story. It was a dreadful evening, and the opening night party ended quickly after the reviews came out later that night. The show had only that one performance and closed the next day.

The Cowans were generous people and great hosts. They would arrange rooms at their hotel for us every New Year's Eve when Liza and Sammy performed. They were a lot of fun to be around, and we did have many great times with them. The Cowans flew to NYC for our son's bar mitzvah, but we gradually lost contact with them.

Liza has very good instincts and has given us wonderful advice over the years. When I was negotiating my business deal with Pfizer, she set up a meeting for me with Mickey Rudin. He had given her advice as her lawyer over the years but was famous for being the person representing Frank Sinatra. His other clients were Marilyn Monroe, Lucille Ball, and Elizabeth Taylor, among others. He was a colorful and feared lawyer and very intimidating to most people. He had a pug-nosed style that frightened people, especially when he joked about "breaking legs" if Sinatra didn't get his way. I expected to meet this hard, tough character who would tell me how to deal with the corporate world. Instead, I found a soft-spoken man. He confided in me explaining that his brashness and toughness were an act he put on to intimidate the mob people and casino bosses he had to deal with. He gave me some free advice, but I decided to let my lawyers handle my business dealings when he told me he was semiretired and not taking on new clients.

Liza always maintained a close relationship with her ex-husbands, except for David Gest. She was with her first husband, Peter Allen, at his deathbed when he passed away at only forty-eight years of age from AIDS. Peter was a lovely guy and a great talent. He had performed with his partner as an opening act for Judy Garland. Judy was very fond of Peter and thought he would be a good match for her young daughter, Liza. When early in their marriage Peter acknowledged that he was gay, they divorced but remained friends. We always loved being around Peter because he had a great personality. Aside from being a fantastic performer, he has written some of the best songs of our generation. "I Honestly Love You," "Don't Cry out Loud," "I Go to Rio," "Quiet Please, There's a Lady on Stage" (about his mother-in-law, Judy Garland), and "Arthur's Theme" with his great lyric "if you get caught between the moon and New York City."

Liza also remained in contact with Jack Haley Jr. until the day he died. We loved Jack and his family. When we first met Jack's dad, who was the Tin Man in *The Wizard of Oz* movie, he hugged us and said that he hoped Liza appreciated his son. In Jack's last year, his body couldn't tolerate his alcohol abuse. He invited me to join him in LA to see what his AA meetings were like. He stood up at the meeting and told everyone he was conquering his problem. Unfortunately, he was lying. The wonderful composer Paul Williams was Jack's sponsor. Paul was such a kind man and tried to help, but maybe he was too nice and could not get his message through to Jack.

In his last days, Jack's girlfriend had become his assistant. Somehow she managed to persuade Jack to change his will, giving her the house. When he died, Jack's sister, Gloria, called me to ask us to testify in their lawsuit. They felt that she swindled the family out of his home. We were not staying at his home in his last years due to his alcohol problems, so we were unable to help them.

Jack was a brilliant producer and director but not always wise in some business ventures. He put up the money for an actor friend named Nicky Blair to open a restaurant called Nicky Blair's on Sunset Boulevard. It became a very hot spot for years, but Jack never got his money back. We spent a lot of time with Nicky and liked him. Jack loved to frequent the restaurant and sit at the main table. We had fun times with him there, with regulars like Tony Curtis, Sylvester Stallone, and George Burns.

Clint Eastwood was a friend of Jack and had his post-Oscar party at the restaurant in 1991. He won the Oscar for both Best Picture and Best Director for his movie *Unforgiven*. Clint was one of the guy friends who would hang around Jack's house, and we got a kick out of spending time with them all.

Nicky was a captivating and colorful character. Tony Curtis and Nicky were best friends, who both wanted to be stars in Hollywood. They each loved the name Tony Curtis and made a pact that whoever landed the first movie role could use the name. When Bernard Schwartz got the first movie role, he became the one to use the name Tony Curtis. They remained friends, and Nicky made his mark as a popular restaurant host, along with some minor movie roles.

One year Liza invited us as her guests to join her on her European tour starting in Cannes. We met at her apartment with our luggage. She arranged for two large SUVs to drive us and her assistants to the airport. She was running behind due to an important phone call. An accident tied up traffic on the highway, and our driver searched for side roads to get to the airport. Our route ended up being slower, and Liza and her assistants arrived there before us and just made the plane. We arrived about twenty minutes later and met the woman travel agent handling the tour. We were late, and the final boarding notice was announced for the Air France flight. We rushed to the gate just as it was closing, but they would not let us board. Our travel agent pleaded with them to no avail. There were no tickets for other flights, and it was the only flight to Nice that night.

We called Liza's assistant on the plane, and he told us that he was desperately trying to find other flights before they took off. We also were racing around the airport, trying to find flights to Paris. Finally, he was able to book us on a flight to Paris, where we would then be able to change planes and fly to Nice. Liza absorbed the cost for all these flights because she felt bad that she caused us to leave her apartment late. Her assistant told us that he would also arrange a car to pick us up in Nice to drive us to our hotel in Cannes. It was a tense long night, but finally, we made it to Cannes. Arlene and I have never forgotten that experience and, since then, always arrive at the airport extra early.

There was another time when we almost missed our flight back home. We were staying with Liza and Mark at her home in Lake Tahoe. Our alarm did not go off, and we overslept. We frantically rushed to pack up and ran to our car with the luggage. We had a late night, and Liza was still sleeping, so we slammed the door behind us. In my haste, I left my car key in our room. The door was locked, and Liza was sound asleep. It was in the days before cell phones, and we started to panic. I walked around the house, found a window that wasn't locked, and crawled into the house. I retrieved my keys; we raced off to the airport and just made the flight.

One of our most memorable concert events was Liza's opening night of a ten-night run at Carnegie Hall in 1979. The audience went wild after every number. After a few curtain calls with the audience standing and screaming for more, she finally left the stage. We went backstage with Halston while she changed and showered. While we waited outside her dressing room, we heard thunderous roars coming from the theater. The audience was still on their feet and would not leave. We told Halston what was going on. He proceeded to go into her dressing room and instructed her to put on a bathrobe as he wrapped a towel around her wet head. He brought her back onstage for her to say goodbye to the fans, who all were still on their feet cheering.

The next night, Steve Rubell organized an elegant formal dinner party at Studio 54 at eight o'clock, before they opened to the public at eleven that night. We arrived to see Studio 54 transformed into a beautiful dining room with flowers and elegant table settings. Every prominent person in the city was there, and when Liza walked in with Halston, everyone cheered. There was no set seating. William B. Williams, who was the number one radio personality of the time and the person who gave Frank Sinatra the title of the Chairman of the Board, was there with his wife, Dotty. He was a friend of ours and asked us if we wanted to join him at his table. Just as he was asking, Liza's assistant came over and explained that Liza would like for us to be at her table. Willie B. remarked that, of course, we should sit with her, and we were seated opposite Liza and next to her father, the famous movie director Vincente Minnelli. We had spent time with Vincente in the past, and we liked him. It was a fabulous evening as every well-known person came over to our table to offer their praise to Liza. After the dessert was served and the tables were cleared, the club was converted back into a disco for the public.

A recent memorable event with Liza happened in April 2018. Italian fashion designers Dolce and Gabbana flew in a mixture of celebrities and clients from all over the world to celebrate the opening of their Manhattan store. There was a three-day series of over-the-top events. The first night was at the New York Public Library, hosted by Sarah Jessica Parker, to show off their high-end jewelry. The next evening was a formal dinner party and fashion show on the stage of the Metropolitan Opera House, with fireworks over the Lincoln Center fountain. On the last night, there was a dinner and fashion show at the Rainbow Room, followed by Liza Minnelli performing.

They hired a private plane to fly Liza back and forth from LA to NYC. She wanted to stay with us rather than at a hotel. She was to be the only person on the plane, along with two assistants. She asked us if we could come to LA a few days before she was to leave, stay with her in LA, and then fly with her to NY. We did and made it a week's vacation in LA and then traveled with her on the flight. We are not good plane fliers and don't like small planes. When we saw the top-of-the-line huge private plane they arranged for us, we felt a lot better. It was the largest private plane we had ever seen, and we enjoyed a comfortable fast trip.

Besides sending the plane, they had paid her an astounding amount of money to show up and sing six songs. They hired a full band and Michael Feinstein to accompany her. She stayed with us four days before the event. Dolce and Gabbana flew in their designers from Italy and LA to come to our apartment. During all the activities over those three days, Dolce and Gabbana were a pleasure to be around, and we enjoyed our time with them. They also sent people to help Liza select outfits and a seamstress to fit the clothes. They brought all their new outfits—each one with shoes, hats, and bags of every color—for her to choose from for her appearance. Our apartment was filled with racks of clothing and accessories. In the end, Liza decided that she would be most comfortable singing in her own black top and pants. After all the many designer outfits were eliminated, Liza agreed to put on a top and some accessories from Dolce and Gabbana to show off their brand. She went on at midnight, and it was a spectacular evening. The limo that picked us up for the event also took her suitcases, and after the performance, she went directly to the airport and back home to LA.

One year later, she received another offer she could not refuse. She was paid an obscene amount of money to come to NYC for the March 2019 opening of the Neiman Marcus store in NYC. It was a six-story department store in a beautiful brand-new mall in a section of NYC called Hudson Yards. It is a completely new area developed on the west side of the city with giant skyscraper apartments, stores, and restaurants. That night was also the grand opening of Hudson Yards, and thousands of celebrities and dignitaries were invited. Whoopi Goldberg, Katie Holmes, and many others came to see the new store, and there were drinks and food served on every level. Liza was sitting with the band behind a round screen on a revolving stage. She was the surprise guest, and when the stage spun around, the spotlight showed Liza sitting on a stool. When she sang "New York, New York," the crowd went wild. She followed that with a few words welcoming everyone, the stage revolved back, and her participation was over.

Liza was supposed to stay for six days. She was so happy being back with us in NYC that she decided that she did not want to leave. However, she had to get back to LA, and they had a plane waiting for her. Our granddaughter Sydney had been accepted into the LaGuardia High School of Performing Arts and was living with us in our apartment. Liza has overcome all her addictions except smoking. We had Sydney move out and stay with her father during the week that Liza stayed with us because Sydney hates being around the smell of smoke. I was worried that we might not be able to eliminate the smell of smoke before Sydney moved back in. I saw an ad for an ozone machine used in hotels to eliminate smoke odors and ordered it. When Liza left, I turned on the machine and prayed that it would work. It was terrific, and Sydney was able to move back in.

Liza bought me a beautiful bathrobe and Arlene a cashmere sweater as gifts for taking care of her those six days. She left a note in the guest room that said, "You both will never know how much your love, friendship, and hospitality mean to me. To have such an endless source of support, cheerleading, and tuna salad—it's worth more than you might know. I count you guys among the biggest blessings in my life."

Liza is always very considerate. We were with her in San Francisco for a concert she was doing there, and with all the stress and preparation, she still had time to surprise me with a cake backstage for my birthday. Before the show, Arlene and I stopped to have a bite to eat in a restaurant a few blocks from where Liza was performing. Arlene got up to go to the ladies' room and found herself followed in by an excited fan of Liza. Because of Arlene's resemblance to Liza, the fan thought that she was her. When the excited fan saw that Arlene was not Liza, she remarked to Arlene that it would be as close as she would ever get to Liza. She asked Arlene to take a picture with her. When we walked out of the restaurant heading to the theater, the girl and two of her friends ran after us. They asked me if I would take a picture of them with Arlene. Somehow they felt a picture with Arlene would be a good memento of their evening.

Liza always has a naturally great radar for the press. Sometimes I would pick them both up after dance class with Luigi, and we would walk home through Central Park. One day while we were walking, Liza said to us that she had a feeling she was being filmed. We figured that she was just paranoid about photographers trying to get pictures of her when she was not made up. Sure enough, we spotted a photographer up on a hill with a telephoto lens. A week later, we were watching *E! True Hollywood Story* on TV, and there was a picture of all of us walking that day in the park.

When Arlene's parents were in their later years and living in Florida, we would spend a lot of time there in the winter. Any time Liza was booked in Florida, we would try to travel with her and her band to her performances in multiple cities. One year we were staying for a few days at an exclusive private club that a friend was able to book for us. It was the Jockey Club, a very exclusive and popular place. After Liza's performance at a nearby venue, we invited her, her assistant, and backup singers to join us there for dinner after their show. Our good friend Obba Babatundé was one of her two backup dancers. He and Liza were great friends as well, and they all arrived to meet us. The door person started to give Obba, who is black, a hard time at the entrance. Obba did not have a jacket, and men had to wear jackets to enter. Liza, sensing some possible discrimination, demanded that a jacket be found for Obba. A waiter said that he had an extra jacket and brought it for Obba to wear. He was four sizes bigger than Obba, and the sleeves were hanging down, but Obba was able to wear it and enter.

Liza had a very strict assistant named Diana at that time. She acted like a dominating mother and always tried to tell Liza what to do. It was a warm night, and Liza had worked hard and was sweating a bit.

Our room had a door that opened up into a private pool area. When Liza saw the inviting pool, she asked Arlene if she had a bathing suit that she could borrow. Diana sternly told Liza that she would not allow her to go in the water because Liza might be chilled coming out and could not afford to catch a cold. That was all Liza had to hear. Like a rebellious teenager, she put on Arlene's bathing suit and dived into the pool. When Liza finished swimming, she got out of the water and defiantly came back into our room and changed while Diana sulked.

Another time, Liza and her band played in venues up and down Florida's west coast. We traveled with them and had a great time. There were clubs with country music, and we learned line dancing. We knew all the band members well and joined all of them with Liza for meals after the shows. One night we went to a large BBQ joint, and the guys in the band ordered the specialty of the house, alligator ribs. They looked great, smothered in tangy BBQ sauce. I joined in the feast, but although they looked great, they did not taste like any ribs I had ever eaten. It would be my one and only attempt at gator ribs.

Liza was very close to her drummer and bandleader, Bill LaVorgna, whose nickname was Blaze. He was the drummer for her mother, Judy Garland. Liza affectionately called him Pappy. When Liza played in Atlantic City, the casino had her stay in a charming home on the water located near the hotel. Liza had Blaze stay in one of the guest rooms, and Arlene and I would sleep in the other room. Blaze was a great cook, and after the shows, we would come back to the home, and he would make fantastic Italian dinners for Liza and us. During the day, he would give me lessons on how to cook Italian-style, and I learned how to prepare some great dishes. Unfortunately, Arlene and I eat out most nights, so my desire to cook at home faded in time.

The day that Bill LaVorgna died from a heart attack, Liza was distraught. The next morning, our close common friend Tony Danza was having his opening live talk show on ABC television. ABC had given him a prime spot on their network to do a live show, and this was to be his first day. Tony was excited about this opportunity, and he wanted to start off with a great guest for his premier show. Liza was happy to do it and asked us to come to her apartment in the morning so we could all go together. Tony was glad that we were going to be with her, knowing that Liza is much more comfortable having friends with her at those appearances. We arrived at her apartment to find her in bed, crying and distraught. She had just received the news of Bill's passing late the night before. She exclaimed that there was no way that she could do a live show. She hadn't slept all night and was exhausted and depressed.

We went into panic mode. We had to find a way to get her to the show because she was advertised heavily as his opening day guest. There was a possibility that Tony would have to go on live without her and find a way to fill in the time. Arlene made coffee to help her wake up, and we tried to explain how important this was to Tony. After thirty minutes of pleading, we managed to persuade her to get dressed. Somehow we got her to the show in time to go on. We had no idea if she would even be able to talk, much less sing. However, once her name was announced and the spotlight went on, she bounced out and was terrific. She summoned up all of her acting skills to get through the appearance without portraying the sorrow that she was going through. Tony later thanked us for accompanying her to the broadcast, but we have never told him what we really went through to get her there.

When Liza, years ago, decided to buy a co-op in NYC, she was concerned about the policy of many co-op boards not allowing entertainers to live in their building. So Liza, instead of picking the many well-known people she knew as references, chose me because I was a dentist. I was someone not associated with those "showbiz types," and she was approved by the board.

We have known most of the important people in Liza's life. When we first traveled on the road with her, Eliot Weisman was her road manager. He eventually became her manager. In 1979, Eliot was the president of the Westchester Premier Theater, and he went to jail for racketeering. There was speculation about Eliot taking the fall for the real gangsters after Eliot was released from jail and suddenly became the manager for Liza, Don Rickles, Steve and Eydie, and Frank Sinatra. Eliot had a rough edge to him, but Arlene and I liked him a lot. He had a major toy train collection and built a small home for it next to his house in Florida. We, along with our children, loved to watch him sit at the controls and run the trains. It is one of the most outstanding train collections in the world and has been featured in magazines.

Eliot's wife, Maria, was a great friend of ours and Liza's. Liza loved stone crabs, and on Liza's day off, Maria rented a boat and stocked it with stone crabs and other delicacies. We had a feast because Maria was a terrific hostess. Whenever there was a break on the Florida tour, we would all go to Joe's Stone Crab Restaurant in Miami. Liza would devour them with such gusto that her hands would be bleeding from the shells.

When Eliot realized his hours managing Sinatra prevented him from giving Liza enough of his time, his assistant, Gary Labriola, took over as her manager. We spent a lot of time with Gary; his wife, Jean; and his friends. We noticed Gary living above his means and were concerned that Liza might be getting cheated financially. A few years after Liza stopped working with him, Gary unfortunately hung himself in his home; the rumor was that he had gotten himself into financial trouble and couldn't handle his situation.

Our friend Jason Strauss is co-owner of the Tao Group. They have many fabulous restaurants and clubs throughout the world, including NYC and Las Vegas. One day he invited us to be his guest at Tao in NYC. Gina Lollobrigida was staying with us, and we took her and Liza to Tao. It was a mob scene, but they both enjoyed it, and we were glad that they were becoming closer friends. As a wedding gift, Gina made two small sculptures of Liza in a pose from *Cabaret*.

One year Jason invited Arlene and me to Tao in Las Vegas and made arrangements for us to have VIP treatment. When we arrived at the VIP rope, they had our names, but Arlene had no ID. Even though we were grandparents, the doorman would not let Arlene in without proof of her age. I found this very amusing and started to take pictures of Arlene being turned away for possibly being underage. Jason finally arrived to get us in, but it was a thrill for Arlene to say that she was refused admission for not being over twenty-one. One other time in Nashville, Arlene was not allowed into a club because she didn't have her proof of age. Even though we had to leave, she left with a happy smile on her face.

In 1991, Saddam Hussein started firing scud missiles into Israel, and we were watching it on TV. I had tickets that night to take Liza to a Broadway show and was looking forward to the diversion of going out to a musical. The show was *Shogun*, a musical about Japan, starring Richard Chamberlain. I was relieved to get away from the explosions I saw on TV of the missiles flying into Israel. However, in this musical, each character would come onstage, sing their song, and then commit hara-kiri. Actors were dying all over the stage as one character after another committed suicide. At intermission, I decided that this was not the way to relax for the night, and we left the show.

We went over to a club nearby that was managed by Chita Rivera's sister. We ordered drinks and food. While we were sitting there, I heard piano music coming from the bar area. Liza commented on how good it was, and the three of us went around the bend to see who was playing. It was a very young-looking guy who introduced himself to us as Billy Stritch. Liza told him that she wanted him to be in her life because she thought he was a terrific pianist. She took down his contact information, and for the next few decades, Billy was her pianist and arranger. Since that time, he has performed all over the world and arranged and accompanied many of the top entertainers of our time. We have traveled on the road with Billy many times while he worked with Liza, and we have remained good friends over these many years. Billy is also a terrific singer, and we love seeing him entertain.

CHAPTER

FORTY

Lindsay Wagner

Lindsay Wagner has been a part of our extended family ever since we met her many years ago while she was dating Jack Haley Jr. She is our most spiritual friend, and we consider her our family guru. Lindsay starred as the Bionic Woman in the very popular TV show of the late 1970s. We bonded with her immediately. When the series ended, she starred in many miniseries on TV.

Lindsay lived in LA, but she had a wonderful large log cabin in Sandy, Oregon. She invited us to come up for a week in 1980. Jack also joined us there later in the week. Lindsay was very well known from *The Bionic Woman* series, but we had never seen it. She is a very spiritual and down-to-earth person. She rarely talked about show business, so it was easy for us to fake the fact that we had never seen her show. We flew into Portland, and she picked us up in her car to drive us to her cabin. When we arrived in the small town of Sandy, she stopped for gas. When she got out to pump gas, we noticed the local people calling out to her and yelling, "Hi, Jaime!" After a few people did this, I asked her if her real name was Jaime and if Lindsay was her stage name.

She looked at me, smiled, and said, "Guess you have never seen my show."

I was busted. I confessed to her that we hadn't, and I stammered and said, "We heard it was terrific." (It was one of my really clever remarks. Fortunately, she didn't throw us out of the car as she must have realized that Arlene looked a lot smarter than me.)

When we arrived at her cabin, which was far more luxurious than any cabin I could imagine, she remarked that she had tapes of her shows. If we were interested in seeing her work, she would be happy to play them for us.

Lindsay is very much against TV violence, and she had a good deal of input into the content of her shows. In 1984, she starred in a TV police drama series *Jessie*. Our friend Tony Lo Bianco was also in it. It did not last long because Lindsay refused to have scenes containing violence in the show, and the public wanted to see more action and gunplay. Ironically, in real life, Lindsay married a stuntman, and both of her sons became stuntmen as well.

For the next few days, we did not turn on regular TV. We watched several of the *Bionic Woman* shows and also went on nature walks. Lindsay wanted us to experience the beautiful outdoor surroundings. The cabin was near Mount Saint Helens, and one day we walked to the base of the mountain. After a few days, I called my mother to check in. She was hysterical on the phone (and not in a funny way). She was very concerned because she knew that we were staying near Mount Saint Helens and told us that it had erupted two days ago and was on every news channel. It was the most disastrous volcanic eruption in US history. The eruption was so large that the debris traveled all the way to the East Coast. I told my mother that we were fine and had no idea what had occurred. When we turned on the TV, we observed pictures of President Carter touring the area and films of the eruption. For some reason, because of the way the winds were blowing, we were never aware of what happened, even though we had walked to the base of the mountain.

The following day, Jack Haley joined us at the cabin. Lindsay wanted us to experience the wonderful feeling of nature and suggested we try some psychedelic mushrooms to enhance our experience. I had never tried that type of mushroom. However, I figured that was the environment to try it. Arlene, who never likes to feel off balance, said that she would pass. Jack took some along with Lindsay and myself, and he went outside to do a large puzzle that he had with him. It was one thousand puzzle pieces of the map of the Los Angeles freeways.

After trying some mushrooms, Lindsay informed me that now I would really feel the wonder of nature. However, I started to feel very strange and felt my legs going numb. Lindsay told me to just enjoy the beauty of nature around me. I replied, "I just want to be able to walk again." I was in full panic mode, and Lindsay stayed with me until the feeling finally passed in a few hours. I never made it outside to explore nature but just sat on the couch, waiting for this awful condition to pass. Needless to say, that was my last experience with mushrooms.

The next day when I woke up, I walked outside. I saw Jack sitting where I left him the previous day, with the puzzle partly done in front of him. I told him about my experience after trying the mushrooms, and he remarked that it had no effect on him. However, I pointed out to him that he was still sitting in the same place with the half-done puzzle for the past twenty-four hours.

Lindsay has always been very spiritual and believes in a holistic approach to health. Even though many of the concepts seem quite far out to us, we have always found them interesting. One year she told us that she was going on a trip to India with her spiritual adviser. She was a doctor named Gladys who was the mother of holistic medicine. For her eightieth birthday, Gladys was taking a group of her disciples to India, where she was born. Her parents were medical missionaries treating lepers in India. Her mother went into labor and gave birth to her on the steps of the Taj Mahal. She was now going to take her followers to India and revisit places that were significant to her. One couple backed out at the last minute, and on impulse, Arlene and I joined the group.

We were quite concerned with sanitary conditions in India and packed canned goods in our suitcases. We were going to be very careful about food outside fine hotels. This group of very holistic people had no concern about that. They would eat any kind of food, regardless of where it was being served. They even ate food served on dirty dishes on broken-down trains. They would eat food from outdoor street vendors, while we would go inside and open a can of tuna fish. They all teased us, thinking we didn't like Indian food. After a few days, they started getting sick one by one.

The second week was partially spent in a fine hotel with upscale restaurants. Arlene and I were able to enjoy wonderful Indian meals. Most of the group were confined to their rooms with upset stomachs. The entire group did not believe in traditional medicine but only holistic medicine. When one of the people started running a fever of 103 degrees, we saw the woman, who was the mother of holistic medicine and a doctor, take out some aspirin. Finally, we thought she was going to use traditional medicine to bring down the fever. However, she took the aspirin and a bandage and taped the aspirin to the center of the person's belly button. She explained that the fever would be alleviated from the vibrations of the aspirin lying on the chakra line. We realized that these people were living in an alternative universe to ours. They all believed strongly in reincarnation, and we were the only two people who did not feel the same way.

Every day one member of our group led us in a discussion of dream interpretation. We took turns describing our dreams to the group for analysis. Lindsay brought her two teenage sons on the trip. There were a few young girls in the group as well. Lindsay's son mentioned to the group that he had a dream where he was in a room with two of the young girls. The group leader explained that, obviously, they were friends in a past life. I raised my hand and said that my interpretation was that he was a young teenager with raging hormones and that he simply had a dream about the attractive young women. This did not go over too well with the group. We did get along well with everyone on the trip, although they thought we were crazy, and we knew that they were all a little nuts.

On the first night of the trip, we all gathered in a room at our hotel to hear a talk from the man who would be our guide for the trip's outings. He explained that he was, at one time, the head of the mountain climbing team from India. He told us that he had medals given to him for leading the first team to ever climb the Himalayas. He spoke about how he led the team in three attempts to climb to the top, and on each excursion, he lost various fingers and toes due to frostbite. He explained that his son died on the second attempt, but none of that stopped him until he finally succeeded. He proceeded to describe each attempt to climb the mountain and the parts of his body that were amputated after each try, as well as the numbers of brave followers who died under his guidance. He showed us the medals that the Indian government gave him to honor the people who died under his leadership. He then told us that part of our trip would include white water rafting, and it may be a challenge for some, but he would get us through it.

When Arlene raised her hand to say that she was afraid of white water rafting, he told her not to worry because he would make sure that she was with him on his raft. That was just what Arlene did not want to hear as he just got through saying how people whom he led had died. Arlene got semihysterical at the thought of being in a raft with this maniac. She ran out of the room and told the assistant on the trip that she would be taking the bus when the group goes rafting.

When they served us some strange-looking food on one of our train trips, Arlene and I opened a can of tuna fish. Lindsay and her sons waved two fingers over the food and declared that the vibrations were good so they could eat it. Two days later, when we went to visit the Taj Mahal, the three of them were too ill to make the excursion. They traveled all the way to India but never got to see the Taj Mahal.

One day our leader took us all on a bus to the school that her parents had founded for children of lepers. We decided to not join the group for lunch in the school and ate our cans of tuna fish on the bus. We sat on the bus and watched the children come out with plates, take dirt from the ground to rub on the plates to clean them, and then bring them back into the school as serving dishes for lunch.

One time we had no choice but to take a short raft trip across the water to reach the tent in which we were going to sleep that night. It was located on the Ganges River, under the Himalayas. We had a small oil lamp as our only light for a few hours at night. In the morning, we had our own yoga instructor, who looked like he came right out of central casting. He had the robes and the beard and led our group in yoga exercises by the Ganges River. (Imagine Arlene with no makeup and me totally exhausted from not sleeping too well in my tent trying to do yoga for the first time at six o'clock in the Himalayas.)

Part of the time, we did stay in some very elegant hotels because Gladys had many connections in India, and we were able to see both sides of India. We traveled to Varanasi to see the place where people came to die. We went out on small boats at night and witnessed the burning of the dead bodies on the river Ganges. In sharp contrast to this, one day we rode on camels into a fabulous resort in northern India. It was like a scene out of the movies, with our large party making this dramatic entrance into the hotel grounds.

Arlene and I separated from the group one afternoon when we arrived in the city of Jaipur because we wanted to visit a well-known jewelry store. They displayed magnificent Indian jewelry, and when they told me the price of pieces I was interested in, I bargained it down to a fraction of what was asked. In New York City, the jewelry would sell for ten times what they had asked me originally, and I was amazed that they said yes to my offer. I thought they had made a mistake and said to Arlene, "Let's pay for this and leave before they realize what they had done."

Much to my surprise, the owner came over to us and told us that he was so happy to see us shopping at his jewelry store that he would like to invite us to his niece's wedding the next day. When I explained that we were with a group and had no transportation, he volunteered to pick us up in his car and take us to the wedding with him. I remarked to Arlene that I probably didn't bargain as well as I thought because he seemed to want to encourage us to be future customers. The next day, he picked us up in his car, drove us to the wedding, and sat us as the guests of honor at this magnificent Indian wedding. The bride and groom came in on horseback, and it was a full day and night of elaborate and fascinating celebrations. (I must have really overpaid for the jewelry to be treated like royalty that day.)

CHAPTER

FORTY-ONE

Neil Sedaka

Neil Sedaka has been my closest friend whom I have known for the longest amount of time. He lived in my neighborhood, and I knew him before he wrote his chart-topping hits like "Breaking up Is Hard to Do," "Calendar Girl," "Happy Birthday Sweet Sixteen," "Oh! Carol," "Stupid Cupid," "Should've Never Let You Go," "The Diary," "The Hungry Years," and "Where the Boys Are." When he moved to England in the late 1960s, we lost contact. His career had stalled during the time of the British music invasion, led by the Beatles.

In 1973, Elton John, who was a fan of Neil, had formed his own record company. Elton produced an album of new songs by Neil called *Sedaka's Back*. It included "Laughter in the Rain," "Solitaire," and "Love Will Keep Us Together." It was a tremendous hit, and Neil was a star again. He moved back to the United States with his wife, Leba.

One day I received a call from him at my dental office. He had an abscess on a front tooth and asked if I could help him. I was able to take care of his dental problem, and we renewed a friendship that has now lasted for many decades. When our children were younger, we gathered all the generations together often. My family and I would go out with Neil and Leba and their daughter, Dara, who is also a fabulous singer, and my mother and Leba's mother. Our two mothers also became very close friends. (Leba's mother, Esther, owned a resort called Esther Manor outside Monticello, New York. One year a nineteen-year-old Neil Sedaka was hired to play there with his band. Sixteen-year-old Leba was working behind the desk at the resort, and it was love at first sight.)

One of our favorite Manhattan restaurants was a Chinese restaurant with the best spareribs, named King Dragon, and our families would go there together on many Sunday nights, and we have spent some holidays with them. (You know people have become family once you share Sunday night Chinese dinners with them.) We would see their son, Marc, who is a talented screenwriter, and his wife, Samantha, when they would visit NYC, or we would visit them in LA. We, of course, would not miss their wedding and flew out to California for the beautiful affair and for their tenth wedding anniversary at the Madonna Inn in San Luis Obispo, California.

Arlene and I have traveled all over the world with Neil and his wife, Leba. We went together to Europe for many years together on a beautiful small luxury ship called the *Sea Goddess*. There was no entertainment on the boat, but they did have a piano. Neil would play and sing at cocktail time most nights because he loves to sit down at the piano. We would meet at the departure port in Europe and spend some time together at hotels before and after each cruise. We enjoyed getting dressed up on this elegant cruise with an international and well-traveled group of people, and it was a special time for us. All the passengers gathered the night before the cruise at a beautiful venue in Europe to have cocktails and socialize.

The last time we took this cruise, we all met at the beautiful Sporting Club in Monte Carlo. That time, it was not the usual international group of travelers. A tire manufacturer decided to reward the top tire dealership salespeople in the Midwest with a cruise as their yearly bonus. Two-thirds of our passengers were the recipients of this bonus. We were dressed in our suits and ties, watching this group in their jeans tell one another how different Monte Carlo was from their small hometowns while downing their beers. We love to relax and have a casual good time as much as the next person; however, this cruise was always a special, elegant week for us. Evenings on the cruise consisted of lectures on how to improve tire sales and quality in the Midwest. We spent a lot of money on a cruise that taught us how to pick out a good tire. That was our last time on that cruise line.

We do have many wonderful memories of those trips. One summer we toured the Greek islands and stopped off at the fascinating island of Santorini. We took a cable car to the top of the mountain to see the main streets and shops. A highlight of visiting Santorini is to go down the steep, winding roads on a donkey to get back to the ship. When they helped Arlene onto the back of her donkey, it suddenly started to bolt and head down the mountain, with Arlene screaming. Neil rushed to the rescue, ran down the road, and stopped the donkey. He became Arlene's hero and savior for the day.

Arlene is a light sleeper and does not always sleep well on cruises. One year on the *Sea Goddess* cruise, our room was situated near the engines. Arlene was unable to sleep, and by the second night, she took her pillow and tried to sleep in the ship's main lounge because it was at the center of the ship and away from the engines. She was too exhausted to care what people thought about a passenger sleeping in the lounge when they passed by her on the way to breakfast. When that didn't help, she decided that the next night she would sleep in the infirmary because the ship was fully occupied, and there were no other cabins available. Her nerves were starting to get frayed from lack of sleep, and she was getting desperate for a few hours of rest.

Neil and I were in the pool when we saw a crowd gathering by the side of the ship while we were docked at a port. When we asked a crew member what was going on, he told us that a passenger had died, and they were removing her body. As unfortunate as this was, I realized this meant that there was an empty cabin for the remainder of the trip. I'm embarrassed to admit that I uttered the word "great" under my breath, rushed to the customer service office on the ship, and changed cabins, and Arlene's sleep problem was solved.

On that cruise, we noticed another ship following along on the same route as ours, and it turned out to be a private yacht hired by Ivana Trump. Ivana was a friend of Neil and Leba, and we all met up at the next port. (We had met Ivana through common friends after her divorce from Donald and had spent some time with her over the years. She had invited us to her beautiful townhouse in the East 60s and was a very pleasant hostess. The only problem we found when being with her was that most of the conversation had to be focused on her. She has a strong personality, and we realized how difficult it must have been for her and Donald to be married, with each having such large egos. One time when Gina Lollobrigida was staying with us in New York, Arlene arranged a lunch for Gina and her with Ivana. Gina afterward told Arlene that it was quite difficult to have a conversation with someone who just keeps talking about themselves nonstop, and that was their last time together. Arlene and I saw Ivana recently at a cocktail party where she was promoting a cookbook that she had written about her healthy home-cooked recipes. After watching her for five minutes trying to lecture about healthy cooking at home, we had a good laugh and left.)

Usually, after our European cruise with Neil and Leba, we would arrange to stay at a hotel near the last port to extend our vacation together. One year we all checked in to the elegant Grand-Hotel du Cap-Ferrat in the south of France. They did not accept credit cards, only cash, so we brought a lot of cash with us for the three-day stay at the hotel. We did not realize how expensive it was. When Neil asked if he could have some ice in his room, he was charged $20 for the ice. We had to go to a bank in town to get more cash before checking out because we simply ran out of cash to pay the extravagant bill at the hotel.

I rented a car to drive us around the south of France. Each time we parked the car, Neil made up a tune and lyrics with the street location so that we could remember where we had parked. Every day we had an original new Neil Sedaka song to guide us to our parking spot.

Sometimes on our vacations, we were lucky to be able to see other friends of ours who were in the same location. We also loved introducing our friends to each other. Years before, we had met Nabila Khashoggi through Liza Minnelli. At the time, Nabila's father, Adnan Khashoggi, was the richest man in the world. Nabila is a beautiful and smart woman, and we have had wonderful times with her. One year she invited us to a party at her father's apartment in Manhattan, and it was one of the most spectacular residences we have ever seen.

Nabila had a home in the south of France and invited us to spend the day with her while we were there. Neil and Leba joined us for the day, along with two other friends of ours who were in the area at the time, Hal and Eunice David. Hal David and his writing partner, Burt Bacharach, are one of the best songwriting teams of all time, so Hal had a lot in common with Neil. Hal and his wife, Eunice, were good friends of ours for many years, and we were glad that they happened to be in the south of France and able to join us for the day to enjoy Nabila's hospitality.

One year we even joined Neil and Leba on a Malt Shop cruise. This was an annual cruise where fans of early rock and roll music could spend a week on a boat with stars from the '50s and '60s. Those performers were still terrific, and every day was filled with live entertainment. The terrific singer Dion, famous for songs such as "The Wanderer" and "Teenager in Love," was on one of our cruises. He had the cabana adjacent to ours, so we had the pleasure of spending time with him. He had many stories about his life and philosophies. He has enjoyed much success and is a member of the Rock and Roll Hall of Fame.

When Dion was twenty years old, he was on "The Winter Dance Party" tour with Buddy Holly, Ritchie Valens, and the Big Bopper. The group chartered a flight to one venue and offered Dion one of the few seats. The cost to him would be $36, and rather than spend the money, he chose to stay on the bus. The plane crashed, killing all on board. Dion's decision not to take the seat saved his life and allowed the world to benefit from his future music. He has experienced both heroin addiction and powerful religious experiences, and we found him to be very interesting to talk to.

We also had a chance to spend time with some of our favorite performers of the past. Darlene Love was quite enjoyable to talk to, and she invited us to see her when she next came to NYC. Darlene had recorded with Jon Fiore, who along with his wife, Moira, was on the cruise with us. Jon is a talented singer, and Darlene was very happy to see him. She played at B. B. King's club in NY six months later, and we visited Darlene backstage after her terrific show.

Brenda Lee was on one of our Malt Shop cruises as well. We had seen her perform a few years earlier as the opening act for Neil Sedaka when he played an arena in Coney Island. During the cruise, Brenda was extremely gracious, extending an open invitation to visit with her at her home in Nashville when she joined us for lunch.

The passengers on the ship were all devoted fans of the music of the '50s, and they waited in lines each night to meet the old-time stars. They dressed up in clothing from that time, and there was even a dance night where a king and queen of the prom were crowned. The passengers would attempt to outdo one another in their outfits, and many completely reverted to their youth during the voyage. There was also a group of Elvis impersonators on the ship who performed Elvis-themed evenings in a showroom each night.

When Neil was one of the headliners one year, we joined him on the cruise and had a ball. Neil is great company on a cruise, but he is not a fan of touring some of the ancient ruins when we dock. He calls it visiting "rocks and rubble," which makes us laugh.

Arlene and I have had many fun times together with the Sedakas. We love to listen to talented singers, but neither of us can sing in tune. One night in New York City, Neil was hired to perform at a charity event. A friend of ours was the chairwoman of the event, and many of our common friends were in attendance. During Neil's performance, he told the audience that he had a special group of backup singers joining him on the stage when he did his next song, "Calendar Girl." The chairwoman of the event, Dennis Basso (a gravelly-voiced furrier from New York), Arlene, and I were the group. We, of course, were terrible, but it was fun, and we raised a lot of money for the charity.

The one other time we participated as backup singers for Neil was on a vacation with him in New Mexico. Neil and Leba were friends with the ex-football-player and broadcaster Don Meredith, who lived in New Mexico at that time. We met Don and his wife at a local restaurant and bar. After a few drinks, Neil got up to sing, and Arlene and I were the off-key backup singers once again.

We have always enjoyed having friends stay with us at our home in Westhampton. Arlene loves to feed people, and she tries to make sure our guests are well taken care of. It gives her pleasure to provide our friends with their favorite meals, drinks, and treats. She takes note of what each person enjoys eating and what they dislike, keeping in mind dietary restrictions and allergies.

One weekend the Sedakas were staying with us, and their visit coincided with the time that Michael Feinstein and his husband, Terrence Flannery, were also staying with us. It is always a delight to sit around the piano while Neil plays and sings, but we also had a terrific concert in our den when Neil and Michael took turns playing and singing. It was difficult for Arlene to figure out what to serve our guests because Neil and Leba enjoy typical American and Italian food, while Terrence and Michael are vegans. Arlene was triumphant in finding and selecting the perfect assortment of appealing food, so our dining room table was divided into sections over the weekend with plenty of variety for all our guests. We did not mind if they didn't share a chicken parmesan platter or vegan soy cheese and lentil casserole as long as they shared the bond of friendship. (I, of course, ate everything.)

Neil and Leba Sedaka have spent many days with us in Westhampton, including some July 4 holiday weekends. Their visit usually coincides with the Wimbledon tennis matches, which Neil loves to watch. He has a pet parrot that he treasures, and a few times, he brought the parrot with him. He put a small leash around the parrot's neck and walked around town with the bird on his shoulder. All the children followed Neil around, and he became known as "the birdman." These children didn't know anything about his career, but he was the most popular man in town.

He was also popular in the theater industry as two different producers were trying to launch a Broadway show using Neil's music. One show ran for a while in England and one in a few cities in the United States. Neil was not thrilled with either, and they never made it to Broadway. I went with him to see a production in the USA, and I felt that the show's writers did not do his music justice. I believed that his music would be so fabulous in a Broadway show, and all it needed was a great script. I decided to try to write a musical concept using his songs. It became another one of my creative projects, but it was very short lived. I had fun thinking of ideas, but I was never able to do a good enough job to impress Neil and Leba. I think that he is one of the great songwriters of our generation, and I believe his music could be the basis for a hit Broadway show. Even though Arlene and I are among the first people to hear every new song he writes because he values our opinions, I think he realized that there were more talented people around for him to use to create a Broadway musical.

We have many wonderful memories of good times with Neil and his friends. We had a lovely evening at the New York apartment of Kathie Lee Gifford. She was always quite nice to be around, and we enjoyed seeing her beautiful home. She was very frustrated with her co-op board that night because she was trying to sell the apartment, and they had turned down three great separate offers. She eventually found a buyer they approved of but not at the price she wanted.

The actress Kirstie Alley, best known for her starring role in the hit TV series *Cheers*, was married at the Sedakas' apartment. Kirstie remained friends with them over the years. Neil invited us to join him for dinner with her one evening, and we had no idea what to expect. We had read about her involvement in the Church of Scientology, and we were concerned with what to talk about during dinner. We were very pleasantly surprised when Scientology never came up, and the conversation was animated and quite normal.

We have spent time with Judge Judy and her husband with Neil, Michael Feinstein, and Terrence Flannery because they are all good friends of hers. We found her to be a dynamic and interesting woman and a pleasure to be with. Every time we have been in her company, she is very friendly and down to earth.

Another memorable day with Neil was spent in Las Vegas when he was performing there. He took us with him to visit with the magicians Siegfried and Roy. Their spectacular magic show, featuring wild animals, was one of the most popular acts in Las Vegas history. Spending time with them and observing some of their tigers was fascinating, and they were both gracious hosts. Seeing how they lived was unforgettable, and we were shocked when Roy was later mauled by his tiger onstage. Roy survived the attack but was never the same. I was saddened to hear of Roy's recent passing.

A less enjoyable incident occurred one night when we left the theater after seeing a Broadway show with the Sedakas. Arlene and Neil wanted to use the restroom, but there was a line at the theater. We went next door to the Hilton Hotel so they could use the facilities there. When Arlene approached the ladies' room, she saw an Out of Order sign. Neil told Arlene that there was nobody in the men's room at that late hour, so she could come in and use one of the stalls there, and he would guard the door. As they were about to leave the restroom, a man walked in. He saw the two of them and started to berate them and accuse them of having sex in the bathroom. Leba and I watched as they exited and started running toward us. Neil wanted to get out of that hotel as soon as possible in case that crazy man called the police. I could imagine the headlines in the paper the next day: SINGER, NEIL SEDAKA AND AN ANONYMOUS WOMAN CAUGHT HAVING SEX IN THE BATHROOM OF THE HILTON HOTEL.

We spent a wonderful New Year's Eve with the Sedakas at the closing of the legendary New York City restaurant Le Cirque. For their last evening, they hired Neil to entertain at a magnificent black-tie dinner for a group of regulars, including Paula Abdul. We had watched Paula on TV each week when she hosted *American Idol* but didn't know her personally. She turned out to be lovely, and she looked great. It was a nice way to spend New Year's Eve with our friends, and we were very nostalgic, knowing it would be our last time at Le Cirque. We had many enjoyable meals at Le Cirque over the years, and it was an NY treasure.

The co-owner of the New York Mets Saul Katz was a fan of Neil and hired him to sing at one of his birthday parties. Saul and his wife, Iris, subsequently became friends with Neil, and he invited us to join them one night for dinner. We found them to be terrific people and developed a friendship of our own with them and their lovely family. I have played tennis with Saul and been to his home, and Arlene and I have enjoyed wonderful times out with them. For Iris's birthday, I connected them to Michael Feinstein, and Saul hired him to entertain at her party.

Since my beloved Brooklyn Dodgers left Brooklyn for Los Angeles many years ago, I have not been much of a baseball fan. However, I must say that going to a baseball game with the owner and sitting in his box makes watching baseball much more enjoyable. I became a hero to my grandkids and children when I was able to bring them to Mets games and have them sit in the owner's box. My family was also able to walk down at any time during the game and use the owner's seats in the first row directly behind the catcher. Besides being great friends, Saul and Iris enabled me to upgrade my status in the eyes of my children. My grandson Justin was such a big baseball fan that he brought his baseball card collection to one of the games and excitedly showed it to Saul, who treated Justin like part of his family and gave him and the rest of us Mets hats.

Neil has come with me to some of the games, but the food and Nathan's hot dogs in the owner's suite are more of a treat for him than the baseball game itself. Neil's passion is tennis, and he knows all the players and watches all the matches faithfully. His knowledge of baseball is not quite the same. One evening Neil was being honored at the New York City Friars Club. While we were sitting with him, a member of the club came over to Neil and told him that Hank Aaron, the legendary baseball star, was at the next table, and the club wanted to take a picture of the two of them together. Hank Aaron was sitting next to an elderly white member of the Friars Club. Neil got up from our table, walked over to the adjacent table, and shook hands with the elderly white gentleman, telling him how honored he was to take a picture with him. Hearing this, I jumped up and took Neil by the arm. I quietly told him that the man he spoke to was probably thrilled to meet with him, but the black man sitting next to the person he was shaking hands with was Hank Aaron. We all had a good laugh afterward.

It reminded Arlene and me about the time in Boston with Liza in her dressing room after one of her concerts. The world's middleweight boxing champion Marvelous Marvin Hagler was in the audience. After the concert, he and his entourage knocked on the door and were ushered in. He very dramatically walked into the dressing room. With great flair, he congratulated "Liza," shook hands with Arlene and everyone in the dressing room, and waved to us all as he exited the room. Liza and Arlene, stunned, looked at each other, and Liza said, "Who was that guy?"

CHAPTER

FORTY-TWO

Sammy Davis Jr.

Sammy Davis had a sign near the door at his home that read, "Everyone with peace and love in their heart is welcome in this home." He always had the latest gadgets, games, and video equipment around to entertain his guests. He loved to cook and built a small kitchen home outside his main house. He enjoyed spending time there cooking because he could keep that house very warm as he hated the cold. Arlene also likes it room-temperature warm, so Sammy would take Arlene with him next door into the kitchen while he cooked.

Sammy lived through the time of segregation in the South, and he told us about many of his experiences. It was the first time we had heard about the "green book," a list of places that black performers could stay at while touring in the South. We had dinner one night in New York with Sammy and the fabulous actor Richard Harris and his wife, Ann Turkel. Richard, who was an Academy Award–nominated actor, also had a very big hit recording of the Jimmy Webb song "MacArthur Park." Richard had a strong and charismatic personality. He told us about the time he was in the audience at a nightclub where Sammy was performing. When a heckler yelled out a racial slur while Sammy was onstage, Richard Harris got up from his seat and punched the heckler, knocking him out. The audience cheered, and Richard and Sammy have been close friends ever since.

Arlene and I remember one other thing from our evening with Richard. Richard's wife, Ann, loved butterflies, and he liked spoiling her. She wore butterfly diamond earrings and a very unusual and dramatic butterfly-shaped diamond ring. I thought of the words uttered by Muhammad Ali, "Float like a butterfly, sting like a bee," after he relayed the story of him punching the guy and adorning his wife with butterfly jewelry.

We became very close to Sammy's wife, Altovise. One day while she was staying with us in New York City, we had an appointment at our apartment to meet with interior designers about redecorating part of our home. We were sitting on the couch with Altovise when the doorbell rang. I answered it and let the two women in. Arlene asked them to sit down, and she brought them some tea and cookies. We discussed possible decorating ideas and made plans to see them again the following week. At the end of our meeting, I walked them to the elevator and remarked that I looked forward to working with them. They replied that they liked meeting us and how impressed they were with the unusual way we treated our "help." They mentioned that they were surprised to see our housekeeper relaxing on the couch while Arlene served them tea. They had assumed, because Altovise was black, that she was our housekeeper and not our friend. It is hard for me to believe how some people saw the world in the 1980s.

When I formed my mouthwash business in 1986, I was looking for a way to advertise my product. I set up a meeting with a top advertising agency, and they proposed the idea of using a celebrity spokesperson. It was, however, very expensive to hire a well-known personality. I told them that I was good friends with Mrs. Sammy Davis Jr. and that she was a former model and spokeswoman for many charities in Los Angeles. I suggested we could hire her for much less money than we would have to pay a star like Sammy Davis and have the advantage of using the famous name recognition. They asked me to obtain some pictures of her, and at the next meeting, I brought them with me. I handed the envelope to the head advertising executive. He opened the envelope, took out the photos, threw them on the desk, and exclaimed, "She's black! Are you crazy?" I fired him on the spot and hired a different agency.

Sammy was one of the most generous people we have ever met. One day he took Arlene and me out for dinner at 21 in New York City. (When I started dating Arlene, I wanted to impress her and take her to the famous 21 restaurant. It was where all the celebrities and the movers and shakers of NYC ate. I had never been there, but I acted as though I had. The maître d' sat us in a casual area, with all sorts of toys hanging from the ceiling. I figured that this couldn't be where the "in people" sit, so I went over to the maître d' and asked him if there was another room where they were serving dinner. He told me that there was an upstairs dining room, but it was pretty empty. I figured that was the place for the well-known customers, and I gave him $20 to seat us there. We had a boring dinner in a near-empty room. I later found out that the fanciful room with all the miniature toys on the ceiling was indeed where the "in people" dined.) Being at 21 with Sammy Davis Jr. was a vastly different experience. We were treated royally, and Sammy also arranged for us to have a tour of the secret downstairs area. During prohibition, 21 had an unmarked door that led customers downstairs to an area where they could imbibe their alcohol.

When we left, Sammy walked us to their small gift counter on the way out and bought us the most magnificent insulated suede picnic suitcase filled with plates and other picnic items, all with the 21 logo. We still treasure it today, along with his watch, as wonderful reminders of his generosity and friendship.

After spending time with our children at Harrah's Marina in Atlantic City, Sammy offered our sixteen-year-old son, Marc, a job working with him backstage on his tour. It would have been a great experience; however, Marc couldn't spend the time because he was in school. We bought Sammy a gift of an apron with the words "Mr. Wonderful" on it because he spent the three days cooking for us.

On May 3, 1985, Liza arranged for her husband, Mark Gero, to have an exhibit of his sculptures at the Weintraub Gallery in New York City. Arlene and I met Sammy at the Waldorf and went with him to the gallery at 4:00 pm. Nobody was really buying Mark's sculptures, but Sammy bought one of his works for $1,500. Sammy, always a sport, wanted to buy something so Liza could witness Mark selling his works and being recognized as a sculptor.

We all went for coffee afterward at the Westbury Hotel. Sammy and Liza had a very special friendship. One night Sammy confided to Arlene and me that someday, when they both are single, he will marry Liza. He looked serious at the time; however, it may have been an extra glass of wine acting as the catalyst for that statement. Sammy loved orange Crush soda and port wine. He would announce onstage to the audience that he was so many months sober and no longer drinking. Then we would meet him in the dressing room afterward, and he'd be having a glass of port wine. He'd look at us and say, "That doesn't count as drinking."

On New Year's Eve in 1985, we took our children to Atlantic City to spend New Year's Eve at Trump Plaza, where Sammy was entertaining. Our children were very close to Sammy and Altovise, and they made us all feel part of their family as we celebrated the New Year together. As a result of our close relationship, we also knew Sammy's mother, who coincidentally lived across the street from us. One day while we were walking with our children in the neighborhood, Sammy's mother, Elvera, came out of her building, and we introduced our children to her. They were surprised to see that Sammy's mother was still alive because he seemed so old to our young children. However, on the side of Sammy's mother, there was a history of longevity. Elvera was in her eighties at that time. You can imagine the shock on our children's faces when she told us that she was heading out to visit her mother. Her mother was one hundred and in a nursing home. It is one reason that we felt so badly when Sammy passed away at such a relatively young age. He developed throat cancer and chose not to operate because he would lose his voice. He did not want to end up not being able to sing and speak. Since I was a periodontist and treated gum disease, Altovise explained all the options to me.

In later years after Sammy died and our son, Marc, was a dentist, Altovise became his patient. Altovise never had children, and they adopted an orphan named Manny. Arlene and I were so happy to see this young boy brought into this wonderful Beverly Hills mansion with every luxury after the hard life that he had. It was such an unfortunate twist of fate that, soon after the adoption, Sammy lost all his money. He died broke due to problems with the IRS caused by crooked accountants.

Sammy's biggest wish was to have black actors accepted in prominent roles on Broadway. He came to New York City for a year to star in the show *Stop the World—I Want to Get Off* in the role made famous by Anthony Newley. His dream role was to star in the show *Phantom of the Opera*. He unfortunately never got the chance but made some wonderful recordings of the songs from that show. We spent hours with him while he played the music from *Phantom* over and over again. He wanted to choose the right songs to record and experimented with various versions of each song until he found what was best for him. He would have been very pleased to know that, eventually, a black actor, Robert Guillaume, did play the role of the phantom on Broadway.

Our common friend Leslie Bricusse, who wrote the lyrics for *Stop the World*, wrote a musical about the life of Sammy Davis. It is called *Sammy*, and we saw a version of the musical in San Diego, starring our friend Obba Babatundé. We loved it, and Obba was as spectacular as Sammy. Unfortunately, it has not yet reached Broadway. Obba can do a terrific imitation of Sammy. He contorts his face and body in such a way that you think he is Sammy. One night in NYC when Sammy was still alive, Obba was doing a one-man show. In the middle of his performance, he announced to the audience that Sammy Davis was backstage and wanted to say hello. Obba walked offstage, and "Sammy Davis" walked out to thunderous applause. He said a few words and started to sing. It took a long time for the audience to realize that the Sammy Davis onstage was really Obba.

Sammy, with all his great success, still had the insecurities that many great performers have. One night we went to see him perform at the Westbury Theater in Long Island. It is a theater in the round, with a large public parking area for its patrons. As people sense the performance nearing the end, some start to head for the exits in an attempt to beat the traffic jam, leaving after the show. Sammy had a very good opening act for him that evening, a lovely female singer. When she finished singing, instead of Sammy coming on, he introduced a very talented young black ventriloquist. Sammy wanted to give him exposure to help start his career. He was excellent, but by the time Sammy appeared, it was already getting late. Sammy put on his usual fabulous performance. However, as it approached close to eleven o'clock, some of the patrons started to head to their cars to beat the traffic jam. Being a theater in the round, the performer can easily see people as they stand up and exit up the aisle.

After the show, Arlene and I went to Sammy's dressing room. He was sitting by himself on a chair with his pants half pulled up around his legs. He looked dejected and sadly said to us, "My audience is starting to walk out on me." We had to explain the car situation, along with the fact that the older crowd is not used to staying up so late for shows. The few people leaving to get to their cars had nothing to do with his performance. In truth, the overwhelmingly large majority of people stayed until the end of his performance, and it went over extremely well despite the very late hour.

In 1989, Gregory Hines starred in a movie called *Tap*, with a theme involving tap dancing. Sammy Davis had a supporting role in the movie. When he came to New York for a few days of shooting, he invited us to join him on the set and keep him company at his hotel before and after the filming each day. It was not a big-budget film, and the producers tried to cut costs as much as possible. They put Sammy up in a hotel close to where they were shooting. When we met him at the hotel, he was very dispirited. He was used to having luxurious large suites whenever he performed. His room was so small that Arlene and I had to sit on his bed while we all were waiting for the car to take us all to the set. The producer put him in one small room at an inexpensive hotel near the shooting location. When the car arrived to pick the three of us up to go to the filming, it was a very ordinary car, not the limousine Sammy was used to. Despite the wonderful role he had in the film, the experience was upsetting to him because he felt he was not being treated like a star.

Although Sammy had a lot of pride, he always was extravagant in his praise for people and generous in the way he treated others. On October 27, 1985, Sammy and Altovise were staying at the Helmsley Palace in New York City, along with friends of theirs from Saint Louis. We were going out to dinner; however, there was not enough room for all of us in the limousine Sammy had ordered. Sammy was experiencing hip trouble at the time and was in some pain and using a cane to help him walk. He was such a gentleman that he insisted everybody go in the limousine, and he would take a taxi to the restaurant. Arlene volunteered to go in the taxi with Sammy, while the rest of us took the limousine.

On December 10, 1985, a photographer friend of Sammy arranged for a group of Sammy's friends to videotape surprise birthday messages for his sixtieth birthday. He arrived at our home, and Arlene and I had him film us in a funny skit that we created. It showed Arlene running into our apartment with many shopping bags from Bloomingdale's while I ran in with my dental uniform and instruments in hand. We both rushed in hurriedly as if we were late for the taping. I'm sure with all the talented and famous friends of Sammy being filmed, ours was low down on the talent ratings. However, we were very flattered to be considered among his closest friends.

FORTY-THREE

Barry Manilow

Lorna Luft has been a close friend of Barry Manilow for many years. They live near each other in Palm Springs. She introduced us to Barry and his husband and manager, Garry Kief. We did not know what to expect when we first met them. Arlene and I arrived at the gate of their home in Palm Springs with Lorna and drove up to their beautiful place on the top of a small mountain. Barry was standing outside his front door, waiting for our car as we drove up. He greeted us warmly and made us instantly feel welcome. Their cook served us cocktails, and Barry and Garry showed us around their home and grounds. They had prepared a wonderful dinner, and conversation flowed easily.

Barry and I both come from Brooklyn, and we had much to reminisce about. It was like being with an old friend, and it was the beginning of years of friendship between us. Garry is very successful and is the president and CEO of Stiletto Entertainment. He is quite good looking and has a very engaging personality. We instantly liked him and loved hearing his witty comments. Garry has a great sense of humor, and his take on things can be very funny.

Lorna is not the only person we have in common with Barry. Our friend Julie Budd has a manager and piano player named Herb Bernstein, whom we also consider a friend. Besides being Julie's manager, Herb has been responsible for producing and arranging albums for many well-known recording stars. Before he went into the music business, Herb was a physical education teacher and basketball coach at the same high school in Williamsburg that Barry attended. Herb had told us that Barry was his student in the school, and Herb realized that Barry was not fond of physical education. Herb not only passed Barry in physical education but, when he found out that Barry was interested in playing the piano, Herb also located a piano in the school for Barry to use. Herb asked us to send his regards to Barry when we saw him. When I told Barry that Herb said hello, Barry remarked that he could only think of him as Mr. Bernstein and could never call him Herb. He looked up to Mr. Bernstein and was actually impressed that I was able to call him by his first name.

When Barry and Garry booked a tour of cities on the East Coast one year, they rented a home in Sag Harbor for the summer months. They invited us over to see their place, and we gave them a list of all the necessary numbers they needed for various services in the Hamptons. Barry could relax there, fly to his booking, and fly back after the show. Barry and Garry have three wonderful dogs, and they looked forward to walking them on the beach and the grounds of their rented home. Barry has very loyal fans, nicknamed "Fanilows." When we tried to show him around the neighboring towns, we saw why he was hesitant to leave his property. He has extremely devoted fans, and they get quite excited when they see him. When it became a problem for him to walk his dogs in town or at the beach, I suggested that he come to our home in Westhampton. We have a private walkway to the beach across the street from our house. The beach is completely deserted because the public has no access to it from that point. They took us up on our offer, and the dogs had a terrific time romping around the beach.

My family enjoyed spending time with them, and our son, Marc, took Garry's daughter, Kirsten, out on our boat and showed her around the area. Kirsten is a dynamic woman who handles many of the aspects of Barry's concerts. While working at his shows, she is always so busy that we rarely get to see her in a normal environment. It was nice to be able to spend some relaxing time with her. We had only seen Barry perform a few times over the years before we became friends with him. As we have grown to know him, we have had the opportunity to attend many of his performances in New York City, Long Island, Las Vegas, and Los Angeles. We observed his amazing fans screaming and jumping up after every song. We had wonderful times with him and Garry during his residency at the Paris Theater in Las Vegas. The hotel even gave him a private area in a disco at the hotel so we could all relax after the shows.

We usually stay with Lorna Luft and her husband Colin Freeman when we vacation in the Palm Springs area. However, Barry and Garry invited us to stay at their home one winter when Lorna was out of town performing. They had us stay in their lovely guesthouse, a few steps away from the main house. We got along so well together that it felt as if we had known them forever. On another occasion, we stayed in a guest room in their main house, and that was equally comfortable. In 2016, we went to Palm Springs to attend a special three-day Coachella Festival. This event was nicknamed "Oldchella" because it featured famous rock performers all in their seventies. The performers were Paul McCartney, Bob Dylan, the Who, Neil Young, the Rolling Stones, and Roger Waters of Pink Floyd. It took place during the presidential election of 2016, and on one of the nights, we left the concert early to watch the presidential debates at Barry's home. Barry and Garry were not fans of Donald Trump, and there was much political discussion that night with Lorna and Colin, who were also there.

In 2018, Barry began a residency in Las Vegas at the Westgate Hotel. He invited us to come to Las Vegas to attend his shows and then fly back with him and Garry on his private plane to their home in Palm Springs after his last show on Sunday night. We had a wonderful weekend in Las Vegas, and it was a treat after the final show to just get on his plane and avoid dealing with the commercial flights at Las Vegas airport.

We had another wonderful time in Palm Springs at their home. A few weeks before going there, we had stayed with friends in Palm Beach, Florida. They made a small dinner party one night, and I was seated next to a very ornately dressed woman named Toni

Holt Kramer. She informed me that she was the head of a woman's organization called the Trumpettes, which she had formed to support President Trump. In the course of the conversation, I mentioned that I was going to Palm Springs the following month. She told me that she has the largest property in Palm Springs, and her home was once owned by Howard Hughes. She said that he bought the property because it had the largest acreage, and he wanted to assemble his airplane, called the Spruce Goose, on the property. It would be the biggest airplane ever made, and he needed room for the tremendous wingspan. She explained that with all her work for the Trumpettes in Palm Beach, she never gets a chance to spend time at her homes in Palm Springs and Los Angeles. Even though I just met her, she offered to set up a tour of her home and grounds with her houseman. She insisted that I call him when I was in Palm Springs. I took down her contact information, but I did not plan to follow up because I didn't know her well.

I saved Toni's contact information on my iPhone. The first day after we flew with Barry and Garry from Las Vegas to Palm Springs, Barry said he would be busy all afternoon working on a musical project. I told Garry about the woman we had met and her offer to tour her home. He thought it might be fun for all of us to see it, so I called her houseman and arranged to meet him. Even though Garry did not like Trump or the people around him, he was curious to see the home and grounds, despite this woman's association. The houseman gave us a wonderful tour of the grounds. He then told us that Toni usually doesn't allow people to tour her home, but she gave him the green light to show us around the estate. Her home was beautiful and decorated very dramatically with ornate prints and furnishings. He brought us into one den where there were large portraits of her dogs hanging on the walls. Garry loves dogs, and when he saw the portraits she had made of her dogs, his attitude toward her softened a bit. However, when he asked the houseman what the dog's name was, he answered "Trump." That was when we knew it was time for Garry to leave, and we all had a good laugh in the car on the way back to the house.

That evening, we were having dinner at a local restaurant, and a woman approached our table carrying a cell phone. Barry started to get up to take a picture with the fan, but to our surprise, she didn't notice him. She had come over to our table to ask if one of us would take a picture of her and her husband at the restaurant. It was our second great laugh of the day.

One of the things we admire about Barry and Garry is their charitable work. Barry strongly believes in the importance of music and arts in schools. He gives a free ticket to anyone who comes to his concerts with a musical instrument to donate to the local schools. Barry and Gary have set up concerts by Barry called "A Gift of Love" and have raised millions of dollars for school music programs. Garry has been honored often for his charitable work for his community and for his college fraternity. They are two great guys who give back to their community.

FORTY-FOUR

Michael Feinstein

Michael Feinstein has come a long way since we first met him forty years ago wearing a white bathrobe in Liza Minnelli's kitchen. He has been the most important person in maintaining the Great American Songbook. Besides performing all over the world, he serves as the artistic director of the Center for the Performing Arts in Carmel, Indiana. Feinstein's nightclubs are in many cities in the USA.

He and his husband, Terrence Flannery, have become two of our closest friends. We flew to Los Angeles in 2008 for their wedding, which took place in their magnificent home. Their home was at one time the Russian Embassy in California, and Terrence did a wonderful job in converting it into a stunning residence. It was a very special wedding. Judge Judy officiated the union, and Liza Minnelli and Barry Manilow sang. It was the first time we witnessed the marriage of two men in a typical Jewish ceremony, including the stepping on and breaking of the glass. Terrence is not Jewish, so Rosemary Clooney's son, Gabriel Ferrer, who is a priest, assisted Judge Judy during the ceremony.

Michael is also the principal conductor for the Pasadena POPS. He and Terrence have recently bought a new home there, and it is one of the largest homes that I have ever seen. We almost got lost inside while seeing it with them during construction. As I said before, Terrence is unusually talented in restoring homes and is turning it into one of the most magnificent homes in Los Angeles. Terrence is extremely bright and very successful in business in his own right. He gives Michael terrific creative suggestions for his career, and they are an amazing couple. They are two of our favorite people, and we think of them as a part of our extended family.

We have also spent wonderful times with them at their ranch and farm in Carpinteria, California. Besides the beautiful setting, they grow avocados. We drove around with them in a small jeep, observing the hundreds of avocado trees on the property. (Every time Arlene buys an avocado in the market and sees how much they cost, she comments on the number of avocado trees they have. I guess we really are that couple whom Jackie Mason describes as counting the seats in a theater or, in this case, avocado trees on the property to guess how much the person is making.)

Michael and Liza Minnelli have remained very close friends, and every time we visit Los Angeles, we look forward to all of us sitting around the piano at Liza's apartment while Michael plays, and they both sing. Those intimate, casual evenings around a piano at home are memorable.

Michael has become the artistic director for the Palm Beach POPS as well. A few years ago, after Michael headed the annual gala for the Palm Beach Orchestra, he and Terrence came back to the Colony Hotel, where we were staying. We took a table in the bar area, and a few other people came over after the gala and joined our table, such as the marvelous actor and performer Alan Cumming. (We met him through Liza and have spent time with Alan over the years. His one-man show is extremely personal, and he always gives credit to Liza for her inspiration. He is a marvelous actor who starred in *The Good Wife* on TV and won a Tony Award as the master of ceremonies in *Cabaret* on Broadway.) There was a piano in the bar at the hotel, and Michael and Alan took turns playing the piano and singing. We were having a good deal of fun, and then another young man, whom we didn't know but was sitting at our table, got up and joined Michael and Alan at the piano. His name was Darren, and he was quite talented. We were impressed that he had the nerve to get up and sing with these two big stars.

Palm Beach is an early town, and the person running the bar told us that we were making too much noise around the piano. It was eleven thirty at night, and we were upset at having to leave the bar. There were two young ladies at the next table dressed in evening gowns. They too had come over for a nightcap after the gala. They announced that their home was only a few minutes away and invited us all over to their place to continue the festivities.

We decided to be spontaneous, as we often are, and got into our two cars and followed their vehicle to their home. It turned out to be a beautiful Palm Beach mansion. We—along with Alan, Michael, Terrence, and Darren—each thought that these two women were friends of one of us. As we asked one another about these two women while walking into their home, we discovered that they were actually complete strangers. We were all in a very festive mood after having a few drinks at the bar and ended up staying. The two women explained that they were sisters, and their husbands were sleeping upstairs. We entered a huge living room, which had a piano, and Alan, Michael, and Darren all continued to play the piano and took turns singing. The alcohol was flowing, and the singing was very energetic. The two women announced that they were going to make some pasta because it was now two o'clock, and we were probably all hungry. They brought us into a large dining room and served a delicious meal, and the party continued.

At one point, I took Michael aside and asked him if Darren was one of the students he mentored at his Great American Songbook organization. Michael answered that his name was Darren Criss and that he was one of the stars of the very popular TV show *Glee*. (A few years later, Arlene and I were amazed while watching the *Assassination of Gianni Versace* TV miniseries to see the name Darren Criss in the credits. His performance was so fantastic in that program, winning him an Emmy and Golden Globe, that we did not recognize him as the fun young singer we spent time with.)

All of us had such a great time that we remained at the sisters' home until four o'clock, a most unusual hour for people to be up in

Palm Beach. At four thirty in the morning, my cell phone rang while I was getting ready for bed. It was Alan Cumming, mistakenly calling me instead of room service at his hotel. I guess he had more to drink than he realized.

We had a terrific time with Michael and Terrence in Nashville. I love country music, and Nashville is one of my favorite cities. Michael was appearing with the Nashville Symphony the same week we were there. For Michael, the leading expert on the music of the Great American Songbook, it was a fun experience going from bar to bar with us and hearing all types of country music. We had a great time, and a few years later, Michael put together an album of him singing songs from the Great American Songbook with various country music stars. Terrence and Michael are both vegans, and our one problem was hunting down a true vegan restaurant in Nashville, but we finally did.

We have a performing arts center in our town of Westhampton. Michael has performed there a few times mainly, he says, so he and Terrence can enjoy a long weekend at our home. Arlene loves to feed our houseguests, and four days of finding good and varied vegan food to serve in the Hamptons is not easy. Terrence and Michael arrived on a Thursday, and his performance was on Sunday night. Arlene managed to find every possible vegan food in Long Island, and our meals were delicious. Terrence and Michael are both slim, and they eat moderately. Arlene and I laughed to ourselves the night of Michael's show on that Sunday when he walked out onstage as, after four days of Arlene constantly shoving food at him, his perfectly tailored jacket was pulling slightly at the waist. He was not able to completely resist the onslaught of vegan temptations Arlene served at every meal. When he dedicated a song to us and thanked us onstage for our hospitality, we were flattered. We commented to ourselves that had he stayed longer, his wardrobe would have to be altered.

Michael and Terrence love to have a good time. One weekend they came to our home with our common friends Tom Postilio and Mickey Conlon. They are two of the top real estate brokers in New York City. They also love to get up at a party and sing a duet. Tom, at one time, did some singing, but he and Mickey are stars in the real estate business. Once a week in the summer in Westhampton, the people bring folding chairs to the great lawn in town for a free concert. We happened to be walking in town when the concert was taking place. There was a big band with a male and a female singer. I lied to Tom, telling him that I knew the organizer of the concert and that I would arrange for him to sing one song with the band. Tom replied that he could not just walk over to the band because they have a set program. Of course, he was right, but it was just a joke that we were all playing on Tom. Michael did his part and told Tom that he knew the organizers of the concert and that he could walk over to the conductor and arrange it.

At intermission, Michael went over to the leader of the orchestra, who was quite happy to talk with Michael Feinstein. All Michael did was compliment him on the first half of the performance. Michael then walked back over to us and told Tom that everything was arranged for him to sing with the band in the second half. Michael explained that the orchestra leader was waiting for Tom to come over and tell him what song he would like to sing. We didn't know if Tom believed us or if he was just going along with the joke. Tom actually did not realize that we were all putting him on, and we watched him walk over to the orchestra leader to discuss what song he would be singing. When the orchestra leader looked at him like he was crazy and told him that one just can't just walk up and sing with an orchestra that has a set program, he became aware that he had been pranked.

In 2008, the Great American Songbook Foundation, founded by Michael Feinstein, set up headquarters in Carmel, Indiana. The foundation houses an archive and reference library and museum. They have an annual gala to raise funds to keep the Great American Songbook alive. One year Terrence and Michael invited us to attend the gala. We were so impressed with the work Michael was doing to preserve the Great American Songbook. Carmel was a charming town, and we had a very enjoyable weekend there. Returning to New York City after the gala was easy because Terrence and Michael spoiled us by flying us back to New York with them in their private plane. Our friend Tedd Firth, the fabulous pianist and musical conductor for Michael at the show, joined us on the plane.

Recently, Tom and Mickey made a birthday party for Terrence at their vacation home on Long Island. It was a terrific day, and there were some delightful friends in attendance to help celebrate with Terrence, including David Hyde Pierce and Jimmy Webb. David Hyde Pierce and his husband, Brian Hargrove, were interesting to converse with. David won many awards in his role on the TV hit series *Frasier*. We had seen him perform in a two-man nightclub show with Michael

Feinstein, and he was fabulous. It's not easy to keep up with Michael Feinstein on a stage, but David sang and performed beautifully.

Arlene and I spent a few private hours with Jimmy Webb and found him fascinating. He talked to us about his career and life. The three of us were sitting in a small den with a piano, and while he was discussing how people in his life influenced his music, he periodically sat down at the piano and played with great emotion. For a few years in his early twenties, he composed some of the great music of our time. He explained how personal experiences and drugs affected his creativity. Some of his songs include "MacArthur Park," "Wichita Lineman," "Galveston," "Didn't We," "By the Time I Get to Phoenix," and "Up, Up and Away." He told us about his love affairs that inspired him for many of these songs. A major love affair in his life was with a close friend of ours, Evie Bricusse. Leslie and Evie have been married for sixty-two years and are one of the most loving couples we know. However, we did hear that many years before we met them, they had a short breakup. A few years ago, Leslie sent us his autobiography, and there was no mention of any breakup. We were quite interested to hear from Jimmy about his relationship with Evie, and he told us to read his autobiography to learn about it. After our stimulating day with him, I did read his book and found it quite informative. I saw him a few months ago when he was doing a concert with Michael Feinstein. He was happy to hear that I enjoyed his autobiography, but I didn't have time to ask him any more questions about it.

Terrence and Michael have a knack for finding unusual and interesting places, and we have joined them for many fun-filled times. One night they took us to an Upper East Side Italian restaurant named Mimi's to hear a unique entertainer. His name was Chicken Delicious. At midnight two days a week, Chicken Delicious performed at a small piano bar in the restaurant. He was one of the most eccentric and unsung acts in NYC. Outlandish masks and costumes were part of his act. For every song and story, he turned himself into a different character. He could be a dog, the pope, Marilyn Monroe, a fairy, or a bib-wearing baby. Besides playing the piano and singing, he related stories of his past and the influence of a mystic in his life. On the nights he performed, he drove up to the restaurant and looked for a parking spot. The show didn't start until he found a spot. (Sometimes that can be a while as you know if you have ever tried to find a parking spot on the Upper East Side.) When we come in with Terrence and Michael, he usually sang a song while wearing a mask with an illuminated sign saying, "Welcome, Terrence and Michael." He made all his costumes and masks and performed songs and stories to fit each one. Sadly, he recently passed away, and no one could ever replace him.

Terrence and Michael also introduced us to the big band sound of Vince Giordano and the Nighthawks. They used to be at the Edison Hotel but are currently playing at Café Iguana in NYC. They play jazz music from the 1920s and 1930s, and they are really fun to hear. Young couples who appear to be professional dancers love dancing to the music of that time on the small dance floor. People from the audience who have any singing talent can get up and sing a song with the band. The last time we were there, Mel Brooks was at the next table. He was having a great time and was very friendly. Michael has used Vince and his band at some of his performances, so we are treated well there.

Since Terrence and Michael are vegans, they have introduced us to many interesting vegan restaurants in NYC and LA. We sometimes have no idea what we are eating, but what they order tastes good.

 CHAPTER

FORTY-FIVE

Tony Danza

Tony Danza is one of our dearest friends in the world. He is an example of how a two-second incident can change the course of one's life. Tony was a pretty successful young boxer with some theatrical training. His professional boxing record was nine wins, all by knockout, and three losses. The producers of a new television series called *Taxi* were looking for a young actor to play the part of a boxer. The casting people went to see Tony fight, and in the first round, his opponent hit him with a solid punch, and Tony went down. Tony told us that while he was on the canvas and dazed, he looked up at the casting people sitting at ringside and felt that his chance of getting the part was fading. He somehow willed himself to get up at the count of eight. He then went on to dramatically win the fight. He eventually was cast in *Taxi*, and it was the beginning of a long and very successful career.

Tony loves to work with kids. In 2009, he taught a tenth-grade English class at a high school in Philadelphia. A&E filmed his experience that year for a reality show. He is doing amazing work in NYC with the Police Athletic League (PAL) youth acting program. He takes children, many from broken homes, and teaches them how to act and perform. He has changed the lives of hundreds of kids, helping them achieve their potential. He also concentrates on strengthening the relationship between the city's youth and the police department. Tony puts on a yearly charity event for PAL called Stars of Tomorrow, featuring a chorus of cops and kids. The cops and kids work and perform together. If more cities followed Tony's lead, there would be less tension between the police and inner-city youth.

For two years, Tony had an entertaining and informative morning talk show on ABC in New York. During that time, we were all fascinated with the TV show *24*, where each episode took place in one hour of actual time. Tony and Liza Minnelli would faithfully watch the show together each week, and we would often join them. Tony, on his live talk show the next morning, would attempt to summarize the plot in sixty seconds each week.

Many of our best moments with him have been in the kitchen. He is a great cook, and Sunday afternoon meals at his place with a few friends are a treat. He wrote a cookbook titled *Don't Fill up on the Antipasto*. We have also had some very memorable long weekends with him at our home in Westhampton. He likes to exercise and cook, and the first weekend that he came to our house, he generously sent over some large exercise equipment, an assortment of knives and a large cutting board, and some bottles of his favorite red wine as a gift. (I bring out the exercise equipment from my garage when he comes and clean it so he won't notice the dust that gathered from not being used.)

One weekend when Tony was staying with us in Westhampton, our performing arts center in town booked the very talented comedian Sebastian Maniscalco. We were not familiar with his work, but apparently, everyone else was because his shows were the most popular ones of the season. As soon as they were announced, they immediately sold out. Tony had recently filmed a TV pilot with Sebastian, and they had become friends. Tony arranged tickets for us and our daughter, Lauren, and her boyfriend Seth, who were already big fans of Sebastian. On the night of the show, Tony invited Sebastian and his wife, Lana, to come to our house for dinner before the performance. Tony spent hours cooking a huge lasagna, and at around four o'clock, Sebastian and Lana arrived. They are a very lovely couple, and Sebastian seemed very quiet and reserved. He was not the typical wisecracking, joke-telling comedian, like the ones I was used to being around in the past. They were charming and polite, and we had a wonderful dinner together.

At seven o'clock, Sebastian left for the theater, which is only five minutes from our home. Our daughter, Lauren, was very excited to see him perform, and she told me that he was hilarious. I mentioned that he did not act like a comedian, and I was concerned that this very polite young man would not be funny enough onstage to hold the audience. At seven forty-five, we all left for the eight o'clock show. When the curtain opened, out came this wild Italian character. Sebastian bounced out on the stage, and for the next ninety minutes, we witnessed one of the most frantic, exciting comedians we have ever seen. He was a totally different person onstage, very different from the reserved person at our home. His body movements and comic delivery was quite an experience to observe.

When we visited him backstage after the performance, he was once again the polite, quiet gentleman we had been with at dinner. During his act, Sebastian did a bit about him and his wife going to people's homes and then talking about them afterward when they left. Lauren asked him if he did that when he left our home and what he said about us. (Tony is a former boxer, so I assume Sebastian didn't make any negative comments in front of him.)

We met one of the most unusual people we had ever come in contact with when Tony's manager, Dan Farah, brought his friend John with him to spend a weekend with Tony and us in Westhampton. John appeared to be right out of *The Great Gatsby*. He came from an extremely wealthy family, owning one of the major baseball teams among other businesses and producing movies. This handsome young man pulled up to our home in a stretch limousine. He and Dan came into our home, followed by the chauffeur carrying many shopping bags. The chauffeur made several trips back and forth from the limousine, bringing in even more shopping bags full of clothing. There were no suitcases.

Dan explained that his friend John never travels with suitcases or any money. If John goes out to a restaurant or club, he has them call his assistant. The assistant pays the bill because John doesn't carry money or credit cards. When John found out that he was going to spend a few days in the Hamptons, he instructed his assistant to order whatever clothing she felt would be appropriate for a long Hamptons weekend. The shopping bags, which now filled the room, contained many sets of matching slacks, shirts, shoes, underwear, socks, bathing suits, caps, jackets, and any other items appropriate for a Hamptons weekend. Everything was brand new, with the price tags still on them. There were also a few cases of soap because he uses a new bar of soap each time he washes his hands or showers. Our daughter, Lauren, was with us over that weekend, and she enjoyed being in his company and hanging around the pool with him and Dan.

Soon after he arrived, a second long limousine pulled up in our driveway. Dan and John were both single, and they wanted to experience some of the clubs in the Hamptons. John kept the two limousines waiting in our driveway for the length of his stay. He wanted the second limousine to be at our disposal, in case Tony, Lauren, Arlene, or I wanted to go in a different direction for the evening. Tony preferred cooking at home, but we all did go to a trendy club with Dan and John one night.

When our limousine arrived at the club to meet up with them, John was seated at the large main table, surrounded by a large group of attractive people. The day John and Dan left to go back to New York City, the chauffeur came into our guest room and removed all the brand-new clothing. Our wastepaper baskets were filled to the top with discarded price tags from his newly bought clothes. Arlene called me into the bathroom of the guestroom to show me that an object was floating in the bottom of the clean toilet bowl. I fished it out and discovered that it was a pair of expensive designer sunglasses. The chauffeur was just finishing placing the last of the packages in the limousine. We told John that we had found his sunglasses, and he exclaimed that they had fallen into the toilet bowl, and he did not want to touch them. His assistant had bought duplicates of every clothing and accessory item, so John had a few other pairs of sunglasses and didn't want this pair. It was a beautiful pair of designer sunglasses, and I gave it to Lauren, along with a large box of soaps that hadn't been used.

John presented us with some wonderful bottles of champagne, and then they went back to NYC, followed by an empty second limousine. We have seen John occasionally over the years, including at the opening party of *Honeymoon in Vegas*, which Tony starred in on Broadway, and read about films he is producing and the success of his family's baseball franchise.

Dan is still Tony's manager and has also produced films and TV movies, notably *Ready Player One* with Steven Spielberg. Dan is a dynamo, and we all feel he will someday head a film studio. He is a terrific guy and fun to be around. He has a creative mind and is constantly thinking of new ideas.

CHAPTER

FORTY-SIX

Joe Pesci–Jack Haley– Bill Cosby–Bob Hope

One night Arlene and I had dinner plans with Joe Pesci. He told us that he had to stop off at a restaurant to pay his respects to a friend who was having a small birthday dinner and asked if we would meet him early and join him for the visit. We arrived at the restaurant to find a few people, including the singer Frankie Valli, sitting at a table with a man wearing dark sunglasses. Joe introduced us to everyone, including the man whose birthday they were celebrating, named Jimmy Blue Eyes. It felt like a scene out of the movie *The Godfather*. We only stayed for drinks, while Joe and Frankie toasted Jimmy on his birthday.

Years later, Arlene and I attended a performance of *Jersey Boys* on Broadway. There is a scene in which Frankie Valli is involved with a mob guy named Jimmy Blue Eyes. We whispered to each other that this show's story is apparently real because we had seen Frankie with Jimmy and Joe at the restaurant. At that moment, an actor playing Joe Pesci entered the scene, and we realized that indeed this story was accurate. We attended the performance with Neil and Leba Sedaka. To further compound our experience that night, another character briefly appeared onstage portraying Neil. In the scene, the record company executive tells the group that Frankie is a good singer, but he is no Neil Sedaka.

On December 15, 1985, we had another memorable dinner with Joe Pesci, celebrating his mother's birthday. Gina Lollobrigida was staying with us, and she joined us at that dinner along with the actor Robert Duvall and a handsome young cinematographer friend of Duvall named Barry Markowitz. We admired Duvall's work and enjoyed being with him. There was some flirting between Gina and Barry, and contact information was shared, but nothing much happened afterward between them.

Pesci is an interesting and fun guy, but he has had some strange personal relationships over the years. One of his ex-wives married a Hollywood stuntman who was murdered at his front door. It turned out that she was accused of hiring a hit man to kill him, and she was arrested. We were shocked because we always liked her and found her to be quite nice. Joe stood by her during the trial probably because he still had feelings for her.

Pesci loves to sing and has made a few albums. He has played some tracks for us from an album that he wanted to record, singing only in Italian, but that didn't happen. Years later, he made an album called *Vincent LaGuardia Gambini Sings Just for You*. The idea originated from his character in the movie *My Cousin Vinny*. At one time, he had talked to me about joining him and Paul Herman as partners in opening up a small piano bar in a location on the Upper West Side where Joe could hang out with friends and sing. That never happened because Joe soon became a huge movie star. As for today, Joe would rather just play golf.

When Jack Haley's movie *That's Dancing!* opened in January 1985, we joined Jack, both in New York City and Los Angeles, for the red-carpet openings. There was a huge opening in Los Angeles, followed by a black-tie party at the Beverly Hilton Hotel. Many Hollywood celebrities attended. We were excited to spend time with two of the most iconic movie stars from the MGM musicals, Fred Astaire and Gene Kelly. They both could not have been nicer, except we felt a little sorry for Fred, who seemed to be dominated by his young wife.

The New York celebration on January 14 for the movie was unusually exciting. It was shown at the Ziegfeld Theater, and a red carpet was stretched across Broadway, from the theater to the opening night party at a hotel. Jack's ex-wife Liza came with Mark Gero, and they sat at a different table from us. Liza and Jack remained friends after the termination of their marriage, and Jack cast her as one of the hosts in the film. Jack brought Lindsay Wagner as his date to the event. We sat with them at his table, along with Henry and Ginny Mancini, Marvin Hamlisch and Cyndy Garvey (whom Marvin was dating at the time), and Bob Fosse and his daughter, Nicole.

That same year, Jack invited us to an AIDS charity dinner in Los Angeles. We sat at a great table with Jack, Connie Stevens, Elizabeth Taylor, Burt Reynolds, Loni Anderson, Altovise Davis, and Lorna Luft. (I should apologize for all the name-dropping in this book, but being with many of these people was just so darn interesting. It brings to mind the very witty comment Tony Danza makes in his nightclub act when he announces to the audience, "I was told not to name-drop by my buddy Bobby De Niro.")

In 1988, we traveled with Sammy Davis Jr. on a tour that he did with Bill Cosby called "Two Friends." Each night they would alternate which performer went on first and last. It was a really fun experience for us. After every show, we went out with Sammy, and Bill went his own way most nights.

As a periodontist, I did gum surgery on most of my patients. In those days, we used cassette tapes. I recorded tapes for my patients so they could hear me describe each step of their treatment. Most tapes that I had them listen to were serious explanations of what the upcoming procedure would be. The most apprehensive visit for everyone was their first surgery, so the tape I would give them describing what to expect on that day was different.

Bill Cosby had created an extremely funny routine about a patient getting a local anesthetic injection in the dentist's office. It was a five-minute piece and hysterical, so I thought to include it at the start of my tape. I would observe each patient nervously listen to the tape and then burst into bright smiles when they heard Cosby's routine. It helped relax them, and then my regular instructions followed on that tape, and I was able to begin my procedure on a much less nervous patient.

When Cosby and Sammy performed each night on the tour, Arlene and I would go to Sammy's room after the show. Then we would all go to Bill's room to say good night. As captivating as Bill was onstage, we did not find him to be very warm or overfriendly. I thought he would be flattered to hear how much I loved his dentist routine and how I used his humor to relax my patients. Instead, he informed me that he was not happy that my patients were listening to his tapes because he did not want them to associate him with dental discomfort. Needless to say, we did not develop a close friendship with Cosby on that tour. I observed that outside their time onstage and the formalities of saying good night to each other after the show, Sammy and Bill went their separate ways when the performance ended each evening.

The years at Studio 54 were magical. It was one continuous party, filled each night with a mix of crazy characters, along with every celebrity who arrived in NYC. Many nights had different themed parties, and you never knew who you would see there. One night Arlene was dressed in all black with a very sexy shiny top, pants, and hat. As we were dancing, we noticed Bob Hope dancing to the disco beat by himself. Bob Hope dancing by himself at Studio 54 was not something we expected to see. I dared Arlene to join him, even though we didn't know him. There were large crepe paper streamers that were cascading down from the ceiling to the floor that night. I stood to the side watching as Arlene danced over to Bob Hope and started to dance with him. We knew about his reputation as a ladies' man, and Arlene, as she danced around him, began wrapping him with the streamers. He was smiling with anticipation at this sexy young girl teasing him. She continually kept wrapping him while they danced, until he looked like a mummy. At the end of the song, she calmly danced away from him. She left him standing there, wrapped up and unable to move.

In 2003, we were invited over to Bob Hope's home in Toluca Lake, California, with our friend Ginny Mancini. (We thought about having Arlene dress in black and bring streamers to remind him of our previous meeting at Studio 54 but thought that, at his age, the excitement might kill him.) His wife, Dolores, was a wonderful hostess and showed us around the enormous home. We never got to see him again because he was one hundred years old and not up to visiting with company that day, so we never brought up what Arlene did to him decades earlier.

CHAPTER

FORTY-SEVEN

Bette Midler–Ron Delsener–Barbra Streisand–Regis Philbin

Bette Midler started her career singing in the Continental Baths, a gay bathhouse in the Ansonia Hotel in 1970. Her piano player and arranger was Barry Manilow. In 1973, Arlene and I went to a club in Downtown Manhattan called the Upstairs at the Downstairs, and an unknown Bette was singing there. We thought she was an amazing talent.

The following evening we were having dinner at Elaine's Restaurant with Ron Delsener, who was becoming the top promoter in New York City. Ron would get us tickets to all his shows at venues like Madison Square Garden and invite us backstage afterward. I reciprocated the favors by having him come over to my apartment and sit down in my bathroom, and I would cauterize the frequent canker sores he would get. We have had many good times backstage with the entertainers he booked.

He invited us to see a young talent who, he said, was going to be a big star. It was Elton John, and he was very friendly backstage at his first Madison Square Garden performance, playfully slapping Arlene on the backside. Another time after a Beach Boys show, one of them tried to hit on Arlene. He was shocked when Arlene showed no interest because they were constantly being mobbed by female fans. One time when Gina Lollobrigida was staying with us, we took her to see the Rolling Stones at Madison Square Garden. Ron told us that the Stones wanted to meet Gina, and he set aside a room so we could all spend time together before the concert. We spent a long time with them as they were fascinated with Gina, and we were fascinated with them.

During dinner with Ron at Elaine's, we mentioned that we had seen this fabulous entertainer the previous night. When we told him her name was Bette Midler, he said he had never heard of her. After hearing our raves, Ron remarked that he would like to go see her and observe for himself. Elaine's had paper cocktail napkins at the bar, Ron asked the waiter to bring one over, and he wrote her name on the napkin. A few nights later, he went to see her perform. The following year, Ron produced her first show on Broadway called *Clams on the Half Shell*. We always felt that we had some part in her success. Her talent was immense, but sometimes you just need the right promoter to see you and recognize it.

A few months after seeing Bette perform at the club in NYC, Arlene and I were in Las Vegas on vacation. Johnny Carson was headlining at one of the hotels, and Bette Midler was his opening act. We were excited to see her perform again and went to the show. She was completely unknown at that time, and the crowd did not react well toward her. They had come to see Johnny Carson and had no interest in seeing this eccentric young girl. Many people were rudely yelling, "We want Johnny," during her performance. We loved what she did, but it was an uncomfortable experience for her as the crowd never showed her any respect. She kept telling them that she would only be on for a short time and that Johnny would be out soon.

In the late 1970s, Bette was starting to become well known in New York City. Lorna Luft was friendly with Bette, and we would often see Bette at various parties that we would go to with Lorna. Bette was going out with a guy for a long time named Aaron Russo. He booked and managed a number of entertainers, including Bette. He was a charming man but a very strong personality. His relationship with Bette was quite abusive, and eventually, they broke up. They seemed to have a rocky relationship, and we witnessed heated arguments between them. Bette would be in good spirits, and we would all have fun until Aaron would say something to get her upset. Aaron told me that he wanted to run for president of the United States but felt that his stance on legalizing all drugs would be a hindrance. He enjoyed promoting drugs, as well as doing them, and definitely had mood swings. I lost track of him but heard that he did produce a documentary against the government's war on drugs, and he even tried to run for governor of Nevada. In 2004, he declared his candidacy for the president of the United States as a Libertarian. He amazingly almost won the nomination to be their candidate but lost on the third ballot.

When I was a teenager, my parents occasionally took me to a most unusual restaurant called Lucky Pierre's. If you ordered steak, the owner would come to your table with a blowtorch and cook it at the table. He did not have a liquor license, but if he knew the customer, he brought you into a back room and served alcohol in coffee cups. The backroom had a small piano and a number of tables. Unknown young performers would come in and entertain the customers for tips. One night a very young girl dressed in thrift store clothing came in to sing. I remembered her name because she was unbelievably talented, and my parents and I were blown away by her singing. Her name was Barbra Streisand.

A few years later, we went to a small nightclub in Greenwich Village called Bon Soir. Each night they had three acts; the last act was the headliner. When my parents took me to Bon Soir, Barbra was the opening act. We went to hear her sing a few times after that, and in a very short time, she moved up to the second act and then to the headliner. She was very bohemian and unique and was already doing the wonderful versions of songs that she is known for today. Over the years, her concerts have become very well organized and rehearsed. To me, she was at her best in those days when she was kooky and unconstrained.

I saw her in 2012 at a memorial for Marvin Hamlisch that she organized along with Marvin's wife, Terre. She sang, along with Liza Minnelli, Aretha Franklin, and others. Whenever I see Barbra at an event, she always looks so serious, a far cry from that young girl I remember.

Terre and Marvin Hamlisch lived near us for a while in Westhampton, and we enjoyed Terre's company. We have lost contact with her since Marvin's death, and she has moved out of our area. Marvin and Liza Minnelli were great friends as teenagers, and he even wrote a song as a teenager for her, which was on her first album. It was great fun being around the two of them, and Marvin was at his most charming self in her presence.

Regis Philbin and his wife Joy were a couple whom we have spent time with over the years. We always enjoyed their company but never developed a very close friendship. He has always been a very popular personality, starring in many TV shows. Regis and Joy loved attending New York events, and we ran into them often, most recently when Tony Danza did a wonderful cabaret act at the Carlyle Hotel in New York. (On a separate note, my family and I returned to the Carlyle the following year when Tony was performing on my birthday, which is a day before my daughter's birthday. Regis was not there that night, but Tony sang "Happy Birthday" to me and Lauren in the middle of his act and sent over a cake and champagne to our table.)

In later years, Regis and Joy would occasionally do a nightclub act together. Our friend Herb Bernstein arranged the music and accompanied them. We had a lot of laughs hanging out with them before and after their performances as they jokingly blamed each other for any mistakes made during the show.

Before Donald Trump became involved in politics, they often flew down with him to Mar-a-Lago. They loved to play tennis. In the winter, we spent a lot of time staying in Palm Beach with our friends Moira and Jon Fiore. They were the best couples tennis players at Mar-a-Lago, and Regis and Joy liked to play with them. I filled in when either Moira or Jon couldn't play. Regis and Joy were not at our level, so they would split up, each partner with one of us. Regis was very competitive and loved to win. We, of course, went easy on him, and they enjoyed their tennis matches at the club.

Regis loved to talk about himself in the first person. He would win a point and yell out, "Good shot, Regis!" Or he'd say, "Great try, Regis." We always had a lot of laughs with them and regretted that his busy work schedule didn't allow us time to become closer friends. We felt sad about his recent passing, but he lived a full and successful life.

CHAPTER

FORTY-EIGHT

Some Very Interesting Friends

I met my friend Albie when he came to my office for periodontal treatment. He listed his occupation as trucking, and I assumed that he was a truck driver. I gave him a low fee because I thought, as a truck driver, he may be limited in what he could afford. When I quoted a fee to him for the four months of work that I had to do, he reached into his pocket and pulled out a wad of hundred-dollar bills. He immediately paid the bill in full. I thought to myself that maybe he was not just a truck driver. He had a rough exterior but had a very affable personality.

On one of his later visits to my office, the nurse informed me that there was a telephone call for me from the Friars Club. I had applied for membership and was waiting to hear from them about an interview with the new members' committee. Albie heard me talking on the phone and asked me when my interview was scheduled.

I couldn't understand why this truck driver had any interest in the Friars Club, which was known for having many famous entertainers as members. When I told him the date of my interview, he simply said, "Don't worry, you are in, and I will see you at the meeting." That was when I realized that he was more than what he appeared to be. I was immediately accepted into the club, and from then on, Arlene and I were at the best table for every Friars event as Albie's guests.

Albie had a gravelly voice and crude manner, but he was a wonderful and extremely likable person. His driver would pick us up in a large gold Rolls-Royce. When we arrived at an event or a restaurant, Albie would give the gun he always carried with him to his driver while we went inside. (For that reason, I never discussed details of his trucking business with Albie.) He also bought the nightclub El Morocco and converted part of it into a restaurant called Elmer's.

He loved to gamble and once took us to Atlantic City with him. They gave him the largest suite that I have ever seen. We had seen beautiful suites when we traveled with entertainers, but the suites given to the high rollers far surpass those. There was a separate dining room in the suite, and a chef was present all day to make whatever foods he desired. Lauren was close friends with his daughter, who was the same age and would often hang out in her wing of the suite. In it was an aqua massage chamber where one would lie down inside and hear music and nature sounds while getting massaged by water from all angles. The modes could be changed from the spray shower to a steam bath and also to a sauna. I thought it was very unusual to have an apparatus inside one's room, but that just shows how decked out Albie's suites were.

One time when the girls were about eleven years old, Albie's daughter got into an argument with her mother, who didn't like the way her daughter was speaking to her, so the punishment was that she was going to ride home in a separate limo without her parents. However, they suggested for Lauren to go with her, so we just followed them. Lauren said that she had the best time in the private limo because it was fully stocked with candy, chips, cookies, and soda, and there was a large selection of movies for them to watch. I wished that I had that kind of punishment growing up.

When Albie decided that he was ready to gamble, two security people accompanied us to the casino. Albie went over to the crap table and put down $10,000 in chips on every roll. He would only play for about twenty minutes. If he lost everything, we would go back to the room alone. If he won, he would be accompanied by the security people back to his room because he would be carrying a lot of cash.

There is a famous restaurant in New York City called Rao's. It is the toughest reservation in the country. The man who ran it, Frankie, was known as "Frankie No" because he turned down everyone who called for a reservation. It is on 114th Street and First Avenue and has many mob people as clients. Rao's only has a few tables, and the regulars have their tables on certain nights for the entire year. If a well-known person wants to dine there, they have to be invited to sit with a regular. The result is a mixture of mob types and celebrities.

They have a jukebox, and people get up and sing on occasion. A few years ago, a woman started to sing, and a young guy who had too much to drink began to heckle her. An old-time gangster stood up, went over to the heckler, and told him that was no way to treat a woman. He then took out his gun and shot him in front of everybody. When the police arrived, the gunman calmly explained that he did it because he was brought up to respect women.

When we walked into Rao's with Albie, they sat us at the bar, informing us that a table would be available soon. Albie got into a discussion with the bartender about a recent funeral for a well-known mob guy. When Albie told him that he was a pallbearer at the funeral, the bartender was very impressed, and we were immediately seated at a prime table.

Rao's is owned by an Italian family, and the mother was the main cook. One year when Gina Lollobrigida was staying with us, Arlene went shopping with her at Bloomingdale's. A woman came over to them and said that she was the owner of Rao's and a fan of Gina's. She invited them to come to Rao's, and I joined them along with our son, Marc. There is no real menu, but the waiter pulls up a chair and sits down at your table. He then tells you the selection of foods they have for the night and takes your order. It is a real New York experience.

Through Albie, I met another unusual character. His name was Frankie Gio, and he has appeared in many movies as a gangster. He complained to me one night at dinner that he was getting bored with his movie roles. He remarked that he shoots someone in the scene, and then they get up and all go together to lunch. He missed the good old days when he could shoot someone in real life, and they didn't get up. I never knew whether he was serious or kidding.

One New Year's Eve, we were with our children in Florida, and Albie invited us to join him and some friends to celebrate New Year's Eve with them. We had a long table, and Frankie Gio and his wife were included in our party. There was another long table near ours with a few Arab couples and their children. The children at the other table were fooling around and kept throwing things, some of which would occasionally land on our table. Frankie got up, walked over to the other table, and asked them to please control their children. (Perhaps his language may have been a little stronger than that.) It stopped for a while, but a short time later, the children once again were throwing things.

Arlene was sitting next to Albie's wife and Frankie's wife. They calmly explained to Arlene that a fight might break out soon if the children did not stop their bad behavior. She explained to Arlene that she and the other women back up their husbands in a fight. They taught Arlene how to take a bottle of liquor on the table, break it on the side of the table, and then use it as a weapon in the fight. Frankie calmly got up from the table and walked over to the man at the head of the Arab family. He threatened, "If one more item hits our table, you will all be dead people." Fortunately, that seemed to be enough to quiet them down, and we were spared the experience of a fight. That was our last New Year's Eve experience with that group.

Frankie was actually a very nice guy and fun to be around. All the actors loved him because he was the real deal. He and his wife had a home near us in Westhampton, and Frankie played tennis at the same club as me. I frankly was a better tennis player and never assigned by the club to play doubles with him. One day as I was leaving, he came up to me and asked if I would like to play a game of singles with him. I was heading home, but I didn't want to insult him and say no. My game is one of strategy; I hit the ball where my opponent isn't. Frankie's game is to serve as hard as he could and then come racing to the net. Each time he did that, I simply lobbed the ball over his head. When we would rally and he would hit a very hard ball at me, I would just do a drop shot and win the point. I won the first five games. As we were crossing sides and passed each other, Frankie looked at me and said, "If you give me one more drop shot, you are a dead man." I didn't know if he was making a joke or serious; however, I decided to let Frankie win the match.

When Tina and Michael Chow opened their restaurant Mr. Chow in London, it became the hottest place in the city. Lorna became very friendly with them when she was living in London. When they opened the branch of Mr. Chow in New York City, we went with Lorna, and she introduced them to us. They became a very popular couple in New York City, and they had a little girl named China Chow. We had some fun times with them, and one day we set up a playdate with our daughters since they were both three years old.

They had a very interesting apartment on East Fifty-Seventh Street above their restaurant. The layout of the apartment was somewhat spooky, almost like out of a scary movie. They had just moved in, and there were no window guards. While we were all talking in the living room, we suddenly noticed that China and Lauren had left their tea party and crawled up onto the window ledge in one of the curved areas of the room. We told them both not to move and quickly grabbed them off the ledge. It was a very strange apartment with many nooks and crannies, and that was the last playdate we had there.

We were close friends with a charming guy named Prince Egon von Furstenberg. He and his wife, Diane, became famous in 1973 when *New York* magazine ran a cover story about them. It was called "The Couple That Has Everything" and described their jet-setting lives and infidelities. Egon was born into wealth and nobility, but he was far from a good businessman. He was a sociable guy and lived only to have a good time. He attended our son Marc's bar mitzvah and danced all night. They had two children together, but the marriage only lasted four years, and they separated. They divorced ten years after the separation.

Diane is a hardworking and shrewd businesswoman, the opposite of Egon. She made the most of the von Furstenberg name and the princess title that came with it. She formed a company using her name and introduced her signature wrap dress, and a fashion empire was born. Both of them had many affairs and were regulars at Studio 54. Diane had a long friendship with the openly gay and extremely wealthy Barry Diller. They eventually married and have been together for many years. Egon was bisexual and very promiscuous and, unfortunately, passed away at age fifty-eight.

We met many interesting people in our days at Studio 54. We spent a lot of time at Studio 54 with Chita Rivera's daughter, Lisa Mordente. Lisa was hanging around with Liza a great deal at that time, and we had enjoyable times together. We had been good friends with Chita for many years, and when Lisa got married in June 1983, we were invited to the wedding. It was a fabulous wedding at an elegant nightclub in the theater district called the Supper Club. She married a fellow performer named Donnie Kehr, and he wrote and performed a song to her on the stage of the club. It was a marvelous party, but the marriage did not last.

Joanne Horowitz was a young girl just starting out in public relations when I met her. Studio 54 hired her, along with a few other PR people, to induce celebrities to come to the club. She was paid in a most unusual way. The club set a monetary amount for each celebrity. If they came to the club, she would be paid accordingly. One name may be worth $50, another may be worth $100, and so on. The money was a huge incentive for those PR people to bring celebrities to the club. The celebrities were treated royally; there was a basement area where special celebrities would have access to drugs of their choice. Arlene and I could be hanging out with celebrities at the club, but if any of them were invited down to the basement, we were never allowed to go with them. They could do what they pleased in private and return upstairs to the club whenever they wanted.

We spent a lot of time with Joanne at the club because she was there most nights. She met and became friendly with a struggling young actor. He had no place to sleep, so she let him sleep on her couch until he could find work. He asked her to become his manager, and she started finding him work. His name was Kevin Spacey, and she remained his manager throughout all his successful career. She arranged the deals for all his movies and shows and for his breakthrough Netflix series *House of Cards*. *House of Cards* was the first original series on Netflix, and its success was the beginning of the rise of Netflix. Their long-term business relationship ended two years before his sexual scandals.

Myra Scheer was in charge of handling the celebrities at Studio 54. Arlene and I have remained good friends with her over the years. She now has a regular show on Sirius radio, along with the former main doorman at the club, Marc Benecke. It revolves around Studio 54 and disco music. Arlene and I have been invited on air a few times to discuss our experiences at Studio 54.

Yeh Jong Son ran the inside access to Studio 54. When the club closed, we invited her to our apartment one night. Our son, Marc, was eight years old at that time. Marc was a terrific boy and very easygoing. Unfortunately, he was sometimes bullied in school and was not a fighter. Yeh Jong was small and thin. Marc was still up when she was at our apartment and came out to tell us about a boy who was picking on him in school. Yeh Jong informed Marc that her father was in charge of a Tae Kwon Do school in Korea and taught her self-defense. She advised Marc that he should learn how to protect himself as she went into a karate stance and did some quick moves. Marc marveled at this little woman who suddenly looked fierce and strong. It turned out to be an experience that changed his life.

The following week, he signed up for a Tae Kwon Do class and started taking lessons regularly. This formerly shy boy suddenly developed self-confidence. A year later, he was at a friend's birthday party. He did not know any of the other boys, and they started to gang up on him. Marc was taught in karate class to avoid conflict if possible, so he ran into the bathroom and locked himself inside. When they started banging on the door, he opened it, and they charged at him. He went into his karate stance, blocked the first boy's punch, hit him in the face, and knocked out his front baby tooth. The rest of the boys stopped and ran away. When we heard what happened, we called the boy's mother to apologize. However, she told us that her son was wrong and deserved what Marc did and that we should be proud of him. Marc was never bullied again and became a second-degree black belt, even forming his own karate school while he was at college.

For several years, we traveled to Gstaad, Switzerland, for a Ciné Music Festival. Our friends Leslie Bricusse and Jack Haley Jr. organized it each year. It highlighted the importance of music in film. An outstanding movie would be shown, both with and without the musical score. It was quite a change when viewing movies without a musical soundtrack. We had fascinating evenings with many noted composers of musical scores for the movies. We would watch some of the great films of all time lose their impact when the music was left out. Henry Mancini, John Barry, Elmer Bernstein, John Williams, and Dave Raksin were some of the composers who attended the event and spent time with us. Watching the marvelous movie *Laura* without Dave Raksin's amazing musical score totally diminishes the film. Watching a James Bond movie without John Barry's fabulous music vitiates much of the excitement. It was so interesting to spend time with these talented composers as they explained their method of scoring films. One year Liza Minnelli joined us, and Leslie arranged for a memorable raclette dinner. (Raclette is a Swiss dish of melted cheese.) We never had time to expand our friendships with most of these composers because they were always working and didn't live in NYC.

CHAPTER

FORTY-NINE

Studio 54 and Other Clubs

In the late '70s and early '80s, there were many terrific clubs that usually became active at midnight and stayed open until the early morning hours. Studio 54 was our favorite, and we got to know the owner, Steve Rubell, quite well. Steve's father was a tennis instructor, and Steve was a very good tennis player. We used to occasionally play tennis at around 4:00 p.m. Mark Gero and Steve would play against Steve's dad and me. We had to play at that hour because that was the time that Steve was able to function after late nights at his club. Steve was taking a great amount of quaaludes, and he was often wasted. I would see a busboy at 4:00 a.m. wheeling him around the club while he was sitting in a small red wagon. Miraculously, by late afternoon the following day, he was able to play a competitive game of tennis.

His partner, Ian Schrager, was rarely seen at the club. We did not know him at all during those days. Ironically, after Ian was released from jail, his dentist referred him to me for periodontal work. He needed gum surgery, and I closed the office for the day and did his entire mouth in one sitting. I found him to be a very nice guy, and he has since built a huge hotel empire. Ian's father was involved in mob activities and was associated with Meyer Lansky. His nickname was Max the Jew Schrager. Ian graduated from law school, and there was no proof of any mob involvement in his clubs. One time in my dental office, Robert De Niro was in one room; and at the same time, Ian was in another room for a cleaning. De Niro was working on a film project about a lawyer involved with the mob and was curious to meet Ian. Ian declined the meeting.

There were many other interesting clubs in New York City during that time. After Studio 54 closed in the early '80s, Rubell and Schrager opened up a beautiful club on Fourteenth Street called the Palladium. We went there often, and it was dramatically decorated but never captured the excitement of Studio 54. Many small clubs became popular, drawing a crowd at 3:00 a.m. after Studio 54 wound down. There was the Mudd Club, Crisco Disco, Roxy Roller Rink, Heartbreak, Club A, and Xenon. Crisco Disco was very popular and was named after its DJ booth, which was shaped in the form of a can of Crisco shortening. (Crisco was often used by gay men as a lubricant. The high-level energy of gay men mixing in with the straight crowds in these years was a key element in the success of many after-hours clubs. The tragic AIDS epidemic in the mid-'80s led to the downfall of many of the clubs, and we lost many friends. We didn't travel downtown often to these clubs and only did so if we were with a celebrity who would guarantee that we would get in.)

One night Liza was invited to an after-hours club, and we went with her. After we navigated our way past the doorman and entered the club, the owner met us and brought us to the dance floor. It was quite active, and the owner mentioned a more private area that he wanted to show us. A bouncer was standing by a door at the side of the room, and he opened it and let us in. It was a small club within the main club. There were a capacity for about twenty people, a very small dance floor, and a bar area with a very chic-looking group of people. We had a drink in this very exclusive club within a club, and then the owner pointed to a door and told us to come with him. We entered a very tiny room, just big enough for the four of us, beautifully decorated with a tiny bar. We had reached the ultimate exclusive area of a club within a club within a club.

Another place that had a long exclusive history in New York City was Le Club and was run by a man named Patrick. He handpicked the very chic membership of people from all over the world. One evening I received a call at home from a friend who was a member of the club. She explained that Patrick was suffering from a gum abscess and asked if I could help him. I kept some instruments at home, picked out a few, and took a taxi over to the club. Patrick was very tall, about six feet six inches. I had him sit on a chair in his private office. I brought a small flashlight, and I was able to see the gum abscess, which I punctured and drained. He became a patient, and from then on, I had VIP access to Le Club.

During our evenings at Studio 54, we socialized with many different people. They would tell us about other clubs and invite people to join them. One night a few people were heading to an after-hours club and asked if we wanted to meet them there after we left Studio 54. We wrote down the address and took a taxi over to the club. We walked in and observed a dance floor with a circular bar in the center. We did not see the people who had told us about the club, so we went to the bar, sat down, and ordered a drink. A nice-looking couple was sitting next to us at the bar, and we were all watching people dancing by. We heard the guy ask the girl to dance, and we watched them head to the dance floor. We noticed that she had a leather necklace with a long chain. He was leading her onto the dance floor, pulling the chain. We now began observing the dancers on the floor and recognized a lot of S-M outfits. We paid for our drinks, realized this was not a club that we were interested in, and started to leave.

As we were walking out, we saw the couples who had told us about the club sitting at a table. We wondered if they knew what a weird crowd this club had because they looked pretty normal sitting there, having drinks. As they got up from the table to greet us, we saw that none of them had anything on below the waist. We explained that our babysitter called us and we had to get home, and we left there quickly.

Even though we were all strangers at Studio 54 and didn't know anything about most people there, we felt a bond. There was an eighty-year-old lady who danced there every night named Disco Sally.

When she married a thirty-year-old bartender at the club, we were all invited to the wedding, which took place at Studio 54. A popular male character who came every night in a dress and roller skates was known as Rollerena. We found out he was a stockbroker during the day.

One night a couple announced to a group of us that they were getting married the following weekend. They invited all of us to stop by the reception at a New York hotel. We thought it sounded like fun. On the day of the wedding, we walked over to the hotel and entered just as the groom was toasting the bride. He then told everybody to please enjoy the celebration, and the bride and groom proceeded to walk through the room, kissing all the guests of both sexes. Then everyone began to get up and started kissing and groping their neighbors. We suddenly realized that we were at a swingers wedding. As the newlyweds approached us, we quickly explained that we just stopped by to congratulate them for ten minutes on the way to another appointment. We ran out of there, and as we glanced behind us, we saw people forming passionate groups on the floor.

CHAPTER

FIFTY

Interactions with Well-Known People

My first encounter with a famous person was at age six when my parents took me out with them for New Year's Eve. Barry Gray was considered to be the father of talk radio and was doing his radio show live from the restaurant that we were dining in. During his broadcast, he called me up to chat with him. He asked what I wanted to be when I grew up. I answered that I wanted to be a dentist like my father because "he seems to make a lot of money, and it looks like a good racket to me." Fortunately, my embarrassed father had a good sense of humor and laughed along with the crowd.

As an adult, I have had many interesting interactions with well-known people over the years. Arlene and I spent many hours at the bar area of Studio 54 with the terrific country singer Tanya Tucker.

331

She was a hoot and could drink and curse with the best of them. She was really fun to be around and wound up having a very tumultuous relationship with Glen Campbell.

Another interesting personality that we spent time with at Studio was Dodi Fayed. His father was the owner of Harrods department store in London, and he was a cousin of Adnan Khashoggi, who was the world's richest man at that time. Our friend Nabila Khashoggi was both a relative and close friend of Dodi. We have many memories of good times in his company. He produced some movies, notably *Chariots of Fire*, but was more known for his romance with Princess Diana. His sudden death in the car crash with Diana was a shock to us all and so unfortunate because he was someone who loved life so much. Nabila's brother, Mohammed Khashoggi, was dating the *Entertainment Tonight* star Mary Hart. She had a great personality, and we enjoyed fun dinners with them both.

My encounter with Tom Jones was a brief one. On the first day of my membership at the New York Friars Club, I decided to visit the steam room. There was one other person in the steam room, and it was Tom Jones. He was quite the sex symbol at that time, and many women would have been happy to be in my place at that moment.

One night friends invited us to their apartment for a dinner party, and we were seated with Ted Kennedy and his sister Eunice. I was surprised to find him not much of a conversationalist, and I was not impressed with his intellect. I left that evening feeling happy that he did not become president because he just did not seem very sharp to me. However, it could have been that he just was not that interested in conversing with me about anything of substance.

When I was spending time with Jackie Mason, he invited me to join him at a bachelor party for a young comedian friend of his. It was not too exciting because it was just a bunch of guys standing around, watching a few strippers. Then of all people, Al Sharpton walked in by himself and joined our group. Reverend Al was already quite the activist at that time, and he was the last person I would expect to see at a bachelor party with a bunch of young white Jewish guys.

One day I was walking up Madison Avenue with Jackie Mason, and Paul Anka was coming down the street toward us. We stopped to chat, and Paul informed Jackie that he had become a part owner of a casino in Atlantic City. Paul told Jackie that if he wanted to come and work at his casino on the weekend, Paul would be happy to book him.

We walked away, and Jackie explained that Paul was trying to act like a big shot and impress him by announcing that he was a part owner of the casino. Jackie knew that certain casinos pay regular performers in such a way that their contract has them listed as a fractional owner, but that is just for tax purposes. Paul just wanted to show Jackie that he was the boss and that less important entertainers could work for him.

Some celebrities whom we have met were not particularly friendly. Spike Lee and Tyra Banks were two people who acted like they were too important to talk to us when we were invited to the same social gathering as them. Some like Dionne Warwick we found downright rude. Dionne and a friend were sitting in the first two seats downstairs at a Michael Jackson concert at Madison Square Garden. We were with Gina Lollobrigida as Michael's guests and sitting in the third, fourth, and fifth seats off the aisle. Arlene wanted to go to the ladies' room before the show started and excused herself to go past Dionne and her friend. Dionne rudely said to Arlene that she didn't like to be disturbed and that if Arlene had to go again later to the bathroom, she should go out to her left. That meant walking about thirty seats down, instead of the two seats to the aisle on her right.

We recently were at an event at the Ninety-Second Street Y in New York City, where Dionne was one of the participants. Two women were waiting outside the door to ask to take a picture with her. Arlene and I stopped to observe if she would be pleasant to them to see if maybe we had encountered her on a bad day in the past. Dionne exited the door, curtly told the two women that she had no time, and got into a car. She might just be friendlier to children because when we were at Sammy Davis's house in LA one night for a party, she did sit down and play a tabletop arcade game with our daughter, Lauren, who was about ten years old at the time.

One night we were having dinner with Lorna Luft at Elaine's Restaurant, and David Merrick, the Broadway producer, was walking out. Lorna had been in one of his shows and said hello. He was with his wife, and when Lorna introduced us to him, he replied, "This is my wife, Mrs. Merrick." Maybe he just forgot her first name?

One night Liza was invited to a small screening room by Harvey Weinstein for a showing of his new movie and brought us along. We were amazed at how everyone catered to him. There was obvious fear of upsetting him in any way, and we observed each person playing up to him. It was one of the few times we were afraid to talk to each other during a movie.

Luci Arnaz is someone we have met on many occasions because she is a friend of Lorna, and her musical conductor, Ron Abel, is a good friend of ours. Onstage, she is a warm and bubbly personality. Offstage, we have found her to be somewhat cold and unfriendly. Liza, before her marriage to Jack Haley, had a romantic involvement with her brother, Desi Arnaz Jr. We found him kookie and fun.

Our close cousins who live in LA, Ellen and Paul Ganus, were friendly with the actor Dick Van Patten and his family. Dick is best known as the patriarch in the long-running ABC television comedy *Eight Is Enough*. Nancy Valen, who married Dick's son Nels, is one of Ellen's closest friends and best known for her role on the television show *Baywatch*. One of Dick's sons, Vincent, was a tennis pro, and I was invited over to their house to play doubles. Desi was one of the players. We started to warm up, and as usual, the other players underestimated me because I did not have the greatest tennis form. Desi made a few remarks about my form and chose to play against me. After I won easily, he was not happy and sulked, but that's tennis. On previous occasions, I always found him to be quite nice.

One of our closest friends appeared regularly on TV for many years. She was very attractive and became friendly with a major male television icon. He told her one day that he and his wife were having a party at their home. She was single, and he invited her to come by herself. They were a very prominent couple, married for many years. When she arrived at his apartment for the party, she discovered that she was the only guest, and his wife was not home. Rather than panic, she thought quickly. She looked him in the eye and told him that she was very flattered that he was interested in her. She calmly stated that she was looking forward to being with him and was excited to let his wife know that she would be moving in with him as soon as their divorce was finalized. The shocked star started to stammer and exclaimed that he only wanted a secret affair and had no idea it would become serious. He apologized to her and meekly let her out of his home. She never brought it up again with him. Their friendship changed, but they remained cordial to each other when they were at social occasions. I am not mentioning their names for obvious reasons but wanted to show an example of what women sometimes encounter.

David Niven Jr. is the son of the actor David Niven and was a close friend of Jack Haley. We had to spend a fair amount of time in his company while we were in LA, staying with Jack. We found him to have a sarcastic, nasty streak, but a number of people found him charming. We always felt that he had a problem living up to his name. One time when we were in Los Angeles with our eight-year-old daughter, Lauren, we took some friends out to celebrate her birthday. We asked Jack and Altovise to join us, and somehow Niven joined our group. David was so sarcastic to Lauren that he actually made the eight-year-old girl cry.

One time we were out with David, and Gina was with us. Gina knew David's father from her days in Hollywood and told David that she thought he looked like his dad. David responded that he didn't like her comment because he was adopted and that Gina should know better. Gina felt terrible that she had offended him. When we returned home and looked it up, we discovered that David was putting her on and was not adopted. He was just being a wise guy. Most people whom we have met over the years have been quite nice, and these few were the exceptions.

We have had many dinners at Elaine's Restaurant with interesting people. One night we had dinner with a young politician named Anthony Weiner. He impressed us and had a lot of charisma and charm. We all thought he had a bright future in politics. He unfortunately threw it all away with his strange sexual habits.

Another night, we were meeting our friend Georgia Witkin at the restaurant. She was single at the time and told us that she was bringing one of the sopranos to dinner. We were expecting a woman opera singer. Georgia walked in with a good-looking young guy whom people at Elaine's seemed to know. It turned out that he was a cast member on the hit TV series *The Sopranos*, which we had never seen. His name was Al Sapienza, his character was just killed, and he was celebrating his last appearance on the show. He was a very nice guy and not at all upset that we hadn't viewed the show. Our good friends Sheila Jaffe and Georgianne Walken were the people who cast the show, and we should have been watching it.

We did have a wonderful dinner with a real soprano a few months later. Lorna Luft met up with us at Elaine's and brought a friend to dinner. She was bright, attractive, and full of personality. Her name was Renée Fleming. She is one of the great lyric sopranos in the world and has been nominated for seventeen Grammy Awards. She also performed the national anthem at the Super Bowl. She has won many awards all over the world, and we have found her very down to earth and personable.

CHAPTER

FIFTY-ONE

My Early Years and Family

One of my early achievements was becoming president of Abraham Lincoln High School in Brooklyn. A senior student named Mort Shuman offered to be my campaign manager when I ran for office. He had a great personality and eventually wound up writing many of the top rock 'n' roll songs in history and was inducted into the Songwriters Hall of Fame. He also adapted the French lyrics of composer Jacques Brel into a successful show called *Jacques Brel Is Alive and Well and Living in Paris*. I lost contact with Mort, but I heard that this Jewish boy from Brighton Beach, Brooklyn, was living in Paris. He was performing songs from his show in French and was seen all around Paris wearing a beret with a girl on each arm.

While I was president of my high school, I arranged a rock 'n' roll dance at the end of the school year. The dean objected to rock 'n' roll because he felt that it was too decadent. I told him we would have a rhythm and blues dance instead, and that he agreed to. I learned that simply using the right wording was often the key to achieving what I wanted.

Another achievement in my youth was winning the best all-around athlete at my summer camp. I loved camp, except for one bad experience. My camp had an honor society called Blue Dragon. Most campers, after a few years, were selected to become a member, but I was one of the few who never made it. It was my only disappointment during my camp years. It turned out that one of the members of the nominating committee could blackball a person and prevent him from being invited into the honor society. Many years later, my closest friend from camp, whom I still saw occasionally, told me that he was living with guilt for many decades. He told me that he wanted to clear his conscience and informed me that he had been jealous of me, and he was the one who blackballed me each year. It was one of the life lessons about people that I never forgot.

My father was a dentist, and I followed in his footsteps, eventually becoming a periodontist. When I was in graduate school, I was offered a part-time position as an assistant professor of periodontics at NYU Dental School when I finished my studies. During my time there, I wrote a textbook called *Periodontal Therapy: A Review*. No one knew about it, and I submitted my manuscript to New York University Press for publication. The chairman of the Periodontal Department at NYU was a very major name in dentistry. One day he called me into his office and informed me that New York University Press had told him about my book. He explained to me that if I wanted to publish it, his name would have to be the first name on the book, and my name would be second. When I told him that he had nothing to do with the book and I did not agree, he informed me that he would stop me from teaching at the dental school. I walked out of his office and would not accept his proposal.

About a month later, I was called into the office of the dentist who was the assistant to the chairman of the department. He let me know that he had read my manuscript and loved it. I had told no one about my work and wondered how he knew. He explained that every department of the university had a secret person who was assigned the task by the New York University Press to read whatever manuscripts that are submitted. It turned out that he was the one who read all dental manuscripts. He approved it; it was published by the New York

University Press and became a standard textbook at NYU and many other dental schools around the country.

The dean fired the department chairman, the assistant who approved my book became the new chairman, and I was appointed a part-time assistant professor at the dental school. The experience became another of my life lessons. When I published the book, I dedicated it to my parents and the dentist who stood up for me and approved the publication. That dentist's name was George Witkin, and I eventually, by chance, became very close friends with his daughter, Georgia.

I always had an interest in the entertainment industry. While I was in school, I read that the very popular pope John Paul II had recorded an album of his teachings. I formed an impressive-sounding company and contacted the producers of the pope's album. I inquired about securing the rights to distribute the album in the Northeast. Surprisingly, they said yes. They would sell the albums to me for two dollars each, and I could make my own arrangements for distribution. I made up a very important-looking letterhead and sent out a letter to all the churches in the Northeast. I explained how the church could sell this album to its parishioners for fundraising. I would sell the album to them for $10, and they could charge their parishioners $19 or whatever they wished. Pope John Paul II was extremely popular, and their parishioners would have a treasured album of his spoken words, and the church would raise money for their needs.

A week after I sent out my letters, I heard from my first church. They wanted to place an order for ten thousand albums. I was ecstatic. I was going to be very wealthy, making $80,000 from the first church that I heard back from. I called the church to make arrangements for the shipping of the ten thousand albums. The person answering the phone had no idea what I was talking about. They came back to the phone to inform me that the minister only wanted to order one album to hear for himself and that there was an obvious misprint in the letter they sent me.

Over the next few weeks, I received an occasional letter requesting one album for them to hear, but not a single church was interested in my proposal. My thoughts seemed perfectly logical to me, but it turned out to be a valuable lesson on the importance of market research when you have a concept for a product. I learned that when you think you have a great idea, it is important to survey the public to see if they also think it is a good idea before manufacturing it. That helped me greatly when I later went into the mouthwash business. I also realized, when I actually listened to the album, that the pope only spoke in Latin. That was obviously an important reason why no church was interested in it.

I love to dance and was a good dancer. When I was in summer camp they put on shows a few times each season. I would be on stage by myself and very upbeat music would play and I would dance wildly. I imitated some of the dance steps I saw famous dancers do on television and made up some of my own. I always ended my performance by jumping off the stage. While I was in dental school, a friend told me that Arthur Murray was training people to become dance instructors. If I was good enough for them to accept me in their training program, I could get free dance instruction from experts at no charge. I went for an interview and did not tell them I was in dental school at that time. It was my school break, and I had a few weeks off. They started giving me personal, advanced dance instruction, and over the next ten days, I learned many steps to different ballroom dances. I had another week remaining to cram in as much knowledge as I could learn before telling them that I changed my mind about becoming a dance instructor. However, they informed me that because I was learning so fast, they had clients lined up for me to start teaching immediately. I left that day and never returned, but I did learn some great moves on the dance floor.

I was an only child, and I had a mother who was a worrier. When my children were teenagers, I introduced them to reruns of *The Honeymooners* TV show, starring the comedic genius Jackie Gleason. The shows were very popular, and fans occasionally gathered together at a venue for a *Honeymooners* convention. One Friday we were driving from New York City to our home in Westhampton during a rainstorm and decided to stop off at a venue where they were holding one of the *Honeymooners* conventions. My son, Marc, got up onstage along with many other fans dressed as the character Ed Norton and proceeded to enter a hucklebuck dance contest. We stayed a few hours before continuing on to our home, arriving there at about eleven o'clock.

It was before the days of cell phones, and our home telephone was ringing as we walked in. My mother was on the other end of the phone, and she sounded hysterical. She knew that we left at around seven o'clock and had been trying to contact us since nine because she was worried about us driving in the bad weather. When we didn't answer the phone, she started calling all the local hospitals and police precincts, wanting to find out if we had been in an accident. She told me that when she explained to the police operator that her son was late coming home, he asked her, "How old is your little boy?" When she answered that her little boy was forty-three, he laughed and hung up.

When I was a senior in high school and president of the school, I was pretty popular. There was a very attractive, very sought-after sophomore girl who lived two blocks from me, and I finally managed to make a date with her. I wanted to come across as a cool guy, so I put on my best outfit and walked over to her house for the date. Her parents answered the door and told me that she would be ready in a minute, and I tried to impress them with my most mature conversation. I was very excited and had planned a special evening. She appeared a minute later, and as I was saying my goodbyes to her parents, the phone rang in her house. Her mother answered it and announced that my mother was on the phone. My mother's message to me was that she heard that it might rain and asked if I wanted her to bring my galoshes over to their house. The girl turned away to hide her laughter. That was our first and last date.

I did meet a terrific girl that year and took her to my prom. She was quite different from the usual high school girls whom I had met. She lived in a different neighborhood in Brooklyn and was in show business. She was a dancer and part of a dance act called Phil Lawrence and Mitzi. They were performing regularly at the world-famous Copacabana nightclub in New York City as the opening act for big-name headliners. She invited me to see her perform, and I had my first early taste of show business. It was exciting sitting at the Copa and watching my date dance. After the show, I would mingle with her and the headliners backstage. Our relationship did not last long because she became involved romantically with Phil Lawrence and eventually married him.

I learned another one of my life's lessons that year while applying to college. I had a best friend, and we were both applying to Ivy League schools. He wanted to go to Yale, and I also applied to Yale, but Columbia College was my first choice because I wanted to remain in the New York City area. We both had two of the highest grade point averages in our class. His average was slightly higher than mine, but I had the advantage of being president of the school. His father was a big-shot type and knew how to pay off the right people at our high school.

One day, my college adviser called me into his office. He told me that he had seen my SAT Spanish language test results, and they were not good. He advised me that Yale would never accept a student with a poor test score in Spanish, and I should cancel my Yale application and only apply to Columbia. I knew that my best friend wanted to go to Yale, and they would probably only accept one student from my high school, so I canceled my application after hearing about my low language score.

The following year, when I attended Columbia and was asked to give them a list of courses that I was interested in taking, I picked Spanish for my language requirement. I was then informed that there was no need to take Spanish for my first-year language requirement because my SAT score in Spanish was so high that I could skip it and go directly into advanced Spanish the following year. My college admissions adviser was obviously influenced financially by my best friend's father. It was an early life lesson on the way the world sometimes works.

My college days were the usual mixture of studies combined with fun times. A fraternity brother of mine was invited by a blind date to go to the year-end gala dance at Bryn Mawr College. He was somewhat surprised that a blind date would invite him as her escort for that weekend's major event. He answered that he would go only if she would fix me up with one of her friends, and she did. The two girls arranged rooms for us, and we arrived to find ourselves with two extremely unattractive blind dates. Bryn Mawr was a dry campus and did not allow alcohol on campus in those days. We smuggled in a bottle of vodka and fortified ourselves for the evening ahead.

There was a large dance floor and a stage. The person in charge announced that the entertainment for the evening was a singing group from Yale called the Good Time Charlies. My friend and I yelled out, "That's us! We are here!" And we drunkenly climbed the steps onto the stage. The hostess of the event announced to the crowd that the Good Time Charlies had arrived, and everyone should be ready for great entertainment from this renowned singing group. They asked what our first song would be, and we told them that we would be singing a popular song at the time, "Five Foot Two, Eyes of Blue." Unfortunately, neither of us can sing a note, and we jumped around onstage singing off-key. The crowd at first thought that we were doing a comedy opening number but soon realized that we were impostors.

The hostess of the event came onstage with a security guard who escorted us out of the hall. The guard walked us to our rooms, watched us pack, and threw us off the campus. Two weeks later, we received a letter from Bryn Mawr College informing us that the school council had voted to bar us from ever entering the town of Bryn Mawr. We wrote back to the student council leaders saying that we had decided to bar them from ever entering New York City. It marked the end of my performing career.

While attending dental school, I had a girlfriend named Honey. She was quite attractive with a fun-loving personality. She was from Austria, and unfortunately, her father was a police chief during the time of the Nazis. He was not too pleased to have his daughter dating a Jewish boy. She couldn't care less and switched her cross to a Jewish star when she met my parents. I took her one night to the Playboy Club in New York City for dinner. She liked it so much that she became a playboy bunny, and her club name was Bunny Honey. She was being supported in New York City by a very famous married producer. He and his partner were major movie producers for many years, and he kept her in an apartment in New York City for which he paid all expenses. Her arrangement was that she had to spend one night a week with him, and the rest of the week she was with me. Besides the fact that I didn't have to pay her rent, I liked the building that he arranged for her to live in. Years later, when I married Arlene and was looking for an apartment in New York, I remembered that building and bought an apartment in it where I still live today.

When I was twenty-one years old and single, I was dating a thirty-two-year-old woman who had two children, ages eight and ten. While I was away on vacation, she wrote a letter telling me how much the children missed me. My mail was still being delivered to my parents' home in Brooklyn, and my mother admitted to me that she opened my mail and was very upset with my relationship. The following year, I decided to teach her a lesson.

I was dating a girl named Rona at the time. I sent myself a Valentine card from Rona, and I addressed it to myself at my parents' home address. The cover of the card read, "Will you be my Valentine?" When the card was opened, there was a picture of a very pregnant woman. The inside caption read, "As if you had a choice!" I knew that my mother would open my mail and read it. I was attending dental school and living in Manhattan.

I waited a few days and called her to say hello. When she asked me if everything was okay, I knew that she had opened the card. I acted depressed and said, "Well, I've been having some problems." I could hear her hyperventilating, and she started yelling for my father to get on the phone.

When he got on the phone, I said to him, "Guess she read my Valentine card."

I grew up in a fairly affluent section in Brooklyn called Manhattan Beach. My father appeared to be a very successful dentist, and I thought I was a rich kid. When I finished my periodontal postgraduate training, I decided to open my own office. I did not have any personal money or the ability to get a bank loan, so I asked my father if I could borrow $5,000 from him to furnish my office. He was a great guy, so I was shocked when he refused, telling me that he started his practice on his own and that I should do the same. I was very close to an aunt and uncle, and they lent me the $5,000. I did not have enough money to purchase a regular dental chair, so I bought a slightly used recliner for $100 to use as my chair. Surprisingly, it turned out to be a wonderful practice builder. Patients would be seated and tell me that they felt very relaxed as if they were in a living room rather than a dental office. My lack of funds for a standard dental chair turned out to be something positive.

My practice grew rapidly, and everything was going well until, one day, my father suffered a stroke. He was sixty-six years old, and my mother and I had no idea about his finances because he never confided in us. I had a duplicate key to his vault, and my mother told me to open it so we could see his financial information. Everyone thought that my father was a multimillionaire because he was busy from morning until night with a never-ending number of patients. I was in shock when I opened his vault and read his financial statements. He was completely broke and owed money to both of his dental laboratories. He had no stocks, had cashed in all his life insurance policies, and had nothing in any bank account. I now realized the financial pressures that led to his stroke and why he could not lend me the $5,000.

When I later examined his patient records, I observed that he either didn't charge or gave breaks to many of his clientele. He was a great guy but a poor businessman. It was another of life's lessons that I learned early on, and I remembered it when running the business aspects of my dental practice. It also taught me how to be tough in business during my later years with my mouthwash company.

The only asset my mother had left was the house in Brooklyn. A few years earlier, he had asked her to change ownership from her name to his; but wisely, she refused because it was the only thing she had in her name. For the next seven years until he died, I supported him and my mom. My mother was a very proud woman, and it was quite hard for her to accept money from me. I would tell her the winter rental in Florida that I arranged for them was $2,000, instead of the real price of $8,000. I tried all types of creative ways to pay for their expenses. I continued to support my mom for many years after that until she sadly passed away in 1998.

When my father first had his stroke, we did not know if he would recover and be able to go back to his practice. His office was in a large building that had many dental offices. A young dentist called me a few days after my father's stroke and explained that he was working for another dentist in the building and had heard what happened to my father. He told me that he would be happy to take on my father's practice until we knew whether my father would return. I realized that the patients would go elsewhere if the office was closed, so I made an arrangement with him. We agreed that he would take care of the patients who came in and keep whatever money they paid him until I could determine whether my father would be able to return.

After two days of him working in the office, I started receiving phone calls from my father's patients. They told me that this new dentist was advising them that all of my father's work was not good and that everything had to be replaced. He was telling children to have their parents sign a blank check and bring it to the office at the time of their appointment. After another day or two of those phone calls, I went to see him at my father's office for a talk. I explained that, after those first few days, I could see that the arrangement was not working out and that I had decided to temporarily close the office. He answered that he intended to take over the practice because I gave him the key and that he now had "squatter's rights." He demanded that I leave because the office was now his. I left the office and contacted the building management to inform them that I wanted him removed. They explained that the office was not mine, they needed written papers from my father, and it might take some time to evict him. I told them that my father could not move his arm due to the stroke and was not able to fill out papers.

I then discussed this situation with the dental society, and they informed me that this innocent-looking young dentist had a terrible reputation of reading dentist obituaries, contacting their widows, and attempting to take over their practices. My father had a close friend who knew about my predicament. He asked me to meet him outside my father's office the next day, and he would handle the situation. We rang the bell to my father's office, and when the young dentist opened the door to let us in, my father's friend took out a gun. He was an imposing tall man and informed the dentist that he was with the police. He ordered the dentist to pack up his things and leave the office immediately while keeping his gun in view while he spoke.

As the dentist walked by me on the way out, he looked me in the eye and said, "I am going to kill you." When I went downstairs to my car afterward, I found that the entire side was scratched with long key marks. For two years after that until that young dentist eventually moved to Florida to practice there, I was concerned for my safety. I even obtained a gun license, but fortunately, I did not come into contact with him again.

I find myself constantly learning about people during my business and personal experiences. I had one very close relative growing up, my mother's only sister. My aunt and uncle never had children, and they were like second parents to me. She was a very outstanding businesswoman. They had a duplex apartment on Sutton Place in NYC. He also was successful but unfortunately died at a young age. After he passed away, I would spend much time with my aunt; and after I married Arlene, she became a second mother to us both.

Things started to change when my father had a stroke. She began acting strangely toward my mother, admonishing her for not always following my aunt's advice. Arlene and I decided to meet with her to ease the situation. I explained that everybody has faults and that none of us is perfect. She then answered that she did have a fault and exclaimed that her fault was that she was too good. This was not like her, and I could not understand this change in her conduct. What I failed to recognize was that she was experiencing the early onset of dementia.

I was her only close relative, but a year later, a distant cousin from Philadelphia was visiting New York City and stopped in to see her for the first time in years. She was a young girl, just out of law school. She arrived at my aunt's beautiful apartment and noticed that things were in disarray. She contacted her parents, who were distant relatives of my aunt, and they traveled to New York City to assess the situation.

That was when the bad side of human nature took over. The young lawyer drew up papers, giving herself power of attorney, and had my aunt sign it. Up to that point, I was my aunt's only heir in her will. They never contacted me about her real situation. I found out by chance, from a neighbor of hers, that they sold her apartment in New York and Florida and put her in an institution. I found out the name, and the next time Arlene and I were in Florida, we went to the institution to check on her condition. It was sad to see this once elegant lady hunched in the corner, disheveled, and completely out of it. They ended up taking all her money and stocks while keeping me completely in the dark.

I maintain our family plot, where my parents and my aunt's husband and brother-in-law are buried. A few years ago, I received a bill from the cemetery, stating that they were doing extra maintenance on the plots, and I would be charged for the five people buried there. I called them to inform them that there were only four tombstones, not five. They proceeded to read me the names of the people buried, and my aunt was the fifth person on the list. The Philadelphia people apparently did not want me to know that she had died and buried her in the plot without a tombstone for anyone to see. It was a disturbing lesson to me about what some people will do for money. This outstanding woman was buried without a headstone to show that she ever existed.

I have many interesting memories of my time as a dentist, even though I have not practiced now for thirty-two years. One time Joe Pesci came into my office late at night for me to recement a temporary cap so he could be back on the movie set in the morning and be able to smile. Cindy Adams, the well-known *New York Post* gossip columnist, came in every six months for her cleaning. She was very close to her mother. Her mother would accompany Cindy to the appointment and insist that I bring a chair into my treatment room for her to sit and watch while I worked on her daughter. I guess she did not want her daughter to be alone with anyone in a room, not even her dentist.

After I retired, Cindy called to ask me if I could recommend a good general dentist for her. I told her that my son, Marc, was the best dentist I know. She has been his patient for many years now. She thinks that he is terrific and often raves about him in her newspaper column. When Liza's ex-husband David Gest died, Cindy asked Marc for Liza's home phone number for an interview because she knew that I had it. I never give out people's private numbers, and I knew that Liza never wanted to talk about David Gest. When Marc told Cindy that I would not give her Liza's number, she had her assistant call me at home. I explained that I would never give out Liza's personal phone number, but if she told me Cindy's personal number, I would give it to Liza, and Liza could call Cindy if she wanted to talk to her. The assistant informed me that Cindy would not give her phone number to anyone, and if I didn't give her Liza's number, Cindy would never talk to Marc or me again. Somehow she felt that it was okay for me to give out Liza's number, but Cindy did not want to give out her own number. It was absurd logic, and since I had no continuing relationship with Cindy Adams, I wasn't concerned if she decided she did not want to talk to me. I don't know if she is still upset with me because I have not come into contact with her in recent years. However, when Cindy realized that she loved Marc's work and really needed him, she disregarded what she said about not talking to Marc and still continues to see him professionally. She invites him to escort her to show openings and special events, and they are great friends.

One day my nurse informed me that a young man had come into the office for his appointment but was not written down in our appointment book. I replied that maybe we had made a mistake and that she should put him in one of the rooms and take a dental history. She sat him in the dental chair, placed the dental apron and cloth around his neck, and asked him a number of questions about bleeding gums and loose teeth. I entered the room, had him open his mouth for a preliminary examination, and looked around with my mirror and explorer. I asked him my usual opening question, which was "Tell me what brings you here, and what can I do for you?"

He answered, "My penis hurts." My assistant and I thought we had heard wrong and asked him again, receiving the same reply. We tried not to laugh when he explained that he was there for a visit with the urologist. Apparently, he had gotten off on the wrong floor. How he went through an entire dental examination before mentioning that to us I never could figure out.

Another crazy time was when a new patient called our office to say that she was given our number by her friend, and she had an emergency. My nurse told her that if she had an emergency problem, she can come right over, and we would see her. Thirty minutes later, a woman walked in wearing a nightgown, a hat, and bedroom slippers and carrying a small purse. My nurse, seeing her dressed only in a nightgown, asked her why she was coming in dressed in her sleepwear. When the woman answered, "You told me to come right over," we knew we had a somewhat crazy new patient.

Over the years, we have introduced our children to the exciting world of entertainment. When our daughter, Lauren, was little, we took her to see Liza Minnelli perform at the Broward Center in Florida. She looked all around the theater and said, "All these people are coming to see one little person."

One New Year's Eve, we took Lauren and Marc to see three of my favorite rock and roll legends perform together. Little Richard, Chuck Berry, and Jerry Lee Lewis were all sharing the same stage. We have had many wonderful times with both of our children, each of whom turned out to be very special.

After graduating from the University of Pennsylvania, our son, Marc, followed in the family tradition and is the third generation of dentists in my family. He was president of his graduating class, and I was so proud to see him speak at his graduation from the New York University School of Dentistry. He has written two books on dentistry and created two popular apps for dentistry. He invented and patented two instruments used by dentists all over the world. He is a leader of advancements in dentistry and is the president of the Academy of Biomimetic Dentistry. This highly specialized area called biomimetic dentistry is the most important new advance in dental care today.

Our daughter, Lauren, excelled at the University of Pennsylvania and then went on to graduate Yale Law School. Even before becoming a lawyer, she was the assistant to Robert Abrams, the attorney general of New York at that time, and she was a judicial intern for Judge Michael Corriero, who recently was one of the judges on Judge Judy's television show *Hot Bench*. Lauren was also a summer associate at Slotnick, Shapiro, and Crocker, where she worked on very high-profile cases. (Barry Slotnick is best known for defending Bernhard Goetz, "the Subway Vigilante.") She became a prosecutor straight out of law school and held the title assistant corporation counsel at the New York City Law Department. She was also an attorney at a top law firm in New York City and, after taking time off for her children, became certified in divorce mediation.

Marc demonstrated what a true romantic he was after the first anniversary with his first serious girlfriend. He met her while he was going to college at the University of Pennsylvania. Her family lived in Philadelphia, so Marc spent a good deal of time with them. He made a collage of every important memento of his relationship with their daughter and had it framed as a gift. When we met her parents at their home for the first time, they showed us the framed collage hanging on their wall at the head of the stairway. Marc included the ticket stubs to their first show, the receipt of their first restaurant date, and every other item that was important in their year together. In the right-hand corner of the collage, we noted another important milestone item that Marc used in the collage. It was the condom wrapper from their first sexual encounter. We didn't quite know what to say to the parents when they proudly showed us this collage that Marc had made for them.

During our first year of marriage, we thought it might be nice to take a course together at the New School in Downtown Manhattan. We noticed a course listed as Encounter: A Group Experience. The course description explained that participants would learn how to meet and interact with people. We thought that this sounded like an interesting course for a newly married couple to take. We had no idea at the time what an encounter group was.

There were about thirty of us in the class, and we sat around in a large circle with the instructor in the middle. He instructed us that it was important that we know nothing about one another's personal lives. He did not want us to use our real names, and we could either choose a name or have the class pick one for us. He explained that the purpose of this class was to learn to tell people our true feelings about everything. It was a ten-week course.

After some preliminary interactions, he then proceeded to go around the room, asking each person what their first impressions were of the person sitting next to them. People would say that the person sitting next to them seemed like a bitch or looked sloppy or appeared to be a dull person. When it came to my turn, I remarked that I had no opinion of the person sitting next to me because I really knew nothing about her. The whole group immediately accused me of not being honest and told me to "get real."

After the first two sessions, I realized that we were the only married couple in the class. We started to get the feeling that the other people were there for inexpensive psychiatric group therapy. At the end of each session, many people from the group wanted to go out for coffee and dessert to keep the spirit going. The waitress would ask our group how she could help us. Someone would admonish her by telling her that she didn't really want to help us but was just doing her job. Arlene and I felt like hiding under the table whenever this happened.

During the second session, the instructor asked one of the girls in the group what she was thinking at the moment. She pointed to one of the boys in the group and announced, "I was mentally having sex with him." The instructor then asked him if he would like to come down to the center of the room and roll on the floor with her. The boy replied that he would not because he thought she was a homely pig and wanted nothing to do with her.

In the third week, one of the girls announced that she had just gotten fired that day. She explained that she told her boss exactly what she thought of him, and he fired her. Each week different people would come in with stories about telling people honestly what was on their minds and described how relationships they had were ending. We learned from this experience that it is not always wise to tell everyone in your life exactly what you think of them. The one thing it did help us realize in our first year of marriage was the importance of being honest about expressing our opinions and feelings to each other. We decided to always discuss with each other how we felt about things, and I believe it was a good start to a successful marriage.

FIFTY-TWO

My Projects

After retiring from dentistry, I involved myself with various projects for my enjoyment. One year I wrote a movie script and even sent it to studios to see if any were interested. No one ever responded back. I realized that if I wanted to pursue my idea, I had to hire an agent and get serious about it. I decided that I didn't really want a career as a screenwriter and abandoned the project.

It was an interesting story about a president of the United States who was having an affair. His mistress had been a serial killer in her early years who managed to turn her life around and lost the desire to kill. New circumstances would cause her to get very upset with the president. He would be her next victim. He was running for reelection against a very conservative Republican with an extremely strong ego. I was somewhat ahead of my time because I developed my script years before Bill Clinton became president and his affairs became public knowledge. It was also long before Donald Trump became interested in politics. If I showed anyone my script today, they would believe that I developed the characters around Bill Clinton and Donald Trump.

I had the opportunity to spend time with Charles Aznavour over the years due to his very close friendship with Liza Minnelli. She looked up to him as one of her mentors and introduced me to his music. Aznavour was revered in Europe in the same way that Frank Sinatra was admired in the United States. In 2007, I decided, purely for my enjoyment, to write what could be a Broadway show utilizing the music of Charles Aznavour. I enjoyed occupying my free time with this project. I did not speak French, so I often had to go to the internet to translate his lyrics into English.

One day I noticed on the internet that someone was producing a show incorporating his music. I thought it was interesting that this project I was doing for amusement was actually being done by serious producers. A few months later, while checking translations of one of his songs, I checked out the progress of the show that was being produced. It was called *AZ*, but there was no longer any mention of it on the internet. On impulse, I called the phone number of the producer, Sybil Goday, listed in the original article. I was curious about what was happening with the project and wondered where I could see it. I was expecting either a disconnected number or a secretary at some agency to answer. Instead, a woman picked up the phone and said, "This is Sybil. Who am I talking to?" I explained that I had seen the information about the *AZ* show on the internet, and I was interested in seeing it because I had been working with Aznavour's music as a fun project for myself. She told me that her husband, Happy Goday, was Charles's agent in America, and Aznavour gave him the rights to his music in the USA. Happy had died, and Sybil inherited the rights. The *AZ* show was the third attempt by people to put together a show using Aznavour's music, but she hated them all.

She told me that she would be interested to see what I was doing and invited me to meet her the following week for lunch. I didn't know what to say since my work on this project was purely for fun. She caught me by surprise, and I blurted out, "Sure."

After hanging up the phone, I thought to myself, *Why not? It might be fun.* In the next few days, I worked hard to put my scattered ideas into the form of a script. By the following week, I had the show more organized and written down for Sybil to see. We met for lunch at Sarabeth's Restaurant on Central Park South, close to where she lived. I did not mention during our lunch that I knew Aznavour or Liza Minnelli. I told her that I was a fan of his and thought his music would be a wonderful basis for a Broadway show. I showed her my concept and outline for the show. Much to my surprise, after reading the pages that I gave her, she told me that she loved it. She exclaimed it was the first time someone used Aznavour's words and music in a way that would make a thrilling Broadway show. She wanted to meet with me again the following week with her lawyer to draw up partnership papers.

I returned home somewhat stunned and told Arlene that I could not proceed on this project without telling Liza what I did. Liza was the one who introduced me to Aznavour's music, and I would not do anything without her approval. The next day, I called Liza and went over to her apartment. I explained what happened and showed her what I had written. She read it and remarked that she thought it was terrific and said she would love to work on the project with me. Liza had never directed before and told me that she would like to direct this show for Broadway and work on the book with me as well. She also had suggestions for some very well-known actors whom she would contact to star in the show.

The following week when I met with Sybil, I informed her of my relationship with Liza and the fact that Liza wanted to direct the show. She was beyond ecstatic at the concept of Liza Minnelli directing a show on Broadway based on the music of Charles Aznavour. She started talking about trying it out the following season in Toronto and then bringing it to Broadway.

Suddenly, things were moving very fast. A few days later, I met with Liza, and she had some fantastic ideas for the show. I had another luncheon scheduled with Sybil, who now wanted to meet with me every week and told me that her lawyers were starting to draw up the papers for our partnership. She informed me that she wanted to have a weekly progress report on what Liza and I were developing. When I went back to Liza and informed her of Sybil's request, Liza let me know that we were not going to show her anything until we had it worked out and ready to be seen. Sybil was not happy to hear that, and my education about mounting a show on Broadway began.

Liza discussed our project with her agent, Allen Arrow, who mentioned that one of his clients would be the perfect person to adapt Charles's music for Broadway. His name was Maury Yeston, and he once taught a class in French music at Yale. Maury had a great track record on Broadway. He had written music and lyrics for three Broadway shows and won a Tony Award for each. We set up a meeting with Maury at his apartment for the following week.

When Liza, Allen, and I arrived, Maury exclaimed that he was so enthusiastic about the project that he took the liberty to update some of Aznavour's lyrics for the show. He sat down at his piano and played some of his new interpretations of the lyrics for us. I thought they were terrific, and on the way down in the elevator later with Allen and Liza, I told them so. Allen agreed that they were great, but Liza was not happy with his changes. She did not like the idea of modernizing Aznavour's lyrics. I remarked that we did not have to use the changes, but Liza felt that she did not have the same concept in mind as Maury.

I was beginning to understand why many shows do not come to fruition and why we read about artistic differences destroying a production. I set up a meeting with Maury the following week at a restaurant near his apartment on Fifty-Seventh Street. He understood my concerns and gave me some good advice. He told me that, in his experience, it can take as long as six years from concept to completion for a musical show to open. He felt that the show had great potential, but I must be prepared to spend considerable time on it and deal with the many different opinions people will have. He wanted me to have a realistic concept of what I was in for.

I had chosen the area of Montmartre in France as the setting for my show because there were bohemian characters that fit in well with Aznavour's music and lyrics. Charles had read my treatment and sent me a letter from France. He explained that he liked my ideas but did not want Montmartre to be the setting. He considered it too obvious a choice, and he insisted on a different location. So I did some rewriting and changed the location to Greenwich Village in New York City.

One day while I was telling my small grandchildren not to bother me while I was working on the computer, I came to a decision. I had returned from separate meetings with Sybil and Liza after talking with Maury. I realized that this project would take me away from my family, possibly for years. I also considered that there was a good chance this project might never come to fruition. I remembered the words of Larry Gelbart, who when he was struggling through tryouts of a musical he was writing in Philadelphia exclaimed, "If Hitler's alive, I hope he's out of town with a musical." I realized that there was a big difference between the fun of creating a show and trying to be a Broadway writer and producer. Sybil, by that time, was driving me nuts, and I ended the venture.

Liza had already started thinking about another project, a show about her late godmother Kay Thompson. A year later, she opened that show at the Palace Theater, playing Kay, and won a Tony for her performance. I still have some regrets about abandoning the show because I think it could have been a big hit and brought Liza fame as a director. It would have given the American public not familiar with Aznavour a glimpse of his talent. However, I am sure that I made the right call because time with my family has been far too precious to give up for a show.

When I formed my mouthwash company, Oral Research Laboratories, I learned many lessons about people's greed. My company occupied a full floor of offices in the Chrysler Building on East Forty-Second Street. After our first year, Pfizer had become a corporate big brother with a financial investment in the company of $20 million for 20 percent of the company. There was an attempt by some people on my board of directors to show our private information to other companies, and as a result, we had armed guards checking everybody in and out of our floor. Someone brought the details of our mouthwash sales to Colgate. We were a private company, so no one knew that my single product mouthwash company was doing more than $100 million in sales after one year on the market. Colgate now wanted to put in a bid to buy the company, and we ended up having a one-day bidding war between Colgate and Pfizer. Teams of lawyers from each company would come into our lawyer's office every half hour and put in a bid.

One of the lawyers on the Colgate team was John McEnroe's father. I recognized him from watching him sit in the player's box at John's matches and always wondered what he did for a living. After a long day of alternating bids, Pfizer made the top offer and won my company. The head of Pfizer loved and used Plax, and he wanted to own it and start a dental division in his company. Colgate was really better suited for it because they were already a major dental product company. In the years after Pfizer's purchase of Plax, the head of Pfizer retired, and Pfizer probably realized that they could make more money from their pharmaceutical products, like Viagra, than they could from dental products. They eventually sold Plax to Colgate internationally and Johnson and Johnson in the United States.

The final week before Pfizer was to finalize the purchase, people were threatening various types of lawsuits. Rival companies wanted to buy us. Pfizer suggested a top lawyer for us to hire, and they would pay all legal expenses. The lawyer charged my company $250,000 for the work his firm needed to do that final week. Pfizer would be paying the bill and approved the amount. When the lawyer began to see the numbers involved in the purchase, he came to me and said that even though he agreed on the previous amount, he would need a fee of $1 million to be able to get the work done in time. When I relayed this information to Pfizer, they told me to offer him $350,000 instead of the original $250,000, even though he was contracted for the smaller amount. When I informed him of the $350,000 new offer, he replied that he was, of course, bound to the agreement, but without the $1 million incentive, he may not be able to get all the work done on time. He explained that with the continuing other lawsuits, there was a possibility that the deal may fall through. Pfizer then advised me to agree to pay him the $1 million.

A week later, when the deal was completed, the Pfizer representative at the signing told me that, now that Pfizer owned the company, he wanted to have one last meeting of the board. I went with him to a small conference room at the Pfizer lawyer's office. He had telephones set up with a few board members online and called the meeting to order. He announced at this last meeting that he would like the board to nominate him as chairman of the board, and I agreed, along with the other board members on the phone. He then declared that there would be one order of business, and that was to cancel the $1 million check to the lawyer. We all voted in the affirmative. The lawyer had made a mistake by not getting his money upfront, figuring he would not have any problem with a large company like Pfizer. When he was informed about the decision to cancel his check, he responded that he would now accept the $350,000 that Pfizer had offered him, but Pfizer would not agree to more than the original $250,000.

While I was sitting around waiting for the final papers to be signed that morning, I casually looked through my large duplicate copy of the many legal papers in front of me. Among all the numerous documents, there was one page that caught my eye. When Pfizer bought my company, they owned all the assets. There was apparently a legal formality requiring them to buy the trademark name for one dollar. To my shock, I noticed that the one-dollar payment was made to the relative whom I put in charge of filing the original papers of the company. He left my name completely out of the original filing. I suddenly realized what his motivation was. The chances of a mouthwash company being successful, competing with major companies like Listerine and Scope, was slim. The overwhelming odds were that it would eventually go bankrupt and fail. With the name Plax being so popular with dental professionals and the public, a major company might pay a few million dollars just for the use of the name Plax. Because his name was the only one on the trademark filing, that money would all go to him. This turned out to not matter only because my company did very well and defied the odds. When Pfizer bought the company and the name that came with it, a check for only one dollar had to be paid to secure the name for legal reasons. I never mentioned to him what I had discovered. He probably assumed that the information was buried in the many pages of legal documents and that I would never notice it. Since it no longer mattered, I saw no reason to bring it up. However, he never quite understood why our friendship ended on my part after that day. For me, it became another life lesson about people and greed.

After I sold my company, I wanted to celebrate. I bought Arlene a new diamond ring, which we jokingly call "the Plax ring." I wanted to splurge on something for myself, and in a moment of insanity, I decided to buy a Lamborghini. I live in Manhattan, and there is no place to drive a car like that. However, we were in Los Angeles on vacation and passed a car dealership with one in the window. Arlene hates fast cars, but she didn't want to deprive me of my fantasy. We went into the showroom and spoke to a salesman, and he offered to take me for a test-drive around the block. It took off like a rocket, and I was almost deaf from the noise of the engine. I warned him to go very slowly when he takes Arlene for a ride. It was hard to see out of the tiny back window, and it was an extremely impractical car for me to consider. I told him that we were going for lunch, and I would return later to sign the contract for the car after talking to my wife.

I was nervous during lunch because we both realized how ridiculous this car would be for me. There was no trunk space, it only sat two people, and it was so noisy that you could not hear music while driving. It was crazy, but during lunch, I decided that I would buy it anyway.

We drove down Wilshire Boulevard, and I spotted an open meter parking spot directly in front of the dealership. The traffic light turned red just as I was about to make the left turn into that parking spot, and a car came from the other direction and took my spot. I watched a very grungy-looking young kid and his girlfriend step out of their car and walk into the dealership. I found a parking spot across the street, and when we got out of my car, I was able to see through the glass window that the couple was talking to my salesman while walking around the Lamborghini. I was hoping these two kids wouldn't scratch my purchase while they were wasting the salesman's time.

I waited until they were no longer visible inside before walking into the showroom. I explained to the person at the desk that I was here to make a payment for a new car, but I didn't see the salesman whom I had made a deal with. She answered that he was in his office with a customer. I waited, and a few minutes later, I saw him walking out of a room with those two scraggly-looking people. When they left the showroom, I remarked that I was ready to give my deposit on the Lamborghini, and he answered that he was sorry, but he just sold it. I explained that I thought we had a tentative agreement. He informed me that this couple walked in, admired the car, and paid the full price in cash. He felt that I was not fully sure about buying the car at the time we spoke, so he could not turn them down. I actually walked out more relieved than disappointed. Thank goodness I missed the green light that would have given me the parking spot. It was a moment of temporary madness, and I eventually bought myself a beautiful new tie instead—that I actually used (although my kids would have preferred the Lamborghini).

I always enjoy getting involved with projects. About fifteen years ago, we expanded the upstairs of our home in Westhampton Beach as our family expanded with grandchildren. We added several additional rooms, and that left a lot of empty white wall space. When I was in my late teens, I did some acrylic and oil paintings. The summer season was about to start, and I now had a home with large areas of bare walls. I decided to go back to painting, so I bought the necessary materials and started to create artwork again. I threw myself into the job, buying large canvases to work on each day. After thirty days, I had completed twenty large modern art paintings. I had enough paintings to fill up the empty walls of my Westhampton home. I signed my artwork "Zarela." I just moved the first two letters of my last name to the end to form "Zarela."

I wanted to get an honest opinion from people about the paintings without them knowing that I had done them. I have been so pleased to hear people tell me how much they like the art in my home. I loved creating the paintings and worked from early morning to late at night on each canvas. However, as soon as I filled up the walls, I retired from painting. I was able to completely decorate the walls in one month, using the colors and subject matters that I felt worked in each room.

In 2012, I attempted to buy tickets for *Matilda*, a show that was a major hit in London. It was coming to Broadway the following year, and I wanted to take my children and grandchildren. I found it impossible to get tickets because it had won all the top awards in England. One day we were having lunch with our friend Fran Weissler. She and her husband, Barry, are major Broadway producers. Fran discussed some of the new shows she was bringing to Broadway the following season and mentioned *Matilda* as one of them. I had never invested with them in the past, but I asked her if I could invest in that show. Aside from thinking that it would be a good investment, I wanted to gain access to house seats for my family. She replied that everyone wanted to be part of this show but that she would give me preference. I did invest in that show, it was successful, and I did make money. I was also able to get house seats for my various family members, and they were very impressed.

She told me at that luncheon that she was also bringing to Broadway a revival of the show *Pippin*. I read the rave out-of-town reviews when it had a run in Boston, and I invested in that show as well. When *Pippin* opened on Broadway in 2013, it received rave reviews, and I made money on that show as well. I also invested in the successful road production of *Pippin*.

Investing in other shows that have already been produced elsewhere was a much easier experience than when I tried to mount a Broadway musical on my own. The one major problem I learned about investing in a Broadway show was that one has no control over the finances. As an investor, I found with my hit shows that my capital investment was paid back quickly. I then periodically received relatively small payments, and my eventual profit for three successful productions was about 10 percent. The investors had no say about when their share of the earnings would be distributed to them. With this formula, the producers could keep the show running longer, maintaining the weekly salaries for themselves, the actors, and other people involved in the production. Instead of closing and distributing the profits, shows are kept running. Eventually, by the time they are ready to close, all the remaining profits are used up to extend the run. I realized that the only way to make considerable money investing in a Broadway show is to have a major hit that runs for many years.

I did have fun at the opening night parties and enjoyed being part of the Broadway community. Of course, I realized that my money paid for those opening night parties. From a financial standpoint, it was another of life's lessons on business. Fortunately, I made money on those investments, but five out of six shows do not pay back their investors. My show *Pippin* did win the Tony for Best Revival of a Musical, but *Matilda* lost the Tony for Best Musical to *Kinky Boots*. *Matilda* won the Drama Critics and Drama Desk Awards for Best Musical, and it did win a Tony for Best Book of a Musical. I loved going to the Tonys that year because our cast members won multiple awards. Patina Miller won the Tony for Best Leading Actress in a Musical, Andrea Martin won the Tony for Best Featured Actress in a Musical, and Diane Paulus won the Tony for Best Direction of a Musical. I enjoyed spending time and celebrating with the casts of both shows that I invested in. I was able to secure house seats for all my friends and family to those shows, but it became a headache trying to arrange good seats for everyone.

I should have known better about investing in shows from an experience I had years before. Liza's husband, Mark Gero, had parents who were both fine actors and producers of many off-Broadway shows. They always had good taste in choosing their shows, and when Mark married Liza, they wanted to help him become a producer. They found an off-Broadway show called *On Golden Pond*. Mark asked each of his friends to invest $10,000 so he could get a producer credit on the show. We would all share, of course, in the profits. It was a wonderful show and received great reviews but made no money. When it closed six months later, we had all lost our investment. We did, however, want to support our friend and did not expect much in return.

In 1981, *On Golden Pond* was made into a movie starring Jane Fonda, Henry Fonda, and Katharine Hepburn. It was nominated for Best Picture at the Academy Awards, and both Henry Fonda and Katharine Hepburn won Oscars for best acting. It was a major box office hit and garnered many Oscar nominations. As an original investor, I figured that I hit the jackpot when the play was sold to the movie studio. I soon learned that, as an investor in the show, I had no rights to the movie profits. I only could receive profits made from the off-Broadway run, which unfortunately were zero.

❧[CHAPTER]❧

FIFTY-THREE

Travels

Arlene never wants to be seen without all her makeup done perfectly. (And she always does it perfectly, although I feel she also looks terrific without makeup.) Even though she is a great natural beauty, she has this hang-up about being seen without makeup and false eyelashes no matter where she is. Her father was a doctor, and we were at his home when Arlene went into labor before giving birth to our son, Marc. He was timing her contractions and informed her that it was time to go to the hospital. She replied that we would have to wait because she did not finish applying her eyelashes and makeup. We nervously arrived at the hospital just in time for the delivery; everyone was stressed, but she did walk in looking great. (It would not have been a pretty picture had she given birth in the back seat of my car on the way to the hospital. However, I believe given the choice, she would still spend the extra time for makeup and take her chances on possibly delivering our baby in the car as long as she looked glamorous doing it.)

Another example of her vanity was the time we went on an African safari. We were by ourselves and staying in a unique resort. It was a circular hotel with glass walls on the outside of every room for beautiful views of the surroundings. The lobby and restaurant were in the center of the hotel. It was located on top of the Ngorongoro Crater in Tanzania. The animals lived at the bottom of the crater, and in the morning, special jeeps would take guests down into the crater to observe them. We did not know anybody at the resort and, after dinner, went into our bedroom for an early night's sleep.

While we were in bed, I heard banging noises outside our window. A loudspeaker announcement sounded in every room, instructing guests to quickly evacuate their bedrooms and go to the center lobby. Two large water buffalos had somehow made it up the crater and could come crashing through the glass windows into the guest rooms. Everyone evacuated their rooms and immediately went to the lobby, except Arlene. Arlene would not leave our room until she finished her makeup and eyelashes in the bathroom. No stranger would see her in anything less than full makeup even if it meant risking her life.

The scariest experience I ever had on a trip took place when I visited Komodo Island. Arlene and I went on a cruise through various Indonesian islands, all of which were very interesting. Komodo Island proved to be very different from the others. Arlene had injured her foot, so she was not able to join our small tour group.

The night before, we heard a lecture on the ship about what to expect on the island. They informed us that the main island inhabitants are Komodo dragons, the largest lizard in the world. They are an endangered species and only live on that island. They are extremely dangerous and were named after the mythical dragon. The lecturer explained that we may or may not see any and proceeded to tell us all about them. They are about twelve feet long and swallow their prey whole. They run very fast and can even leap onto a tree. Their venom is poisonous and can kill you with one bite. A small number of natives live on one side of the island, and they keep a supply of goats available as food for the dragons. If the dragons do not get enough food, they are known to come into the village and devour some people.

The next day, a group of about thirty of us went by tender to the island. Komodo dragons are an endangered species, and guns are not allowed on the island. The young boy who was our guide was allowed to carry only a small V-shaped stick. If the dragon was in our path, he could approach and push the stick against the dragon's neck, forcing him out of the way. The stick is the only weapon allowed on the island.

We started to walk along a path in the sand, and there was a sign saying, "Caution, dragon crossing." We all got a laugh out of that sign and proceeded to take pictures of one another under the sign. We continued to follow the young boy along the path. Suddenly, we saw in front of us a monster that looked straight out of *Jurassic Park*. It was about twelve feet long with long claws, a large jaw with many teeth, and a tongue that kept jutting out toward us. We froze in our tracks, and the young boy calmly walked over with his stick and pressed it against the animal's neck, and it slowly moved off the path. I was shocked that the stick worked because I believed that if the dragon was hungry that morning, our tour would have been cut short for lack of a guide and maybe a few tourists. This was not a creature behind a cage; we were all completely out in the open and very vulnerable.

We walked a little way up a small hill and looked around. About thirty feet away from us was a large group of these monsters staring at us. The only thing between us and them was a six-inch-high wire fence that defined the pathway to the dragons. We were told that, once a week, the natives take live goats and tie them to a tree. The dragons come out, kill the goats, and swallow them whole. We hoped that they were fed recently as they started to crawl closer to us. We took some pictures, and all of us huddled together in a frightened group until the guide thankfully led us back to the boat. You have never seen a tour group walk so fast back to the boat as our group that day.

We were one of the early groups to visit that island. When we returned home, I read up on the history of the Komodo dragon. I learned that one of the first tour groups from Germany followed the same path that we took. A member of the group exclaimed that he was tired, sat down to rest, and said he would catch up with the tour in a few minutes. When he never showed up, they went back to look for him. All that remained was his camera and one shoe.

Years later, I read that Sharon Stone visited the LA Zoo, where they kept a baby Komodo dragon. Her boyfriend at the time was a newspaper reporter, and he posed for a picture with the baby dragon. The dragon bit him on his sneaker. One tooth went through the sneaker, and because the venom was so strong, his foot swelled up for weeks. He was hospitalized and lucky to be alive. How they are allowed to bring tourists to this island I'll never know, but it was certainly a memorable experience.

We had another scary travel experience that involved humans instead of animals. On our first trip to Bangkok, Arlene and I were a young couple, and we stayed in a very elegant hotel. We dressed up for dinner and had the concierge write down the name and address of our restaurant on a piece of paper. When the doorman hailed a taxi, we got in and gave the driver the paper with the name of our restaurant written in the Thai language. He, in turn, handed us a large piece of paper that looked like a menu. On it were a series of items in English, describing various sex acts. Each had a price and included everything from children and animals to various mixtures of people for us to choose from. All we wanted was a good dinner, so we politely declined. How he had the nerve to present this list of depraved sex choices to a well-dressed couple heading out to dinner I have no idea. Bangkok was a beautiful city, but some weird things occur there as we found out on our next Asian trip years later.

There are so many beautiful and interesting sights to enjoy in Thailand that we returned a few years later. The buildings and monuments were magnificent, and observing people living full time on the water was fascinating. We decided to see as much as possible and hired a guide with a car for daily tours. At the end of the second day, our guide asked us if we would like to use him at night to show us around the city after dark. We only planned to go to dinner and therefore didn't need a guide. He recommended that we see the Patpong area at night while we were in Bangkok. He told us that the Patpong area has an open market for tourist goods, as well as a red-light and entertainment district that is unusual. He offered to not only show us all the sights but also take us to see "Ping-Pong." I declined his suggestion because I felt that, coming from NYC, I could experience nightlife without the need for a guide.

After dinner with Arlene, I suggested taking a taxi to the Patpong area and exploring it ourselves. When we arrived, we observed a large market in the center of the street with many clubs on either side. In the windows were beautiful young girls dressed in sexy outfits to fit a different theme for each club. Each club had its own look, and inside, there was music and dancing. As we looked inside through the open glass, we saw attractive young girls; and obviously, they were expecting to get paid. We decided not to venture inside because we saw enough from the street, and we settled on browsing for souvenirs in the markets.

We were looking for a taxi to return to our hotel when a young boy approached us. He asked if there was anything that we wanted. Apparently, the young girls in that area were prostitutes, and the young boys acted as their pimps. We explained that we were not interested and were walking away when he suddenly remarked that he would show us "Ping-Pong." Our guide from the afternoon had mentioned that he wanted to show us Ping-Pong, so we were curious about what that was. We asked the young boy about seeing Ping-Pong but let him know that we would not go anywhere off the well-lit main street. We had no idea what Ping-Pong was, but he told us that it would just cost $10 to see and pointed to a brightly lit club across the street.

Instead of going into one of the clubs on the ground level, he walked us up one flight of steps to a small club. I asked the man at the door how much the cover charge was, and he said $10 for the first drink. We went inside and were seated at a table in a very darkly lit room. I ordered two glasses of wine, and all we could observe in the place was a tiny stage. The room was so dark that we couldn't see people at any other table. Two very old and ugly women came over to us and asked if we were interested in either of them. They looked like two witches out of a horror movie, and we declined. The contrast between them and the beautiful young girls behind the glass walls of the clubs downstairs was dramatic. Within a few minutes, two equally ugly women walked out on the small stage. They started to do disgusting sex acts, including blowing cigarette smoke out of their private parts. We then discovered what Ping-Pong was when they took turns blowing out a Ping-Pong ball from one woman's privates to the other.

We both started to get nauseous watching these revolting displays, and I immediately asked my waitress for the check. We were only there for about fifteen minutes, but we had more than enough. When I was presented with the check, it read $80 instead of the $10 I was told. I explained this to the waitress and reminded her that we had only been at the table for fifteen minutes. I put $20 on the table, and we got up to leave.

Suddenly, the man who let us in blocked our way out. As I looked around for help, I realized, as my eyes got accustomed to the dark room, that we were the only customers in the small place. The one exit out was now blocked by our waitress, the man who let us in, and the two old ugly women. I heard that life can be cheap in Bangkok when it comes to money, and we were very frightened for our lives. I came to the area with only $110 in cash and no jewelry or wallet. I told the man that if he allowed Arlene to go out of the door, I would give him all my money. He refused to let her out until I paid him what he wanted first. I had no choice but to decide to give him the money he asked for and hope that he would let us go. I gave him $100 and held my breath. He took the money, and the other people took their hands off the door and allowed us to leave.

We ran down the stairs into the bright street filled with tourists. Arlene wanted to look for a policeman and report them. I believed that the police knew what was going on, and I just wanted to get back to safety at our hotel. We walked to the corner and found a cab, and I had just enough money left for the ride back to our hotel. Years later, we went to see the Broadway show *Miss Saigon*. There was a musical scene showing the decadent clubs in the city. In the background of the dancing, there was a Ping-Pong ball periodically flying up in the air. I guess "Ping-Pong" is done elsewhere and not just in Bangkok.

Early in our marriage, I took Arlene on a trip to Morocco. She was just twenty-two, and we were exploring new places together. We stayed in the beautiful hotel La Mamounia. It was very elegant, and after three days, we hired a car and driver to take us to Fez. It was a four-hour drive, and Arlene wanted to go to the bathroom during the trip. When I asked the driver to take us to the nearest restroom facility, he informed me that the nearest bathroom would be two hours away. When I asked what local people we observed used as a bathroom, he pointed to the fields and trees.

After a long drive, he finally informed us that we arrived in a town with a bathroom. He drove up to a beautiful white mansion and told us that this was the only bathroom in town, and it was in the office of the mayor. In front of the mansion was a well-dressed man who was the outside guard. Our driver told him that Arlene wanted to use the bathroom, and he said he would escort her there. He handed

Arlene a copy of an Arab newspaper. She thought that it was nice of him to give her reading material. She followed him around to the side of the building, where he opened a door. When the door swung open, Arlene saw only a large hole in the ground and a long chain hanging on the wall to hold on to. Arlene realized that this hole was the only toilet in the town, and the newspaper was the toilet paper. The mayor's residence contained the sole toilet until we arrived in Fez.

We went from there to the south of France. It was May when we arrived in Cannes, and we saw signs in our hotel promoting the opening night of the famous Cannes Film Festival. We asked the concierge if there was any way that we could attend. He said that it was an event for invited guests only, but for a price, he could get us two tickets in the balcony. The problem was that it was formal, and we had no formal clothing. I did have one jacket but no tie. The waiters in the dining room dressed in suits and formal bow ties. I gave one waiter money to borrow his bow tie for the evening. I had bought Arlene a caftan in the market in Morocco. We went to our room, and Arlene turned her decorative gold-threaded Moroccan caftan into a dramatic formal dress. Arlene wore her hair long in those days and carried with her a long braid to attach to it. She fastened the braid so that it fell over her shoulder and went down to her waist. She looked very exotic, like an Indian movie star.

On opening night, the steps of the theater were lined with paparazzi from all over the world. As each movie star walked up the steps, flashbulbs exploded, and the waiting crowds yelled with excitement. I left Arlene downstairs, and I walked up the steps to the top. I took out my camera and stood among the press. Arlene started to slowly walk up the stairs. The press had no idea who this movie star was, but she looked so dramatic in her caftan and exotic hair that flashbulbs went off while the crowd cheered. It was an exciting moment for us, and I still have the film of her entrance. I met her at the top step, and we went inside to our seats in the balcony to watch the movie. Arlene's "Cinderella at the ball" moment was over, and instead of meeting a prince, she was left sitting in the balcony with me.

I had a patient who was a major gambler. He was invited by the casinos on all-expense-paid trips that were set up for high rollers. He asked me to join him on one of those trips as his guest, telling me that because he was such a big gambler they allowed him to bring friends. Arlene was somewhat apprehensive, but I explained that we had no obligation to gamble. It was a trip on a chartered plane to Las Vegas, and everything—including food, drinks, hotel room, and plane trip—was free. We all met in a private lounge at the airport before boarding.

Frank was the man in charge of the trip, and he had a very good-looking assistant named Rick. We started chatting with Rick and discovered that he lived across the street from us. He appeared to be a very outstanding gentleman, impeccably dressed in a suit and tie. He explained that he worked on the trips as a way of earning some extra money. Arlene and I were impressed that this young man seemed so levelheaded as we watched him organize all the people. Frank seemed to rely heavily on him. Arlene's sister was single at the time, and we concluded that he would be a great guy to fix her up with.

When we were all seated on the chartered flight, Rick went up and down the aisles, letting each of us know the details of the check-in at the hotel. We tactfully asked him if he was single, and he answered yes. We mentioned that Arlene had a sister who was also single and inquired if he would be interested in meeting her when we returned to New York City. He replied that he would love to and gave us his contact information. Rick promised to call Arlene's sister when we returned from the trip. We thought what a great match they would be, and he lived a few steps away from us.

We arrived in Las Vegas at around 4:00 p.m., and cars were waiting to take us to our hotel. When we arrived, Frank and Rick gave us our room keys. They told us to book any shows we wanted to see and that everything was free for us. Rick said that he would be at the bar area in our hotel if we needed anything, and when we returned, we should give him the phone number of Arlene's sister. He said that he was looking forward to meeting her.

We went to our room and dressed for the evening. We had a delicious dinner at the hotel and then traveled to a nearby hotel to see a great Las Vegas show. When we arrived back at our hotel, we stopped at the bar area to give Rick the phone number of Arlene's sister. We spotted Frank, Rick, and a blond woman sitting at a table with a big bottle of champagne in front of them. Frank invited us to have a drink with them because they were celebrating Rick's marriage. He introduced us to the flashy blonde sitting at the table and told us that they just got married an hour ago.

When Rick and his new wife left to go to his room, we were quite confused and asked Frank what happened. Frank explained that

Rick had smoked a joint, and he and Frank were having drinks in the bar area. A blond woman was sitting at the bar, and she began flirting with Rick, who then invited her to join them at their table. They had some drinks together, and she let them know that she was a hooker and was working the bar area. She and Rick took some puffs of a joint and started getting very friendly. Frank described them getting drunker and drunker and suddenly deciding on impulse to get married. They went to a chapel in the hotel and got married six hours after meeting. Rick was taking the next day off to drive with his new bride to meet her parents, who lived in a nearby town.

We asked Frank how Rick could pick up a hooker in a bar and then marry her. Frank answered that Rick was a smart guy and would probably put her to work in New York City to supplement his income. We were dumbfounded. This was the outstanding, stable young man we sized up as a date for Arlene's sister.

On the trip back to New York a few days later, Rick came over to us on the plane. He invited us to have a drink with him and his new wife at his apartment in New York City the following week. We did go to his place out of curiosity and walked into an apartment filled with the aroma of marijuana. We spent five minutes, congratulated the newlyweds, and told them we had to leave for an early dinner appointment. It was another life lesson, teaching me to never judge a book by its cover.

Arlene and I do not gamble, but I figured I could do a very small amount of gambling on the trip since all my expenses were free. I thought maybe if I showed that I played at the tables, I might get invited back on future trips. I figured I could fool them into believing that I was a player by buying some chips, playing a few hands, and then cashing in the chips at the cashier's window. I did the same thing each day, so it looked like I was losing money. Arlene kept warning me that these trips are run by mob people and that I shouldn't try to fool anybody. I replied that no one was paying attention to me and that she should just relax and enjoy the vacation.

Just then, the phone rang in our room, and I was told that Frank wanted to see me privately in his room. We both went into somewhat of a panic mode. I told Arlene that if I wasn't back in an hour, she should call hotel security. I went to Frank's room, and I was as nervous as could be. When I entered, Frank asked me to sit down. He told me that he heard I was a dentist, and there were no physicians on the trip.

He needed to have an injection in his buttocks for some medical issues he was having. He figured, as a dentist, I was used to giving injections and hoped that I could help him out. I was never so relieved in my life and happily did it. When I returned to my room, Arlene and I decided that, as great of a time as we had on this trip, I should never try to pretend that I am a gambler.

CHAPTER

FIFTY-FOUR

Experiences with People in The Entertainment Industry

When I first became a dentist, my picture was featured in *Time* magazine but not for any achievement on my part. I was going to a well-known New York City barber (also known as a hairstylist for any of you high-class readers; to me, coming from Brooklyn, the person cutting my hair will always be a barber, especially since the hair I have remaining doesn't leave enough to "style"). My barber had a business concept using glue-on mustaches and goatees. His idea was that a clean-shaven dentist during the day could change his appearance and go out at night with various types of facial hair. The story in *Time* magazine featured me with no facial hair during the day, becoming a bearded and mustached man about town at night. They showed before and after photos of me, but the fad never became popular. My friends and family did get a kick out of the article.

I also had my picture featured in Andy Warhol's *Interview* magazine. The editor, Bob Colacello, wrote a front-page article about the reopening of Studio 54 after it had closed when the original owners went to jail. The headline was STUDIO 54 REOPENS, AND EVERYONE WAS THERE FROM HALSTON TO MY DENTIST! There was a large picture of me on the dance floor with both arms in the air.

We spent a lot of time in those days with the marvelous photographer Francesco Scavullo. All the celebrities wanted to be photographed by him because he made everybody look so good. He was a wonderful and charming man, and we loved being with him and his companion and assistant, Sean. *People* magazine published a picture of him, Lorna Luft, and Arlene at a restaurant together. The caption explained that Lorna was out with Francesco and her dentist's wife, Arlene Lazare.

One year the Sunday Magazine section of the *New York Daily News* featured a story about me. It described the many celebrity patients who had been treated by me. When it was published, I received a call from the New York Dental Society, admonishing me for advertising in newspapers. I explained that I was not advertising but was approached by a reporter requesting an interview after hearing about my practice while doing an article on a well-known movie star.

A famous New York City agent named Swifty Lazar was such a great dealmaker that, after making three amazing deals in one day, his client Humphrey Bogart gave him the nickname "Swifty." His client list was legendary, and he was by far the most powerful agent in the country. When I made a restaurant reservation, I often received a very good table. Although I did not know him, I was happy to have the same name (except for the spelling) and the advantage it gave me when making reservations. When I finally did meet him and told him about all my perks in sharing his last name, he actually was flattered. Ironically, we had the same birthday, so I always felt a certain kinship with him.

One other legendary New York agent was Sam Cohn. His clients included Paul Newman, Woody Allen, Meryl Streep, Sigourney Weaver, Whoopi Goldberg, Cher, Jackie Gleason, and Dame Maggie Smith. Sam held court at the main first table in the Russian Tea Room every day for lunch. That was a major celebrity hangout for many years. Sam represented many of the most outstanding playwrights and actors in the New York City area. He was also well known for two of his peculiar traits. One was that he never dressed in fancy clothes, and his sweaters often had torn sleeves. The other was that he never returned anybody's telephone calls promptly. Famous people would call to talk to him, and he would not get back to them for days. This difficulty of getting through to him only served to make him more important in the eyes of his clients.

One day his dentist referred him to me for periodontal treatment. Ordinarily, I would observe a person sitting in my chair with a torn sweater and baggy old pants and feel sorry for him. However, I knew about Sam Cohn because he was Liza Minnelli's agent. Sam became not only a patient but also a good friend. I believe that I gained his respect when he called to speak to me at the office with questions about a procedure, and I did not return his calls immediately. I purposely did to him exactly what he did to his clients, and I guess that made me look important in his eyes.

One year Sam had to travel to Philadelphia to negotiate a deal for Liza to appear in an extended run there. He invited me to drive with him. True to his image, he picked me up in a broken-down old car with junk in the back seat. We planned to have dinner in a very famous seafood restaurant in Philadelphia after he negotiated his deal and then return to New York City after dinner. Sam was used to always having the best table at any restaurant he went to in New York City. When we arrived in Philadelphia at this well-known restaurant, there was a line waiting to be seated. They informed Sam that it would be about an hour's wait because they were running behind. He didn't know what to do as this never happened to him before. This restaurant had no idea about his connections, and Sam suggested that we just go to a coffee shop down the block since the wait was too long. I walked over to the maître d' and gave him $20, and we were seated in two minutes. Sam, who never needed to tip a maître d' to get a table, was impressed, and we proceeded to enjoy a great lobster dinner.

During our first few years of marriage, Arlene and I did not have many friends in Los Angeles. On our first trip there, we stayed at the Beverly Hills Hotel. The Polo Lounge at that hotel was the top spot for celebrity watching. The popular time there was the cocktail hour when celebrities would stop in to have drinks and meet up with each other. We stopped there every night before going out for dinner and recognized many famous faces. Every night when we arrived, we noticed a single man sitting by himself at the first prime table by the entrance. He was not someone whom we recognized.

On our third night while waiting to be seated, we smiled at him, and he invited us to join him for a drink. He introduced himself to us as Fishel Banks. He told us that he and his wife would come there every evening for cocktails for many years before she passed away at an early age. He explained that they were very much in love, and when he observed us the first few nights, he felt that we reminded him of himself and his late wife. While we sat with him, we noticed that most people said hello to him as they passed by. We had an enjoyable time talking with him, and he extended an invitation to sit with him on any future visits.

We loved our stays at the Beverly Hills Hotel and checked in there for a few days whenever we returned to Los Angeles in the early years of our marriage. Each time, we would see Fishel at the Polo Lounge and join him for a drink. He told us that since his wife's death, he had not been interested in a serious relationship with any other woman. On some nights, he did have a date with him and occasionally a few bachelor friends. He was obviously well connected and successful, and finding women to go out with was not a problem.

One of his bachelor friends whom we met was Max Factor. Max was a very charming man and, with that famous name, had no problem meeting women. We were impressed to meet Max Factor. As we got to know Fishel better, he told us the true story of his friend Max. It seemed that his father was the original Max Factor, and he had three sons. When he got older, he decided to make one of his sons the figurehead for his business. He picked the son with the least interest in the business and changed his first name to Max. Even though the other two sons were better at running the business, the son he named Max possessed a fabulous personality. So that son became "Max Factor" and the face of the business.

Fishel had many connections and arranged for Arlene and me to go to a very exclusive private club called On the Rox. It was situated on Sunset Boulevard, above the Roxy Theater. There was a private elevator that took us upstairs to a small darkly lit room. It was so exclusive that only a handful of top celebrities were admitted. We walked in and saw, among others, Jack Nicholson and John Lennon. We found it exciting to sit in this small intimate club and observe famous faces interacting with one another. (Years later, when I formed my mouthwash business, one of the young women working for me to help demonstrate my product was May Pang. She was John Lennon's lover for eighteen months, but I never discussed him with her.)

We started to frequent some of the hot spots in Los Angeles. There was a very popular celebrity hangout on Rodeo Drive called the Daisy. Sitting by himself almost every time we went there was a very overweight Orson Welles, the legendary actor, producer, writer, and director of possibly the greatest film of all time, *Citizen Kane*.

Our favorite store in LA was Giorgio. It was the first luxury boutique founded on Rodeo Drive in Beverly Hills by Fred and Gayle Hayman. Besides having wonderful fashions, customers were treated in a very special manner. They had wonderful cappuccinos, a pool table, a reading room, and an oak bar. Their clientele was the Who's Who of Hollywood. Our friend Lindsay Wagner starred in a very popular three-part miniseries called *Scruples*. It was about a boutique owner dealing with Hollywood's world of high fashion, quite similar to Giorgio.

When we became good friends with Jack Haley, he invited us to stay with him whenever we visited LA. Our times with him were special, and we learned about many aspects of the film industry. Debbie Reynolds was a close friend of Jack, and she was chairman of the Thalians charity organization, which raised money to help with the mental health of people who were in the military. Jack brought us to some wonderful Thalians events. We attended very exciting evenings honoring people like Bing Crosby, Dorothy Lamour, Bob Hope, and Rita Hayworth. Debbie was a delight to be with, and we enjoyed her company.

We were also invited to the LA Friars Club. Dinah Shore was the host of the dinner, and Arlene sat next to her. Arlene found her to be down to earth and enchanting.

Share is another charitable organization in LA that helps women with breast and ovarian cancer. It was started by the wives of major Hollywood male stars, along with some other women who were in the entertainment industry. People came dressed to Share's annual charity event in western attire. We attended a few of these evenings with Jack Haley and Ginny Mancini. One year we went with Lorna Luft during the time she was dating Burt Reynolds. We did enjoy spending time with Burt, who could be very charming when he wanted to be. Burt bid $5,000 for Lorna to sing a song of his choice. Major Hollywood stars would perform something after a person in the audience made a bid. The entertainment was followed by a fabulous western-themed party. I talked to Johnny Carson at one of the parties and was amazed at how extremely shy he was in public. His wife was very active in Share and got him to host it several times, although he seemed uncomfortable mingling with the crowd.

In 1982, Wolfgang Puck opened up Spago, and it quickly became the hottest celebrity restaurant in town and another restaurant Arlene and I frequented on our trips to LA. Wolfgang's wife, Barbara Lazaroff, walked around wearing the craziest outfits, but she was an effective hostess. The combination of innovative foods and celebrities made Spago an instant hit. It was right down the road from Jack Haley's home, so we went there often.

Jack, after divorcing Liza, was dating the actress Carol Lynley, and she was a sweetheart. Carol is best known for her roles in the films *The Poseidon Adventure* and *Blue Denim*. Jack, at one time, was engaged to Nancy Sinatra. They always remained friends, and the first time we went over to her home with Jack, we found her to be very lovely and warm. She treated us so wonderfully that we felt like old friends while we were in her home, but we never socialized with her outside her residence.

Another great LA institution was Matteo's Restaurant, especially on Sunday nights. We would go there with Tony Martin and Cyd Charisse and Ginny and Henry Mancini, who were regulars on Sunday nights. Milton Berle, George Burns, Frank Sinatra, and John Wayne were often there at our dinners. Sinatra would eat there with a group of friends any Sunday that he was in LA. It was a great, old-fashioned Italian restaurant. When the owner, Matty, had a stroke, many of the celebrities started going elsewhere.

When Mr. Chow opened a branch of their very successful restaurant, it instantly became a major celebrity hangout. Through our friendship with Tina and Michael Chow, we were able to get reservations when we were in LA. The unique Chinese food there was and still is fabulous. The only problem has always been the bill. Mr. Chow is the only restaurant I know where the check comes, and the bill states only the word "food," followed by a dollar amount. When some people complained that they wanted to see an itemized bill, they honored the request but wrote the entire bill in Chinese. To the majority of their customers, that doesn't seem to matter. Diners love the food, and the people watching is terrific. We went there on our latest trip to LA with Neil Sedaka and spent some enjoyable time with a very friendly Jamie Foxx at the next table.

Hal David was one of the most soft spoken and sweetest men we have ever met. We have wonderful memories of the time we spent with him and his wife, Eunice, both overseas and in the United States. Whenever we were in LA, we were invited by Hal and Eunice to Hillcrest Country Club for lunch. Most of the old-time Hollywood stars and producers are members. We loved meeting George Burns, who was in his late nineties and sharp and funny.

In 2011, when Hal received his star on the Hollywood Walk of Fame, we flew out to LA for the event. Our friend, the talented singer and producer Steve Tyrell, was also at the event. Steve always spoke to us about how important Hal was to his career. That occasion would be the last time that we saw Hal. He passed away the following year.

In 2012, we attended a special memorial to Hal where he was saluted by many people, including his two most famous collaborators, Burt Bacharach and Dionne Warwick. Hal was president of the Songwriters Hall of Fame. In 2004, he was awarded the Towering Song Award for his iconic song "What the World Needs Now Is Love." It was a very special evening. Presenters included Bill Cosby, Regis Philbin, Hall and Oates, Stevie Wonder, and Dionne Warwick. It was especially memorable to us because my closest friend Neil Sedaka was honored with the Sammy Cahn Lifetime Achievement Award at the same event.

We still see Eunice David both in New York City and LA for dinner. Since Hal's passing, Eunice has been dating an interesting man named Sidney Kibrick. Sidney was a child actor who appeared in the famous Hal Roach series *Our Gang*. For the past twenty years, we have been staying with Ginny Mancini at her beautiful duplex apartment when we visit Los Angeles. Eunice is her next-door neighbor, so we only have to walk a few steps to say hello.

One of our memorable dinners with Hal and Eunice was at a restaurant with two other couples. One of the other couples was the former secretary of state Al Haig and his wife, Patricia. Haig was a very strong and opinionated person. He was secretary of state under Ronald Reagan. When Reagan was shot, Haig famously announced to the country that "I am in control here." Eunice arranged the seating at the table and put Arlene next to Al Haig as his dinner companion. This normally would make for a fascinating dinner conversation, except for one problem—Arlene had laryngitis and was completely unable to talk. She came to the dinner with a notepad and pen and tried to make conversation with Haig by writing notes to him during dinner on her pad.

During the years that we hung out with Jackie Mason, we spent a fair amount of time with Rudy Giuliani. Rudy got a kick out of Jackie, and Jackie loved to talk politics with him. Rudy liked to go to a popular NYC cigar bar, so we usually passed on those nights. Rudy had a close friend and supporter named Howard Koeppel. Howard was a very successful automobile dealer in New York City and a loyal friend to Rudy. When Rudy and his wife, Donna Hanover, ended their relationship in 2001, he moved out of their apartment and did not have a permanent place to live. Until he found one, Rudy moved into a guest room at Howard's apartment.

Howard was gay and lived with his partner, Mark Hsiao. When Howard and Mark decided to get married in 2009, he asked Rudy to officiate. According to Howard, Rudy said he would be happy to as soon as a marriage between two males was allowed in NYC. When that came about in 2011, Howard was quite upset when Rudy never returned his phone calls about performing the ceremony, and it harmed their friendship.

We had met the author Barbara Taylor Bradford and her husband, Robert Bradford, through Lindsay Wagner. Barbara Taylor Bradford is one of the most prolific and well-read authors of our time. She has written thirty-five best-selling novels, and her novel *A Woman of Substance* sold thirty-six million copies worldwide. It is one of the ten best-selling novels of all time. Her husband, Robert, was a producer, and he turned many of her novels into TV miniseries. When Lindsay Wagner finished her years as the Bionic Woman on TV, Robert Bradford chose her to star in the TV miniseries *A Woman of Substance*. Lindsay became great friends with them, and every time she came to New York and stayed with us, we would all spend time together.

We always found them to be a very pleasant and stimulating couple to be with. We have spent time with them in Europe as well because Barbara does a tremendous amount of traveling to formulate ideas for her novels. The apartment they had in New York City when we first met them had one of the best views of the East River that we have ever seen. However, they wanted a larger apartment and moved into a magnificent apartment in the River House in New York City.

Lindsay Wagner is a strong believer in holistic medicine and is very much an earth mother. She has raised two wonderful sons and is a firm believer in breastfeeding for as long as possible. One day we were with her and her four-year-old son Dorian and our young teenage daughter, Lauren. Dorian was walking next to Lauren and pulled on her shirt, saying, "Hungry, Mommy." (She must have been doing something right or had Bionic Woman breast milk as Dorian is now a six-foot-six-inch stuntman.)

We have been through some interesting times with Lindsay and some of her dates. When our daughter, Lauren, was sixteen, Lindsay was dating Fred Segal. He owned several very popular Fred Segal boutique stores. When he came to New York City with Lindsay, he gave Lauren a beautiful bracelet from his store as a sweet sixteen gift. Lauren was quite upset when that relationship ended. Besides liking Fred, she anticipated having perks at his store in the future.

Lindsay dated the actor Bruce Davison while he was starring on Broadway in *The Elephant Man*. He spent a good deal of his time onstage in a large bathtub. Lindsay has a playful nature and managed to arrange with the stagehands to leave him fun notes from her in the tub while he was onstage.

When our daughter, Lauren, had her bat mitzvah, our friend Sheryl Lee Ralph flew in from Los Angeles. She was wonderful with the children and had them gather around her while she sang "We Are the World" with them. Her date for the evening was a very good-looking, sharply dressed man named Rashid. He was a very popular school guidance counselor and teacher and part-time black male model. Lindsay Wagner had also flown in from Los Angeles for the party and had come without a date. Somehow during the evening, Lindsay and Rashid hit it off. We ended up taking Sheryl home from the party at the World Trade Center with us, and Rashid and Lindsay left together. They then dated for a few years whenever Lindsay came to town.

They made a terrific couple, except that Rashid was always very formal, and everything had to be perfect. He was a nice guy, but we all wanted to loosen him up a bit. He spoke with perfect English pronunciation and was very neat. We went with them one night for dinner at the Algonquin Hotel, and all night, Rashid was critical of the sloppy service. He announced that the next time we all went out, he wanted to take us to one of his favorite restaurants, where the service and food presentation was impeccable. Lindsay, Arlene, and I decided that we had to try to loosen this guy up and make him more fun.

I came to the dinner with an assorted number of items hidden in my pockets. I had imitation bugs, a plastic ice cube with a fly inside, a used Band-Aid, and a twisted piece of wire. Rashid proceeded to order his favorite dishes, letting us know how perfectly they were served at this establishment. When he noticed a fly floating in my water, he immediately called over the waiter to remove the glass. He was speaking very formally, describing in eloquent terms the beauty of their salad presentation. When he finished talking, he noticed a Band-Aid in his salad and tried to remove it without any of us noticing. Lindsay had slipped it into his salad while he was talking to us. When Arlene pointed out a bug floating in her soup, and I found a piece of wire in my salad, Rashid was mortified. He apologized profusely to us, stating how embarrassed he was. He explained that this restaurant was always perfect in their food presentation, and he demanded that the waiter bring over the maître d'. We could no longer hold back our laughter, and Rashid finally realized that he had been set up. He started to laugh along with us, and from that day on, our relationship with him changed. He loosened up, and we remained friends for a number of years, although his relationship with Lindsay came to an end partly because she lived in Los Angeles and he in New York City.

We had met Liz Derringer many years ago through Lorna Luft and her husband Jake Hooker. Jake was in a British rock group and wrote the very popular song "I Love Rock and Roll." He took the last name Hooker as his stage name, but Lorna didn't want to be known as Lorna Hooker. She kept her name, and when they had children, she took the name Richards as their last name. Lorna didn't want her children to have the last name Hooker either. Jake's group was called the Arrows, and they were friendly with the Rolling Stones. Lorna liked Keith Richards's last name better than Jake's, so she used Richards as the name for her children.

Liz was married to a famous rock musician Rick Derringer, best known for his song "Hang on Sloopy." That marriage did not last, and Liz later dated the creator of the Benihana restaurants, Rocky Aoki. We found Rocky to be an interesting guy, and we had some fun dinners together, but that relationship also did not last. Rocky has a daughter named Devon Aoki, who became a top model, and she goes to our son, Marc, as a dental patient.

Liz went to work for the artist Peter Max. Peter is one of the most famous pop artists of the '60s. His paintings sell for a very high price, and his art is extremely colorful. Arlene and I always loved his work, and Liz invited us to his studio in New York City. The man running the studio gave us a tour of the place, showing us many of his works. We had spent some time with Peter and Liz over the years and found him to be a very nice person. He liked to doodle on napkins while we were in restaurants and had given some to us. The man running Peter's studio made me aware that if there were any works of art that I liked, he would give us a considerable discount if I paid for them in cash. We bought a number of paintings that we liked, all of which hang prominently in our home today. Even with my discount, it was still very expensive. The studio manager offered to have me pay a part in cash and the rest in checks made out to cash.

In 1997, I received a call from an IRS agent. He advised me that Peter Max was under investigation from the IRS for not declaring income. He explained that my name was given to the IRS as one of the purchasers of Peter's art. He wanted to meet with me at the IRS office in Manhattan and ordered me to bring my checking account records. I told him that I did not want to get involved with their case against Peter because he was a friend. The agent firmly explained to me that if I did not fully cooperate, they would investigate me next. I felt terrible about having to produce financial information that would hurt Peter.

When I went to my interview with the agent, he asked me which paintings I had purchased. I named a few but left out some. He looked me sternly in the eye and proceeded to remind me about some paintings I had mistakenly left out of my discussion with him. I realized then that someone from Peter's studio obviously had squealed on him to the IRS, and they knew exactly which paintings I and others had purchased. Fortunately for me, I did not use unreported income cash, but I had a clear record in my checking account of checks that I cashed to pay for the paintings. The agent took my checks and told me that he would make duplicates for me. When I remarked that I would like my original checks back, he explained to me that I did not have a choice.

That day, I learned a lesson about the power of the IRS. I was later required to give that same information to a grand jury, which was looking into Peter's financial affairs. I felt bad for him when it turned out that the man running his studio was the one who reported him to the IRS. Peter had donated paintings for many of the major events in our country and must have had great connections. He served a jail sentence for only a few months and was back to work soon afterward.

Steve Rossi was part of a famous comedy duo in the '50s and '60s called Allen and Rossi. I met him in Palm Beach through friends years after his act had broken up. He was a charming and witty guy, but I witnessed him using his charm to live off other people. He would be the entertaining houseguest or storytelling dinner companion. When he learned that I had sold my company, he began trying to persuade me to invest in memorabilia he had from the old Allen and Rossi act, which he wanted to merchandise to the public. He lived in Las Vegas with a girlfriend who was a singer. He kept telling Arlene and me to meet him in Las Vegas and offered to show us around the town. When we mentioned that we were coming to Las Vegas in a few months to meet up with Liza, he said we must call him. He insisted on taking us to his favorite restaurant. We were arriving in Las Vegas the day before Liza's opening, so we figured it might be fun to take Steve up on his offer. He sounded excited to hear that we were coming to Vegas and invited us for a very special dinner that he arranged.

When we met him at the restaurant, he apologized for coming without his girlfriend because she was singing in one of the lounges in town. He announced that he would order everything and proceeded to give our waiter instructions on what food and wine to bring out. We were amazed at how extravagant he was as platters of food started to arrive. He remarked to the waiter that his girlfriend loved their food and gave him a list of dishes for a takeout order for Steve to bring to her.

When we finished our main dish, Steve told the waiter to bring out some special desserts. He then informed me that he was sorry to leave our dinner before dessert was served because he had to meet up with his girlfriend at the lounge, where she was performing. He took with him the large takeout order of food and reminded us to enjoy the special desserts he ordered and to meet him later at the lounge to hear her sing. All through dinner, he bombarded us with stories about the famous entertainers he hung out with and had worked with. When he walked out of the restaurant, we commented to each other that we must have misjudged him as he proved to be quite a big sport.

We finished our meal and got up to leave. The waiter stopped us, telling me not to leave because the check was on its way. Steve left before dessert so we would be stuck with the check, which included the large takeout order for his girlfriend. That was the last we saw of him, although he still tried to contact me to invest in his memorabilia business.

David Gest was another person who knew how to get things for free. He put together evenings that appeared to be charity events, but all the proceeds went to him. He had a large bevy of old-time movie stars who would accept his invitation of free plane flights and hotel rooms in exchange for appearing at his events. He would give the event some official-sounding name, misleading people into believing that it was a charity evening. None of the old-time movie stars were paid for their appearances.

We met many film stars from old Hollywood movies and did get a kick out of spending time with them and hearing their stories. I found Jane Powell and Dickie Moore to be an adorable, charming couple. They lived near us, and we would see them from time to time. I had a great time with Jane Russell in London. We got to know her quite well after spending a week with her there. We were surprised at how well Arlene Dahl could still sing and have been friends with her and her husband, Marc Rosen, for many years now. Her dog and Liza's dog actually mated, and each of them received puppies from the union. We have been at Liza's apartment when the dogs would get together for playdates.

Kathryn Grayson, Esther Williams, and Mickey Rooney were some of the other movie stars whom we met through David. Mickey was not easy to deal with, and Esther enjoyed her alcohol, but David handled them all. David dragged Liza and us to some really dingy restaurants during the time they were together because he was not a big spender.

We had good times in London with David, Liza, and Joan Collins, and her husband Percy Gibson. Percy is thirty-one years younger than Joan, but their chemistry together really works well. In New York, they invited us to one of their favorite Italian restaurants, Isle of Capri, and they held hands throughout dinner. They are also good friends with Neil and Leba Sedaka and Leslie and Evie Bricusse, and we all had lovely times together.

A few years ago, Joan did a tour of her one-woman show. When she appeared at the Regency Hotel in New York City, she invited us to attend. We couldn't imagine what she would do, but we were very pleasantly surprised. She showed many film clips from her movie and TV work. Joan became an international superstar with her role as Alexis Colby in the TV series *Dynasty*. She has appeared in countless films and television shows over her long career. In 2015, Joan was made a dame by Queen Elizabeth II for services to charity. Joan has a very sharp wit and knew when to criticize herself if her performance was not deserving of an Academy Award. She told some wonderful stories and totally captivated and charmed the audience. Joan has aged better than any actress we know and is still a remarkable beauty.

In October 1985, I was invited to speak at the annual meeting of the American Dental Association in San Francisco. During my presentation, I discussed for the first time a revolutionary new mouthwash called Plax. I did not mention my involvement in its development but merely reported the results of clinical studies that were done at the University of Pennsylvania. Some people from my newly formed company traveled to San Francisco, and we began the rollout of Plax on the West Coast. Within one year, my new mouthwash product exceeded $100 million in sales, becoming the third most popular mouthwash in the country behind Listerine and Scope.

Ironically, that year, the American Dental Association hired our friend Julie Budd to perform at one of the evening events. I loved the idea that I was able to celebrate this important beginning of my business venture with my good friend. Earlier that year, I had tested my mouthwash on several of my patients. Farrah Fawcett and Ryan O'Neal, who would come into my office holding hands, were two of the people I asked to evaluate it. Farrah loved the product and wrote a wonderful note thanking me for giving it to her. She and Ryan took Arlene and me out to dinner at the Carlyle Hotel, where they were staying, as a thank-you for giving them samples of Plax. They were a very sought-after couple for the paparazzi to photograph at that time, and they didn't want to venture to restaurants out of their hotel. It was nice spending personal time with them outside my office environment, and they were a delightful couple.

Another interesting and unique patient was Peter Beard. Peter was a well-known artist, photographer, and writer. He was very handsome, adored by the ladies, and quite a playboy. At one time, he was married to the supermodel Cheryl Tiegs. For part of the year, he lived in Manhattan and was seen at all the chic places in New York. For several months of the year, he lived in Africa as a wildlife photographer. The *New York Times* referred to him as the "last of the adventurers." His death-defying photographs of African wildlife were legendary. Whenever he was back in New York City, he came in regularly as a patient.

One year he could hardly walk and hobbled in on crutches. He explained that an elephant had rolled over on him while he was photographing it. Often, I noticed this handsome guy sitting in the chair, scratching different parts of his body where he had rashes from his experiences in Africa. This visual didn't quite fit with his reputation as a sophisticated man about town. Peter spent decades as an amorous and pharmaceutically inclined man about town. Unfortunately, in his later years, he developed dementia and was recently found dead in the woods in Montauk after he had been missing for three weeks.

So many celebrities end up in financial difficulty because they have an incompetent or crooked money manager taking care of all their finances. A good example of how many celebrities have no idea about bills being paid was when one of Debbie Reynolds's children came to my office for a consultation. She needed extensive work, and I gave her my fee for what would entail four months of treatment. She never went ahead with the work because she was not going to be in New York City for that length of time. She told my receptionist to send the bill for the consultation and my recommended treatment plan to her mother's financial adviser. A few weeks later, my office received a check from Debbie Reynolds's financial adviser for the total amount of the four months of work that I had recommended. We, of course, returned the check since I never did the treatment. That is a perfect example of how some people allow money managers to handle their funds without them knowing where their money is going.

I witnessed what happened to Sammy Davis Jr. when he allowed his financial adviser to handle all his money. Instead of sending payments to the IRS for Sammy's taxes, the money manager kept the funds for himself. As a result, Sammy had a tremendous IRS debt, compounded by penalties incurred when the initial payments were not made.

In 1989, Billy Joel fired his manager and former brother-in-law, suing him for $90 million for misuse of Billy's money. Billy was quoted in the media as being upset with his lawyer, Allen Grubman, for not protecting him properly. Allen is the most powerful lawyer in the music business. His clients include Bruce Springsteen, Madonna, U2, Rod Stewart, Elton John, Mariah Carey, and Jennifer Lopez. I met Allen many years ago through common friends. We always found him to be an interesting guy with a very short attention span, which made it difficult to socialize with him over the years.

At the time I met him, he was dating a girl who lived near us in Westhampton. He asked if he could sleep over at our house one weekend after a late evening with her. Early Sunday morning, I got up early to play tennis, and Allen was sitting in our kitchen. I was not a coffee drinker, and when he asked me to show him how to work the coffee machine, I had no idea how to use it. We were two sophisticated men about town who had no idea how to make a cup of coffee.

Allen wanted to read the *Sunday Times*, so he decided to go into town to get some coffee and the Sunday papers. When he returned and opened the newspaper, I realized why he was up so early and anxious to see the papers. The front-page story that morning in the *Sunday Times* was how Grubman organized a deal that forced Walter Yetnikoff out of his position at CBS, and Allen's friend Tommy Mottola would be the new head. Allen had not said a word about it all weekend. Yetnikoff was the flamboyant and volatile president of CBS Records, the most successful label of its time. (Michael Jackson, Bruce Springsteen, the Rolling Stones, Bob Dylan, Billy Joel, Paul Simon, Barbra Streisand, and James Taylor were some of the artists under contract.)

Allen always enjoyed being around Jackie Mason. He loved Jackie's humor, and we had fun moments together during the years I was spending time with Jackie. I still see him around town, and he still is the most prominent entertainment lawyer.

 CHAPTER

FIFTY-FIVE

Our Parties

Arlene and I have a large group of friends who are not in the entertainment industry. We always enjoyed making fun parties, mixing entertainers with people who are not in the performing arts. We often plan unusual themes for our parties. During our first year of marriage, we saw two street musicians in our neighborhood playing on the corner for tips. Our apartment had a terrace, and we invited some friends over for a party. Arlene was somewhat hesitant to have two strangers in our apartment, but I asked them to come and play for our guests. I set a price and only requested that they shower before they come. (They did give off quite an odor, but they played outside on the terrace and worked for little money, so on balance, it seemed good to me. I somehow sensed that Arlene wouldn't let me get off so easily for future parties, and I was right.) It turned out to be a fun time, with everybody singing along with them, and that was the beginning of our love for throwing parties.

For our next party, we asked everybody to dress in Asian attire. We called up the China Institute in NY and hired some musicians to play Chinese music. There was a very flamboyant gay male working at Arlene's beauty parlor. We hired him to come dressed as a geisha. He showed up with a gigantic wig, over-the-top makeup, and long artificial fingernails. We announced that there would be a prize for the best costume. I chose my squarest male friend as the recipient of the prize for the best costume. The prize would be a massage in our bathtub by a beautiful geisha. I set the bath and provided him with a bathing suit. I then revealed that the beautiful geisha masseuse was actually the flamboyant gay male. My friend was a good sport, and we all laughed as we watched the fun, but it was a very short massage. At another party with the theme "Come as your favorite fantasy," our cousin Fred, who is a very religious, outstanding doctor, came dressed as his nurse.

During the Studio 54 days, we would have a party in our apartment, and then invite our guests to join us after dessert at Studio 54 if they wanted to continue the party and stay out late. One year we were doing some extensive decorating in our apartment and had a considerable number of mirrors installed that afternoon, just in time for the party. Our contractor warned us that the large mirrors were glued in place that afternoon, and people should be careful not to touch them.

Two of our guests that evening were Milton and Amy Greene. They were close friends of Marilyn Monroe, and Milton was famous for taking all the outstanding Marilyn Monroe photographs. Marilyn lived with Milton and Amy for a while and formed Marilyn Monroe Productions with Milton as her partner. At the time of our party, Milton and Amy were going through a very unpleasant divorce. Amy was also dating a much younger man. Milton came by himself to the party and was having a wonderful time until he spotted Amy and the young boyfriend enter our apartment around dessert time. We were making a birthday party for Jack Haley, and being somewhat devilish, he invited them both.

When Amy walked in with the boyfriend, Milton started to glare at them and said to me, "I'm going to hit him." I begged Milton to please not start a fight because new mirrors were just installed that afternoon. I managed to keep them at opposite ends of the apartment for the remainder of the evening.

We invited any guests who wanted to join us at Studio 54 to meet us there, and everyone made their way out of our apartment. As Amy and her boyfriend walked out of our door into the hallway, Milton ran out after them. He took a swing at the boyfriend, and after a few blows, we managed to pull them apart. While I was restraining Milton, he turned to me and said, "I waited until I was in the hall so I wouldn't damage your mirrors."

One year a very huge, four-story karaoke club opened in the Broadway area. We had a big dinner party there. They had a stage on one level where our guests could get up and sing any song they wished. There was a screen in front displaying the words, and the club had professional backup singers onstage with various outfits to accompany them on whatever song they chose. There also were costumes and props that our guests could use for their song. Cameras were filming each person, and every guest went home with a video of themselves performing. Some of our guests, like Neil Sedaka, were so entertaining that people wanted copies of those videos as well.

One of our favorite clubs in New York City is Birdland. Birdland is run by a good friend, Gianni Valenti. On Monday night, there is an open mic evening for Broadway entertainers to perform with the band. It is called Cast Party and run by a longtime friend of ours, Jim Caruso. We met Jim many years ago when he was doing some work for Liza Minnelli, as well as performing with her. He observed the great times we all had around the piano at Liza's apartment. He created a similar feeling with a great trio at Birdland on Monday nights. Jim is a very charming and witty host and knows how to create a really fun evening.

We decided to allow our friends who are not professional entertainers an opportunity to have the experience of getting up onstage and singing with a professional band. We took over Birdland on a Sunday evening for a dinner party and entertainment. We advised people that they could pick any song they liked and then perform it with the band. They could bring their own musical arrangements, and the trio was capable of playing almost any song and in any key. I had Jim Caruso host the evening, and I gave him a list of friends who wanted to sing. We also invited a number of our entertainer friends to sing as well. Mixed in with our friends who were not performers were Tony Danza, Peter Cincotti, Ann Hampton Callaway, Billy Stritch, Johnny Rodgers, Neil Sedaka, Liza Minnelli, Hilary Kole, Sheryl Lee Ralph, Nicolas King, and several others. Some of our nonprofessional friends went up in small groups and had a ball singing with the band. Some of our friends, unfortunately, were intimidated when they saw professionals up there singing and took their names off the list.

One of our friends, Pamala Morgan, always wanted to sing. For her wedding gift, we gave her singing lessons with Julie Budd. She performed at our party and had such a good time that she continued with singing lessons. Recently, she started doing a one-woman show at a small nightclub in New York.

One person out of all the entertainers received the biggest standing ovation. His name was Arnie Greenberg. He nervously explained that, growing up very poor, he worked as an usher in a Broadway theater. Every night he would hear Ezio Pinza sing the hit song from the *South Pacific* musical show "Some Enchanted Evening." Even though Arnie could not sing, his life's ambition was to one day sing that song to the woman he loved. Arnie and two of his friends from Brooklyn opened up a small deli. They had an idea for a new drink and decided to manufacture it. They called it "Snapple." It turned out to be one of the most popular drinks ever and made all three of them multimillionaires. Arnie explained to all the guests at our party that he still had not achieved his one ambition of singing that song to the woman he loved. He took out a sheet of paper and, with shaking hands, dedicated the song to his wife, Roberta. He sang "Some Enchanted Evening" in front of his wife and friends. It was not a fabulous rendition, but he received a standing ovation from everybody in the room. He was a very lovely, sweet man and was definitely the hit of the evening. He told me later that he was sorry he was not able to rehearse because he would have been less nervous.

He had a magnificent home in Southampton, and Arnie decided to throw a big party there the following summer. After dinner, he invited his guests outside to the back deck. He had hired a band and rehearsed all week with them. Arnie wanted to recreate his Birdland moment in front of his friends but, this time, after rehearsing with his own band. He finished singing "Some Enchanted Evening" and received some polite applause. He was not much of a singer, and in that atmosphere, it didn't really go over well. He told me afterward that he realized that his experience at Birdland was very special and could not be duplicated.

We had a few more parties at Birdland but stopped after we observed that our guests who were not entertainers were embarrassed to sing when the professional singers performed. One party coincided with our anniversary. The fabulous singer Ann Hampton Callaway called us up onstage with her. She asked everyone to yell out any words that came into their minds. She then proceeded to create an original song about us using the words that people shouted out. In addition to her vocal talents, she has the ability to compose a song on the spot. Ann is a dear friend and a very talented songwriter, and among the songs she has written is the theme to the TV show *The Nanny*.

One of our guests, Bobby Zarin, brought his daughter, who was quite shy in public. I was shocked when Jim Caruso informed me that she was on the list to sing at one of our parties. She sang a fair version of a song that she chose. When she finished, our friend, the talented singer Sheryl Lee Ralph, walked up onstage and called her back up. In front of everybody, Sheryl asked her to sing the song again, only this time Sheryl advised her to look directly at the audience, maintain a good posture, and sing out. The girl did the song again, and this time, she was terrific. I believe that evening positively changed her life.

Every year for the past number of years, I have been celebrating my birthday with Judy and Rod Gilbert. Judy and I were both born on March 28, so we usually gather some people together and celebrate. Rod is a fun-loving guy and a terrific person. He was a star hockey player for the New York Rangers. He was the first New York Ranger player to have his number retired and is the leading Rangers scorer in both goals and points. For my last birthday, he gave me an autographed jersey of his, along with an autographed puck as a birthday gift. Rod is constantly making appearances for various good causes, and he and Judy are always involved in charitable work. Rod is still working with the New York Rangers, making appearances at events for them. His outgoing personality and popularity with the fans make him the perfect person to represent the team. Rod always has an endless amount of new jokes, and an evening with him is never dull. He's great with kids as well, and our grandchildren Justin and Devin loved kicking a soccer ball around with Rod at our Westhampton home when he visited.

Some of our dinner parties, when we first were married, didn't always go so well. We met a lovely young married couple in our building named Linda and Sam. We decided to invite them over for dinner to get to know them better. We had asked a third couple to join us, but they could only stay for cocktails. It was the early '70s, and the use of drugs was becoming popular, but Arlene and I did not partake in it. The couple who could not stay for dinner brought us a gift of a bag of marijuana and a rolled-up joint. We thanked them and figured we would dispose of it after they left since we had no desire to try it. We are not prudes, but smoking anything does not interest us. Sam and Linda had also never tried marijuana.

When the other couple departed, we sat down for dinner. Linda looked at the joint and said that she had never tried marijuana and asked if it would be okay if she took a puff. I answered that it was fine with me, and she and Sam each took two puffs of the joint. Arlene and I passed on the experience. Suddenly, Linda announced that she was feeling dizzy. She got up from her chair, started to sway, and fell on the carpet. Arlene looked at me with daggers and admonished me for allowing them to do that in our apartment.

I had no experience with the effects of marijuana on a person and tried to comfort Linda. Her husband, Sam, also tried to comfort her. But then Sam announced that he was also feeling dizzy, and he sat down on the floor next to Linda. Arlene panicked and wanted to call for an ambulance. I informed her that I could not believe that two puffs on a joint would cause anything that was life threatening. The first thing I did was take the bag of marijuana and flush it down the toilet. In case an ambulance was needed, I did not want to have illegal drugs in my possession and run the risk of losing my license as a dentist.

I somehow was able to urge Sam to stand up. Lenox Hill Hospital is just four blocks from my home. I had Sam and Arlene help me get Linda up on her feet, although she was quite wobbly. We managed to walk Linda to the elevator, and when we got downstairs, Sam and I supported Linda by the arm while Arlene hailed a taxi. In the cab, I emphasized to Linda, "Whatever you do, do not say that you received any marijuana at my apartment." Besides my fear of being arrested, I was in a panic at the possibility of losing my dental license. I mentioned this a few times while we pulled up to the emergency entrance.

I called out to the attendants to help us with a woman who was not feeling well. When they reached Linda, they asked her what happened. She pointed to me and said, "He gave me a cigarette." They placed Linda on a bed and wheeled her into the hospital. The female attendant looked at me and laughed. She informed me that this happened dozens of times a day, and it was only a panic reaction to the experience. Sam came out after seeing his wife to let us know she was fine. The original attendant was correct in diagnosing the panic attack that Linda had after feeling light headed from puffing on the joint.

A few months later, Linda notified us that she was divorcing Sam. They appeared to be a well-matched couple. However, Linda felt that Sam did not give her the proper attention that evening, and arguments ensued daily after that.

Arlene doesn't take any drugs mostly because she never liked the feeling of being off balance. In all the years of our marriage, I have only seen her tipsy twice. Once was at our home in Westhampton, when Lorna Luft and her husband Jake were staying with us. Arlene had never tried tequila, and Lorna suggested that they do some shots. I was in the living room when I noticed Arlene crawling across the floor, heading toward the bathroom. The two shots of tequila made her dizzy and sick, and she managed to get to the bathroom on her hands and knees. We all were hysterical at the sight of Arlene, who is always in perfect control, unable to stand up.

The other time when Arlene was off balance occurred at a dinner party where the hostess served cauliflower au gratin as a side dish. Arlene is not much of a cauliflower fan, but she loves au gratin, and she scraped it off the top and ate it. What we didn't know was that the stupid hostess thought she was being cute by mixing hash in with the au gratin. Arlene could hardly stand up, and I and two friends helped her into a cab, and we went home. Arlene was unable to walk, but she did not want the doorman to see her looking stoned. Two of us supported Arlene under her arms, and we walked into our building with Arlene moving her legs as if she was walking. We were totally lifting her, and her feet never touched the ground. She was able to go past the doorman looking elegant, with her head held up high.

One major party we threw was almost a disaster. On December 16, 1975, I made an anniversary party for my parents at the Blue Angel nightclub on East Fifty-Fourth Street in NYC. It was the most spectacular nightclub in town, featuring dinner, dancing, and a big production show. They had two shows that night, and I booked the early show. My entire family was there, including every conceivable relative. The only two family members not present were our two young children, ages one and five, who were at home with our nanny. It was a fantastic evening of great entertainment and family bonding.

After the last of our guests left at ten thirty, I paid the check as a small crowd entered for the second show at eleven o'clock. We filled the club with our family for the first show, but the second performance only had about thirty-five people in attendance. We took my parents home and then went to our apartment. For the next few hours, my home phone did not stop ringing. At the beginning of the eleven o'clock show, a fire broke out in the club. Faulty electrical wiring under the stage ignited a fire that burned through the curtains and consumed the room. People attempted to flee in panic through the one fire exit. Out of the thirty-five people attending the performance, seven died, and six were hospitalized. Had that faulty wiring ignited two hours earlier, my entire family would have been wiped out. The later show had a small audience, so many were able to fit through the fire exit. If the fire occurred with the packed first show, most people would have died. My relatives, hearing this major news story on the evening news, thought that Arlene and I were trapped in the fire because we stayed after they all had left. As I assured each caller that we were safe, I realized how lucky we were.

The day we had our first child, we made arrangements with Arlene's sister, Susan, to raise each other's children should something happen to either of us. We also had backup family members to help raise our children in case of our early demise. We never could have foreseen an occasion where our entire family would be destroyed in one night, leaving only two babies alive. Those two hours made all the difference between a disaster and a celebration. I still shudder at the thought of what might have happened. The one bright spot was that I paid the very expensive bill with my American Express card, and all records of that purchase went up in smoke. (If I suddenly get a bill from American Express after forty-five years have elapsed since that incident, I might regret writing this book.)

I have tried to organize interesting parties for Arlene's birthdays with her girlfriends. One year I had Liza Minnelli host a birthday luncheon for Arlene and sixty of her girlfriends at the Park Avenue Café. Liza gave a touching speech, telling everyone how special Arlene was to her.

Another year, I invited Arlene's girlfriends to her birthday dinner at a place called Bathtub Gin. It is on Ninth Avenue downtown in New York City and is set up like an old-fashioned speakeasy. There is no sign on the door. When you knock, they let you into a very small candy shop. After you give your name to the person, a back door opens, and you enter into a small nightclub. At the front is a bar area, followed by a room with a number of tables. At the end of the room is a large bathtub. Arlene's girlfriends were served drinks and were given a menu for food. During the meal, a scantily dressed woman walked out with a microphone. She welcomed everyone to the party and proceeded to introduce a series of exotic female strippers who performed between courses. The last one stepped into the bathtub, which was partially filled with water. She did a very acrobatic striptease act in the bathtub, splashing water about when flipping her hair. The food and drink and atmosphere were all great, and the women enjoyed a different type of birthday celebration.

There was a unique Japanese restaurant and nightclub in New York called Sushi Roxx. We asked everyone to dress in Asian-style and took over the entire club. The main rooms had many multimedia video screens, and there was a dance floor in the center of the room. Every twenty minutes, a new group of terrific performers entertained with song, dance, and acrobatics. There was great dance music playing in between the performances for everyone to get up and dance.

On another occasion, we threw a party at Swing 46 Jazz and Supper Club in New York City. They have a big band sound from the '40s and a dance floor. We had dance instructors in between sets, teaching our guests how to do the Lindy Hop and dance steps from the '40s. The band had some terrific singers, and a few of our entertainer friends also got up to sing. One of our favorite people Tomaczek, who has performed all over the world, started the party by having everyone stand and sing the national anthem. Nicolas King, Hank Stampf, and Pamela Morgan also sang, and the big band was terrific.

Arlene's father, Dr. David Levin, lived to 102 years of age. When he turned 100, Arlene and her sister, Susan, made a party for him. The theme was "From cars to Mars," and they explained that when he was born in 1904, cars were just invented. When he died in 2006, we were sending astronauts into outer space. All our family was there, and Arlene and Susan hosted a wonderful celebration. He was a remarkable doctor and person, and he is always in our thoughts.

₰[CHAPTER]₰

FIFTY-SIX

Real Housewives of NYC

When Sol Kerzner invited us to the opening of the Mohegan Sun Hotel and Casino, we met a couple who would become close friends. Bobby and Jill Zarin lived near us in NYC and the Hamptons. They became part of a group of about forty couples whom we have socialized with over the past twenty years. Jill and Bobby threw a Fourth of July party every year at their home in the Hamptons.

One year as we were entering their property, we were stopped by people at the entrance. We were asked to sign forms allowing us to be filmed for television. We thought it was a joke but discovered that they were filming a pilot for a possible TV show. It was called *The Real Housewives of New York City*. We were surprised anyone would be interested in filming any of the parties that we attended with this group. They were lovely people, but I assumed the public would be interested in observing celebrities interacting, not everyday housewives. Boy was I wrong! The various "real housewives" filmed in many cities have been extremely popular for many years now.

The following year, Jill invited us to a party in Midtown Manhattan celebrating the first show. I sat in a restaurant with TV screens overhead, watching Jill tell her daughter to play up to her stepfather to obtain extra money from him. Just as I was commenting to Arlene that Jill must be mortified to realize that her private conversation was now being seen by everyone, including her husband, Jill walked over to us. She pointed to the television screen and exclaimed, "Look, I am on TV!"

Most of the "real housewives of NYC" have been people we have known for years, leading relatively unknown lives. Mario and Ramona Singer were a couple we had been friends with for twenty years. We thought that they were a great couple together. Mario is a terrific tennis player and loved to tease me about my poor tennis form. Unfortunately, their marriage broke up during the filming of the show.

When we were throwing our parties at Birdland, some of the "real housewives of NYC" asked if they could sing and film it for the TV show. We declined because I wanted to keep our parties private. They did organize a similar evening to ours at a later time and had it filmed for the show. At one of our parties, Ramona asked me to have Mario sing with the band because that was on his bucket list. I agreed, and Mario had a friend write an original song for him to sing. He was pretty good but not professional enough to pursue a singing career.

Luann, better known as the Countess, always wanted to sing, and she performed at our party. She is not the best singer in the world, but her enthusiasm and style help her put on an entertaining performance. The year after our party, she invited us to a restaurant in New York City called Josephine, where she sang a tune that she recorded for her first CD. She has subsequently formed a nightclub act, with our friend Billy Stritch as her pianist and arranger. Because of her popularity on the *Housewives* show, she has become one of the most popular and successful nightclub acts in the country.

Ramona, with no real theatrical training, has become a terrific natural actress. She invited us to go with her when she took a small part in an off-Broadway show, and she was wonderful onstage. During our time in London with Liza Minnelli and David Gest, we met Dorinda Medley at a party hosted by Sol and Heather Kerzner. We were surprised to bump into her at a restaurant in Southampton a few years ago, sitting with Ramona. We went over to hug her and say hello, only to realize that they were filming an episode for *The Real Housewives of New York*. Dorinda had moved to New York City and was going to be the new housewife that season. She became a popular and energetic personality on the show.

At the July 4 party at Jill Zarin's house, which became the initial *Real Housewives of New York* TV show, we met a girlfriend staying with Jill. Her name was Bethenny Frankel, and she appeared to be somewhat of a lost soul. Jill and her mother looked after Bethenny, who was a talented chef but had not been successful yet. Bethenny was one of the women being filmed as part of the *Housewives* show. As it turned out, Bethenny became the breakout star of the first season. She had a biting wit and a confrontational personality. Bethenny held nothing back, wearing her emotions on her sleeve and fearlessly taking on everybody. When her Skinnygirl brand products made her a multimillionaire, she began to clash on the show with Jill. After a few seasons, Jill was off the show, and Bethenny became the star. Bethenny is now a popular media personality and entrepreneur.

We have known most of the "real housewives of New York City" for many years now, and we are amazed at the worldwide success of that show. One year we were in Russia, and our hotel had only one English-speaking channel. The *Housewives* show was the one English-speaking program on the air.

When the second season of the show aired, Jill asked if she could spend an evening with Liza Minnelli and us. She wanted to ask Liza how she handles her fans so Jill would be able to better deal with her public. We never set up that meeting because we felt that Jill didn't have the same superstar status as Liza. However, every time we walk down the street with one of the women from that show, we are amazed at the tremendous fan reaction, and they all have become major celebrities.

One of our other friends, a beautiful tall half-Japanese girl named Jules, joined the show. It turned out to be a disaster for her. Under the scrutiny of the camera, her marriage broke up, and she left the show after one season. We have had another friend, Sonja Morgan, sing at our parties as well. She is quite an exhibitionist and has become a standout star on the *Housewives* show. Our son, Marc, was her dentist, and they filmed an entire episode of the show at his office with Sonja as his patient. Unfortunately, the episode didn't fit in with the story line of the season, and it was never shown. Since these women are part of the group of people we socialize with, we are constantly being filmed at parties with the housewives. I am amazed at how many people stop us in elevators to tell us that they saw us on the *Housewives* show. We started taping the show at home because people would call us to inquire about an episode that they saw us take part in.

CHAPTER

FIFTY-SEVEN

Liza and Friends

Leslie and Evie Bricusse have a beautiful home in Saint-Paul de Vence in the south of France. We have had wonderful times staying there with Liza Minnelli and Mark Gero. One year Gina Lollobrigida traveled from Rome to join us all. Leslie hosted a wonderful lunch at La Colombe d'Or Restaurant. Besides fabulous food and a great setting, it has a priceless collection of art. Leslie and Evie are terrific people to be around, and we have had many great experiences with them. They were even good sports to go on my boat in Westhampton with me, even though I am not skillful at boating. ("Not skillful" is a kind description of my boating skills. "Dangerously incompetent" will be a better description.) A few years ago, Leslie revived his hit musical version of *Jekyll and Hyde* on Broadway. He invited us to the opening, and it became another one of his successes.

Liza always surrounds herself with very interesting people. Marisa Berenson was in Liza's movie *Cabaret*, and they have remained close friends over the years. Marisa is a very special person, and we saw her often with Liza until she moved to Paris. She had a lovely sister, Berry, who tragically died while she was a passenger in one of the plane crashes on 9/11. We recently spent time with Marisa in Los Angeles, and she was as elegant and beautiful as always. Mia Farrow was another close friend of Liza's. We found her engaging but somewhat strange and kooky.

In 2014, we took Liza to see the movie *Dallas Buyers Club*. She thought the performance of Matthew McConaughey was fantastic. When one of the entertainment television shows interviewed Liza and asked her what performances she liked that year, she raved about Matthew's performance. Liza exclaimed that if he did not win the Academy Award for his performance, she would give him her Oscar. His manager saw the interview, and when Matthew came to New York City to do publicity for the movie, he invited Liza to join them at a press dinner. It was held at the Monkey Bar Restaurant in New York City, and Liza invited Arlene and me to come with her.

We sat with Matthew and his wife, Camila, and they were terrific to be with. They spoke a lot about their family, and I was impressed with their values. We were thrilled when Matthew won the Oscar for Best Actor that year. Jared Leto, who had the other major male role in the movie, was also at the dinner. He had an odd style of dress and was somewhat eccentric, but he was interesting to talk with and extremely friendly. Arlene, Liza, and I were happy when he won the Oscar for Best Supporting Actor for the same film.

One night we went with Liza Minnelli to a nightclub called Rainbow and Stars to hear Maureen McGovern perform. She is an excellent singer and, during her show, acknowledged the presence of Liza in the audience. Liza does a rendition of a very difficult song, "If You Hadn't But You Did," in her act. It is a great, fun song but one of the most difficult songs to perform because of the very complicated lyrics and fast tune. We are always amazed when Liza performs that song because it is so difficult. It is a real showstopper, and when Maureen McGovern announced that it would be her next song, we whispered to Liza that we hoped she would be able to do it. Halfway through her rendition of the song, Maureen couldn't keep up with the frantic pace. She lost her way with the complicated, rapid-fire lyrics and called out to Liza sitting in the audience to help her. We all were hysterically laughing because we knew it was almost impossible to get through that song. We enjoyed a good laugh with Maureen after her show.

One performance by a friend of Liza's, named Sam Harris, was not so much fun. Sam is a talented singer and has known Liza for a long time. We had spent a lot of personal time with Sam and also enjoyed his shows. A few years ago, Sam appeared at Feinstein's/54 Below nightclub in New York City, and we went with Liza to see him. Liza, Arlene, and I were seated in the center booth when Sam came out to start his show. He sang a few songs, and Liza, Arlene, and I enthusiastically applauded. He then announced to the audience that he had just published his autobiography and wanted everyone to hear some excerpts from two of the chapters. Both chapters involved Liza, and the three of us sat openmouthed as he started to read. The first chapter that he read from described Liza and David Gest's wedding day. Sam mockingly made fun of the way David and Liza kissed. Then he made disparaging remarks about the wedding party, making cruel fun of Michael Jackson and Elizabeth Taylor. Liza, who was sitting between Arlene and me at the table, was stunned. The second chapter he read from described visiting Liza when she was at a rehab facility. When he started to relate details about her in rehab, Liza said to us, "Let's get out of here." We left as quietly as we could, but it was really uncomfortable because the audience had to notice our exit.

What made it even worse was that Sam was staying in her apartment. Liza didn't want to have anything to do with him after seeing that performance and stayed at our place that night. When Sam finished his show, he tried calling Liza on her cell phone and then me on mine. Liza did not want to speak with Sam and instructed her assistant to tell him to leave her apartment the next day. We could never understand why Sam did that onstage, especially in front of Liza, but it ended their friendship.

Liza has cooked for us over the years, although her busy work schedule limited her free nights. She still makes her terrific pot roast for us whenever we travel to LA. Liza has all her recipes categorized alphabetically in a large loose-leaf binder. A few years ago, she discussed with me the idea of publishing a cookbook. I went online and obtained a copyright for her. We thought she could sell it, along with her recording of the song "I Can Cook Too" included in the package. I informed her agent, Allen Arrow, and he offered to handle it, but nothing ever happened.

Arlene and I had many fun times with Liza over the years. One year we were with her in Las Vegas, and she sat us with Goldie Hawn and Kurt Russell during her show. We all then went out for dinner after the show and had a wonderful evening of laughs. We found both of them to be lovely, and it was like being with old friends. They were extremely warm, but unfortunately, they lived in LA, and both had very busy work schedules, so we were never able to establish a friendship with them.

One year we traveled with Liza and Joel Grey when they went on a tour together. Joel insisted on doing many songs from *Cabaret* in his half, forcing Liza to leave out some of her standards. She is so generous to other performers that she told him it was fine, and everything turned out well. The two of them sang some songs together, like "Money Makes the World Go Round," which was wonderful. We spent time with Joel recently when he performed at an event in Pasadena honoring Liza. He and Liza did a number together, and the magic was still there.

Arlene and I joined Liza for dinner one evening with Vic Damone, who, when he heard I had developed Plax, spent the evening telling me about his inventions. Vic had many number one songs on the charts and had appeared on every major television show. Arlene loves his singing, but his passion seemed to be inventing. He had a series of products he invented, from creams to pain reliever to a brassiere that prevents breast cancer in women. He took my contact information, and the following week, large packages filled with multiple products, including brassieres, arrived at my home daily. I eventually contacted him to tell him that I was not interested in getting involved with another product launch. He eventually married a very wealthy woman in Palm Beach, retired to live a life of leisure and golf, and appeared to give up the desire to invent anything. His wife, Rena, was part owner of a restaurant in Palm Beach called Café L'Europe, and when she died, Vic took over her shares. We would often see him at the restaurant entertaining friends, and he was always quite friendly. He was one of Arlene's favorite singers, and we were sorry when he passed away in 2018.

We also had dinner with Liza at Joe Allen Restaurant in NYC with his ex-wife, Diahann Carroll. Diahann was a wonderful singer and actress who was the first African American woman to win a Tony Award for Best Actress for her role in the Broadway musical *No Strings*. Her title role in *Julia* was a milestone as it was the first American television series to star a black woman. Diahann was married four times and also had long-term affairs with Sidney Poitier and David Frost. We were looking forward to spending time with Diahann as she was someone we greatly admired. We found her to be very nice but quite different from what we expected. She was fun to talk with but somewhat eccentric.

We had a lovely night at Joan Rivers's apartment with Liza. We were amazed at the opulence of her apartment, much different from her image. A few years before that evening, Arlene and I were having dinner with a couple at Elaine's Restaurant. Joan Rivers was sitting at the next table with another couple. The woman at Joan's table accidentally spilled some red wine on Arlene. It was an accident, and we told her not to worry about it. They left the restaurant before us. When we asked for our check after dinner, we were told that Joan had paid the bill. She was a mensch.

We spent a good deal of time over the years with some very outstanding friends of Liza Minnelli. Kay Thompson was her godmother and the best friend of Judy Garland. She was the author of the *Eloise* books, which were really inspired by Liza as a child. She starred in the movie *Funny Face* and also headlined the highest-paid nightclub act in the world. Andy Williams and his brothers were her backup singers before Andy became famous. She was the vocal arranger for all the MGM movies and the vocal coach to their stars, like Judy Garland. Kay was very eccentric, and we loved being around her.

When Kay became ill and was hospitalized in 1993, the doctors told Liza that Kay was dying. Liza did not want to see Kay die in a hospital and moved Kay into a guest room in Liza's apartment. Liza hired nurses full time and brought in a motorized wheelchair for Kay. We were at the apartment the first day Kay tried to figure out how to control the wheelchair. She turned it on and promptly rolled all over the apartment, spinning around, with us jumping out of the way. Liza thought Kay would be there for just her last months, but Kay thrived under Liza's care and lived there another five years until 1998. It was very hectic having the eccentric Kay, along with her nurses, at the apartment. When Liza had to study a script, she periodically moved into a hotel for a few days of quiet.

Another fascinating friend of Liza's was Martha Graham. We spent many hours with her and Liza. Martha was a very spiritual and interesting woman. She spoke to us often about her theory of blood memory, genetic memory codes that are passed down from generation to generation. She used it as the title of her autobiography. Her dance company and its role in the history of dance is legendary, bringing modern dance to a new level of popularity in American culture. In her later years, she gave up much of the control to a younger man whom we never trusted. She was respected by everyone, and it used to upset us when we were with her to observe him not treating her well. He eventually took control of her company, and there were many legal problems for the company when she died in 1990, at ninety-five years of age. We loved the time we spent with her, and we learned a lot about life from her.

In 1977, Arlene and I were in LA on vacation. There was a major charity event, and Liza was the final performer. She had just finished filming the Martin Scorsese movie *New York, New York* with Robert De Niro. She chose for her closing song the Kander and Ebb title song from the movie. It was the first time that the song was heard because the film was not yet released. When she finished the song, we—along with the audience—were stunned. The cheers were deafening. We rushed backstage and told her how much we loved the song. Liza told us not to move, and she rushed over to Scorsese, who was standing off to the side. She brought him over to us and gushed, "Martin, they love the song, and he's a dentist!" Martin, who is always nervous to begin with, had been anxiously waiting backstage to hear the audience's reaction to the song. The fact that a dentist and his wife loved it allowed him to actually relax and smile. Weeks later, we attended the NYC premiere of the movie *New York, New York*, along with Liza, Scorsese, and De Niro. We all went after the screening to a fabulous party for the film at a popular disco, aptly named New York, New York. Liza and Martin were good friends, and we loved the few occasions we were able to spend time with him.

My family and I have had many Christmas and New Year's Eve celebrations with Liza. She always had a beautifully decorated Christmas tree in her apartment. We have great pictures of Liza sitting around the tree, opening gifts with our two young children, Marc and

Lauren. One picture shows Liza hugging three-year-old Lauren, who is her goddaughter. We have another picture taken at her apartment almost thirty years later of Liza sitting under her Christmas tree, hugging Lauren's three-year-old son Devin. Every season is special with Liza.

One summer when Liza was staying with us in Westhampton, we took her to a restaurant called Oakland's, which is on the water. When the owner saw us come in with Liza, she gave us a table with a great view of the bay. Since Arlene resembles Liza, the owner told Arlene that she was glad to meet her sister and was a fan. We chose not to tell her that Liza was not Arlene's sister. We figured that when we would come back in the future, she would give us a good table.

A few years later, Liza's real sister Lorna Luft was staying with us in Westhampton. We took her to Oakland's, and when we arrived, the owner asked Arlene how her sister Liza was doing. Arlene said, "Fine." And we quickly went to our table. Lorna heard her asking about Liza and wondered why she asked Arlene about how Lorna's sister, Liza, was doing. We explained that the owner was a "little ditzy" and came out with strange things sometimes.

We met Lauren Bacall several times with Liza at her apartment. She came off as a tough lady with very strong opinions. She gave off an unfriendly vibe, and we felt that she would be difficult to be around regularly.

When we first met Cynthia McFadden, the ABC television news anchor and NBC news correspondent, at Liza's apartment, we did not recognize her. She was hosting *Nightline*, but at the apartment, she looked totally different from her TV image. When we arrived at the apartment, she greeted us and asked if we wanted anything to drink while turning on the living room lights. She then busied herself lighting candles throughout the apartment. Liza loves to create an atmosphere with the glow of candles in the apartment, and Arlene and I thought that Cynthia was a new housekeeper. When Liza appeared and introduced us, we were embarrassed that we did not recognize her. She was doting so much on Liza that we thought that she was hired help. It turned out that she just wanted very much to be Liza's friend. As we got to know her over the years, we found her to be intelligent and interesting. (She was very close to Katharine Hepburn and was the executrix of her estate.)

CHAPTER

FIFTY-EIGHT

Friends and Encounters

There have been many celebrities whom we have met and spent time with over decades in various situations but do not see regularly. There have been others whom we have had brief but interesting encounters with. When Johnny Mathis played the Hollywood Bowl with Henry Mancini, we went with the Mancini family to the concert. We found him to be extremely likable and left the evening impressed with what a fine person he was.

When Neil Sedaka was receiving an award one time, Connie Francis was there, and we sat with her. Neil wrote some of her best-known songs such as "Stupid Cupid" and "Where the Boys Are." We found her to be very friendly, but she seemed emotionally fragile. When Connie was young, she had a long-term affair with the singer Bobby Darin. She has had a very traumatic life and wrote a book about her experiences that she wants to turn into a movie. One of our friends, Nicolas King, is a very talented singer and actor. Connie has taken a liking to him, and if her movie is ever made, she would like Nicolas to play Bobby Darin.

Nicolas started performing when he was four years old. He had important roles on Broadway in three major shows before the age of twelve. His grandmother Angela Bacari was hired by Liza Minnelli as a vocal coach. She traveled with Liza for many of her performances, and we got to know her very well. We spent many weeks with her on the road and met Nicolas when he was a very young boy. When Nicolas was in his early teens, Liza asked him to open for her on many of her shows because she recognized how talented he was. Nicolas was always very mature for his age. He lived in Rhode Island with his family, but when he would come into New York City to perform, he would call us. It was somewhat strange having lunch with a fourteen-year-old and discussing all aspects of show business with him. He is now only in his late twenties, so my family and I have known him for most of his life. We consider him a great talent and an interesting person to be around, even with the vast difference in our ages. We have brought many of our friends to hear him perform, like Gina Lollobrigida and Tony Danza. Tony had a wonderful time, even getting up onstage and singing with Nicolas.

Ginny Mancini has twin daughters, Felice and Monica Mancini. While Henry was alive, Monica did not show any interest in performing. After Henry died, Monica started to sing in public, and she has a great voice. She is married to a marvelous musician named Gregg Field. Gregg is a very accomplished drummer and has played for many of the greats, including Count Basie and Frank Sinatra. He is also a multiple Grammy Award–winning music producer. Monica now appears all around the world, singing the beautiful music of her father, Henry Mancini. We have spent so much enjoyable time with all the members of the Mancini family that we feel like a part of their family and try to join them in as many of their family gatherings as possible.

Norman Lear, who is now in his late nineties, is a close family friend of the Mancinis. We have been privileged to spend evenings with Norman at the Mancini residence, and we have always found him to be a likable and modest man to talk to. He is a legendary pioneer in television, creating shows like *All in the Family*, *The Jeffersons*, *Maude*, *Good Times*, *Sanford and Son*, and *One Day at a Time*. With all his tremendous success, there has been one negative in his life, and that was the lack of support and respect from his parents. Even at age ninety-seven, he has still not gotten over the rejections from his mother and father throughout his life. What he does have is the respect of the entire world and the other members of his family.

I mentioned previously that, through Ginny and Henry Mancini, we spent time with John Glenn and his wife, Annie. Having dinner with the former senator and first American to orbit the earth was memorable. He was modest and unassuming, a true American hero. The Mancinis have introduced us to many outstanding people. Quincy Jones is another longtime friend of the Mancinis, and we have always found him interesting to talk to, although at times it is somewhat hard to follow his convoluted thought process. We spent some time with the actress Sharon Stone at one of Ginny's events in Florida and found her quite nice. Polly Bergen was also a close friend of Ginny whom we loved being around. She was always fun, with an upbeat personality.

Bobbi and Jack Elliott were good friends of the Mancinis, and Jack created and presided over the Henry Mancini Institute. Jack was a talented composer and was the musical director for the Academy Awards, the Emmy Awards, the Kennedy Center Honors, and the Grammy Awards. He was the musical director of the Grammys for thirty consecutive years. We always enjoyed being with him and hearing his comments on contemporary music. Over his thirty-year span conducting the Grammys, Jack was witness to the changing musical tastes of the nation. As the years went on, Jack had to conduct music that he did not care for. He loved the Great American Songbook, and much of the new rock music did not appeal to him.

Rosemarie Stack was a good friend of Ginny, and we had the pleasure of spending time with her. She always invited us to lunch when we came to LA. Her husband, Robert Stack, won an Emmy Award for Best Actor while starring in the popular TV series *The Untouchables* from 1959 to 1963. He has appeared in many films and was nominated for Best Supporting Actor in 1956 for the film *Written on the Wind*. In 1988, he starred with Jackie Mason in the comedy film *Caddyshack II*. During our dinners with Robert and Rosemarie, we traded many Jackie Mason stories. Although Robert and Jackie were quite different personalities, Robert told me how much he enjoyed being in Jackie's company.

Our friend Angela LaGreca was a producer at the *Today Show* for many years. When she had her baby shower, we met Hoda Kotb and Meredith Vieira. They were two extremely friendly and lovely people. Angela is also close to Joy Behar, and we met Joy at Angela's home in East Hampton. Joy has a great personality on TV, but I found her to be cold and unfriendly. The first time I met Joy was when I was seating people as an usher at Liza Minnelli's wedding. Most of the celebrities attending the wedding were quite easy to seat. Joy just marched in with a stern face, totally ignored my seating suggestions, and walked right by me with a dismissive attitude. As far as the level of importance at that time of the celebrities in attendance, Joy was near the bottom of the list. We felt the same unfriendly vibe on the occasions we have seen Ellen DeGeneres at the Polo Lounge in the Beverly Hills Hotel and other social settings. (I do understand that many celebrities build a wall around themselves to avoid constant contact with fans. As a dentist, I never had that problem as most people would put their dentist at the bottom of the list of people they would like to see, except for maybe undertakers.) Many of the charismatic and outgoing comedians on TV are not the same in real life.

We were present many nights with Sammy Davis at his suite in NYC when well-known comedians would come over and trade stories with one another. Some tried to impress Sammy to get a job as his opening act, and some were friends. Many were surprisingly insecure and moody and were competitive with one another. Those evenings were really fun, observing each comedian trying to top the next with their jokes.

We have spent some brief time with people like Jimmy Fallon and Meghan Trainor at places like the Polo Bar Restaurant in New York City and the Friars Club and found them to be extremely delightful and personable just as they appear on television. We had one very fun evening at the Polo Bar in New York City. Arlene and I were having dinner with Ginny Mancini and our daughter, Lauren. Sitting behind us was the very famous record producer Clive Davis, who was the president of Columbia Records, the founder and president of Arista Records, and founder of J Records. We had met him many times in the past and said hello to him once again. He was sitting with Meghan Trainor, who is a talented singer-songwriter who won a Grammy Award for Best New Artist in 2016. Clive introduced us to Meghan, who was extremely friendly and initiated a conversation with

Lauren. Meghan Trainor commented to Lauren how tempting her cheeseburger looked and wished she could order it, but she was trying to watch her weight. (It was not "All about That Bass" [the name of her hit song] at that moment but was all about that burger.)

Just as we were all laughing, Jimmy Fallon walked over from across the room to say hello to Clive and Meghan. They introduced us to Jimmy, and we informed him that Ginny was Henry Mancini's wife. He said he was a fan of Henry's, Lauren said she was a fan of Jimmy's, and we all formed a little conversational group by Clive's booth. Lauren was thrilled because she not only enjoys watching Jimmy on television but she also loves Meghan's music.

Just as we were about to return to our respective tables, Lauren pointed out that Lorne Michaels, the producer of *Saturday Night Live*, was standing behind Jimmy and was more of an observer than a participant in the conversation. Lauren waved as he walked away, and he waved back. (We all wished we had noticed him earlier because he would have been interesting to talk to considering he has received nineteen Primetime Emmy Awards and produced *The Tonight Show* since 2014 and the *Late Night* series since 1993, in addition to creating and producing *Saturday Night Live*.)

We soon saw Clive walk out with Meghan and commented on how we had an exciting evening. About fifteen minutes later, Clive returned to his same table next to us but this time with Mariah Carey. Lauren wanted to meet her, but it was awkward because we had just finished speaking with Clive. Lauren turned her head toward Mariah and smiled; I don't know whether Clive informed her that he knew us, but she smiled back at Lauren and gave her a wink.

We see Ralph and Ricky Lauren occasionally at his restaurant, the Polo Bar. We have had warm encounters with them due to our daughter's friendship with their daughter, Dylan. The first time that we went over to say hello at the restaurant, Ralph's brother was with them, and he offered me a bite of his corned beef sandwich. He told me that it was made exactly like Ralph had growing up and was the best thing on their menu. I tasted it, and he was right.

One year when Jack Haley was producing the Academy Awards, he invited Lorna Luft and her husband Jake and us to the show. It is always exciting to be in the audience at the Oscars, especially in the producer's seats. However, this particular evening, there was some extra excitement for us. Our friend Skye Aubrey was going through a contentious divorce. In 1976, she married Ilya Salkind, and they had two young children, Anastasia and Sebastian. The marriage only lasted three years, and Skye was suing Ilya for child support. Ilya and his father, Alexander, were prominent Mexican film producers. They were responsible for the very successful *Superman* movies. Their movie was nominated for various awards that season. Ilya had been doing everything possible to avoid the legal papers Skye was trying to serve him. Skye figured that he would show up at the Academy Awards, and she gave the four of us the assignment to locate him in the audience and serve him with the papers. While everyone was networking on the red carpet, we were searching for signs of Ilya. The four of us split up, and each covered different parts of the theater. Between the Oscars and our detective adventure, it was exciting; however, we never were able to locate Ilya.

A good friend of ours worked in production for ABC children's television. She and her husband invited us to a party in NYC for ABC television affiliates. All the major personalities were there, and she introduced us to them all. One of the couples we met was a major nightly news anchor and his much younger wife. We were introduced to them as Dr. and Mrs. Lazare. When we walked away, the newscaster's wife inquired of our friends what kind of doctor I was. The husband decided that bringing a dentist to the party wasn't very impressive, so he told her that I was a world-famous psychiatrist.

She approached me while I was conversing with people on the other side of the room. She asked if I could have a word with her in private. I had no idea why she had singled me out as I had just been casually introduced to her. When she took me aside, she frantically blurted out the most intimate details of her private life. She mistakenly thought I was a renowned psychiatrist, and I had no idea why. She hysterically told me that she was having sexual problems with her husband and explained that it was because she had an incestuous relationship with her father. She didn't know who to turn to and hoped I could help her. I was dumbfounded and told her that I was getting a drink and would be right back.

I raced over to Arlene and our friends and quickly tried to explain what happened. When our friend's husband let me know what he had told her about my profession, I understood why she sought me out. I had no time to be angry with him as the four of us made our way out of the party before this desperate woman found me again. It can be harmful to lie about what you do, and I felt very badly about what transpired. I subsequently read that they divorced, and he remarried.

Many years ago, Lorna Luft introduced us to Hugh York. He was a Hollywood hairstylist for such people as Farrah Fawcett, Cher, Candice Bergen, Diana Ross, Dame Judith Anderson, Sophia Loren, Princess Grace, Diahann Carroll, Cybill Shepherd, Neil Diamond, and Cheryl Tiegs. Hugh was a very good-looking man, and it was suggested that Warren Beatty's character in the film *Shampoo* was based on Hugh. Hugh, in real life, was gay; and the first time we went with Lorna to his LA apartment, he had just finished a bitter argument with his partner. We entered to find Hugh breaking every dish in his kitchen. There were hundreds of pieces of broken china covering the floor. It was a unique way to first meet someone, but after that incident, we spent many enjoyable times with him.

I have always had a problem leaving food on my plate. (I was the only child of a Jewish mother—enough said.) Arlene is constantly imploring me to not feel the need to finish every last bite. Hugh was her idol in self-control at the dinner table. Every time he ordered food in a restaurant, he would tell the waiter to charge him for the full meal but only bring out half. He would order eggs Benedict, and if a full portion was brought out, he would separate half and return it. After every meal with Hugh, I would receive a lecture from Arlene about portion control. I grudgingly had to admit that Hugh possessed great willpower, and he had a perfect trim body. It was the image he needed for his beauty business.

After a few years of friendship, we lost contact with Hugh. I then heard that his business had declined as new stylists now served the fickle celebrities. I also was told that Hugh was extremely heavy because he stopped watching his diet when he lost his clientele. As bad as I felt upon hearing this news, I must admit that I felt pleasure in informing Arlene that Hugh was now heavier than me. He could not sustain the willpower to continue to eat half portions, and I was now able to finish my delicious meals without a lecture. Hugh unfortunately passed away at only fifty-three years of age.

Steven Tisch is a film producer and part owner of the New York Giants football team. Lorna Luft sang at one of his charity events, and he invited her to dinner at his magnificent home. We were invited to join Lorna, who was staying with us at our New York City apartment. It was a beautiful dinner party, and my dinner companion was the actress Lisa Kudrow, best known for the TV show *Friends*. While sitting next to Lisa all night, I regretted not seeing more of the *Friends* TV show so I could have been able to discuss it with her. She was a lovely person, and her very charming French advertising executive husband, Michel Stern, sat across from me, next to Arlene.

We also enjoyed spending an evening with Lorna's friend, the singer Lesley Gore. Lesley lived near us, and we drove her home after dinner. We never connected with her because she seemed very private.

We spent an evening with Alan Alda and his wife, Arlene, at the Carlyle Hotel after a terrific performance there by Tony Danza. While we were talking together in Tony's suite, we both realized that we were the only Arlene and Allan couples that each of us knew. Alan really got a kick out of meeting another Allan and Arlene, and we had a lot to talk about. Our daughter, Lauren, who was with us, suggested that it would be fun to have a picture of the four of us, and Alan thought that was a great idea and gathered our group together for her to take the photo. He, of course, starred as Hawkeye in *M*A*S*H*, which was written by our friend Larry Gelbart.

One of the most down-to-earth and loveliest people we spent time with was the actress, Joyce DeWitt. We met her after she had starred in the TV show *Three's Company*. At that time, she did not seem too interested in continuing her television career; and although we liked her, our friendship didn't last long.

We also were friendly with the actress Anne Archer and her husband Terry. Her son Tommy was similar in age to our children, and they enjoyed playdates together. Anne was a beautiful woman and talented actress, nominated for an Academy Award for Best Supporting Actress in the film *Fatal Attraction*. We had nice times together, but after a few years, we lost contact with her. She and her husband became members of the Church of Scientology, and her son Tommy also became active in it.

One night we were out to dinner with Lorna Luft, and on the way into the restaurant, she stopped to say hello to John McEnroe and his wife Tatum O'Neal. My one previous encounter with him was not pleasant. I was walking down the aisle at Madison Square Garden, heading to my seat for a concert. I had to pass a seated John McEnroe, and he acted quite bothered that I was trying to get by him on the way to my seat. He never stood up to let me through. I figured that I caught him on a bad day and squeezed by him to go to my seat. I am a fan of his tennis game and love his commentary when covering the tennis matches on TV. He and Tatum were very friendly to Lorna, and they invited us to join them for dessert on our way out. John seemed totally different from my first impression of him at Madison Square Garden and was quite pleasant. I was looking forward to getting to know him and spend time with one of my tennis idols. I ordered quickly and asked for the check after our main dish. I was anxious to join John and Tatum.

As we got up from the table, the maître d' came over and told me that I had a phone call. It was my daughter, Lauren, telling me that she received a phone call from our son, Marc, and he was in the hospital. Marc was living in Philadelphia while attending the University of Pennsylvania. He was not feeling well, and the resident at the hospital told him that he thought Marc had meningitis and had a 50 percent chance of dying. We rushed out of the restaurant and headed home to get my car to drive to Philadelphia. Fortunately, my father-in-law was a brilliant doctor; and when told of the symptoms, he diagnosed it as mononucleosis. He advised us not to have the resident doctor there take a spinal tap and suggested the diagnostic procedures for them to do. The emergency room head doctor called later to inform me that my father-in-law was correct. I drove to the hospital and brought Marc home to rest while he recovered from mononucleosis. We were happy that Marc was fine, but I never was able to get acquainted with John and Tatum, who eventually broke up. (It does seem that Larry Gelbart was right when he said that "marriage is not all it's cracked up to be and is probably the main cause of divorce.")

I have many fond memories in my life that took place with Lorna Luft. We have been with her everywhere from the Carnegie Deli in NY to Shanghai, China. For many recent years, Lorna toured in the Irving Berlin musical *White Christmas*. Several times, we traveled with her and the cast to various cities. One memorable year, we joined Lorna and the cast for Thanksgiving dinner on their day off in Las Vegas when the show played the Smith Theater. For two people like Arlene and me who have no performing ability, it was a treat to be around the many talented performers in that cast.

When John Lennon was shot, we joined Lorna at Strawberry Fields in Central Park for his very emotional memorial. We have spent time over the years with Lorna's brother Joey. We knew that Lorna's dad, Sid Luft, was Jewish, so one year when Joey was in NY, we invited him to join our family for a Passover Seder at our home. It was his first and only Seder. Lorna has been performing often these days in NYC, and we love having her stay with us each time. Both Lorna and her husband Colin are great cooks, so meals at home on her nights off are terrific.

One of our most interesting experiences with Lorna took place in Florida. She had a contact number for two women living near the Miami area that kept many rescue lions and tigers at their home. Lorna was appearing in Florida, and the day after her performance, she arranged for the three of us to visit the women's home. They had animals that were abused in circuses and other venues, and they tried to rehabilitate and raise them. We arrived to observe two very glamorous women surrounded by cages full of lions, tigers, and other big cats. (They looked a lot better than Carole Baskin, the star of the television series *Tiger King*.) They told us that they bring the lions and tigers into their home but never turn their back to them. They explained that even though they have raised and fed them, lions are still animals with a certain inherent instinct to attack. We watched their assistants throw red meat into the cages and witnessed the animals fiercely devouring the food.

They asked if we would like to take pictures with the animals. I had to sign a form, agreeing that they were not responsible for my life should I be attacked. I didn't know what to do because it was a once-in-a-lifetime opportunity, and frankly, I was somewhat frightened. Arlene declined, but Lorna and I filled out our forms. They brought out a huge tiger, and it had a long chain around its neck, which they fastened to the wall. They gave me a large baby bottle filled with milk. I fed the tiger while Arlene took photos. The women warned me to never turn my back to the tiger. As I was feeding the tiger and the bottle was starting to empty, I quietly asked one of the two women to please take over. It was a unique experience, and I have terrific photos of myself with the tiger. When I left, I realized that it was somewhat of a risky thing to do.

Years later, we spent time in Las Vegas with Neil Sedaka. After his show, we went with him to visit with Siegfried and Roy, the world-famous magicians headlining for many years in Las Vegas. They were so nice and showed us around their place. When Roy was mauled by the white tiger onstage years later, I thought about my experience in

Florida with the big cats. Lorna recently arranged for Arlene and me to have a much less threatening evening.

Hugh Jackman was performing in a one-man show at Madison Square Garden. Lorna and her husband Colin arranged tickets for us and a personal meeting with Hugh before his performance. He could not have been nicer, spending time with us before he went onstage. He had played Peter Allen in the Broadway show, *The Boy from Oz*. Since Peter was married to Liza and was Lorna's brother-in-law, we had many things in common to talk about. Coincidentally, a good friend of ours worked as a personal chef for Hugh Jackman and his family while he did the Broadway show in New York City. She raved about what a wonderful family they were and how nice he was to work for.

A few of our friends had interesting personal relationships. While Robert De Niro was under my care as a patient, he was having a relationship with the supermodel Naomi Campbell. He was a hard person to contact, and everything had to go through his assistant. (This was before the days of cell phones, text messages, and emails.) The beeper device had been invented, and De Niro gave one to Naomi as a gift so he could page her when he was free and wanted to be with her. I met her one night in Elaine's Restaurant and was stunned by her beauty.

We were friendly with the legendary New York radio personality William B. Williams and his wife, Dotty. He had an eye for the ladies, and they eventually divorced. One time when we were with him, we introduced him to our friend Melonie Haller, who was a very sexy young actress. It was quite awkward for us when he began having an affair with her while still married as our introduction was merely just that and not a setup. He was a very personable guy and dean of the NY Friars Club. We even had him escort Gina Lollobrigida to our son Marc's bar mitzvah.

Some of the people whom we enjoyed fun times with had another side to them when it came to business. One night we walked into Elaine's Restaurant in New York City with Bob Wachs, who at the time was producing all of Eddie Murphy's movies. At the first table entering the restaurant, we spotted our friend Danny Aiello, a wonderful actor. Danny starred in numerous films, including *The Godfather Part II*, *Once upon a Time in America*, *The Purple Rose of Cairo*, *Moonstruck*, *Harlem Nights*, and many others. He was nominated for an

Academy Award for Best Supporting Actor in the Spike Lee film *Do the Right Thing*. I went over and hugged Danny, and he was all smiles until he saw Bob Wachs. He apparently was in one of the movies that Bob produced and felt that Bob had given him a bad accounting of the money owed to him.

Danny was a former bouncer before becoming a movie star and started to verbally berate Bob. I then saw a side of Bob that I hadn't seen before. Bob started screaming at Danny, telling him that he would never work in Hollywood again, and Bob threatened to have Danny blacklisted. Danny was furious and told me that he refrained from punching Bob only because he had walked in with me. It was an embarrassing shouting match, and being afraid of violence, I quickly ushered Bob to a table in the back.

Arlene's cousin, Howard Marren, is a talented musical composer. Years ago, he was working backstage at the Broadway production of *Dracula*, starring Frank Langella. Frank has won four Tony Awards, been nominated for an Oscar, and has starred in countless movies, television shows, and plays. *Dracula* had marvelous special effects, and Howard arranged for us to see the show and come backstage afterward with our children. Marc and Lauren loved the show, and we met Howard at the stage door. He showed us around and then offered to have us meet Frank. He told Marc and Lauren to make sure they had the theater programs with them for Frank to sign. They replied that they really were not interested in collecting his autograph. Howard explained that the autograph was not for them. He wanted them to ask for the autograph for Frank's benefit because Frank had a strong ego and thrived on people asking for his autograph. It was before the days of the cell phone, so there were no opportunities to take pictures of Frank and the kids.

When we entered the dressing room, Frank was very happy to autograph the children's programs, which they promptly threw out when we left the theater. I also was never into collecting autographs. When I was a child, I was with my father at a gas station in Brooklyn while he was getting fuel. The car next to us belonged to Jackie Robinson, who was my idol. My father asked him to say hello to me, and Jackie gave me his autograph. As much as I worshiped Jackie, when I returned home, I threw out the autograph. Maybe my lack of interest started when I was taken by my parents to my first Broadway show. The famous comedian Jack Benny was sitting directly in front of us, and before the show started, my father asked Jack to please sign an autograph for me. Jack very curtly told my father not to bother him.

I love to play tennis, and I took a camera with me when we had a charity tennis event in the Hamptons. My assigned partner was Billie Jean King, and I did get a kick out of spending time with her. I have a picture of us together as a memory of that day. Our former NYC mayor David Dinkins loved to play tennis. He was a member of the same tennis facility that I used. I had the pleasure of playing doubles with him several times. He gained weight over the years but maintained a good tennis game. He was a delight on the court, always smiling, and everyone loved being in a game with him.

Arlene and I enjoyed many great nights at a nightclub called Rainbows and Stars at the top of Rockefeller Center. We have known Lainie Kazan casually over the years and went to her opening night one year at the club. The venue invited some opening night guests for a meet and greet with her after the performance with a buffet and drinks. When Lainie finished her show at Rainbows and Stars, the special friends were told that she was going to shower and change, and the drinks and buffet would start in thirty minutes in another room. Arlene and I had time to kill, so we decided to head up to that room early and get a drink. We walked into the room, which was set up with a buffet table, and saw one other person in the room. It was Lainie. She had piled up a few plates of food and was gobbling them down at a small table by the buffet. She must have been too hungry to shower and change and was eating alone in a darkened room. We helped ourselves to some food as well, and we all had a good laugh together.

Lainie then excused herself to change her clothes, and we waited for the other guests to arrive. Lainie always had an eating problem, and her added weight makes her look older. In fact, she often played mother roles when she was quite young. She's a great actress and singer. She was Barbra Streisand's understudy on Broadway in *Funny Girl*. Lainie became well known in the industry for not getting a chance to perform onstage because Streisand never missed a single performance. She was either very dedicated in the role or didn't want any understudy to ever go on in her place. Barbra had a cousin, also with the last name Streisand, who was a patient of mine. I asked her what Barbra was like, and she told me that her side of the family had no relationship with Barbra.

We have known the columnist and critic Rex Reed for many years. He is a strongly opinionated man, and we always enjoy his company. His movie and music reviews can be quite tough, and he can be venomous if he does not like something. A few years ago, he went to see Steve Tyrell sing at the Carlyle in New York City. Rex did not like the performance and wrote one of the nastiest reviews I have ever read. He not only composed a vicious review but Rex also sent emails of his review to many people in the entertainment industry. People we know were quite shocked that a critic would do something like that. Steve is a friend of ours, and we have never mentioned to him that we are friendly with Rex.

A few years ago, we were heading home after dinner and passed a club named the Beach, which featured singers a few times a week. As we walked by the window, I thought I saw Rex Reed on stage. The owner had just wandered out, saw me looking in, and invited us to have a drink at the bar. Arlene and I did not know that Rex could sing, and we were curious to hear him. He was up on a small stage accompanied by one of our favorite people, the fabulous piano player Tedd Firth. We assumed it was the end of his performance and thought it would be interesting to hear him sing one or two songs. His theme for the show was unknown songs by famous songwriters. He would tell a brief interesting anecdote about each composer and then sing a song. He managed to pick out the worst song that each of these songwriters wrote, and since Rex was a better writer than a singer, we hoped that we only would have to sit through one or two songs. Unfortunately, he went on for another full hour after we walked in, and we were too embarrassed to walk out on him.

After the show, he rushed over and asked us how we enjoyed his performance. We lied and told him we thought he was wonderful. He has known Liza Minnelli for many years and knows how friendly we are with her. He wanted us to let her know how great he was, so I called Liza on my cell phone and put him on with her. He was so happy to tell her all about what he was doing, and when he returned my phone to me, Liza simply remarked, "Rex sings?"

The next time we saw Rex, he informed us that the club wanted him back, but he was unable to find a pianist to accompany him. He asked me if I knew anybody who might be available, and I told him I would check. I had a feeling that anybody in the profession may not be too happy playing the piano for someone who was not a professional singer. We felt sorry for Tedd Firth, who had to sit through the two hours of Rex singing totally obscure songs. It's amazing that Rex, who is such a critic of music, will not see the weaknesses in his own vocals and song choices. Years ago, he had made extensive tapes of all his favorite singers as a gift for us, and his taste was terrific.

Rex is a very popular and respected movie and theater critic. Because of his clever wit, in the late '70s, he was offered a job to appear as one of the panelists on a silly but popular TV program called *The Gong Show*. It had great ratings, and Rex was paid well. However, he was somewhat embarrassed to be a participant in this crazy show. One day Arlene and I were watching Rex being interviewed on television about his distinguished career. Rex was stating that despite all his learned reviews and many articles, he feared history might remember him only for being a member of "the stupid *Gong Show*." Just then, our two young children walked by, saw Rex being interviewed, and remarked to us, "Isn't that the guy on *The Gong Show*?"

We have spent time over the years with some very interesting personalities. One unique guy is Chuck Zito. We first met him when he was working as a part-time bodyguard for Liza Minnelli and Lorna Luft. Chuck looks and talks a lot like Sylvester Stallone and has worked as a body double for Stallone in some of his movies. Chuck is a good actor and was a regular on the HBO prison drama *Oz*. Chuck was the president of the Hells Angels Motorcycle Club and is a very intimidating person. A low point in his life was being sent to prison for drug conspiracy in Japan, but Chuck has always landed back on his feet. We have known him for decades and always enjoy spending time with him.

Chuck is someone who does not "suffer fools gladly." He lives by a code of ethics, and if insulted, he will not argue with someone. He will simply throw one punch and lay them out cold. If treated with respect, he is a warm and engaging person, and he has always gotten along great with our children. He loved showing our son, Marc, his fighting moves. He became a minor celebrity after an altercation at the Scores club in NY with Jean-Claude Van Damme in 1998. Jean-Claude was sitting at a table with a few other people, and Chuck walked by and greeted him with a friendly hello. Jean-Claude was quite well known at that time as a martial arts champion and starred in many films as such. Jean-Claude completely ignored Chuck and waved him away. Chuck commented that he found his behavior rude, and Jean-Claude stood up and told Chuck to stop bothering him. Chuck didn't argue, but with one punch, he completely decked Jean-Claude, who found himself sprawled out on the floor. The paparazzi had a field day, and the picture was on the front page of many newspapers. Chuck has appeared in a number of films, and Hollywood celebrities love him as do we. However, I would never want to be on his bad side. I read his autobiography, and he proved to be a good writer who explained his views on life quite well.

CHAPTER

FIFTY-NINE

Close Friends—Experiences

Arlene and I have gotten to know and like Rod Gilbert and his wife, Judy, very much. Rod has great stories about his glory days with the New York Rangers when he was the most famous of the hockey players. Rod is a very good-looking man, and in his single days playing with the Rangers, he had the nickname "Mr. February." He explained to me that in all the other months of the year, baseball, basketball, and football receive the most headlines. The single players in those sports get most of the attention from the ladies during their peak seasons. Joe Namath was the most well-known New York City bachelor in the '60s and '70s due to his role as quarterback for the New York Jets. Broadway Joe was the top sports bachelor until the Super Bowl ended in early January. The single baseball players, like Ron Darling, were most popular with the ladies during the baseball season from April to October. From March to June, the NBA basketball stars ruled the city. However, in February, hockey took center stage. That was when a handsome hockey star like Rod was king of the bachelors. I didn't know him then, but apparently, he did well enough with the ladies to earn the nickname "Mr. February."

We have become quite friendly with a very talented performer named Haley Swindal. Her first important Broadway show was the musical *Jekyll and Hyde*, written by our friend Leslie Bricusse. Lorna Luft introduced Haley to us, and we have been great friends ever since. Haley married a top theatrical agent named Jack Tantleff, and they had a beautiful wedding. Our common friend Steve Tyrell serenaded the couple at the wedding. Haley's grandfather George Steinbrenner was the renowned owner of the New York Yankees.

One year Haley was starring as Nellie in the musical *South Pacific* at a dinner theater in Westchester, New York. After her Friday night performance, as she removed her wig after the show, her head snapped forward. Her mouth hit against the mirror, and she fractured her front tooth. It was eleven o'clock on a Friday night, and she had two shows on Saturday and two shows on Sunday. She called us in a panic to see if we knew of anybody who could help her. A number of her family members were coming to the show on Saturday, and Haley couldn't imagine how she could go on with a cracked front tooth. By chance, our son, Marc, had dinner with us that evening. Before heading back to his home in Long Island, he planned to stop by his New York City dental office to pick up some items. I called Marc and explained the situation. Marc offered to wait in his office for Haley. She arrived at Marc's office at one o'clock, and he worked on her until three. He was able to completely restore the tooth, and Haley was thrilled. She even commented that the restored tooth looked even better than it did before the accident.

The positive outcome of his good deed was that our family is invited to Yankee games, and the seats are in the owner's box. My grandkids are thrilled to be able to attend the Yankee games and enjoy the marvelous dining arrangements for the guests of the Yankee owners. There are also special seats from which my children and grandchildren were able to watch the games, next to the Yankee dugout. When the players come into the dugout, they occasionally throw a ball to the kids. My grandkids now have a drawer full of balls from Yankee games, along with multiple Yankee hats and other Yankee paraphernalia.

We recently took our children, Marc and Lauren, and our grandchildren to a Yankee game with Haley. Sitting in the owner's box with us that day was the actor Adam Sandler and his wife and children. They were very friendly and down-to-earth people, and we all had a great time together. Adam took many pictures with our family, and then we noticed his wife taking multiple photos of him with a bald black man. We were curious why she was taking so many photos of them. Our grandson Justin then recognized that the man was Reggie Jackson when he put on his Yankee cap. Reggie and Adam then posed with all our kids.

The ex-baseball star Mickey Rivers was also in a nearby box with the Gilberts, and Judy introduced him to Lauren and her children. He was so friendly and gave them autographed pictures of himself and took photos with them. It was a memorable day for our family, spending time with both baseball and film stars that they admired.

Haley is a big fan of Judy Garland, Liza Minnelli, and Lorna Luft. She recently performed at Feinstein's/54 Below nightclub, and her show was a wonderful tribute to Liza Minnelli. It was the sixtieth birthday of Haley's mother, and she had many tables of her friends and family at the show. I called Liza and had her record a personal "happy birthday" message to Haley's mom. In the middle of her performance, Haley played Liza's message to her mom, and it made the evening extraspecial.

A few years after we were married, I booked a two-week cruise for us on a boat called the *Oceanic*. We did not go with any other couples whom we knew, and the first few days of the cruise were quite boring for us. Arlene was just twenty-two years old, and almost everyone on the ship was many decades older than her. After two straight nights of bingo, we were wondering how we would be able to survive two full weeks on this boat by ourselves. The only lively people whom we observed on the boat were a small group of three young couples who appeared to be having a great time.

On the third night, Arlene told me that she would solve our loneliness problem on the boat. When one of the women in the group of young couples headed to the ladies' room, Arlene followed her. Ten minutes later, I observed Arlene exiting the ladies' room with the other young woman. Arlene motioned for me to come with them, and we joined the other couples' table. The woman Arlene spoke with was named Lillian Shiller, and her husband's name was Bryant. They lived in Montreal, Canada, and for the rest of the cruise, we spent every day with our new friends. One of the other couples, who were also from Montreal, was Maury and Diane Cohen. After we returned home from the cruise, we remained friendly with both Canadian couples.

We traveled to Israel with Maury and Diane, and they were a fun couple. Maury was an outgoing guy with a very big personality. One year he traveled to New York City on business, and we took him to Elaine's Restaurant. He wanted to meet Elaine, who was the most well-known restaurant owner in New York City. We warned him that she was a tough lady unless she knows you. When she walked by our table, Maury got up and approached her. He announced, "I am Maury Cohen, and I flew all the way in from Montreal to have dinner at your restaurant."

Elaine stared at him and said, "Big f——king deal." And she walked away.

We have lost contact with Maury and Diane over the years due to us living in different countries. The other Canadian couple, Bryant and Lillian Shiller, bought a place in Palm Beach, Florida. The Shillers have remained two of our closest friends ever since that first meeting on the cruise. We spend a considerable amount of time with them in Palm Beach every winter. They have introduced us to many interesting people there.

In the winter season, Palm Beach has a frantic social life. A woman whom the Shillers introduced us to is a good example of how much importance is placed on the events going on every day. She was a wealthy widow, very involved in the many charitable and other social events in Palm Beach. The previous year, her husband had died in December. It was the start of the social season in Palm Beach. She didn't want a funeral and mourning period to stop her from taking part in the many charity events and fancy parties. She had his body frozen until March. She attended all the nightly social events and then had his funeral in March when the season was over.

We have traveled the world with the Shillers, and we stay at each other's homes throughout the year. They are a couple whom we consider part of our extended family. When their son, Doug, married his wife, Sonya, in 2002, they requested that everyone share their favorite recipes with them for a cookbook that they were putting together. In the cookbook that they gave out to all their wedding guests, they printed out each person's best recipe. There were many fabulous dishes listed. We were at a loss to figure out what to include from us as we eat out all the time, and Arlene rarely cooks home. (That was until this current pandemic when we were forced to eat in, and I discovered that Arlene is really a good cook. She's no dummy, and downplaying her cooking skills all these years led to delicious dinners in restaurants without the need to prepare meals and clean dirty dishes. In all fairness, she did make wonderful meals for the children, either by cooking or with takeout. My cooking skills are limited to the microwave. Our kitchen features his and her microwaves. A big part of our social life was dining out with friends.) The Shillers live in Montreal, and many of their French friends submitted marvelous recipes for the cookbook. Arlene's recipe for all to share was on page 47 of the wedding cookbook. Page 46 was poached salmon with orange mint sauce from the Lampes of Phoenix, Arizona. Page 48 was pasta puttanesca from the Lenarciaks of Montreal, Canada. Page 47 featured two recipes from the Lazares of New York. The first recipe was "Tea Arlene." It stated, "Heat water to boil then add teabag of your choice." The second recipe was "Toast Arlene." It stated, "Put a piece of bread in the toaster and set time to high . . . Remove when burnt."

Bryant is involved in real estate but trained as an engineer. He is unusually bright and, for years, was working on a book that he wanted to publish about the origin of life on our planet. He was constantly speaking about his theories on the rational design hypothesis of life based on engineering principles. Bryant would talk about his ideas at dinner parties, cruises, vacations, and other social gatherings. One day we were in our pool in Westhampton, and Bryant started expressing some concepts to me. I stated that if Albert Einstein had Bryant's social life, he would have presented his theory of relativity as E equals M. Einstein never would have gotten around to the full E equals MC squared. The cocktail parties and vacations wouldn't have allowed him time to complete the full theory. Bryant understood my message and, for the next few years, concentrated on his book. It was published and titled *The Fifth Option*. He presents in detail his opinion on the origin of life. Bryant's theories have been well received by the scientific community, and now he can once again enjoy his dinner parties and vacations.

We went on one vacation with another couple, and that trip did not turn out so well. Since that time, we have been very careful whom we travel with. We learned that it is important when spending long periods with other people to make sure everyone is compatible. Early in our marriage, we planned a very interesting trip that included Athens and the Greek islands. We were having dinner with a couple we didn't know that well, and I mentioned that we were going on a trip in two weeks. They had never been overseas and seemed quite interested in the places we were visiting. They remarked that it sounded so exciting and that they would look into joining us. I did not think it was possible to sign up at the last minute, and I didn't quite know how to respond. I answered that, of course, they could join us. I was quite surprised when they were able to duplicate our bookings, and off we went together. Although we hardly knew them, we had a number of common friends, so I figured it would work out fine.

On our first night in Athens, we all went to a very nice restaurant. In the middle of dinner, the couple had a huge fight at the table, and she stormed out of the restaurant. We thought they were a happily married young couple, but obviously, they had some problems.

The next day, we boarded a small ship to take us through the Greek islands for the next week. The captain of the vessel was straight out of central casting, a very handsome Greek man named Spiros. On the first day, when the passengers met the captain and crew, our female traveling companion commented to us how good looking he was. On the second day of the cruise, she confided to us that she had a crush on the captain. Since it was a fairly small cruise ship, each night the captain would invite a small number of passengers to have dinner with him, instead of at their regular table. In that way, over the course of the one-week cruise, he would have one dinner with all the passengers on board.

On the third night of the cruise, Arlene and I received our invitation to dine with the captain that evening. We assumed that the other couple we were traveling with also received a similar invitation. Sure enough, in a short time, the other female we were traveling with burst into our room, all flushed and excited. She told us that she had been flirting with Spiros for the past few days, and he invited her to have dinner with him that night. She had no idea that the captain would invite every passenger on the ship for dinner, so we played along. We remarked that we would try to join her and her husband with the captain and help divert her husband while she was flirting with Spiros. Of course, we already had our reservation for dinner with the captain, so we knew that we would be sitting with them.

At dinner, she made sure to be sitting next to the captain, with her husband on her other side. Arlene and I were sitting opposite them, and I let her in on my plan. I was sitting in a seat where I was able to take my leg and rub it across her leg under the table at such an angle that she thought it was Spiros making advances to her. Later that night, she took Arlene and me aside and told us about the captain's advances during dinner.

The next day, she sought out Spiros and made an overt pass at him. When he explained that he was a happily married man, she was devastated. Arlene and I tried to make excuses to avoid dinners with her and her husband in the other cities on our itinerary. We also vowed to be much more careful about whom we traveled with in the future. Needless to say, they are no longer a couple.

One winter night, we were having a late dinner at Elaine's Restaurant with our friend Obba Babatundé. (Obba is a talented actor and dancer, and his portrayal as the director of a musical called *A Tale of Two Cities* on the third season of *Friends* made him very recognizable. When the character Joey lies about his dance experience to get a part in the musical, Obba's character has him take over the dance class, and the choreography, or lack thereof, was hysterical. The episode became one of the most popular ones on *Friends*.) There was no coat check at Elaine's, but there were coat hooks near every table to hang your coat. I was wearing a very nice long black cashmere winter coat with a beautiful scarf and cap in the pocket. When the three of us stood up to leave, I took the remaining black garment off the hook and realized it was not mine. Someone at an adjacent table took my coat and left theirs. When I tried to put it on, I discovered it was a very small woman's cloth coat. A woman had taken my beautiful coat and left hers on the hook.

When I told Elaine what happened, she informed me that two young women were sitting at the next table, and she had the phone number they used to make the reservation. I dialed the number and explained the situation to the woman who answered. She curtly replied that her roommate's friend must have taken it, and I could come over and talk with her. I explained that it was a cold winter night and asked her to please have the girl return the coat to me at the restaurant. She excused herself and, in a minute, came back on the phone to tell me that the friend refused to come to the restaurant. I would have to walk the ten blocks to their apartment to exchange the coat. I had no choice, so Obba, Arlene, and I walked over to the apartment.

I draped the short women's coat over my shoulder to ward off some of the cold wind. When we knocked on the door, we were met by a very rude young girl who informed me that her friend was asleep and could not exchange the coat at that moment. Our friend Obba, who is a lovely, sweet guy and an immensely talented actor, whispered to me that he would handle this. He immediately changed his character from his normal affable self into a tough black gangster type. He proceeded to sternly inform her that if the coat didn't appear in the next few minutes, they were in for trouble from him. He was so menacing that, sure enough, my coat and cap suddenly materialized. My scarf was missing from the pocket, but since Obba was really only an actor and not a gangster, I decided not to push the issue further.

One of our unusual encounters featured two strangers in Westhampton. We had dinner with another couple and invited them back to our home for dessert. When we pulled up to our driveway, I noticed a strange car parked there. I parked at the end of the driveway and told the women to stay in the car in case we were being robbed. The other fellow and I cautiously walked past the parked car to check on my house. As we passed the car, we noticed what looked like a person in the car. As we approached, the back door of the car opened slightly, causing the car lights to go on inside. We observed two naked people making out in the back seat.

After a minute, a man opened the door and exited the car. I asked what he was doing in my driveway. He explained that he and his girlfriend were living in a group house down the road. He left her at home to go to a party and met the girl who was now getting dressed in the back seat. He wanted to have sex with the girl he picked up, but they couldn't go to his house. While driving down the road, he noticed my long driveway and a darkened house. He figured that he wouldn't be too long, but unfortunately, we arrived home early. I motioned to Arlene and our other friend that it was safe to leave our car. After the stranger and his pickup date exited their car, they seemed so nice that I invited them to use our bathroom. I figured they would want to clean up before going home to their respective partners.

I had a neighbor who had a similar surprise when returning home. They had a beautiful home near me on the bay in Westhampton. They would stay in their home on the weekends and then return to NYC during the week. One week at the end of the summer, they decided to come back to Westhampton on a Wednesday night to spend a long weekend. Upon entering their bedroom, they found a couple sleeping in their bed. The startled couple explained that they observed the home was dark all week, so they opened a window and climbed into the house. For the past few weeks, they lived in the house as if it was theirs. On Friday mornings, they restored it, so our friends were unaware of what was happening. They didn't call the police but warned the couple to leave and never return. The following week, they installed a gate and security system.

When we first met Sheryl Lee Ralph, she was starring in *Dreamgirls* on Broadway and dating our close friend Obba Babatundé; but eventually, they broke up. We have remained close friends with both of them over these many decades. Sheryl married a French clothing manufacturer and has two amazing children from that union. After getting divorced, she is now happily married to an outstanding local state senator from Philadelphia named Vincent Hughes. She is a wonderful entertainer and actress and has starred in many television shows and movies, including the popular television series *Moesha* with the singer/actress Brandy and movies like *Sister Act 2* with Whoopi Goldberg. Sheryl even arranged for our daughter, Lauren, to see the taping of one of the episodes of *Moesha* when she was in LA and to meet Brandy. We see Sheryl often, and she has become part of our extended family. Thirty years ago, she created a charity organization called Divas. She produces an event every year called Divas Simply Singing to raise money for HIV. We try to time a vacation in LA to attend whenever we can.

Rita Cosby and Tomaczek Bednarek are one of our favorite couples. Tomaczek comes from a family that has served our country as part of the military. He is a fine singer and is very patriotic. Rita is a television news anchor and correspondent, radio host, and best-selling author. She has done historic back-to-back interviews with Palestinian leader Yasser Arafat and Israeli prime minister Ariel Sharon. Her interviews with boxer Mike Tyson, Michael Jackson, and serial killer David Berkowitz all made headlines. We have had many wonderful times with them both over the past few decades. When we recently took our grandkids Hunter and Sydney to Washington, DC, Rita arranged for us to have a private tour of the White House and chambers of Congress. It was a very special experience, and our grandkids loved it.

Tomaczek has started some of our parties with a patriotic song, and he has performed with many well-known entertainers. Rita has written a best-selling book about her father, titled *Quiet Hero*. She was estranged from her Polish father for twenty-five years because she thought that he had deserted the family. In 2008, Rita discovered an old suitcase belonging to her father. It contained World War II possessions, including his Polish resistance armband and prisoner of war identification. He had kept this all a secret from her and her family. She reconnected with him when she realized that he was secretly one of the great Polish war heroes. In his last years, he was honored by the Polish government for his services. We celebrate our common birthdays and other special occasions together every year. Rita is a dynamo, always full of nonstop stories because of her knowledge of much of what goes on in Washington.

CHAPTER

SIXTY

Diary, 1982

Arlene and I recently found three of our diaries from the years 1982,1983, and 1985 in the back of a shelf at my home. For a few years, we tried keeping a diary of our activities. On many of the days, we jotted down notes about what we did. However, there were times that either we were too tired to write down the day's activities or we just forgot to do so. After 1985, we stopped because we lost interest in trying to write down what we did each day.

On the following pages, I will describe some of our notes from those years to present a picture of our social life at that time. It would be too long to detail every single day. Some of the events described are repeated in other chapters earlier throughout the book when I wrote about experiences with various people. These next chapters are included to show a chronological diary of our social lives over those three years. As I go through the days, I will sometimes add related thoughts of experiences from other occasions as events trigger memories.

We started the new year on December 31, 1981, in Florida at the Diplomat Hotel as guests of the owners, Marge and Irv Cowan. Yul Brynner and his son, Rock, joined us to watch Liza Minnelli entertain at the hotel. Rock is one of the smartest people we know, and many times in long evenings spent with Rock and Liza, we were overwhelmed with his knowledge. When Gina Lollobrigida starred in the movie *Solomon and Sheba*, Tyrone Power was her leading man. Tyrone Power suffered a heart attack and died during the filming. Yul Brynner replaced him as Gina's leading man. Gina told us about what went on during the filming when they had to redo all the close-ups after Tyrone's death, so it was interesting talking to Yul about it.

After Liza's performance, we all went to the Cowans' home for another of their all-night parties. I played tennis at their home on New Year's Day, and the Cowans served Liza's favorite Florida dinner, stone crabs. We flew back to New York on January 4 to greet Gina Lollobrigida at our home and ordered in her favorite dinner, Chinese food. Gina loves NYC Chinese food. Gina bought Arlene some wonderful fabrics from Italy to use for making dresses. Gina was having some dental problems, and Arlene went with her the next day to her dentist.

Gina described how, at the height of her popularity, there were such huge crowds that she needed a police escort in New York City to go anywhere. One time when she was riding in the back of the police car, one of the policemen mistakenly thought that she was a hooker they were taking to jail, not someone being driven to the opening of an event.

On January 7, Gina had a business dinner, and we stayed in. I have mentioned that Jack Haley had a devilish sense of humor. That same night, our doorman rang up to tell me that there were two women downstairs. When I answered that we were not expecting anyone, he told me the women said that they were a "gift" from Jack Haley. We didn't know what Jack was up to, but they were at our building, and we had them sent up. They arrived with two massage tables and said they were here to give us a couples massage as a New Year's gift from Jack.

Arlene and Gina went to a fabric store the next day to pick out fabric for Gina to make a dress for herself. She is terrific at making fabulous gowns for herself and needed something very special to wear in February for an event called the "Night of One Hundred Stars." We went for dinner that night with Gina to celebrate Arlene's birthday at Monsignore Restaurant.

After dinner, we went to Café Central to meet up with Liza Minnelli, Mark Gero, Mark's friend Waldo, and Lisa Mordente. Lisa is Chita Rivera's daughter and had become very close to Liza. Gina had made Arlene a beautiful red Chinese-style suit from material she had bought in the fabric store the last time she was in New York City. Arlene wore it that night, and Liza loved it so much that she made Gina promise to make one for her as well.

Liza and Mark had a third wedding anniversary party at their apartment in early January because they couldn't do it in December. Gina Lollobrigida was staying with us at the time, so we brought her with us. It was a great party with Diana Ross, Beverly Sills, Truman Capote, and Lucille Ball among the guests. (In 1979, Liza divorced Jack Haley Jr. and married Mark Gero. Jack came from a show business family; his father was the Tin Man in *The Wizard of Oz*. Jack was a brilliant film producer and was very much a Hollywood person. We remained good friends with him until the day he died. Jack was a special person whose life was unfortunately cut short by alcohol. When Liza and Jack divorced, many of their common friends gravitated toward Liza, but we remained close to Jack too, and Liza respected us for that. Mark Gero worked as a stage manager with his parents, who acted in and produced off-Broadway shows. He was also a sculptor and very much a non-Hollywood guy. He was younger than Liza, and he had a loyal group of friends who had nothing to do with show business. That was in sharp contrast to Jack, who lived and breathed show business. I am still in contact with Mark to this day, although after divorcing Liza he remarried and moved to Croatia.)

On January 16, Arlene and I went to Halston's showroom at the Olympic Tower in New York City. Liza was receiving the Martha Graham Award from Gregory Peck. It was a wonderful crowd, including Polly Bergen, Christopher Walken, Cher, Karen Black, Cheryl Tiegs, and Peter Beard. We found Gregory Peck to be a modest, classy man. When I told him how much I admired him in his movie roles, he replied, "I'm very popular with the blue-haired set." (We have spent many fun times over the years with his lovely daughter, Cecilia, a successful film producer. We recently spent time with Cecilia at her home in LA at a party that she made for an Italian film festival where Gina Lollobrigida was honored. It was great to reunite with her and our longtime friend Marisa Berenson, who was also there. Al Pacino was at the party with his young girlfriend. He was very friendly to us, and he seemed quite taken with his girlfriend. However, a short time after this party, I read that he and his girlfriend had broken up. Ted Danson was also at the party, and although we hadn't met him before, he was very open and warm to us. We always admired his work on the hit TV series *Cheers* and his recent appearances on Larry David's HBO series *Curb Your Enthusiasm*. Claudia Cardinale, who was one of the sexy Italian movie stars who were popular after Gina Lollobrigida, was also being honored at the party. I remembered her as being so beautiful, but I didn't recognize her when they introduced her and Gina to people at the party. She sat with Gina and us at Cecilia's party and was very friendly, but she was far different from her glamorous image. Even though she was ten years younger than Gina, she looked much older.)

On January 18, we went with Liza to see *Dreamgirls* on Broadway. It was a hit show about a fictional girl group similar to Diana Ross and the Supremes. We were good friends with Obba Babatundé, a wonderful actor, singer, and dancer whom we met when he was a backup dancer for Liza. (We have remained close friends with him for over forty years.) Obba had a role as a brother of one of the girls in the group.

We went back to Liza's apartment after the performance with Obba and his girlfriend. We all sat in Liza's apartment while she analyzed every line that Obba spoke and gave him suggestions on his performance. He greatly appreciated her remarks, and even though his role was not the main one, he was terrific in his part. His girlfriend was casually dressed in jeans and a top, and her hair was pulled back in a ponytail. She was quiet and seemed like a lovely young girl. Liza realized that she, Arlene, and I were directing all the conversation to Obba and his performance while ignoring his girlfriend. So Liza said to her, "And what do you do?" to be nice.

She answered, "My name is Sheryl Lee Ralph, and I play Deena Jones in the show." We were all stunned because that was the lead role in the musical, the part based on Diana Ross. Sheryl was the star, and we did not recognize her without her large wig, costumes, and makeup. After our embarrassment, we all had a good laugh. We left at

5:00 a.m. (Sheryl and Obba eventually broke up, but we remain close friends with both of them individually to this day.)

On January 19, we went over to Liza's apartment because she wanted me to take her to my office that evening for a gum treatment. Liza always tried to stall for time before having any dental work done, so we had some vodka and orange juice. We first left her apartment for my office at 11:00 p.m. At the office, she acted like a director, and I gave her a large mirror to hold so she could see what I was doing. She told me that she had to cancel a show she was planning to do with her ex-husband Peter Allen because they could not agree on an opening number. At three o'clock, we were still hanging out in my office after I worked on her. She had called Chita Rivera's daughter, Lisa Mordente, who came over to join us as well. We had many late evenings that month that we named "Clockers" when we saw the sun came up in the early morning.

We finally had an early evening on January 22 with Julie Budd and her pianist and musical conductor, Herb Bernstein. We ate fried chicken and pizza and watched the movie *Fatso*, starring Dom DeLuise.

On January 23, I played poker at Liza's apartment with Mark Gero and his friends. Arlene came over with a lasagna that she made. Liza lived near us in NYC, and her place became a second home. Cher arrived soon after to join Liza, Mark, Mark's friend Waldo, and Arlene and me for dinner. Cher came dressed in a black leather miniskirt, fishnet stockings, and green hair clips. She had some rocky relationships and was in between boyfriends. I told her that I knew some nice guys for her, but she said that she was not interested in dating a dentist. I tried to explain that my friends were not dentists, but I recognized that I was not cut out to be a matchmaker for Cher.

Liza gave Cher a tour of the apartment. Liza told Cher that when she visited her in her home in LA, the house had oak paneling, and Liza felt that the decor didn't reflect Cher at all except for her bedroom. Cher explained that it was all Sonny's influence, and she didn't really think for herself in those days.

After dinner, we all went over to Café Central to meet up with Bianca Jagger. Bianca was always friendlier to us when we were with Liza, so it was a fun time. We often found Bianca not to be too talkative, and friends explained that she is sometimes shy. Suddenly, at two o'clock, Cher announced to all of us that she was leaving to go over to Studio 54. We were enjoying the time at Café Central, so off into the night by herself went Cher. We later decided to go to Paul Herman's apartment upstairs from the restaurant. He had a piano, and we stayed and had some drinks until five o'clock.

We then returned to Liza's apartment. Mark went to sleep, and we remained up with Liza and Mark's friend Waldo until eight. Liza told us that if she dies before us, we should make sure that she has fireworks at her funeral. We also discussed what we needed for the Super Bowl party that Liza and Mark were hosting at their apartment the next day.

The Super Bowl was on January 24, 1982. (Liza's husband Mark Gero loved sports in contrast to her other husbands who loved the entertainment industry. Mark and Liza spent many weekends at our home in Westhampton, where I have a tennis court. I'm a good player, and Mark wanted to learn how to play tennis because he was such a very athletic person. He was so frustrated when I would beat him. This was only because tennis was new to him and not easy to master quickly. After losing, he would run all the way into town to ease his frustration. In time, he became a very good tennis player and eventually would beat me regularly. It helped that, being married to Liza, he was able to become friendly with tennis stars like Jimmy Conners, who gave him lessons.) Liza made an onion dip, and we also served the remainder of Arlene's lasagna at the Super Bowl party along with a deli platter.

While we sat around the living room watching the Super Bowl, Mark introduced us to a young man who he said was a great boxer. The man was very personable and polite, although he looked like someone I would not want to face in a ring. His voice was very high pitched and did not fit his look. That was my first meeting with Mike Tyson. He had just started out and was unknown to the public at that time. Our very young daughter, Lauren, who was with us, asked me, "Who was that man with the huge neck?" (Years later, I was at a business lunch meeting with Pfizer executives, and someone in the group I was with excitedly said, "Look, that's Mike Tyson sitting over there by himself." Mike was now the heavyweight champion of the world. Imagine their shock when I got up from the table and went over to Mike. He invited me to join him for a while until I finally excused myself to go back to my meeting. When everyone asked me how I knew him, I casually said, "Oh, he's an old friend." They all gave me a lot of respect for the duration of that meeting.)

On January 26, Robert De Niro came over for drinks to Liza's apartment at 8:30 p.m., and then we all went out for dinner. On Friday, we went with Liza to see the *Dreamgirls* show on Broadway again. After the show, our friend Obba came back to Liza's apartment with us. Liza spent a lot of time going over Obba's role in the show while giving him creative suggestions. Mark called in for pizza, and then he went to bed. Liza didn't want Obba to leave, but he had a matinee the next day. She kept Arlene and me up all night, talking. She brought Arlene into her closet and gave her some clothes that no longer fit her as a gift. We stayed up all night, and Liza came over to our home on Saturday morning for breakfast. I was exhausted, and I had to go to work that day. Arlene stayed with Liza at our apartment.

Liza was meeting a musician friend from Brazil, Edu Lobo, who was a world-renowned guitar player. He came over at around noon and gave her guitar lessons all afternoon. Arlene, Edu, and Liza watched Liza's HBO special together. The next day was January 30, and Liza was nominated for a Golden Globe Award for her role in the movie *Arthur*. At night, I had a poker game with Mark and his friends at Liza's apartment, and afterward, we all watched the Golden Globes. At one point, Liza went into her closet and took out a tenor saxophone. She couldn't really play very well but said that she wanted to learn. Liza knew that she wasn't going to win, but we watched until her nomination. We were exhausted and went home to sleep.

The following day, Edu came over to our apartment with Liza, and she sang along with him while he played for us. The times that Liza sang at our place or hers accompanied by talented musician friends in a casual relaxed atmosphere are very special memories for us. Somehow in the middle of these hectic three days, Arlene managed to take our young daughter, Lauren, to a roller-skating party and the Ice Capades show. Those were some of the days and nights from January of that year.

On Monday, February 1, we joined Liza and her guitar-playing friend, Edu, at Halston's place. They played guitar and sang together, and we had dinner at Halston's. Then we all went to Café Central and met Lisa Mordente. We stayed until three o'clock and finally went home to collapse.

On Wednesday, February 3, 1982, I received two calls about dental work. Gina Lollobrigida called me from Rome about a TMJ dental joint problem, and Robert De Niro called for an appointment at my office for the following Friday. On Thursday, February 4, I had lengthy conversations with Liza. Her husband Mark was upset with some of the clockers (all-nighters) of the last week. On Saturday night, February 6, Liza called at nine o'clock to inform me that she was in New York Hospital for stomach problems. She asked us to visit with her and bring pizza with the works and wine, so I guess her stomach problems didn't seem that bad. We watched TV with her until midnight, and we had a miniparty at the hospital.

On Thursday, February 11, Gina Lollobrigida flew in from Rome. She was in New York City for an evening at Radio City Music Hall, called the "Night of 100 Stars," which actually had 230 stars in attendance. The event organizers put everyone up at the Helmsley Palace Hotel in New York City. We met Gina there and went out for Chinese food at a restaurant called David K's. After dinner, we went back to Gina's hotel and called Sammy and Altovise Davis, who were also in town for the event. Gina wanted to take pictures of Sammy for an Italian magazine. Gina is a world-class photographer and was also photographing all the stars at the event for *Life* magazine. Sammy had just flown in from Phoenix and invited us to come over. We went to Sammy's suite at the Waldorf, and Gina took some terrific pictures of him. We all had a great time sitting around, talking, and we were joined by Patrick Hermès.

Gina related a story about how years ago when she was dining at Maxim's in Paris and was upset about something, she went to the ladies' room three times to cry. Sammy Davis was at the restaurant and walked into the ladies' room to see what was wrong. Gina remembered the incident because Sammy said to her, "What am I doing here trying to calm you down when I have two beautiful blondes waiting for me at my table?"

On Friday, February 12, when I finished working on Robert De Niro in my office, I met Arlene at Sammy's hotel at six thirty. He had us meet there early, so we could watch him rehearse at Radio City Music Hall for his performance at the "Night of 100 Stars." Sammy would be performing his signature song, "Mr. Bojangles."

We then went with him and Altovise to see James Earl Jones and Christopher Plummer in *Othello* on Broadway. Sammy even got a seat in the theater for his bodyguard, Brian, who went everywhere with him. The production was not typical Shakespeare, and Sammy was not happy with it. Sammy was gracious enough to have us all go backstage to congratulate the cast.

Afterward, we went to the restaurant and nightclub Regine's, and Regine was a great hostess. She invited us all to her place the next night for a Valentine's Day party. At Regine's, Sammy asked Arlene to do the twist with him on the dance floor. Sammy spoke about being a follower of Satan for a number of years and remarked that he even had one red fingernail. We didn't know if it was true or just the alcohol talking.

We returned to Sammy's hotel room, and the actor Pernell Roberts, from the TV show *Bonanza*, joined us, along with some others. We called Gina, who was at our apartment, to invite her over, but she was just going to sleep. After everyone left, Sammy asked us to stay, and it was another late evening. (Whenever we were at Sammy's suite in New York City, entertainers and celebrities were always coming and going throughout the evening.)

The following night, Lorna Luft returned to New York City after filming the movie *Grease 2* in Los Angeles. She was in a limo with her husband Jake and had the limo stop off at our apartment so she could see us before going home. She invited us to join them for their anniversary dinner two nights later.

The next night, we met Sammy and Altovise at Regine's. When Regine, the legendary owner of clubs named after her all over the world, was in town, she invited fabulous people for dinner parties at her club. We had a great table of people join us for dinner, including Julio Iglesias, Roger Moore, Peter O'Toole, Joan Collins, and Peter Falk. Later, we all went to Sammy's Waldorf Hotel suite, and some other entertainers also stopped by, including Pernell Roberts and Robert Guillaume.

(We had many wonderful nights at Regine's over the years. One night we had been out with Sammy at a Broadway show, and he informed us that Regine wanted to see him while he was in town. We were starving and hoped that she was inviting us to a dinner party. When we sat down, Regine—assuming we had eaten—brought over a huge tin of beluga caviar, thinking that we might have a little as a snack. While she and Sammy were in animated conversation, Arlene and I started eating the caviar. No other food came out, so our dinner that night was spoonfuls of caviar until we returned to Sammy's for some leftovers from his cooking. We probably consumed many hundreds of dollars of caviar but would have traded it all for a juicy hamburger at the time.)

The following night, Lorna and Jake came over for drinks before dinner on their fifth anniversary. We opened a bottle of Dom Pérignon and went to dinner at the Box Tree Restaurant. Later, we went to Studio 54 and then to a new place called the Red Parrot. They featured live parrots in cages and a swing music orchestra. The following day, Arlene met Lorna at Paramount to see the beginning of the *Grease 2* movie. They had lunch with Rex Reed, who was interviewing Lorna for *Gentleman's Quarterly* magazine.

On Thursday, February 18, we went to our son Marc's sixth-grade Greek festival at school. We then attended Lorna's party celebrating the opening of the movie *Grease 2*. We went with her to a dinner at a restaurant, followed by a party at Studio 54. Liza attended the opening of Cher's show on Broadway (*Come Back to the Five and Dime*) and then made an appearance at Studio 54 in time for pictures with Lorna and Lorna's dad, Sid Luft. We later joined Liza and Mark for a drink at Café Central with Kate Jackson, Cher, and Cher's daughter, Chastity. Cher was upset by the bad reviews, but Liza was very diplomatic and told her that the show was not that bad. Cher was disturbed about one bad personal review she received, but Liza raved about how good she was, and that made her happy.

On Friday, February 19, we went to school to see our son Marc's grade perform a Greek play. We then brought him to Serendipity for lunch and then to the electronic and toy departments in Bloomingdale's. In the evening, we took Gina Lollobrigida to see Cher's play. The critics were right, it was awful. We left at intermission to go to Elaine's for dinner. We did not stay late because Gina had to fly to Los Angeles the next day to tape *The Bob Hope Show*. He was featuring many of his leading ladies from the past. Gina checked out of her hotel, and we took her luggage back to our apartment. She was coming back to stay with us after Los Angeles. Gina was also planning to meet with people from the Metropolitan Museum about a photography exhibit. I was able to set up the meeting for her because the head of the museum's mother was a patient of mine.

On Saturday, February 20, Arlene made tacos and veal parmesan, and everyone came over to our apartment for dinner. Liza, Mark, Waldo, Kate Jackson, Lorna, Jake, and Jake's bandmate Alan Merrill were there. Mark's best friend, Waldo, was now dating Kate Jackson, although he lived and worked in NYC, and she was in LA. Alan Merrill was the cowriter with Jake on the rock classic "I Love Rock and Roll." We all gathered in our bedroom to watch Lorna's tape of her movie *Grease 2*. Lorna had gone to see Cher's show that afternoon and also walked out at intermission.

On Sunday, February 21, we went with Liza and Mark to see the act High Heeled Women. Liza enjoyed it and wanted Kander and Ebb, who wrote most of her shows, to see it. We always loved being around Fred Ebb, who had a brilliant wit, but he was a nervous wreck. Fred's great sense of humor rubbed off on both Liza and Chita Rivera, who used many of his expressions. We had wonderful moments with him, and even though he was always tense, it was stimulating to observe his creative juices flowing. Lorna and Jake and the star of *Grease 2*, Michelle Pfeiffer, and her husband joined us, along with four girls from Liza's Broadway show *The Act*.

On Monday, February 22, Gina arrived from Los Angeles to stay with us. We had some Chinese food at home, which is her favorite NYC meal. The next day, Gina had us send a telegram to Henry Kissinger, who always had a thing for Gina, we believed. Henry had recent heart surgery, and Gina sent him well-wishes.

On February 25, Liza appeared at a charity event at Carnegie Hall. There was an after-party at the Japanese restaurant Hisae. Dinner was with Helen Hayes, Faye Dunaway, Melba Moore, and Joe Pesci. It was a fabulous grouping of people, and many paparazzi were circling our table all night (probably wondering who Arlene and I were and how they could cut us out of the photos). After dinner, we went with Liza and Joe Pesci to Café Central. (Liza and Pesci were close friends, and we have spent many great times with Joe over the years.)

The following week after Gina returned to Europe, we met Liza and Mark at a west side tennis club on March 2. They took a lesson first, and then we played doubles. We went back to our apartment for piña coladas, and Arlene served a taco casserole, which she had made earlier. Liza asked Arlene to join her for an exercise class with her trainer. She wanted to get into good shape because she was possibly going to have to be in a nude scene for an upcoming movie, something she never did before. Arlene was happy when the exercise trainer canceled the next day because Arlene really did not want to go.

The following day, March 5, Liza called us to come over at 5:45 p.m. because Mark was playing tennis, and she wanted company. John Belushi just died, and we were watching TV together to get details. Liza made us shrimp scampi, potatoes, and an onion dip. It was good to just relax for an evening because it was another hectic month.

On March 27, 1982, we celebrated Lauren's early birthday at home, and she invited three friends to sleep over. Later, we had dinner at Elaine's with Mark, Liza, and Waldo.

On Sunday, March 28, we took a ride with the kids to New Haven to see our cousin Howard Marren's new musical play *Luv*. Howard is a talented composer and has won many honors for his musicals. That night, for my birthday, Liza hired a limo. She took us to a wonderful French restaurant on East Seventy-Ninth Street and ordered all the specialties of the house and three bottles of wine. She really made it a memorable birthday.

The next night, I played poker at Liza's apartment with Mark Gero and his group. Arlene went with Liza to Halston's apartment to watch the Academy Awards. Liza had a rough day because she found out that Mark's mother might need breast surgery and was checking out doctors. After poker, I picked Arlene up at Halston's and took her home. The following Sunday, Lorna, Jake, and Mark came over for brunch. Liza wasn't feeling well and stayed home.

On April 7, we left for Rome to spend a week with Gina Lollobrigida. Gina's chauffeur, Celestino, picked us up at the airport. We stayed in Gina's guest quarters at the lowest level of her house. An enormous fish tank divided the room that we stayed in from our bathroom. It was lavishly decorated, like being in Morocco. Gina's home is huge, and it is filled with magnificent works of art, beautiful carpets, and tiled floors. It is like visiting a wonderful museum. Her home is in an area called Via Appia Antica, where ancient columns and ruins line the roads.

Her chauffeur drove us into the center of town, and we went shopping. Because Gina is so revered in Rome, she rarely is able to leave her home. She felt comfortable going out with us and loved walking through the streets of the city. We shopped until eight o'clock.

Gina has a screening room in her home, and over the course of a few days, she showed us some of her movies, including *Solomon and Sheba* and *Go Naked in the World*. Gina is an amazing actress, and she even did some of her own stunts on the trapeze in the famous movie *Trapeze*, which she starred in with Burt Lancaster and Tony Curtis. She has a photography studio and darkroom in her home and showed us her photographs and equipment. Gina has published many books of her photography, and they have been very successful.

On Sunday, a well-known Italian man flew Gina and us to Sardinia and put us up at the San Marco Hotel. We celebrated Easter Monday at a picnic where they roasted a pig and a goat. The next day, we flew back to Rome and spent a few more days at her house. Gina screened one of her famous Italian films called *Bread, Love, and Dreams*. It was only in Italian, so she gave a running commentary in English while we watched the movie. A friend of Gina's, Massimo Gargia, throws a party filled with well-known international celebrities every year called the Best. We went to a beautiful Italian club to attend the party with Gina.

On April 15, we flew back to New York City. Liza had left messages for us at our home, and we went over to see her that evening. We caught up on things while enjoying piña coladas.

On Sunday, April 18, we went over to Lorna's apartment for dinner. She gave us gifts from the *Grease 2* movie to give to our kids. Lauren walked into her third-grade class that year with her arms filled with new school supplies, all of which said in bold letters, "Rydell High." (Thirty-five years later when Lauren was dressing as a character from *Grease* for Halloween, Lorna happened to be staying with us. She helped Lauren with her costume and styled her wig.)

Arlene went with Lorna to P. J. Clarke's (her favorite hamburger restaurant, which was established in 1884; her father and mother used to go there regularly with her, and she has fond memories of time spent there with them). Lorna's marriage to Jake had been somewhat shaky, but we all went out to the movies together to see *The Diner*. We ran into Lorna's first conductor, Gene Palumbo. Gene was also Judy Garland's conductor when he was just starting out at age nineteen. We had a fascinating time hearing them both reminisce about stories of Judy Garland on the road.

We spent the following weekend with our children in Westhampton. On Sunday, April 25, we returned home to Manhattan and attended two charity affairs. Lorna was singing at Fight for Sight. Liza was entertaining at Carnegie Hall, doing a charity event for the Tappan Zee Playhouse. Lorna's event was earlier, and after hearing her sing, we went out for drinks with her, Jake, and Gene Palumbo. At ten o'clock, we went over to Carnegie Hall in time for intermission. After intermission, Dudley Moore and Liza Minnelli performed. We went backstage after to meet up with them. Arlene wore a forties-style outfit with a hat and veil. Liza changed into simple black pants and a top with little makeup. As we left Carnegie Hall, everyone waiting outside thought that Arlene was Liza, and Liza got a big kick out of it. We left with Liza to meet Joe Pesci at Café Central. Liza was anxious to do *Gypsy* on Broadway and wanted Joe Pesci in that show with her. (But that never happened.)

On Tuesday, April 27, we went over to Liza's apartment and had Chinese food with her and Mark. Liza had taken a double acting class with Herbert Berghof. She was really focusing on her acting because she wanted to obtain the rights for *Gypsy* and do it on Broadway.

The next night, on April 28, we had dinner with Truman Capote. We picked him up at his apartment at UN Plaza, and he gave us one of his early books as a gift. He took us to one of his favorite restaurants La Petite Marmite. We loved our dinners with Truman because he told the most fascinating stories. We never knew if they were real or not, but they were so interesting that we didn't care. Later that night, Arlene modeled along with the Broadway cast of *Sophisticated Ladies*, *Dreamgirls*, and Lucy Arnaz at the Red Parrot. It was a fashion show by the designer Tony Chase.

On Saturday, May 1, we left for the Hamptons with Liza and Mark. Mark and I played tennis, and Liza and Arlene made BLT sandwiches. We went to our local movie theater at night and saw *Victor/Victoria*. The theater manager was so happy to see Liza that he let us in without paying. Later that night, we received a phone call from Mark's best friend, Waldo, informing us that he just married Kate Jackson that afternoon while she was on a break from her *Charlie's Angels* set. Arlene made tacos for dinner.

On Sunday, Mark and I played tennis, and Liza relaxed and read the book *Hawaii*. Liza talked again about wanting to do *Gypsy*. (And she would have been great in it. It remains a disappointment for her never to have done it. Liza tears down the house at her concerts when she performs songs from that musical.) I brought in steamers and pizza for dinner. We sat around watching TV. Ironically, the program was of Liza's ex-husband Jack Haley, *Ripley's Believe It or Not*. (We had spent a lot of time with the host of the show, Jack Palance, during our time at Jack's home. We found him to be quite a character and definitely someone not easy to work with because he had very strong opinions. Palance loved to show off in front of us, doing multiple push-ups.)

We drove home on Sunday night and received a late-night phone call from Lorna informing us that her marriage to Jake was not going well. The next night, May 3, was Jake's birthday, and she invited us to join them at Mr. Chow Restaurant for dinner. Besides not being a good husband to Lorna, Jake had an affair. The next day, May 4, we had lunch with Lorna at P. J. Clarke's and later saw the trailer for her movie *Grease 2* at the Baronet Theater. Lorna was trying to find shoes for the movie opening and eventually received a pair from Liza. The following day, May 5, we went to a birthday party at Studio 54 for Julie Budd, who turned twenty-eight.

On May 10, Gina Lollobrigida flew in from Rome to stay with us. On May 11, our friend Aldo Cipullo invited us to a party in honor of him creating the Cartier Love bracelet. It was at the apartment of the new owner of Studio 54, Mark Fleischman. We invited Gina to join us, and Aldo was thrilled. Lorna and Jake and Liz and Rick Derringer were also there. (When we invited Aldo the following year to our son Marc's bar mitzvah, he kept telling us that he wasn't sure if he could make it. He explained that he hadn't been feeling well and never did attend. He was the first person we knew that came down with AIDS and sadly passed away that year. A few years earlier, we had gone to Fire Island with Lorna and Jake to see Aldo, who had a home there. I took my boat from Westhampton, and when we got to Fire Island, there was a big tea dance going on. Aldo, who was the nicest, friendliest guy, was in a very strange relationship with a man there. It was the only time he ever acted unfriendly to us. It was not like him, and when we all saw him next, he apologized profusely. He explained that his lover didn't allow him to talk to others. He gave Lorna a Love bracelet as an apology gift.)

The next day, Gina stopped at my office for a dental checkup and then flew to Boston for a business meeting. The following day, Lorna came over and gave *Grease 2* T-shirts and signed posters to our kids. *People* magazine was doing a spread on her for its next issue. Liza was spending the day doing an eight-page spread for Italian *Vogue*.

On Friday, May 14, Lorna came over for a few hours to show us her schedule for the promotion of the *Grease 2* movie.

On Saturday, May 15, Waldo and Kate Jackson drove Arlene to our home in Westhampton. I drove out in the afternoon, and Gina Lollobrigida came from the airport in the evening as well. I barbecued steak and veal, and we had a great dinner. Gina took pictures of the newlyweds, who were embracing and kissing all the time. At eleven thirty, we went to the local pizza place Baby Moon for pizza and wedding pictures. Waldo and Kate blew out candles from a cheesecake because this was actually their honeymoon. We had a great time, but Kate got upset when a local woman took two pictures at the restaurant, and her mood changed. Kate was a very big TV star at that time and didn't want her picture published. She insisted that the local person take the film out of her camera, and everything turned happy again. The next day, Kate and Waldo went to town and bought us some gifts, including "sickness bags" because we had to watch them making out so much.

On Sunday, May 16, we all went back to the city, and Gina had her usual favorite meal of Chinese food with us at home. We watched Jack Haley's three-hour TV special *The Gift of Laughter.*

On Monday, May 17, Arlene went with Gina to the Westbury Hotel to watch girls modeling designer clothes for *Best* magazine. Cornelia Guest was the debutante of the year, and she was one of the models. We first met Cornelia when she was very young and a muse of Andy Warhol. (Over the years, she has become a very outstanding woman with many accomplishments.) Also modeling that day was our friend Prince Egon von Furstenberg, and Arlene was also asked to model some outfits. In the evening, we went with Gina to the Pierre Hotel for a fur fashion show. Gina's furrier from Rome, Soldano, was there. I bought Arlene a stunning long red fur coat from him at a great discount because of his friendship with Gina. We stopped off to see Lorna before she left for her promo tour for the movie.

The next morning, on May 18, Arlene went with Gina to the Brooklyn Botanic Garden, where she wanted to take photographs. That evening, we took Gina to Elaine's Restaurant for dinner and spent some time there with George Hamilton. George is very charming and always fun to be with.

On Wednesday, May 19, Gina spoke with *People* magazine about selling them some pictures of Kate Jackson and Waldo. At night, we went with my friend Albie and his wife to his restaurant, Elmer's, for dinner with Gina. On Friday, May 21, we took Gina over to Liza and Mark's apartment, and Arlene made tacos. On Saturday, May 22, we took Gina to Wolfe's Deli for frankfurters so she could experience a New York deli. We later had dinner at Regine's. On Monday, May 24, Arlene went with Gina to watch film footage that she had taken in the Philippines for a documentary she wanted to produce. Her photography book on the Philippines was a best-selling book. Earlier in the morning, Gina was interviewed on the *Good Morning America* television program. On Tuesday, May 25, we had dinner at il Valletto Restaurant with Gina and some artist friends. She decided not to sell the pictures of Waldo and Kate to *People* magazine because they offered too little money.

On Wednesday, May 26, we went with Gina to see Tommy Tune in the show *Nine* on Broadway. At dinner afterward at Ted Hook's Backstage Restaurant, Gina told us about her dates with Tom Jones. Ted Hook ran a fun restaurant in the Broadway area. Performers would come in after their show and sing a song. He had small lamps at each table and would put one out with the name of any performer who came in that night. On Thursday, we went with Gina to see Al Pacino in *American Buffalo* on Broadway, which we hated.

On Friday, May 28, we went to dinner with Gina and a very talented Italian painter named Mago. He was an amazing artist but just lived in the wrong century. He painted in the style of the great Italian painters of old but was unable to sell any paintings here in the United States. He did not speak any English, and Arlene did not speak any Italian. They decided to have some lunches together so she could learn Italian while he learned English. (After a few lunches, he was starting to speak English very well, but Arlene could not learn Italian. When she realized she was not learning Italian and he was getting a little too attached, Arlene ended the lunch meetings. He unfortunately never had success as an artist, even though he was a very gifted painter.)

Over the summer, we had friends like Lorna and Jake, Liza and Mark, and Jack Haley come to stay with us in the Hamptons. In September, we came back to NYC on the tenth for Mark Gero's thirtieth birthday party. Liza's father, Vincente Minnelli, and his wife Lee traveled to NYC for the celebration. There was a great group of people in attendance, including Gregory Peck, Ryan O'Neal, Farrah Fawcett, Robert De Niro, Al Pacino, Marisa Berenson, and Obba

Babatundé. Liza made a beautiful buffet and had a birthday cake shaped like a shark because Mark's nickname was "the Shark." Mark's best friend, Waldo, couldn't attend because he flew to Los Angeles to be with his wife, Kate Jackson.

When Waldo returned on Tuesday, September 14, we did another small dinner at Liza's, and Arlene made tacos. Farrah Fawcett and Ryan O'Neal joined us along with Steve Rubell. Steve's father was a tennis pro, and a few days later, we played tennis together. I played with Steve's father against Mark and Steve, who was quite a good tennis player. In the evening, we went over to Liza's to watch the Emmys and ordered in pizza.

On September 21, we went to the opening party at Studio 54 for the new season there. We sat with Obba Babatundé, Eartha Kitt, and Phyllis Hyman. A few people came over to Arlene, thinking she was Liza because we were sitting in the VIP section. Liza often remarked that she was written about in the press for spending more nights at Studio 54 than she really did because of Arlene being mistaken for her.

The next night, we met Liza and Nabila Khashoggi for drinks at Café Central. We then went to the disco Xenon. (Nabila has been a great friend for years and is a lovely girl. At the time, her father was the richest man in the world. For her nineteenth birthday, he bought her a nineteen-carat diamond ring.) The following day, we took Nabila to lunch at Le Cirque Restaurant. The next night, she took us to her father's birthday party at his amazing apartment on the top two floors of the Olympic Tower. It was one of the most opulent apartments we had ever been to, and there was heavy security.

The following day, Gina Lollobrigida came to New York for a few days, and we had wonderful times together. Her English had improved tremendously from her many trips to New York since meeting us. (When she was making movies, they told her in Hollywood not to learn any more English because they loved the charm of her accent in the movies.) Jack Haley arrived in NYC and invited us to a party for Raquel Welsh. It was nice to meet her, and we found her very friendly. Another night, we went with Jack and Gina to Regine's with Jack Palance, who was starring in Jack's TV show *Ripley's Believe It or Not*.

For Thanksgiving that year, Lorna cooked dinner and invited all our family, including my mother. Liza came also, and later, everyone went to Halston's for nightcaps. The following day, we joined Liza for the weekend at her shows in Worcester, Massachusetts. Lorna also came to Worcester, and on the second night, Liza brought her onstage with her to sing a duet.

The next day, we drove home with Liza and met Robin Williams at Café Central for dinner. He was unbelievably funny and eccentric. We met the same group the next day at Café Central, and Steve Rubell and Halston joined us. The following night, we went with Obba Babatundé to the theater and then to Studio 54 for a party theme of "Night of One Hundred Trees."

The next night, we had dinner with Liza and Mark, and the actress Susan George and her boyfriend at Elaine's. Jack Haley was still in town, and the following evening, we went to dinner with him at Elaine's. We sat at the same table where we sat the previous night with his ex-wife, Liza. We were afraid the waiter would say something, but he didn't. The next night, Julie Budd opened at a nightclub in New York, and we went there with friends.

Our year ended with us traveling to Rome with our children for Christmas with Gina. We all flew together to spend New Year's in Gina's home in Crans-sur-Sierre in Switzerland. The kids had a fabulous time in Rome and Switzerland. Gina's home had beautiful views of the mountains and was right on the ski trail, so the kids could go skiing every day right outside the house. Gina is a great cook and, at night, made pasta for us. The home also had a wonderful wine cellar, and we had terrific samplings of great wines.

On New Year's Eve, we went to the home of one of Gina's friends who owned many hotels in Italy. We had a beautiful dinner and watched Liza perform a live show on German TV that night. We have spent many New Year's with Liza, so we felt good about at least being able to see her perform on New Year's Eve. We drove back to Rome from Switzerland on New Year's Day. We stopped overnight at the fabulous Hotel Splendido in Portofino. When we arrived in Rome the next day, we had dinner at Gina's home and flew back to New York City on January 3.

CHAPTER

SIXTY-ONE

Diary, 1983

When we returned from Rome in January 1983, our long nights of clockers continued. We brought our son, Marc, over to Liza's apartment at 7:30 p.m. because she wanted to show him around. After I took him home, we went over to Halston's place with Liza. Halston informed us that Martha Graham's dance company was running out of money, and he was trying to figure out how to help. We all went to Café Central and stayed until three.

The next day, we went with Liza and Mark to a party that our friend George Martin was throwing at Studio 54 for the tennis great Guillermo Vilas. It was another late night. The following day, we went to Liza and Mark's apartment to watch tennis and the Jets game. After the game, I took Liza to my office to clean her teeth. We went back to her apartment afterward, and Mark fell asleep around 1:30 a.m. Liza wanted to continue talking, and we sat around the kitchen table until four thirty. At that point, I thought that it did not pay to go to sleep, and we all stayed up until seven thirty. I went home to shave and then to my office to work.

The following weekend, I played tennis again with Mark Gero and Steve Rubell. Arlene made lasagna at home to bring over to Liza's apartment on Sunday for the Super Bowl. Lorna and Jake had broken up, and we met her and her new boyfriend, Jim, at Mr. Chow for dinner. Leslie and Evie Bricusse were staying with Liza as houseguests, and it was great seeing them the next day at the Super Bowl party. Mark's friend Kevin Wade was there as well. We always liked Kevin and were happy that he won a Golden Globe Award for Best Screenplay for his movie *Working Girl*. He has also written many other successful movies. It was Leslie's birthday, and we all sang "Happy Birthday" to him. We planned to take him and Evie to Café Central, but at 1:45 a.m., Liza was still not ready to leave, so we went home. I had a poker game the next night with Mark and his group and needed some rest.

Two days later, we went to Liza and Mark's to have farewell drinks for Mark's friend Waldo. He was moving to LA the following day to try TV producing along with his new wife, Kate Jackson. (That idea failed, along with the very short marriage. Within a few months, Waldo was back at his family business in New York City.)

The following Saturday, we went to Café Central with Liza, Mark, Bill LaVorgna (Liza's drummer and musical conductor), and Desi Arnaz Jr. (Liza's old boyfriend from years ago, who was in town). We stayed until three o'clock, and then Liza arranged for a limo to drive us to a late-night club called Crisco Disco. When we arrived, we were escorted to a special upstairs VIP room and offered a lot of drugs, but no one took anything. It was somewhat uncomfortable all evening having both Liza's husband Mark and former boyfriend Desi at the same table. We heard that Desi had a drinking problem, but he did not drink at all and only had espresso and sparkling water. Liza was in a great mood, but we were concerned that there might be words between her and Mark when they returned home after spending an evening with her ex-boyfriend.

The following Sunday, Arlene took the kids to see the show *Merlin* on Broadway. Chita Rivera was the star, and Arlene brought the kids backstage afterward to see her. (Our kids were used to seeing our friends in shows. They actually were surprised whenever we brought them to a show and didn't go backstage.) The following week, we took the kids to see the off-Broadway show *Snoopy*. Lorna Luft was starring in it, and afterward, we went with her and some of the other cast members for a bite to eat at a place called JR's.

On Saturday, February 26, I went to see the movie *Forty-Eight Hours* with Mark Gero. Liza had gone to see Lorna in *Snoopy*, and Arlene met us all back at Liza's apartment. Paul Herman, who ran Café Central, came over to the apartment with Mohammed Khashoggi (Nabila's brother) and our friend Jimmy Russo. (Jimmy was starring with Farrah Fawcett in the off-Broadway show *Extremities*. It was a very physical show, and Farrah broke her arm during its run. That was when I started supplying Farrah with my Plax mouthwash because her arm injury made brushing difficult. I was developing Plax, but it was not yet on the market. She was very thankful the rinse helped keep her famous smile bright, and she became an early advocate for it.)

After everyone left Liza's apartment, Liza asked us to stay. She played a tape from her father's eightieth birthday tribute in Palm Springs, California. Kirk Douglas was the host and asked Liza to perform a whole new act for the occasion. They wanted Liza to perform music from all of her father's movies, and it was the first time she sang her mother's songs in public. Liza told us how her mother, Judy Garland, always trained to go onstage with a killer instinct. That night, she did not overdo it because she did not want to upstage her father. Vincente actually sang "Embraceable You" that evening.

We arrived home at six thirty, and the sun was shining. We were able to rest all day on Sunday, February 27, until the evening. We had our children's Dalton School benefit that night. The children of our friend Neil Sedaka also attended Dalton. He was the entertainer that evening at the Milford Plaza Hotel, and we took our children. As usual, Marc and Lauren were used to seeing our friends performing in public and were quite comfortable at the event. The following afternoon, we had lunch with Lorna Luft at a restaurant near us called Grass.

On March 2, Liza invited us to an evening at the Metropolitan Museum where her father was being honored. The main celebration had been in Los Angeles, but New York City also wanted to honor Vincente on his eightieth birthday. The next day, Liza called to tell us that her father was taken to the hospital and was unfortunately diagnosed with kidney cancer.

That day, Thursday, March 3, Gina Lollobrigida arrived from Rome to stay with us. We had our usual first-night dinner of Chinese food. Gina gave Arlene a magnificent necklace of two strands of pearls with rhinestones and gold that Gina made for her. (Gina has given Arlene fabulous jewelry over the years that she made herself. She is an amazing talent, and her paintings, drawings, photography, and sculptures fill our homes.)

The following night, Friday, March 4, we went with Gina to see Julio Iglesias at Radio City Music Hall. We spent time with him afterward before heading out to dinner at Elaine's, and he was quite charming. One of the people whom Gina wanted to photograph was Gregory Peck, and coincidentally, he and his daughter, Cecilia, were having dinner at Elaine's at the next table. We have been friendly with Cecilia for many years, and we always found Gregory Peck to be humble and down to earth.

The next night, Saturday, March 5, Gina had a business dinner, and we went to dinner at Elaine's with Jack Haley and his girlfriend Kelly. They were in town for Jack's new television show *Ripley's Believe It or Not*. On Sunday, our kids wanted Gina to make fettuccine carbonara for them, and she did. It was delicious. (She taught me how to make it, and I attempted it a few times, but the kids preferred that we wait for Gina to return to have it again, and I got the hint.) We watched the movie *The Rose Tattoo*, which Gina wanted to do on Broadway. The last time Gina was in NY, she went to Trader Vic's Restaurant and broke a tooth on something in her food. She filed a lawsuit against the restaurant and had a meeting with her lawyers about it.

Jack Haley was filming episodes of *Ripley's* in New York City, one featuring a man who offered rides on llamas. Jack filmed our children and us as the people on the llamas. The filming went well, and we were featured on the *Ripley's* TV show episode "Chickie the Llama." (That was the beginning and end of our family's television career, except for Lauren, who was flown to LA to appear on a TV show called *The Weakest Link* shortly after she graduated law school.)

On Saturday, March 12, Arlene took Gina to see Bette Midler's show on Broadway, and she loved it. (We were in the audience years before when Bette opened for Johnny Carson in Las Vegas. The audience only wanted to see Johnny, and Bette was unknown. They didn't understand her at all and kept yelling for Johnny. We, on the other hand, had seen Bette in New York and were probably the only people in the room who came to see her. During her performance, Bette kept telling the rude audience that Johnny would be on soon and promised she would only be on for a short time. We hated to see her treated that way, but Bette soon became a major star and had the last laugh.)

On Tuesday, March 15, we went with Gina to photograph Andy Warhol at his studio. We had a stimulating day with him and the various interesting characters at his place. (I am sorry that I did not realize how much his art would be worth because he was always offering to sell it to us or paint our portraits for very little. For $25,000, we could have had a personal Andy Warhol portrait of us.) On Wednesday, March 16, Gina and her assistant, Tonino, took us to a new hot restaurant, the River Café, in Brooklyn. (It is still very popular today.)

On Thursday, March 17, Lindsay Wagner arrived in New York City. We invited her over to our place for dinner with Gina and our family. Lindsay was in town with her mother, Marilyn; her makeup artist and his wife; and her baby Dorian. She brought Dorian's diapers for us to wash because she did not believe in disposable diapers. Lindsay's husband, Henry Kingi, was a stuntman in Los Angeles, and he arrived the following day. We had a wonderful dinner with them both. They couldn't stay at our place with the baby because we had Gina staying with us. On Sunday, March 20, we had brunch with Lindsay and her family. We then went with her and our children to the Metropolitan Museum costume exhibit. We all took a horse and buggy ride back to Lindsay's hotel.

The following day, we had dinner with Lindsay at the Russian Tea Room and met up with Lorna Luft. Lorna was flying to Houston the next day, because her father, Sid Luft, was undergoing heart surgery. The next day, I played tennis with Mark Gero and lost. He was determined to be a good tennis player and began beating me regularly. On Wednesday, March 23, Lindsay came over with the baby, and our children enjoyed playing with him. (Today that little baby and Lindsay's other son, Alex, are six-foot-six stuntmen and actors.) Lorna called from Houston to tell us that Sid had triple bypass surgery and was doing well.

On March 24, we went with our children to Los Angeles and stayed with Jack Haley. We went to sleep early because Jack was shooting the last episode of his TV show the following day. The actor Ricky Schroder was on our airplane, and the kids got a kick out of seeing him because they watched him regularly on TV in *Silver Spoons*. They went over to say hello to him, and he was very nice. On Friday, I took the children to Disneyland.

In the evening, we went with Jack, his girlfriend Kelly, and the actor Michael Callan and his wife Karen to Trader Vic's Restaurant. Michael was best known for creating the character Riff in *West Side Story* on Broadway. They were a fun couple, and we enjoyed zombie drinks. Jack usually held his liquor well, but that night, he almost drove into his house when we went home. Jack was a great guy, but we were starting to get concerned about his problem with alcohol.

The following day, we took our children to Universal Studios for the tour. That night, Jack threw a great party at his home. Before the party, Arlene and I went over to Sammy Davis's house. Our first stop every time we went to LA in those days would be to say hello to Sammy and Altovise if they were in town. Sammy had just returned home from the hospital after suffering from pneumonia. He had gone to bed earlier but got up to spend time with us. On Sunday, March 27, Sammy was feeling better and invited the children and us to come over to his house. Altovise spent a lot of time with the kids, playing in the pool house and on all of Sammy's gaming equipment. She put out a huge buffet of fried chicken and homemade potato salad and took pictures with the children and Sammy. Sammy turned on the first episode of *The Thorn Birds* on TV, but it was boring. The theme music, by Henry Mancini, was the best part of the show.

Monday, March 28, was my birthday. My daughter Lauren's birthday is March 29, and we celebrated our joint birthdays at a Japanese restaurant called Yamato. Altovise, Jack, and Jack's friend David Niven Jr. joined us. Sammy was still not feeling well enough to go out and was suffering from some back spasms. We had a fun time and, after dinner, stopped off to see Jack's mother. She was a lovely woman, and she gave Lauren a candy doll with balloons.

For Lauren's birthday the next day, I took the kids to the amusement park Knott's Berry Farm. Arlene had lunch with Altovise and Skye Aubrey. Skye was a great friend of ours. Her father, Jim Aubrey, was president of CBS television and, later, head of MGM. He was one tough guy, but his daughter, Skye, was a sweetheart. Later that evening, we met Lindsay Wagner and her husband Henry, and we went with all the children to the Mandarin Restaurant for dinner to celebrate Lauren's birthday.

On Wednesday, March 30, I took the children with Arlene to Magic Mountain, another amusement park. Jack was busy working that evening on one of his TV projects, and the kids stayed home with him. Arlene and I went over to Sammy Davis's house. Sammy wasn't up to going out, so Altovise called in for sushi. Sammy had a projectionist show us a film, and we talked until 3:00 a.m.

On Sunday, March 31, I took the children to Disneyland. Arlene spent time with Karen and Michael Callan at Jack's house. Karen and Michael took us out to Sonny Bono's popular new restaurant, Bono's, for dinner. The following day, we flew home to NYC.

On Monday, we went to see the movie *Flashdance* with Lorna Luft. At the box office, we bumped into Christopher Reeve and his girlfriend, Gae. We sat with them at the movie, and afterward, we all went to Sombrero, a Mexican restaurant, for a bite. Chris loved to fly his own plane and urged me to go up with him. That was something I was definitely not interested in. He only played *Superman* in the movies and, in real life, would be little help to me if there was any trouble with a small plane.

The next day, Tuesday, April 20, we had lunch with Sheryl Lee Ralph before she went to the theater for her starring role in *Dreamgirls*. The following day, we spent the evening at the theater to see Noel Craig, who was appearing in an off-Broadway show. Noel was with Lorna when we first met her on Halloween, and we had a casual dinner with him after his show to catch up. (A few years after this dinner, Noel would unfortunately pass away from AIDS.)

The next night, we had dinner with Lorna and her new boyfriend Jim. She was upset because she had received a letter with words pasted together from newspapers, telling her that she would be killed. (Fortunately, that turned out to be a prank, and nothing ever came from it.) The following night, we went with a group from Lorna's off-Broadway show *Snoopy* to see her movie *Grease 2*. Our friends BarBara Luna and Randon Lo joined us. (BarBara is a talented actress, best known for her roles in *Star Trek*. We met Randon when she appeared in *Stop the World* on Broadway with Sammy Davis. After the opening night party for that show, Sammy invited all the cast to his suite for an after-party. Randon was in the bathroom and forgot to lock the door. I opened the door to use the bathroom, and she was sitting there on the toilet. We were both shocked, but when she came out, we all laughed about it. I introduced her to Arlene, and we became close friends for many years.) Lorna came to the screening with a bodyguard because of the threatening letter that she had received the day before.

Two nights later, we had dinner with Neil and Leba Sedaka at a Japanese restaurant in the Waldorf Hotel. Neil was having a dental problem and came to my office the next day. He was playing Atlantic City that weekend, and I was able to take care of his situation. The following night, we went to Café Central with Lorna. The superagent and movie producer Allan Carr had just offered her a part in his new movie remake of *Where the Boys Are*. BarBara Luna joined us, along with Dick Cavett and Michele Lee. Dick is a great conversationalist, and Michele has a very vibrant personality, so it was a stimulating evening. Michelle had received an Emmy nomination for her role in the popular TV show *Knots Landing*. (We have spent wonderful times with her over the years, and she has recently moved to LA, where we see her when visiting the West Coast.)

Lorna also invited Chuck Zito to join us. This former head of the Hells Angels and part-time actor had been helping as a bodyguard for Lorna that past week. He is one of our favorite people, and he often demonstrated fighting moves to our son, Marc, when he was learning karate. Afterward, we all went to Studio 54, and Chuck brought along his mother. The following night, BarBara Luna and some friends came to our apartment for a screening of her new movie *Concrete Jungle*. We made it really easy and just served deli sandwiches.

The next night, we went back to Café Central with Lorna and Chuck Zito to celebrate Lorna signing to do the movie *Where the Boys Are*. She didn't care for the script but felt that it could be a popular film. The original film in 1960 was quite popular, and the hit song was written by Neil Sedaka and sung by Connie Francis. (This 1984 remake turned out not to be as good as the original, but Allan Carr threw a great opening night party at a special area in one of the New York City train stations.)

May was also a busy month. We went to a nightclub called Freddie's to see BarBara Luna. Afterward, Arlene and I went to Café Central to meet Liza, Mark, and Joe Pesci. We had something to eat and drink there and then went to a club called Rare Form. They had a piano, and Liza and Joe both sang. We departed there at six o'clock.

The next day, Lindsay Wagner called from Oregon. She used a special homeopathy doctor in Oregon and told us that he was just shot by his ex-wife when he went to visit with his kids. Lindsay reminded us to see her TV movie the following night, *I Want to Live* (which was an ironic title after just hearing the tragic news about the homeopathic doctor).

On Thursday, May 12, Gina Lollobrigida arrived from Rome to stay with us. That Sunday night, we went to dinner at Elaine's with Gina. (Gina surprisingly did not request Chinese food.) Diana Ross was there, and we joined her for dessert at her table. Our daughter, Lauren, had played with Diana's daughter Chudney when they were in preschool, so we had things in common to talk about.

The following Tuesday, we took Gina to see the Broadway show *A View from the Bridge*. Our friend Jimmy Hayden was becoming a star from his role in the show. Tony Lo Bianco was nominated for a Tony for his role in the show, and we went to see him backstage afterward with Gina. Gina was interested in Tony for the male lead in her Broadway project *The Rose Tattoo*. Tony played a detective in a TV series that Lindsay Wagner produced and starred in, so we have known him for many years. Lindsay is against violence of any kind, and her TV show did not last long because she insisted that all violent scenes in the detective drama be eliminated. (It is ironic that someone disliking violence so much was married to a stuntman, and both of her sons are stuntmen today as well.) (Tony is a great guy, and we still see him and his wife occasionally. We spent New Year's Eve with them two years ago in Palm Beach.) After the theater, we went with Gina to Café Central to meet Michael Callan, who flew in from LA to do the show *Pal Joey*.

The next day, we had lunch with Gina Lollobrigida at the Russian Tea Room. At night, we went with Gina to see Tommy Tune and Twiggy in the Broadway show *My One and Only*. After the show, we met Joe Pesci at Café Central. He was interested in the male lead opposite Gina in *The Rose Tattoo*.

On Friday night, we went with Gina to see Elizabeth Taylor and Richard Burton in the Broadway show *Private Lives*. We spent time backstage with them both after the show. We didn't know what to say because all three of us thought that Elizabeth was not good in her role. We tried to find things to compliment her on and must have been successful because we all got along great. Lorna Luft arrived from Florida for one day, and we met her after the show for a late bite.

On Saturday, May 21, we had dinner at Elaine's with Gina. We asked our friend, the famous radio personality and dean of the Friars Club, William B. Williams, to join us because we wanted him to meet Gina. Julie Budd and her husband, Alan Ramer, came with us as well. Lucille Ball was at the next table. We didn't know her, but she stopped by our table to say hello to Gina.

On Sunday, May 22, the Friars Club was honoring Elizabeth Taylor. My friend Albie sent his chauffeur to pick Gina, Arlene, and me up. Gina wore a magnificent white beaded dress and a matching white cape. The event was at the Waldorf, and we sat at the front table, which Albie always had. The Friars either love mob-type guys or were in awe of Albie. He always had the best table at every event, and that evening, we were his guests. Gina was seated at the main dais along with the other celebrities, including Frank Sinatra, Roger Moore, and Janet Leigh.

The following day, Arlene went shopping with Gina on Madison Avenue. Gina was wearing a chimpanzee coat, and one man started yelling at her. After that experience, Gina decided to never wear that coat again. They had lunch at La Côte Basque Restaurant. For the next two days, Arlene and Gina did a lot of shopping. (It proved not to be a highlight of that week for me when I received the bills.)

On Tuesday, May 24, we took Gina to see Farrah Fawcett in the off-Broadway show *Extremities*. After the show, we all went to the restaurant Orso. The famous agent Swifty Lazar was there with Irwin Shaw and Arlene Francis. We joined them for dessert. I got a kick out of spending time with Swifty because of the similarity of our last names.

Gina told us about various experiences with Ted Kennedy, Cary Grant, Orson Welles, Howard Hughes, the Spanish bullfighter El Cordobés, pioneer heart transplant surgeon Christiaan Barnard, Bulgari, Yul Brynner, Rock Hudson, Tom Jones, Castro, Marcos, and many other famous people. (But I'll leave those stories for her autobiography, although I would have loved to tell you about a few that were really quite interesting.) The next day, Gina flew to Washington, DC, to photograph panda bears.

The following week, Lindsay Wagner arrived to spend the weekend with us before flying to England. We were having a chicken dinner, but Lindsay would not eat chicken because she did not like the way they were killed. Her two young children were with her, and the youngest had diarrhea. Lindsay doesn't believe in traditional medicine, so she called her homeopathic doctor. He prescribed juice from boiled brown rice and some homeopathic tablets that dissolved in the mouth. Lindsay had written a vegetarian cookbook and, for breakfast, made fabulous healthy whole wheat pancakes. For many decades, Lindsay has been a spiritual guru for us, and she has many fascinating ideas, although some can be pretty unusual.

On Sunday, June 26, we returned to New York City from Westhampton Beach to celebrate our anniversary (which was the day before). Liza and Mark invited us over for champagne. Chita Rivera and her daughter, Lisa Mordente, came over to help us celebrate. We always love spending time with Chita because she has one of the best personalities of anyone we know.

On Tuesday, we went to the Garden State Arts Center to see Liza perform. It was a totally new show, with a special section devoted to songs from movies directed by her father, Vincente Minnelli. After the show, Mark, Mark's brother Chris, and Liza drove back to New York City with us, and we went to El Sombrero, a Mexican restaurant.

The next night, Wednesday, June 29, we traveled to Liza's show again in New Jersey. Afterward, we went with her to Elaine's Restaurant, along with her conductor, Bill LaVorgna. Farrah Fawcett and Lisa Mordente joined us at the restaurant. After dinner, we all went over to Café Central to meet up with the actor Jimmy Hayden and some other people. Liza asked Arlene to go shopping with her the next day for bathing suits.

The following night, Thursday, June 30, we met Obba Babatundé at Café Central. Lorna had attended a dinner for Peter Allen earlier and met us there. Later, Liza, Halston, Steve Rubell, and Farrah also joined us. Liza asked Arlene to come to her apartment the next day and wake her at twelve thirty to go shopping. Liza arranged for a limo to take them to Bloomingdale's and some other stores on Third Avenue. (As I read these diaries and see all the references to shopping, I realize why I was working long hours in those days.) I went to Liza's apartment later to meet them. Gina Lollobrigida called from Rome to inform us that it looked like the deal was set for her to star in *The Rose Tattoo* on Broadway.

Liza and Mark were staying at Halston's house in Montauk over the July 4 weekend. On July 3, we drove up to the house, and I played tennis with Steve Rubell and Mark. The home and property were owned by Andy Warhol, and Halston was renting it. It was a fabulous piece of land with water surrounding much of the property. Halston was a wonderful host and told us that he was looking to build his own home in the area. He gave us a tour of the house and grounds and served a sumptuous lunch.

On Tuesday, July 5, Lorna joined the cast of "Extremities," along with Jimmy Russo and Farrah Fawcett. We attended the opening, and after the show, we all went to Café Central.

On Thursday, July 7, there was a special showing at Radio City Music Hall of the movie *A Star Is Born*. It was the restored, uncut version. When it was originally shown, the movie theaters cut the length of the movie down so they could have more showings. The powers that be felt that the original was too long, and they wound up eliminating many key scenes. It certainly was a factor in denying the Academy Award to Judy Garland. Lorna's father, Sid Luft, who produced the film, was there. Liza, Rex Reed, and James Mason, who starred in the movie, also were present. After the showing, we all went to Elaine's. Liza sat next to Sid at the restaurant, and after dinner, all of us went back to Liza's apartment. Everyone left at three o'clock, but Mark's brother Chris, Arlene, and I stayed until seven forty-five. Chris had written a movie script called *Pipeline*, and Liza talked about everything from her suggestions regarding the script to her marriage to Jack Haley.

The following night on Friday, July 8, we went to Westhampton with Liza and Mark. Liza had appointments at eleven and two o'clock during the day. She managed to get through them, even though she had very little sleep. Mark drove Arlene and Liza out east after her appointments. Liza gave Arlene a gift of a jade bracelet that her father had given her twenty years before. She told Arlene that he had brought it back from Africa after directing a movie with Audrey Hepburn there. Liza explained how very special it was to her, and she wanted Arlene to have it. I drove out by myself, and in the evening, we made piña coladas. Liza did not want to eat because she was watching her weight. Mark went to bed early, and Liza, Arlene, and I stayed up all night talking. We finally went to sleep at six thirty.

On Saturday, July 9, I played tennis with Mark. Liza confided to us that they had a terrible fight, and she wanted to go back to NYC. She hired a seaplane to pick her up in the bay behind our home and fly her back to New York City. She told Mark that she was not feeling well. Mark was very cool about everything and stayed. He drove back to NYC on Sunday, July 10.

On Wednesday, July 13, Jack Haley met us for dinner at Elaine's. He had spent the weekend in the Hamptons at his friend Jamie Niven's home in Southampton.

On Thursday, July 14, Sheryl Lee Ralph took us to lunch in New York City. It was her first day on the TV show *Search for Tomorrow*. She had a photo session the next day and spoke with us about an act that she wanted to put together showing off her singing talent. At night, we met Lorna at our favorite hangout, Café Central.

Arlene stayed in the Hamptons for the second half of July with Lauren while our son was at sleepaway camp. Julie Budd came to visit one week and Lorna Luft another. During the week, I was working in my office in New York City. (Remember how I described all the shopping days that I had to pay for.)

On Monday, August 1, Liza and Mark invited me to their apartment for hot dogs and hamburgers. Later that evening, we went to the dance club Heartbreak, along with Jimmy Hayden. Heartbreak was a popular club, decorated like a school cafeteria. It played music from the '50s and '60s. Monday night was very special there because they had a live band, and many celebrities would show up to dance.

On Tuesday, Arlene and Lorna took the jitney bus back from the Hamptons to New York City. Gina Lollobrigida called us from Rome complaining that she was having trouble securing the theater that she wanted for *The Rose Tattoo* show on Broadway. She also let us know that she would be flying in from Rome for our son Marc's bar mitzvah in October.

On Wednesday evening, August 3, we had dinner with Liza and Mark. They planned a romantic dinner at Mildred Pierce Restaurant. We picked up Liza and met Mark at the restaurant. Liza spoke about how talented her father was and became very emotional. She had been suffering from a stomach ulcer and a hiatal hernia recently and, during dinner, went back to her apartment with Arlene to pick up her medication. She and Mark were very happy together at the restaurant, and after dinner, we went with them to their apartment.

Liza told us that she was looking forward to going to our son Marc's bar mitzvah in October. She discussed a new Broadway show that she would be doing with Chita Rivera called *The Rink*. They were good friends, and it was somewhat awkward because Chita would be playing Liza's mother. (It eventually turned out fine; our daughter, Lauren, was happy to see not one person but two people she knew onstage; and Chita won a Tony for her role in the show.) Liza also informed us that she just received the highest money offer ever for a performer in Atlantic City and would be doing two weekends there in the fall.

On Tuesday night, August 16, we met Lorna at Café Central, and she announced that she was one month pregnant. She would be due in April and asked us to be the godparents. On Thursday, August 18, Mark Gero's brother Chris was celebrating his thirtieth birthday at Café Central. We attended his party, and since Lindsay Wagner was flying in from LA to stay with us, she met us there after she landed in New York City. We had a great weekend with her and the kids. We went one night to see the show *Little Shop of Horrors*. Lorna Luft and Farrah Fawcett were both having tough times doing the show *Extremities*. It was a very physical show, and Lorna developed a bad back from it, and Farrah broke her wrist.

Lorna and Jake stayed with us in the Hamptons over the Labor Day weekend. On Friday, September 9, Farrah Fawcett and Ryan O'Neal came to my dental office, and I took care of both of them.

On Monday, September 12, Julie Budd went with Arlene to a baby shower for the comedian Marilyn Michaels. Lorna Luft, Sheryl Lee Ralph, Rip Taylor, and Loni Ackerman were also there.

On Friday, September 16, we met Farrah Fawcett and Ryan O'Neal at the Carlyle Hotel, where they were staying. She had been to doctors all day for opinions about her broken wrist. The doctors were concerned that if they reset it, there might be a deformity, so Farrah was mulling over her options. We had drinks in the galleria part of the hotel, and after drinks, they took us for a wonderful dinner in the main dining room. Ryan told us that Liza respected Mark Herron, a former husband of Judy Garland, because he didn't want to write a book about her. Then Ryan mentioned that he and Farrah were reading a screenplay about a relationship between two people similar to Judy and Mark Herron. Ryan told us it was not obvious that it was based on Judy Garland, but we were skeptical. (It never got made.) We later went over to see Liza and Mark and had a very fun night with them.

The following day, we went to a party at Studio 54 with Lorna and Jake in honor of Rick Derringer's new rock album. I called Farrah Fawcett, who told me that she had the cast removed and was concerned that her wrist looked deformed.

On Monday, September 26, Gina Lollobrigida flew in from Rome to stay with us. She gave our children, Marc and Lauren, gold good-luck bracelets as gifts. She also gave Arlene two beautiful gold and pearl necklaces that she made for her. Gina had taken pictures of the children and us, and she had blown them up to hang in our hallway. Our daughter, Lauren, who was nine, wrote a beautifully sensitive poem about how close she was to Arlene and me. Lauren described how we were like two shoelaces tied together.

On Tuesday, September 27, Gina had a business dinner with her agent, Lionel Lerner, and the producer Harry Rigby about her Broadway show *The Rose Tattoo*. Liza and Mark picked us up in a limo, and we went to dinner with them at a Mexican restaurant in SoHo. Mark brought us to the studio where he did his sculptures. After dinner, we went home, and Gina was back from her business meeting. We put her on the phone with Mark Gero. He is Italian and wanted to speak with her only in Italian because he wanted to learn the language.

On Wednesday, September 28, I took Gina to lunch at Elmer's Restaurant. Then we went with her to see the dress that Arlene would be wearing to Marc's bar mitzvah, made from fabric Gina had given Arlene. At night, we took Gina to Elaine's for dinner. Gina had published a best-selling book of her photographs of Italy, called *Italia Mia*. She had a series of book signings in honor of the upcoming Columbus Day holiday.

On Friday, September 30, Liza and Mark invited us to see a one-man show by Eric Bogosian. One of my patients, Melissa Finley, was there. She was a fabulous dancer and had her own dance company. After the show, there was a party in the Broadway district at a place called Panache. We sat at the party with Liza, Christopher Walken, and his wife, Georgianne. Georgianne was one of our friends, and she was coming to our son Marc's bar mitzvah by herself on October 8 because Christopher would be working on a film.

On the day of Marc's bar mitzvah, we had lunch at our home. Gina stayed at the Saint Regis Hotel that weekend because it was quite hectic at our place. The evening party was at El Morocco. It was a fabulous evening, and we even had Liza and Gina dancing the hora together at the party. Our friend William B. Williams escorted Gina to the affair. Liza came directly from her rehearsal for the upcoming Broadway show *The Rink*, and she was in great spirits. Liza informed us that Chita Rivera hurt her back during the routines and had to leave rehearsals early. Our son, Marc, handled himself wonderfully both at the temple and the party. Nikki Haskell, who had a cable TV show, filmed our bar mitzvah. It was later shown on her TV show and was called the "jet-set bar mitzvah." The other feature on her show that week was the opening of the Trump Tower in New York City.

On Monday, October 10, Arlene went shopping with Gina, and they had lunch at the Russian Tea Room. (Notice the shopping pattern when friends come into town.) It was Columbus Day, and the following evening, we had dinner with Gina at Elaine's.

On Wednesday, October 12, a videotape of a commercial that Gina had done for AT&T was delivered to our home, and it was great. We took her to dinner at Csarda Restaurant with Arlene's parents. Over the next few days, we had dinners with Gina at Café Central and Café Luxembourg. (When I see all these dinners in our diary, I wonder how I managed to stay so trim. Okay, it's my book, and maybe I could get away with that statement if you don't look at the photos in the book and notice my belly.)

On Sunday, October 16, we went to the opening of the Broadway show *Zorba*. Gina called Anthony Quinn's wife Jolanda at their apartment at the Adams Hotel and arranged tickets for us to attend. The opening night dinner was at the Tavern on the Green. We sat with Gina and the show's producer, Ken Greenblatt, and his wife, Sandy. Over the next few days, we had lunches and dinners with Gina. One evening we took her to see the show *Cats*. Sitting two rows behind us was a Russian former lover of hers, and she described her time with him (another revelation I wish I could report on).

After our week with Gina, we traveled with our children to Boston on Friday, October 21, to see Liza Minnelli perform at the arts center. She did a fabulous show, which included a tribute to her father. We took our children to dinner before the show. After the show, we had a late dinner with Liza's manager, Eliot Weisman, and other members of her entourage at Anthony's Pier Restaurant. We met up with Liza later at the bar of the hotel and went back to her room, along with Lisa Mordente, who also came to Boston for the show. The four of us stayed up all night, talking about various topics such as our son's bar mitzvah and the rehearsals for Liza's next Broadway show *The Rink*.

On Saturday, October 22, we took the children to the science museum during the day; and in the evening, we saw the show again. John Kander, who wrote the music for many of Liza's popular songs, came to see her show. He is a lovely and fine man, and we always enjoy being with him. We spent time with Liza at the bar after the show and then hung out in her room with her. The hiatal hernia was bothering her, so it was not one of our all-nighters.

Gina didn't want to come to Boston for the weekend, and we returned to New York City to meet up with her the following day. On Monday, October 24, we went with her to the Helmsley Palace Hotel to see an exhibition of Anthony Quinn's artwork. In the evening, we all went to see the Broadway show *La Cage aux folles*. We spent the next few days with Gina.

One night we saw a movie called *Carmen*. It was a dance version of the well-known story, starring an old boyfriend of Gina's, named Antonio Gades. He was one of the most famous Spanish dancers, and Gina told us all about their relationship. (We love all the stories that she tells us concerning her relationships with these famous people. In her youth, she was considered one of the most beautiful women in the world, and famous men from all walks of life courted her. All the stories she told us will remain private between us. Once again, I apologize to the reader for having to omit some really great stories. Please just use your imagination about what happens when the most alluring woman in the world meets some of these amazing men.)

One of the dinners that week with Gina was with our friend Bob Wachs and his wife Linda at Elaine's. Bob had become quite important in show business, managing Eddie Murphy and Arsenio Hall and producing all of Eddie's movies. Gina was having meetings with Harry Rigby, the producer of her upcoming Broadway show *The Rose Tattoo*. She complained about how cheap he was being with her expenses and her wanting a limo. One day Arlene went with her to Ossining botanic gardens so Gina could take pictures of the fall foliage.

On Sunday, October 30, I played tennis with Mark Gero, who was now beating me easily. Liza was home from her tour, and we went to their apartment. Arlene brought ingredients for tacos, and we made them along with piña coladas. Liza had hurt her bac, and was supposed to be in Milwaukee but rescheduled her show. She was in very good spirits, and she and Arlene had a good time making tacos together. Later, we watched TV until the early hours of the morning. Gina was still in NYC at the Saint Regis Hotel, studying her script for *The Rose Tattoo*. We had an early dinner with her on Monday, October 31.

It was Halloween, and Lorna, Jake, and Noel Craig came over to our apartment. Halloween was always special for us because that is the day Arlene and I met Lorna and Noel. We ended October of that year at a wild and fabulous Halloween party at Studio 54. No party in the world on Halloween was as creative as the ones at Studio 54.

On Wednesday, November 2, we took Gina Lollobrigida with us to see Sammy Davis and Bill Cosby at the Gershwin Theater in New York City. We all had a great time together after the show. On Friday, November 4, my mother took our children to see the show. They loved it, and Sammy was wonderful to them after the performance. We went with Gina to Elio's Restaurant in New York City for dinner.

On Saturday, November 5, Arlene spent the day with Gina shopping and then took her to 40 Central Park South to look for an apartment, which she would need while doing her Broadway show since she was planning on staying for a very extended period. Liza had rented an apartment there in the past, so we knew the building. We spent many nights there with Liza and had some interesting times with tenants living there, like Johnny Cash and his wife June. There was an Indian restaurant, Shezan, in the building, and we had dinner there.

Gina left for Rome on Sunday, November 6, and we took Lorna to dinner at Elaine's. Woody Allen was always there at his regular table that everyone had to pass. Even if he knows or has worked with our dinner companions, he nods hello and then turns away. I find it strange that someone who wants privacy always sits at the most prominent and well-trafficked table.

On Wednesday, November 16, Lindsay Wagner arrived with her baby Dorian and her mother, Marilyn, to stay with us. She was in town to meet with her agent about doing a Broadway show called *Papa Hemingway*. Anthony Quinn would star in the show, and he and his wife Jolanda came to our apartment to meet with Lindsay. It was a three-character play, and the third actor would be Treat Williams. Anthony Quinn had become such a popular artist that he was actually making more money from his art than from his films and shows. The following night, we had dinner with Lorna at Café Central and ran into Treat Williams, who told us that he was excited about doing the Hemingway show.

On Monday, November 21, we went out with Lorna and Jake for Lorna's birthday. Liza and Mark joined us, and Mark picked up the check for the evening. There was some tension between him and Liza during the evening, and there were uncomfortable moments.

On Wednesday, November 23, we went to Liza and Mark's apartment. Her stomach was acting up, but she felt better as the evening progressed. Lisa Mordente came over, and we all went to a new disco called Area, downtown on Hudson Street. It turned out to be another late night.

On Thursday, November 24, Arlene made a holiday dinner at home for Thanksgiving. My mother, Lorna, Jake, Liza, and Mark were our guests. Later, we all went over to Halston's for dessert and drinks (except for my mother as drinking at midnight at Halston's was not part of her lifestyle).

On Sunday, November 27, Jack Haley flew to NYC to stay at the Sherry-Netherland Hotel. He was in town for the opening of his movie *That's Dancing!* We went to dinner at Elaine's with him, David Niven Jr., and Gene Kelly, who were both involved with the movie. Gene is someone we greatly respected, and we felt honored to be in his company.

On Tuesday, November 29, Gina arrived from Rome. On Wednesday, November 30, we invited Gina to join us for dinner at a restaurant called Auntie Yuan. We went with Jack Haley, David Niven Jr., Lorna, and Jake.

On Saturday, December 3, we went to Liza and Mark's apartment for their fourth wedding anniversary party. We brought Gina, and Arlene wore a gold link tunic, which Gina gave her as a gift. It was a costume from one of her movies and very dramatic. It was an exciting party with a really great crowd. Diana Ross, Beverly Sills, Jennifer Beals, Karen Black, Truman Capote, Rex Reed, Lucille Ball, and Lucy Arnaz were among the guests.

On Tuesday, December 6, Arlene joined Gina for lunch at the Russian Tea Room with the producer of her Broadway show Harry

Rigby and her agent, Lionel Larner. After lunch, Gina told Arlene about her experiences with Cary Grant and Orson Welles. (But that information will remain private, and once again, I apologize to the readers who must hate me for holding back. I have been trying to talk Gina into doing her autobiography.)

On December 7, we saw a Tennessee Williams play on Broadway, *The Glass Menagerie*. We then went with Gina and a well-known group of Italians to a dinner organized by Massimo Gargia.

On Thursday, December 8, Lorna invited us to a screening of her new movie *Where the Boys Are*. In the evening, we had dinner with Bob Wachs and his wife Linda at Orso. Afterward, we watched Sheryl Lee Ralph's new nightclub act at a place called Silver Lining. Bob was managing Eddie Murphy and recently signed him for a $15 million payday on a movie. Bob let Sheryl know how much he enjoyed her act and told her to call him for a meeting.

Gina left in the morning to fly to Florida for the opening of a new hotel and a new Regine's nightclub. They pay her a lot of money to make those appearances. (Nobody ever pays a dentist to make an appearance at these openings, except if someone has a toothache.) I played tennis on Friday, December 9, with Mark, and Arlene and Liza joined us for dinner at Pancho Villa Mexican Restaurant. Gina returned to New York City the next day, and we had dinner at Elaine's.

On Wednesday, December 14, Marge and Irv Cowan invited us to the premiere of their Broadway show *Peg*, starring Peggy Lee. We took Gina to the show, and there was a party afterward at the Tower Suite. The show was awful and closed that same night. Peggy Lee was a great talent, but it was a one-woman show where she simply sat in a chair, sang a song, sat in another chair, and sang another song. The critics understandably hated it. When the reviews came in, the party ended abruptly. (They couldn't have lost too much money. The only scenery was two chairs.)

On Thursday, December 15, we flew with our children to Madrid, Spain. Gina left the same day for Rome. We planned to meet her in Switzerland. We had a scary flight to Spain on Iberia Airlines, and the turbulence and the breaking of the automatic pilot function frightened us all, especially our daughter, Lauren. We had a great time with the children and took them via hydrofoil to the casbah in Tangier and the Rock of Gibraltar. When we arrived at the Rock of Gibraltar, a group of native children started to all hound us for money. When we kept walking, they yelled at us, "Jew bastards!" Our children asked me how they knew that we were Jewish. I explained that they didn't know, but that was how they were taught to curse strangers they didn't like.

On December 24, we met Gina at her home in Switzerland for the second year in a row. Gina had been in Spain at the same time as us but was appearing on a TV show in a different city. At Gina's home, she was very happy and comfortable and made us terrific spaghetti carbonara. We enjoyed side trips to Gstaad and a few dinner parties with her friends but mainly relaxed at Gina's place through New Year's and ended a very busy and exciting 1983.

SIXTY-TWO

Diary, 1985

For New Year's Eve on December 31, 1984, we took the children to Atlantic City with Sammy and Altovise Davis. Sammy did his New Year's Eve show at Trump Plaza, and afterward, he threw a fabulous party for his guests. For many years, we had spent New Year's Eve with either Sammy or Liza. For two straight years, they both appeared together at the Diplomat Hotel in Florida, and those two New Years were extraspecial. (We often took our children to see our many talented friends perform in Atlantic City, Florida; the Concord Hotel in the Catskills; and various other venues. Arlene always told them that since they were sitting in the front row, their friends would notice if they were not paying attention. Luckily, our kids were always interested and well behaved. It helped that they were very familiar with all the songs, and they would sing along. Liza herself taught

Lauren to sing "Liza with a Z," which Lauren still memorizes to this day.)

On Thursday, January 10, Jack Haley arrived in New York City, and we had dinner at Elaine's with him, Ginny Mancini, David Niven Jr., Karen O'Toole, Jamie Niven, and Debbie Chenoweth. They were all in town for the opening of Jack's movie *That's Dancing!* on January 14. Jack and the people involved in the movie were staying at the Saint Regis Hotel.

We all had dinner on January 12 at a new restaurant called Prima Donna. Karen Callan joined us, and she and David Niven Jr. had a bad fight. David can be very nasty at times, and after he left, Jack made excuses for him, explaining that he had a difficult childhood. Jack told us that when David was seven, his parents were playing hide-and-seek games at someone's house. His mother opened what she thought was a closet and ended up breaking her neck in a fall and dying. David also had to live up to his famous Academy Award–winning father in Hollywood, being named David Niven Jr.

On Sunday, January 13, we watched Lorna Luft's appearance on Angela Lansbury's TV show *Murder, She Wrote*. On January 14, Lindsay Wagner also arrived in New York City for the premiere of the movie *That's Dancing!* We met her, Jack Haley, David Niven Jr., and Ginny and Henry Mancini for lunch at the Oyster Bar. There was a big party after the film's opening at the Ziegfeld Theater. Gregory Hines and a group of dancers entertained. We sat at Jack's table along with Marvin Hamlisch; Cyndy Garvey; Bob Fosse and his daughter, Nicole; and Ginny and Henry Mancini. Liza Minnelli and Mark Gero were at another table.

After all the work and planning Gina Lollobrigida did for *The Rose Tattoo* show on Broadway, the producer, Harry Rigby, suddenly died. On Sunday, January 20, Gina flew in from Rome; and Monday, January 25, was Harry Rigby's funeral. He owned the rights to the show, and his death ended the hopes for Gina doing the show on Broadway. All that week, we had a series of lunches at the Russian Tea Room with Gina's agent, Lionel Lerner, and dinners with lawyers at Elaine's, but all possibilities of doing the show faded. On Sunday, January 25, Gina flew to Los Angeles to be a presenter at the Golden Globe Awards. She was nominated for Best Supporting Actress for her role in the TV show *Falcon Crest* but lost to Faye Dunaway.

On Monday, February 4, Lorna Luft came back to New York from Los Angeles to work on a channel 13 TV special, "Judy Garland Concert Years." We had dinner with her and her father, Sid Luft, at Prima Donna Restaurant. We missed celebrating Liza's birthday with her on March 12 because she was back in the Hazelden rehab center. Liza went there on March 4 after a relapse but was doing well. We sent her an inflatable birthday cake greeting. Gina flew into New York because I was going to escort her to Pres. Ronald Reagan's White House dinner for the president of Argentina.

On Monday, March 18, we drove with Gina to Washington, DC, for the presidential dinner. We stopped on the way at a McDonald's, and Gina loved it. In Washington, we all stayed at the Hay-Adams Hotel across from the White House. On Tuesday, March 19, I escorted Gina to a welcoming ceremony for Argentina president Raul Alfonsin. Gina wore a bright pink Chanel suit with a matching pink hat and looked stunning. The state dinner in the evening was an unforgettable experience (a little different from the McDonald's meal the day before). Gina sat with Secretary of State George Schultz. When he asked her for the first dance, it received a lot of press. Gina and I entered the main ballroom as the honor guard announced, "Presenting Dr. Allan Lazare and Miss Gina Lollobrigida." And they escorted us both into the room. It was very exciting. Arnold Schwarzenegger, Irene Cara, and tennis great Guillermo Vilas were also at the dinner, along with all the members of the White House cabinet.

I had the best time talking with Nancy Reagan, who wanted to know all the gossip about things going on in New York City. She told me that she missed her good times in NYC and her friends there. We communicated for a long time, and I came away feeling that if she wasn't the First Lady, I could have a good time hanging out with her. I felt bad that Arlene had to remain in our hotel room during the events. On Wednesday, March 20, we drove back to New York City; and the next day, Gina flew to England for a TV appearance.

On Friday, March 22, we took our children away on a vacation to Los Angeles. Jack Haley's home was being renovated, so we stayed at the Beverly Wilshire Hotel. Lindsay Wagner picked us up at the hotel, and we went to dinner with Jack at Le Dome Restaurant. Tramp, the private club from London, opened a branch at the Beverly Center, and we met Lorna there after dinner.

On Saturday, March 23, Lindsay Wagner picked us up in her large jeep; and we drove with her, her son Dorian, and our kids to Rancho Mirage, near Palm Springs. We stayed at the Rancho Mirage Racquet Club. Lindsay kept getting lost on the way, and her young son, Dorian, repeatedly asked every fifteen minutes, "When do we get to the pool, Mommy?" It became a running joke, and we kept saying, "It's right around the bend," for the next hour. At night, we called in for pizza and watched Lorna hosting the TV special about her mother, Judy Garland. The next night, we went with the children and Lindsay into Palm Springs. We dined at a Moroccan restaurant where they had no silverware, and we ate everything with our fingers. (We had many very intimate personal conversations with Lindsay about significant events in her early life, and that will remain private between us.)

On March 26, we went with Lindsay to Malibu for a few days. We stayed at the Casa Malibu Motel. It was very private and didn't even have a phone in the room. (When Lindsay was doing *The Bionic Woman* TV show, she cherished her privacy, and this was the place she would stay in that area.)

We drove into LA to have dinner with Lorna, Jake, and Lorna's dad, Sid, at Spago. Sid was a very charming guy as long as you didn't do business with him. (Years later, when he was taking medication for cancer, he tried to convince me that it was growing hair on his head. He wanted me to invest money with him to manufacture a version of that medication to sell as a hair restorer. I politely declined.)

On Wednesday, March 27, I took the children to Disneyland while Arlene went with Lorna to a Share rehearsal. Share was a popular charity organization, and many of the female Hollywood celebrities were active in it. At night, Lindsay made dinner for us at her Malibu home. She made vegetarian lasagna and salad and invited some of her interesting homeopathic doctors and chiropractors to dinner. It was a stimulating evening of conversation, with many theories about health and energy that were quite foreign to us.

On my birthday, March 28, we celebrated my birthday and Lauren's at a Chinese restaurant, Chinois. Altovise Davis, Jack Haley, Lindsay, and a friend of Altovise joined us.

On March 29, Lindsay had her nanny take all the kids to Knott's Berry Farm for the day. We went to Lorna's house to celebrate her brother Joey's thirtieth birthday. Lorna arranged for a stripper telegram for him as a surprise.

On Saturday, March 30, we visited Ginny and Henry Mancini's beautiful home. Henry gave us a tour of the house and grounds. He was working on music for a new Santa Claus movie, and we had lunch with Ginny at Bistro Garden. In April, we celebrated the fortieth anniversary of Arlene's parents at Regine's. We bumped into Fran and Barry Weissler there, along with our friend Ben Vereen. Ben was starring in the Weisslers' new Broadway show called *Grind*. They were having an opening night party for the show, but when the bad reviews came in, they all left. We had no involvement with the show, so we stayed and had a great time.

On Friday, May 3, we met Sammy Davis at his hotel suite in the Waldorf at 4:00 p.m. Liza rang up a little later, and we went in her limo to the Weintraub Gallery to see her husband Mark Gero's sculptures on display. Sammy ended up buying one for $1,500 (so typical of Sammy as he was always trying to help and support friends; he wanted Liza to see that Mark was selling his sculptures). Then we all went to the Polo Bar at the Westbury Hotel for coffee. Sammy and Liza were talking about "one day at a time" to control drinking and other temptations.

The next day, both Sheryl Lee Ralph and Obba Babatundé were in New York City. They were no longer a couple, so it was a bit awkward finding time to see them both. We took Sheryl to lunch at the Russian Tea Room, and then Arlene invited Sheryl to a Dennis Basso fur show. That night, we went out with Obba for dinner.

The following weekend, Julie Budd and her husband, Alan Ramer, and his son, Jordan, came to spend time with us and our children in Westhampton. On Friday, June 7, we went to Liza Minnelli's run-through performance at the Edison Theater for her new show. She would be touring twenty-six cities. In the evening, we brought the children to a Madonna concert. (They wished we were friends with her so they could go backstage, but we told them sarcastically that they would have to settle for going backstage to see people like Liza and Sammy.)

In June, we took the kids to Atlantic City to see Sammy Davis perform at Harrah's Marina. Sammy traveled with all the latest video game equipment, and our children loved playing the games. (Our daughter, Lauren, has fond memories of playing on one of Sammy's video game units against Dionne Warwick at his home in Los Angeles.) Sammy put on his usual great show, and afterward, we went back to his room, and he cooked for us. Sammy traveled with his own kitchen equipment and utensils wherever he went. As a gift, we bought him a cooking apron that said, "Mr. Wonderful."

On Thursday, September 5, we had dinner at Ferrante Restaurant with Paul Herman and Mikhail Baryshnikov. (Liza was a close friend of Mikhail, so we had spent time with him in the past.) Gina wanted to do an interview with Mikhail for RAI Italian TV, but he did not seem very receptive to the idea, and it never came to fruition.

On Tuesday, September 10, we went to Jones Beach to see Liza perform. Arlene drove out with Obba Babatundé and his girlfriend Tamar, and I met them at the venue. It is an outdoor theater, and it started to rain during the performance. After a short rain delay, Liza came out and did a fantastic show. The *New York Post* had just published an article stating that she was pregnant. Liza told the audience that she wished it was true, but the story was false.

On Friday, September 13, we drove with our children to Atlantic City to see Sammy Davis perform. Our friend Chita Rivera had an 8:00 p.m. show in Atlantic City. We went with the kids and Altovise to see it. Afterward, we attended Sammy's late show. On Saturday, we took the children to Sammy's early show. Sheryl Lee Ralph was also doing a show in Atlantic City, and we all saw that as well. Whenever we took the children to a show, they expected to see one of our friends entertaining. On Saturday, Sammy spent time with Marc and Lauren during the day. Marc was fifteen, and Sammy asked him if he wanted to observe what went on behind the scenes. Sammy offered Marc a summer job working backstage on the road with him. Marc enjoyed the private time with Sammy in between the shows and observed the late show from backstage.

On Wednesday, September 18, Arlene flew to Los Angeles to work with Gina Lollobrigida on the interview that she was doing with Sammy Davis for Italian TV. Altovise arranged for Arlene to fly to LA on the same plane with her and Sammy. She didn't tell Sammy that Arlene would be on the plane, so they were able to surprise him. When the plane landed, Sammy invited Arlene to come to his house in his limousine. After spending time together, Sammy had his driver take Arlene to her hotel. Sammy invited Arlene for dinner, but she had made plans to meet Lindsay Wagner. Lindsay had an office at Orion Pictures and spent some time there with Arlene before going to dinner at Madame Wu's Restaurant. After dinner, they met up with Lindsay's boyfriend Fred Whitehead, who was president of Orion TV.

On Thursday, September 19, Arlene visited Lorna Luft on the set of the TV show *Trapper John*. Lorna was appearing in an episode, and at the break, they went for lunch at the commissary. They also viewed rushes from the previous day, and Arlene enjoyed time on the set with the cast. That morning before going to the studio, Arlene got a ticket for jaywalking and thought that the policeman was just kidding. (Arlene didn't take it seriously and forgot about it. Weeks later, when Arlene was back home in NYC, she received a letter threatening that she would be sent to jail if she didn't pay her ticket, so she quickly did.)

That evening, Arlene was meeting Gina to attend a big affair at the Beverly Hilton Hotel for an AIDS benefit. Gina had her passport stolen in India, and her flight from India was delayed. She had to go directly to the AIDS dinner from the airport. She wore her formal gown on the plane and departed the plane looking quite elegant. A limousine drove her directly to the dinner from the airport, picking Arlene up on the way. Arlene sat at Jack Haley's table with Elizabeth Taylor, Burt Reynolds, Loni Anderson, Altovise, Lorna, and Connie Stevens. At the dinner, Gina made arrangements to interview Burt Reynolds for the Italian television program she was doing. Arlene contacted our friend Eliot Weisman, who was managing Frank Sinatra. Gina was able to arrange an interview with Sinatra for the Italian television program. Lorna stopped by Arlene's hotel in the morning so Arlene could say hello to her son, Jesse, who is our godchild.

After they left, Arlene and Gina invited Lindsay Wagner to the hotel for lunch. Gina showed Lindsay her photographs from China, which were fabulous. Gina told Lindsay that she would love to have her on her TV special, but *Bionic Woman* played on a rival station in Italy, and the network wouldn't approve.

On Friday, September 20, Arlene and Gina went to Burt Reynolds's home to discuss Gina's upcoming interview with him. It was a beautiful Spanish-style home with Indian paintings and sculptures of his grandfather. He discussed the possibility of doing *The Rose Tattoo* with Gina as a TV special. Loni Anderson came into the room toward the end of the discussion. Arlene found Burt quite engaging and witty, but he changed his demeanor when Gina asked him about rumors concerning him having AIDS. Burt told Gina that he wanted to have fun with the interview and that she should not bring that subject up.

On Saturday, September 21, Arlene and Gina went over to Sammy Davis's home to discuss her interview with him for Italian TV. On Sunday, September 22, Arlene went back with Gina to Burt's home to film him by the pool and in his living room near the fireplace. Gina was disappointed that there was only one cameraman present, and Burt's agent kept rushing them through the interview. Burt's interview was not so interesting because his usual great sense of humor didn't show through. In the evening, Arlene went with Gina to the Emmy Awards. Fans behind barricades were yelling, "Gina Lollo!" And she signed some autographs.

On Monday, September 23, Gina filmed at Sammy Davis's home for RAI TV. Sammy organized everything and was very enthusiastic. He directed Altovise to answer the door when Gina rang and had her say, "No, it can't really be her." Then Sammy went to the door, Gina took off her sunglasses, and they embraced. The interview started at his bar area, and Sammy showed her all his jewelry. He then took Gina into his separate kitchen area. Sammy directed everything that went on and was really into the interview. He told Altovise to say, "How about cooking some pasta for lunch?" Then he proceeded to show all his pots and pans to the camera, and it turned out to be a really fun interview.

On Tuesday, September 24, Arlene was set to fly back to New York City and Gina to Rome. Gina changed her flights so she could accompany Arlene on her flight to New York City because she knew that Arlene was fearful of going by herself on the plane. She took a later flight from New York City to Rome.

On Sunday, September 29, Lindsay Wagner came to New York with her new boyfriend Fred Whitehead, head of Orion Pictures. We all had lunch at Café des Artistes. They were very lovey-dovey, but nothing ever came of the relationship. A few days later, Gina Lollobrigida flew to Washington, DC, to tape Jacques Cousteau for RAI TV.

On Saturday, October 12, I took the children to Westhampton for the weekend. Arlene went with Gina to the Golden Nugget Hotel in Atlantic City to meet with Frank Sinatra. Dorothy, Frank's secretary, arranged for a limousine to pick them up. Frank organized dinner and show tickets, and they spent time with him before his 11:00 p.m.

show. Gina asked Frank if he was interested in singing for the pope at the Vatican, and Frank told her to call him at the Waldorf in New York City after the weekend. Gina and Arlene sat with Frank's wife Barbara in her booth at the show, and she was extremely friendly. They spent time with Frank after the show. His opening act, comedian Tom Dreesen, walked them to the limo at the end of the evening.

Arlene did not get much sleep, and on Sunday, October 12, Arlene went with Gina to the RAI TV studio in NYC to watch tapes of the interviews. Gina dubbed her part in the interview and taped an introduction to the show. On Wednesday, October 16, Gina flew to Los Angeles to interview Bo Derek, who had become internationally famous for her role in the 1979 film *Ten*, for the Italian television show.

On Wednesday night, October 16, we went to a festive party at the Palladium nightclub for Liza in honor of her TV movie *A Time to Live*. The following week, Sammy and Altovise Davis came to New York City, and we had dinner with them at the Helmsley Palace Hotel on Friday, October 25. We went back to see them at the Helmsley Palace the next day on Saturday, October 26. Altovise's parents were there, and we ate deli in Sammy's room. We had spent time with Altovise's parents over the years and found them to be wonderful people.

Sunday, October 27, was the New York City Marathon. Sammy Davis had friends from Saint Louis running in the marathon, and we all met up at Sammy's room at the Helmsley Palace Hotel. We went to my friend Albie's restaurant, Elmer's, for dinner. Sammy was a classy gentleman when it came to going to the restaurant. He had hired a limousine, but all of us could not fit in. He sent everybody in his limousine, and he took a taxi with Arlene to the restaurant. He was having hip pain and using a cane. He actually looked very dapper with his cane. He had a large collection of elegant-looking canes as a hobby and picked an interesting one for the evening. The pain was traveling down his leg to his thigh and groin. During the dinner, he was in considerable pain, and he left early to go back to his hotel.

On Friday, November 1, we flew to San Francisco with members of my new mouthwash company. That area of the West Coast was our first market for my mouthwash, Plax. I did nine radio and television shows in a few days to help promote my product. We timed the product launch for the American Dental Association's annual meeting, taking place that week in San Francisco. I was one of the speakers at the meeting and used part of my time to introduce Plax to the dental community. We allowed time on Sunday, November 3, to watch Lorna Luft on the *Trapper John* TV series because she had a major role in the show that evening. The rest of November was a very hectic time for me, starting my new mouthwash business. I was working around the clock, between seeing patients at my office and involvement in a new business. (Someone had to pay the bills for Arlene's shopping days detailed in these diaries.)

We did have time on December 7 to take a break for the weekend to spend time with Liza Minnelli in Atlantic City while she was performing there. On Tuesday, December 10, we taped a message for Sammy Davis Jr.'s sixtieth birthday at Josh Green's studio in New York. All of Sammy's close friends were taping messages to surprise him on his birthday. We did a skit about dropping everything to come to the taping of his birthday. Arlene pretended that she rushed out of Bloomingdale's and dropped all of her shopping bags while rushing to the taping. I entered with knives in my hand, pretending that I rushed out of surgery for the taping. It actually was pretty good considering I'm a dentist and not a film director.

Gina Lollobrigida arrived from Europe on December 11. On Thursday, December 12, we escorted her to a formal event for the organization the Best. (This organization obviously did not believe in modesty.) On Friday, December 13, we went with Lorna and her father, Sid Luft, to Columbus Restaurant. The people who ran Café Central opened a new restaurant named Columbus when Café Central suddenly closed. It immediately became a New York City hot spot, and many celebrities like Regis Philbin, Mikhail Baryshnikov, and Neil Sedaka invested as partners in the restaurant.

(Sid Luft was a larger-than-life character, a likable con man. He was great fun to be around but not to be trusted. He was once an amateur boxer and not one to be pushed around. He was the producer of his wife Judy Garland's great comeback film *A Star Is Born*. When Lorna wrote a book about her life, Sid was not happy. He claimed that it was his story and wanted to discourage publication. He managed Lorna early in her career, and when she realized her father might not be the best person for her, she hired new management. Lorna always acted with class and tried to maintain a good relationship with Sid. At the end of his life, Lorna felt that even after any disagreements between them, he was still her father, and she treated him with respect in his later days and at his funeral.)

On Saturday, December 14, Nikki Haskell made a dinner party for Lorna at a friend's Park Avenue apartment. By chance, Gina was also invited by someone else, so she joined us at the dinner party.

On Sunday, December 15, Joe Pesci invited us to his mother's birthday party at Ferrante Restaurant. We took Gina and sat with her at Robert Duvall's table. We were excited to spend time with Duvall after seeing him in the *Godfather* films. Robert had invited a young cinematographer he worked with, named Barry Markowitz, to the dinner. Barry and Gina hit it off and exchanged numbers. (However, they never developed a relationship.)

We ended the year with a vacation in Saint Martin with our son, Marc. Our daughter, Lauren, was still afraid to fly after the scary plane trip to Madrid. She stayed home with my mother, and Marc was thrilled to have the second bedroom all to himself at the resort. When we returned home, we took both children to the Concord Hotel in the Catskills. Our daughter, Lauren, was thrilled when she went to one area of the hotel where they had children's rides and activities, and she played with Keshia Knight Pulliam, who played Rudy on *The Cosby Show*. The young actor Alfonso Ribeiro seemed to be overseeing Keshia in the play area, and Lauren loved meeting him as well. (Our children were both fans of the show *Silver Spoons*, and Alfonso was on that show with Ricky Schroder before later playing Carlton on *The Fresh Prince of Bel-Air*.)

Those last few chapters provided insight into my life in the early 1980s. The next few chapters describe some of my times at Studio 54, which was a big part of my life in the late 1970s and early 1980s, even though I have included several references to the unique nightclub throughout the book.

❧ CHAPTER ❧

SIXTY-THREE

Studio 54

When Studio 54 closed in February 1980, after Steve Rubell and Ian Schrager went to jail, I thought that part of our life would be over. But in September 1981, it reopened with a new owner, Mark Fleischman. He did not have the charisma of Steve, and although he kept Studio 54 running until 1985, it never returned to the glory days when Steve and Ian were in control. However, we did have many wonderful evenings over those years, just not as regularly as before. There still were many great parties with fabulous celebrities, and Mark tried to recreate the glamour of Studio 54 as best as he could.

To avoid the crowds out front, we learned to go around the block and enter the West Fifty-Third Street entrance. On the reopening night, all the regulars were there. We partied with Rollerena, the Dupont brothers, Disco Sally, and celebrities like John Belushi, Andy Warhol, Jack Nicholson, Cher, Brooke Shields, Liza Minnelli, Lorna

Luft, Ryan O'Neal, Farrah Fawcett, David Geffen, Paul Simon, Diane von Furstenberg, and Calvin Klein. We were happy to be there with all the people we missed over the past year, and we brought Gina Lollobrigida and Julie Budd with us to the opening. At this second reincarnation of Studio 54, Calvin Klein gradually became the prominent fashion face as Halston's presence diminished.

Marc Benecke was still the person out front for the first months of the reopening. Steve Rubell was still showing up because the success of the club would assure that Fleischman made enough money to complete his financial obligations to Steve and Ian. Quaaludes, cocaine, and poppers all continued to be present throughout the club. They were dispensed to well-known celebrities in the basement area, where most of us regulars were not allowed. We observed the relatively quiet and bland new owner, Mark Fleischman, change during the years he owned Studio 54 into someone caught up in the drug scene.

The crowd at the new Studio 54 never reached the exciting level of the original. However, because the club first allowed its patrons in at eleven o'clock, there were some fun and interesting early night themed parties organized there each week before the doors were open to the general public. Part of the dance floor was curtained off, and at midnight, the curtains opened so the people from the private VIP parties could mingle with the regulars. An overhead bridge was built, and entertainers would perform on it. Partygoers could walk across it and look down on the throngs below. The DJ booth was also a very popular place for celebrities like Michael Jackson, Mick Jagger, Cher, and Liza.

We loved spending time in that area, watching them enjoy the music. We had great nights on the dance floor next to Liza and Baryshnikov, Liza and Goldie Hawn, and Cher dancing with everyone. Michael Jackson and Mick Jagger preferred to spend more time in the DJ booth rather than on the dance floor. Alana and Rod Stewart loved to sit in the special banquet area on the dance floor, along with Bianca Jagger, Truman Capote, and Calvin Klein. We were lucky to be allowed in that area but knew when to give up our seats if it became too crowded with celebrities.

There were many special themed parties because they tried to encourage celebrities to show up. Famous names in the press helped extend the life of the new Studio 54. For us, it was exciting hanging out with Elizabeth Taylor, Bob Hope, Prince, Steven Tyler, Madonna, Tanya Tucker, Iman, and Grace Jones in a fun casual setting. We were good friends with the fabulous photographer Francesco Scavullo. He was a great guy and made all the celebrities look terrific in his photographs. Everybody wanted to be photographed by him. We would sit at the banquet, and every well-known person would stop by to say hello to him.

Carmen D'Alessio was one of the original people hired by Steve Rubell to help promote the club. Carmen knew everybody who was important internationally and brought many celebrities to the club. One wild party took place when Carmen celebrated her birthday. She stood on the bridge above the dance floor, and a giant birthday cake was brought out. After everybody sang "Happy Birthday," she proceeded to take handfuls of cake and throw them down to the people below on the dance floor. It was a messy scene, but everybody was smiling.

Sylvester Stallone was at Studio 54 many nights, but people thought he was there more than he actually was. Our friend Chuck Zito, who did some body double work for Stallone in his movies, was often there, strutting his stuff in a manner similar to Stallone. Some of the celebrities did not quite match up in person to their image. The handsome movie star Tony Curtis looked bloated with a bad toupee and often seemed somewhat spaced out.

When not on the dance floor, our favorite place to hang out was the ladies' room, which was filled with people of every gender and persuasion. It was a great place to take a break from the pounding disco beat. Another place to escape from the loud music was the balcony on the upper level. We would order a drink at the bar and then sit down and relax. We would watch the scene below on the dance floor. (Although many people went up there to make out, Arlene and I could wait until we arrived home and enjoy our privacy.) There was a separate section in the balcony called the rubber room, but that did not interest us. It was designed to be scrubbed off after each night's sexual activities in that area.

We would love to go with Liza or Halston to the DJ booth, especially when Michael Jackson was hanging out. There was not much conversation, but it was exciting to feel the electricity of his presence. Our friend Joanne Horowitz was responsible for bringing many celebrities to Studio 54. She would walk in with notables like Sylvester Stallone and later collect a fee for bringing them in.

About ten years ago, there was a one-night reunion at Studio 54, which has since become a Broadway theater. Joanne and our friend Myra Scheer invited us to the event, and the theater was redesigned as the old Studio 54 for the night. The young people who came to the event reveled in the stories we told them about what went on. Rollerena showed up in his dress and skates, and Ian Schrager was there as well. Many of the old effects, like the coke spoon and the man in the moon over the dance floor, were recreated. We reminisced about the old times, and it was a nostalgic evening.

A terrific party at Studio 54 was for Cornelia Guest's twenty-first birthday celebration. Studio 54 became a Swiss village for the night, and Stevie Wonder sang to guests like Calvin Klein, Oscar de la Renta, Carolina Herrera, and Diana Ross. In the 1980s, Cornelia was the most talked-about young woman of the time and part of the Andy Warhol crowd. Her mother was C. Z. Guest, a leader of NY society. Cornelia was close to Jack Haley because she was considering a movie career, so we spent time with her in those days. (We recently ran into Cornelia Guest at a charity party in New York City. We hadn't seen her in years, and she has turned out to be a delightful woman. She no longer lives in Manhattan but still visits the city.)

Prince Egon von Furstenberg was a fun-loving friend of ours. He attended our son Marc's bar mitzvah and brought Marc a very extravagant gift of an antique clock. His wife Diane was a smart businesswoman and became very successful in fashion. She was pretty wild in those days, quite different from her current image. After her fashion empire became so well known, someone persuaded Egon to open up his own fashion business. He gave me a number of his suits as gifts, but his clothing line was cheaply made and soon failed. Business was not really his thing, but he loved a good party. When Egon opened his fashion business, we attended a fabulous dinner party for him at Studio 54. The private dinner was elegant, with his family crests displayed on large banners while violinists serenaded us during dinner. At eleven o'clock, the tables were cleared away, the regular crowd was allowed in, and thousands partied through the night.

There were many evenings at Studio 54 celebrating fashion icons. When Yves Saint Laurent launched his Opium perfume, Studio 54 had an elegant party with Yves, Halston, and Gianni Versace from the fashion world, joining guests like David Geffen and Cher. There were orange lanterns, hundreds of fresh orchids, and multicolored streamers throughout the club. New Year's Eve parties would feature acrobats and aerial dancers hanging from the ceiling and railings around the club while tons of silver glitter and balloons rained down on the crowd at midnight. Paloma Picasso, Diana Ross, and Karl Lagerfeld were some of the celebrities joining us at the banquets one year. One New Year's Eve, Studio 54 hired an actor to dress up as Baby New Year and lowered him down on a swing from high up on the ceiling while a brass band played on the bridge. Then twenty-five dancers came out on the bridge and threw gloves and beach balls down to the crowd before finishing with a kickline dance.

Jerry Rubin was a famous antiwar activist in the 1960s, along with Abbie Hoffman. By the 1980s, he became a business networker. He ran weekly early parties at Studio 54 to attract his followers, and we found them pretty dull. Abbie Hoffman hosted one charity party at Studio 54 that we did enjoy. It was a strange mixture of aging hippies, along with celebrities like Grace Jones, Mick Jagger, Warren Beatty, Joe Namath, Jack Nicholson, Joan Rivers, and Carly Simon. It was one of the parties at Studio 54 in the early 1980s that rivaled those of the late 1970s under Steve and Ian. In the 1980s, the nightly parties weren't always exciting, but I still have great memories from the many that were. Other clubs were opening to compete, but when AIDS hit in the mid-'80s, the party scene at these clubs was not the same.

In the last years of Studio 54, as I mentioned, Calvin Klein had replaced Halston as the major fashion face in the club. Calvin was an iconic fashion designer and had a strong presence at the club. He threw his daughter, Marci, an amazing sweet sixteen party there with multiple grand pianos lined up in the entranceway to the club. There were giant birthday candles, enormous bows, over-the-top decorations, and elegant dining tables. All the servers were dressed in tuxedos, and after dinner, dozens of dancers in top hats and tails performed on a huge staircase. Calvin Klein and Marci walked down the staircase while confetti and balloons came down from the ceiling.

Eddie Murphy also hosted a fun party one night. My friend Bob Wachs was managing Eddie Murphy and producing his movies. When his movie *Forty-Eight Hours* opened, Eddie hosted *Saturday Night Live*. We were invited to the party Eddie threw for the cast at Studio 54 after the show. The *SNL* cast was a crazy group, and along with Lionel Richie, Eddie threw a really wild party.

Studio 54 was trying every theme idea to keep the magic going. When Raquel Welch appeared on Broadway in *Woman of the Year*, she hosted a great party at Studio 54 in honor of her show. Christie Brinkley hosted a *Sports Illustrated* wet T-shirt night, which was really fun. Yul Brynner invited us to a private party for his show *The King and I*. All the children in the cast attended, and there were all sorts of candies and cakes laid out for them. Some celebrities not usually seen at Studio 54, like Frank Sinatra and Jerry Lewis, were there. Michael Jackson sat with Yul at his table and in the DJ booth. Our friend Chuck Zito brought members of the Hells Angels to several parties. It was fun but somewhat intimidating to hang around with these "angels." Cast members from *Saturday Night Live*, especially John Belushi, would often show up at Studio 54 after their show's regular after-party.

There were memorable evenings of live performances by the most popular singers of the day. We enjoyed great nights of entertainment by the Village People, Grace Jones, Gloria Gaynor, Stevie Wonder, the Temptations, the Four Tops, Chubby Checker, and the Weather Girls. (We recently spent time with Randy Jones, the cowboy from the original Village People, and he amazingly looked the same.)

We went with Lorna Luft to a creative party at Studio 54 for the movie remake of *Where the Boys Are*, which she appeared in. They brought in enough sand to turn Studio 54 into a beach in Fort Lauderdale. We entered on a wooden boardwalk, surrounded by girls in bikinis, boats, and surfboards. One memorable night in 1983, Michael Jackson's "Thriller" video was shown on a large screen at Studio 54. Michael Jackson was in the DJ booth while it was being shown, and he came out and danced along the bridge over the dance floor. When Michael Jackson starred in the movie *The Wiz*, Studio 54 made a party to honor Michael and the Jacksons. Michael danced down the floor accompanied by four models dressed as scarecrows to the song "Ease on down the Road." Many party night themes involved various model agencies because that brought beautiful women into the club.

On any particular night, there would be rock legends like Rod Stewart and the Rolling Stones rockers Mick Jagger, Ronnie Wood, and Keith Richards hanging out on the couches with us. At some point, they would disappear downstairs to the basement, where we were not allowed. On rare occasions, a celebrity we were with invited us to join them. I only went a few times out of curiosity because we did not want to get involved with the drug scene there.

We met a young girl named Victoria Leacock because she was an obsessed fan of Liza Minnelli. She came often to Liza's concerts and was very sweet. Victoria eventually worked for Mark Fleischman at Studio 54 and was responsible for running many parties there. She invited us to a terrific party in honor of Marvin Gaye. Celebrities like Mick Jagger were there, and the crowd loved Marvin's music, but Marvin did not mingle with the people.

A really fun night was when Paul Jabara had his hit song "It's Raining Men" debut at Studio. The Weather Girls sang it live with backup dancers on the bridge while we all danced below on the dance floor. Paul was a great guy and a wonderful talent who died too early. Some of his other hits were "Enough Is Enough" and "Last Dance." We always liked him, and years later, our friend Bob Wachs obtained the rights to his life story. Bob tried to get me to invest in a musical about his life, but I declined, and Bob unfortunately died before it could be made.

Arlene and I love dancing to Gloria Gaynor's recording of "I Will Survive." The night she sang it live on the bridge was one of our unforgettable nights at Studio 54, and the crowd went wild. The Village People singing "YMCA" and "Macho Man" were other disco idols who rocked the place whenever they sang live in the middle of a party. Grace Jones was a uniquely popular entertainer, and we loved seeing her perform at Studio 54 very late at night. Boy George, Duran Duran, and New Edition were some other artists who would appear suddenly, singing live in the middle of a night of dancing. One night I sat with Halston, watching a relatively unknown Madonna singing on the bridge above the dance floor. She performed songs from what would be her first album.

In the early years of Studio 54, Bianca Jagger was a major presence. Pictures from her birthday party at Studio 54 were seen all over the world when she entered the club riding a white horse. That generated a great deal of publicity for the club. That animal theme would continue at other parties. Another year, Halston and Steve Rubell threw a party to celebrate her birthday by having a man enter leading out a black panther. If the crowd wasn't frightened enough, that was followed by a leopard and the release of one hundred white doves. Bianca loved animals because she said that they "represent the freedom we have lost." We were there with Liza, who gently patted the leopard, which was, of course, on a chain with a handler. Barbara Walters, Carrie Fisher, and even a prince from Saudi Arabia were there.

We went with Liza to the first anniversary party of Studio 54 in April 1978. Issey Miyake put on a fashion show, and Liza sang to Steve Rubell. Andy Warhol, Halston, Bianca Jagger, Tennessee Williams, Margaret Trudeau, Shirley MacLaine, Mikhail Baryshnikov, Farrah Fawcett, Lauren Bacall, and Diana Vreeland (former editor in chief of *Vogue* magazine) were among the guests.

Another unique experience at Studio 54 was the opening night of Arnold Schwarzenegger's movie *Conan the Barbarian*. Men and women wearing loincloths walked around Styrofoam mountains. We viewed seminaked girls in cages while Arnold and his wife, Maria Shriver, walked across the dance floor. Roy Cohn, the infamous lawyer, was very involved with Studio 54. We were invited to a birthday dinner for him, along with people like Donald Trump and Barbara Walters. I tried to fix up Barbara Walters that night with a handsome friend of ours who managed a hotel, but she was not interested. (I guess she, like Cher, also did not trust my matchmaking capabilities as a dentist.) She appeared to be all business and said that she was only there because of Roy Cohn. I think that Roy wanted to be seen with her so people would think that he was straight.

In those days, no one had cell phones or cameras, and celebrities could wander freely throughout the club. Studio 54 could not exist in this day and age with its mixture of celebrities and raucous activities. The club could not allow tabloid photos of zonked-out celebrities and public heroes passed out on the couches.

Another memorable party had Studio 54 decorated as an evening on the *Titanic*. The entire place was transformed into what appeared to be a giant ship. At one point in the evening, Peter Allen danced out on the bridge with a long fire hose and doused water on everyone dancing below. People were getting soaked, and the ship was tilted to look like it was sinking. As the ship went down, Eartha Kitt and an orchestra appeared at the back of the dance floor. She performed for the crowd, opening with the song "I Want to Be Evil."

Valentine's Day every year was celebrated with amazing parties. One year numerous gold harps lined the entrance hall, which was filled with a video installation featuring over one hundred television sets playing iconic love scenes from great Hollywood movies. Busboys dressed as Cupid welcomed guests like Bill Murray and Gilda Radner from *SNL*. Giant hearts that people could sit in on the floor filled with candy echoed the heart theme of the invitation to the party, which was an inflatable heart. (Studio 54 often had unusual invitations to special parties. For their reopening party after renovations in September 1978, they sent out the invitation printed on a clear Lucite box filled with black confetti. For Roy Cohn's birthday party, the invitation looked like a subpoena from the state of New York.)

In 1983, the movie *Psycho II* was released, starring Anthony Perkins. Anthony; his wife, Berry; and the rest of the cast had a fabulous movie premiere party at Studio 54. We were good friends with Berry's sister, Marisa Berenson, and were invited. As we walked into Studio 54, we noticed dozens of bathtubs with shower curtains and water, like in the original shower scene from the first *Psycho* movie. As guests opened the curtains, they observed barely dressed men and women behind each curtain, each with a prop knife imitating Janet Leigh in the original movie. Even Mayor Ed Koch was at the party, along with Leonard Bernstein (a talented conductor and composer best known for the Broadway musical *West Side Story*), Kenneth Jay Lane (a well-known costume jewelry designer), and Ursula Andress (a Swiss actress best known for her role as Bond girl Honey Ryder in *Dr. No*, the first James Bond film).

In the last few years of Studio 54, we did not go as frequently but picked nights when there was an interesting themed party. My patient Bob Colacello, who was the editor of Andy Warhol's *Interview* magazine, invited me to many fabulous parties at Studio 54 over the years. One party hosted by Patti LuPone drew an interesting mixture of celebrities. Where else could you be on the dance floor with David Bowie, Richard Gere, John Travolta, Phil Collins, and Keith Richards? These people were not making a press appearance; they were partying along with the rest of us.

One year Andy Warhol and Truman Capote hosted an Academy Awards party. They put large palm trees throughout the club, so we felt like we were in California. Television sets lined the dance floor showing the award show. Mick Jagger came with his new girlfriend Jerry Hall.

Another special party that my patient Bob Colacello hosted and invited us to was for the Best. It is an elegant international group whose events we have attended with Gina over the years. This evening featured a jungle decoration with trees and vines and busboys wearing loincloths. Claus von Bülow, the socialite accused of murdering his rich wife, was there. Donald Trump, Frank Sinatra, Brooke Shields, Richard Gere, and Valentino were part of the crowd. Toward the end of the party, a machine on the bridge shot down confetti along with real money all over the dance floor. At first, we thought it was phony money, but it turned out to be real. (I did not notice if Trump bent down to grab any money, but I did.)

One night we spied the singer Prince hanging out with a few people at the side of the dance floor, but he never danced. A highlight each night at Studio 54 were the partygoers themselves with striking outfits meant to stand out in a crowd. (Arlene has kept many of her outfits, which she can only wear now to Halloween parties.)

The top gossip columnist of the day Liz Smith was very close to Liza. We were invited to a dinner party at Studio 54 for Liz. Kathleen Turner, Elaine Stritch, opera soprano Beverly Sills, Liberace, Marvin Hamlisch, Gloria Steinem, and Diane Sawyer were there. Because Liz was from Texas, we wore cowboy outfits, and Studio 54 was decorated in a western theme.

On many nights, we would shuttle back and forth from Studio 54 to Café Central and Columbus. Regulars at both places included Robin Williams, Christopher Reeve, Christopher Walken, Joe Pesci, Danny Aiello, Lorna Luft, and Paul Herman. If it was a quiet night at Studio 54, we would hop over to Café Central or Columbus. If we were at Columbus, someone might say, "Let's check out Studio." And off we would go in the early hours of the morning. Many other clubs came and went during those years, and we tried them all. There was a time when the Roxy Roller Rink became popular, and we would roller-skate to disco music.

We often saw Ahmet Ertegun, who headed Atlantic Records, at many Studio 54 evenings. He would be with various artists like the Rolling Stones, and we even saw him there one night with Luciano Pavarotti. Ahmet had a socialite wife, Mica, but he was usually in the company of beautiful young girls.

Margaux Hemingway was a popular model and the granddaughter of Ernest Hemingway. Ernest was a big game hunter, and Studio 54 threw a party for Margaux when she made her first movie. It was decorated with giant stuffed animals and foliage, and it felt like we were in a jungle. Any time an actor or celebrity had a birthday, it was an excuse for Studio 54 to throw a party for them. These parties would take place behind a curtained-off area, and the celebrities had the choice of staying to mingle with the crowd when the curtain was opened or leaving through a back entrance.

One night Francesco Scavullo, the celebrity photographer, invited us to a birthday party for Maria Burton, the daughter of Elizabeth Taylor and Richard Burton. They didn't show up, but Christie Brinkley and Christopher Walken were there, dancing away on the floor. Tom Cruise, Rob Lowe, Matt Dillon, and Debbie Reynolds were other people we observed at various birthday parties at Studio 54. Some stayed and enjoyed the festivities, and some just came for a short time to observe the scene.

Everyone in the world was curious to see Studio 54, from heads of state and royalty to blue-collar workers. Sammy Davis told us that he went twice just to observe, but he did not care for it. He experienced so much in his life that a few times there was enough for him. The new owner of Studio 54 invited us to his birthday party, with the duo Ashford and Simpson hosting. Lionel Richie, Chaka Khan, and Eddie Murphy sang "Happy Birthday" on the bridge above the crowd. O. J. Simpson and Nicole Brown were among the partygoers. When people ask me how I could spend so many nights at Studio 54, I simply answer that I did not want to miss this unique time in history. We never knew what to expect on any particular night or who we would encounter there. Nobody took pictures or asked for autographs, so celebrities and regular partygoers could just enjoy themselves and have a good time. Studio 54 did allow certain photographers to attend the special events and controlled all the photographs that appeared in the press.

Halloween was always a fantastic party night at Studio 54. One year we walked in on a surface of clear plexiglass, with live rats running underneath. We had to walk through a graveyard, and various monsters popped out along the way. The entire club was turned into one big haunted house.

Another night, Elizabeth Taylor celebrated her birthday, sitting on a float of gardenias, while the Radio City Rockettes performed on the bridge above the crowd. The birthday cake was a life-size portrait of Elizabeth. The designer Karl Lagerfeld held an eighteenth-century birthday party totally lit by candlelight. The waiters were in eighteenth-century court dress and powdered wigs. One Valentine's Day, the club was turned into a flower garden, with picket fencing and multiple women playing harps. The designer Valentino had a party at Studio 54 that he turned into a circus ring, with sand on the floor and mermaids on trapezes. Valentino dressed as the circus ringmaster, and various celebrities and socialites came dressed as circus performers.

In 1980, to honor Giorgio Armani, there was a ballet performance by the Trockadero Gloxinia Ballet Company. A string orchestra played on the bridge while pink rose petals floated down from the ceiling. The floor was covered with faux snow, and dozens of violinists dressed in white tie and tails serenaded the entering guests.

When Dolly Parton performed in New York City in 1978, Studio 54 made a fabulous party for her. Studio 54 was turned into a giant farm with haystacks throughout the area, and horses, donkeys, and mules were running through the club. There were giant wagons filled with hay and even a chicken pen with live chickens. Dolly Parton was somewhat overwhelmed by the scene, and Steve Rubell ran around, asking people if they had any extra quaaludes to give her for "diet purposes." I believe the quaaludes were not meant for Dolly but for a stressed-out Steve.

Allan Carr was one of our favorite people, and he was quite a unique character. He started out as an agent and eventually became a movie producer. He really knew how to throw over-the-top parties for his film openings. For one of his parties, he took over a complete New York City subway station, and we had a party on the train platform. For his 1978 movie release of *Grease*, the Studio 54 entranceway was transformed into a high school locker room. After passing through this area, we walked into the main club to find multiple vintage convertible cars from the '50s. Many of the guests were jumping in and out of the old cars, and I don't know how many old cars survived the party.

The night before Steve and Ian went to jail, they threw an amazing send-off party for themselves at Studio 54. We went with Lorna Luft and joined Halston, Andy Warhol, Truman Capote,

Richard Gere, Reggie Jackson, and Sylvester Stallone. Diana Ross sang to Steve and Ian from the DJ booth, and then Liza Minnelli performed "New York, New York." Steve was holding on to Bianca Jagger and was stoned. He took the microphone and kept telling everyone how much he loved Studio 54 and all of us, and it was a very emotional evening. Steve stayed at the club all night, and in the morning, he went off to jail.

I recently observed on the internet a series of pictures from the Studio 54 days. In one of them, I was photographed talking with the famous heavyset, bald drag queen Divine. Divine had just come off the dance floor after dancing with Elton John. It was at the *Grease* party attended by Olivia Newton-John and Elton John. After Elton and Olivia posed together, Elton started dancing with Divine. (Divine was a larger-than-life celebrity and became well known starring in female roles in films by John Waters. His real name was Harris Milstead, and he died at age forty-two from an enlarged heart.)

Many of the parties at Studio 54 would be politically incorrect in this day and age. At one Halloween party, we entered the club to find walls with windows set up in the entranceway. We looked through the various windows and observed various groups of midgets sitting at tables, having a formal dinner party. Over the years at Studio 54, sexual acts were going on in various areas of the club that are not suitable for print. I will always have fond memories and be grateful to have experienced those crazy and fun years at Studio 54.

CHAPTER

SIXTY-FOUR

Newer Friends—Older Friends

My feelings about the people I have met throughout my life can be best summed up by a quote. It is from a book of poetry titled *The Other Side of My Face*, just published by my brilliant seventeen-year-old granddaughter, Sydney Paige Lazare. In her dedication, she writes, "To every single person I've known forever, known for a second, known briefly, shared a smile with, shared tears with, and everyone in between. Whatever their impact, collectively they inspired something in me."

In the last fifteen years, we have become close with a large circle of about forty couples, most not in the entertainment business. This group loves to throw parties and go to restaurants, shows, and nightclubs. We enjoy bringing them to venues where our entertainer friends perform.

When we first met some couples from this group, they invited us to join them on Christmas week in Saint Bart's. All the couples went there to celebrate the holidays, and there was a different party organized every night. Two of the people, Andrea Wernick and Fred Stahl, had milestone birthdays that year. We did not know many of them that well but wanted to join them because they seemed like fun people. There was a big party on the first night, and Arlene decided, instead of her normal short dark hairstyle, to wear a blond wig for variation. It is a very attractive look for her and is also extremely youthful looking. When I walked in with her, nobody in the crowd would acknowledge me, and most looked away. At first, I could not figure out why they were so unfriendly until I realized that they assumed I brought a young date instead of my wife. After we walked over to everybody and assured them that it was Arlene, we bonded and have been friends with this crowd for the past fifteen years.

Between our friends in the entertainment industry and our other friends who love to go out, we have kept up a very active social life to this day. Some people may think this is tiring, but to us, it is our relaxation and enjoyment. I realized when I became a dentist that a dental office is one of the places few people want to be. It may be somewhat more appealing than going for a colonoscopy but definitely not high up on the list for popular activities. I believe that there is a good deal of negative energy felt by dentists daily, and that will explain the fairly high rate of suicide and depression in dentistry compared with other lines of work. Rather than come home each night and think about my day, I enjoyed going out to restaurants and entertainment venues. Every night I loved feeling the positive flow of happy energy. Even if I came home late, I would be energized, happy, and refreshed.

I also did not want to socialize with people who constantly talked about negative things and their various aches and pains. I searched for and found people whose company I enjoy. I learned a wonderful philosophy from Ginny Mancini. Ginny compares people in her life to audience members in a theater. There are some people and relatives that sit in the front rows of your theater. There are other people you come in contact with that you put in the back of the orchestra and others whom you move to the balcony. There are some people in your life you actually move out of the theater completely, whether it is friends, acquaintances, relatives, coworkers, lovers, or anyone you come in contact with. This is a constantly changing dynamic as relationships change with time. Sometimes you meet a person and seat them in your balcony, but as you get to know them better, they can be moved into the back orchestra and eventually to the front row. There are, conversely, people who are in the front orchestra seats of your life that over time you move farther back in the theater. Many wind up out of your theater altogether after years of sitting in the theater of your life.

Some of our friends in this newer group whom we have become closer to have been involved in the entertainment industry. Wendy Federman is a multiple Tony Award–winning producer. She often arranges tickets for all of us to attend her many Broadway productions. Lucia Hwong-Gordon is an outstanding composer and has created the score for the hit show *M. Butterfly*. Her mother is an internationally famous actress, Lisa Lu. Lisa Lu recently starred in the popular movie *Crazy Rich Asians*. Leesa Rowland has made a number of movies and has a cult following from her many horror movie roles. Elyse Slaine became the latest addition to *The Real Housewives of New York* TV series and became a fan favorite. Elyse is an extremely bright person and is involved in the financial world. After her first year's experience with this combative television show, she decided that reality TV was not for her.

Jacqueline Murphy has had minor roles in a number of movies. Jacqueline won numerous awards for her 2017 short film *The Admired*. She wrote, directed, produced, and starred in that movie. Steve Boxer, until recently, was the major partner in the popular restaurant Phillipe. We met Dennis Basso in the Studio 54 days. He has become a very successful worldwide furrier and is a major star on the QVC shopping network. Adrien Arpel has been a successful fixture on the Home Shopping Network for many years now. Bob Roberts's late wife, Lucille Roberts, created gyms all over the country bearing her name, and Bob kept them going after her passing. Jeff Allen we have known for a long time because he has been a very successful talent agent. He was the agent for the legendary entertainer James Brown, and today he is co-owner of Universal Attractions. Jerry Kremer served in the New York State Assembly for many years. Besides being a lawyer and political consultant, I was surprised to learn that he was very important to the new owners of Studio 54, securing a liquor license for them after Steve and Ian went to prison.

Consuelo Vanderbilt Costin and her husband, Rafael Feldman, are two of our new favorite friends. Raf is a fine actor and singer and a wonderful film editor. Consuelo is a terrific singer and has written and recorded some wonderful songs. She is a great businesswoman and is a descendant of railroad tycoon Cornelius Vanderbilt. Consuelo created a company called SohoMuse and has made it a very successful international entertainment company. When people all over the world need performers, artists, technicians, and so on for their event, SohoMuse will supply them.

Our attractive longtime friend Mattie Roberts gives beauty advice on the internet. Her videos titled "The Care and Feeding of Divas" are very popular. Carole J. Bufford has become one of the most popular performers in the cabaret and jazz scene. She is as charming offstage as onstage, and we love seeing her when she performs in NYC. Larry Herbert invented the world-renowned color-matching company Pantone. He and his wife, Michele, recently divorced after many decades of marriage. Michele is an excellent dancer, and for Larry's eightieth birthday party, she hired the dancing stars from the TV show *Dancing with the Stars* to dance with her at the party. She wore a different outfit for each dance and threw a great three-day party in Palm Beach. However, all didn't end well when Larry divorced her when he was eighty-eight years old.

Our great longtime friend Lew Pell has owned some of the finest restaurants in New York City. However, the restaurants are just a sideline for him; he uses the spaces to have periodic meetings with top medical experts from all around the world. He flies in people who have discovered various medical advances to give presentations to him in New York City. He has his own panel of experts who help him evaluate the inventions that are presented to him at meetings in private areas in his restaurant. If Lew believes the medical invention is a worthwhile project, he will financially back it and become a partner in the venture. He has built a reputation in this area and is a very successful owner of many major medical companies. Lew is also a great wine connoisseur, and our evenings out with him and his charming wife, Lynn, are highlighted by superb wine tastings.

When we first met Jon Fiore, he was a very successful jingle singer for commercials. Our friend Neil Sedaka's daughter, Dara, was also a jingle singer. Dara is a marvelous singer, who had a number one duet hit with her father called "Should've Never Let You Go." Dara recorded some wonderful albums, but she didn't like performing live. One of our closest friends, Moira, met Jon at a party, and they exchanged numbers. Moira, however, was not sure that she wanted to date him. Neil performed at our local theater in Westhampton one summer and stayed with us for the weekend. We threw a party for Neil at our home after his show. Moira and Dara both attended our party, and when Moira heard that Dara knew Jon from their jingle singing days, she asked about him. Dara spoke so very highly about Jon that Moira decided to get to know him. They dated, married, and are a terrific couple. Jon, who never had children of his own, became a father-in-law to Charlie Sheen when Moira's daughter, Brooke, married Charlie. Jon is a fabulous singer and has made some terrific albums. Recently, Jon decided to become an actor and just shot his first film with Lee Majors. Lee is best known for his days starring as the Six Million Dollar Man on TV.

Robin Cofer is a wonderful ballet and interpretive dancer with a great style sense. She is also an ordained swami priest. Trish Bacall is a very talented singer and has sung at all our family weddings. Deanna Amato and Rick Passarelli are a delightful couple to be around. He owns and operates Bobby Vans Steakhouse in NYC, and many of our friends love dining there.

Carrie White is known as a hairstylist to the stars in LA. We were fascinated by Carrie when we met her because she was a very attractive and young-looking seventy-year-old woman who was dating a handsome younger man in his thirties. They are a charming couple and very much in love. When we first met Carrie, we found her quite interesting and wanted to know more about her. She told us to read her autobiography and sent us a copy. Carrie, in her younger days, was the top hairstylist in Beverly Hills. Her clients included every major celebrity, such as Elizabeth Taylor, Elvis Presley, Goldie Hawn, Brad Pitt, and Sandra Bullock, to name just a few. However, Carrie traveled in such a fast crowd that she became addicted to drugs and wound up living on the street. Miraculously, Carrie pulled herself up from near death, raised seven children, resurrected her career, and became successful once again.

Most of our other friends from this large group of interesting people are outstanding people who also like to have a good time. They come from all walks of life, and many are involved in doing charitable work. George Spadoro is a lawyer who was the mayor of Edison, New

Jersey, for three terms. He and his wife Christina DeSimone love going to music venues with us. Christina is the founder and CEO of Future Care, a maritime and telemedicine health service. Gary and Colleen Rein are wonderful designers, and Gary has invented many terrific products. He is also a talented artist. Suzan Kremer, Arlene Reed, Andrea Wernick, Jaye Roter, Suzanne Turkewitz, Mark Roter, Shirley Wyner, Zach Tunick, Nicole Tunick, Amelia Doggwiler, Carole Koeppel, and Nancy Pearson are all successful real estate agents. Marnie McBryde is the head of McBryde and Partners, a top executive search service firm. Larry Wohl, Fred Schwabe, and Fred Stahl are all important people in real estate. Cynthia Hochman has been a mainstay on the board of our local performing arts center in Westhampton. Jane Pontarelli is a former playboy bunny who is very social and is invited to parties every night with her popular husband, Joe. Jane is a dynamo and is the life of every party. Dennis and Susan Erani run a tennis charity event at their Quogue home every year, which includes many of my tennis buddies. Mitchell Doshin Cantor is a former classmate in dental school who became a Buddhist monk and outstanding photographer. Jim Palmer is the owner of Malibu Vineyards. His wife, Irene Dazzan, has been called the "the Queen of Coastal Real Estate." We love their magnificent home and sampling Jim's fabulous wines. Barbara Edelstein and her husband, Ken Goldman, are outstanding doctors. Cheri Kaufman is the widow of George Kaufman, the owner of Kaufman film studios in Astoria. Glenn Myles is a principal in the First Wall Street Capital team and has financed many entertainment projects. We met him in his bachelor days and attended his wedding to Jennifer, which was televised on *The Real Housewives of New York* TV show.

Growing up in Brooklyn, I had a next-door neighbor named Herb Sherry. He was a popular bandleader, and he and his band performed at my wedding. In the summer, Herb would lead the band at Brown's Resort in the Catskills, where Jerry Lewis often performed in the showroom named after him. Herb's sons, Marc and Greg Sherry, are currently the owners of the popular Old Homestead Steakhouses in New York and Las Vegas, and we see them whenever we go to their restaurants.

We spent time with Jerry Lewis when he appeared in a show with Sammy Davis in Las Vegas. In his later years, Jerry Lewis's nightclub act was not that well received in many venues. Sammy told us that he booked the two-person show with him and Jerry purposely around the time of the Jerry Lewis muscular dystrophy telethon. Sammy explained that, in the two weeks before the telethon, Jerry Lewis became the biggest name in the business because of publicity surrounding it. The other fifty weeks of the year, Jerry Lewis was a tougher sell to the various venues. We saw Jerry Lewis at the New York Friars Club a few years before he died. They were naming a room at the club after him. We found him quite different from his image as a funny, zany comedian. He wasn't overfriendly and was actually quite serious.

Artie Schroeck and Linda November are a couple we have known for a long time. Linda is one of the most famous jingle singers. Artie is a wonderful composer and arranger for many of the major stars. We love his song "Here's to the Band," which he wrote for Frank Sinatra. When he and Linda got married, they formed an act together. One year we were in Atlantic City with Liza Minnelli while she was performing there. Artie had arranged an act for Liza Minnelli, and after Liza's show, we all went to see Artie and Linda perform in the lounge at Harrah's Casino. They have moved to Las Vegas, where they now perform, and we have not seen them in many years.

We have been friendly with Mickey Palin and Jerry Wolkoff for many years. They were both very successful real estate owners. Jerry sadly just passed away from a rare neurological disease that only affects four people a year. He was a vital, dynamic person, lost too soon. He was one of the largest home builders in NYC, with a twelve-million-square-foot portfolio in NYC and Long Island. Mickey was partnered with my friend Albie in the El Morocco nightclub and Elmer's Restaurant. Mickey's late wife, Carole, and Jerry's wife, Michelle, are the daughters of the legendary owner of the Sands Hotel in Las Vegas, Jack Entratter. Entratter ran the hotel in its prime when they headlined the Rat Pack, featuring Frank Sinatra, Sammy Davis, and Dean Martin.

Cassandra Seidenfeld is a talented and gifted actress. Sheila Rosenblum started Lady Sheila Stables in 2009. Sheila had been a pioneer in female-owned racing stables, with forty-five thoroughbreds, and she heads a successful all-female investors' group. Peter and Marion Goodman are an outstanding couple, each with great business successes. Michael Schmerin is an outstanding gastroenterologist and his wife, Daphne, is a superb teacher. Ann Markelson was vice president of Pressman Toy Corporation. Her brother, Ed, is a successful film producer of many outstanding movies such as *Wall Street*.

We first met Linda Marx many decades ago in Palm Beach, Florida. She and her brilliant late husband, Jack Cole, had a very popular daily radio talk show at that time. Linda is a regular contributor to *People* magazine and the *New York Times* and has been one of our dearest friends for many years. We love being in her company, but unfortunately, she has a fear of flying that prevents her from coming to see us in NYC. She is knowledgeable and smart and someone we always enjoy talking to.

Paula and David Roth are another Palm Beach couple who have been friends of ours for years. David is one of the top lawyers in Florida, and he also knows his wines. Sher and Don Kasun are terrific people who, every year, invite us to wonderful dinners and events in Palm Beach. Holly and David Dreman are another great couple from Palm Beach. David has written four books on investment strategy and is a regular consultant on investing for many TV networks.

Our two favorite cousins live in Los Angeles. Ellen and Paul Ganus are both accomplished actors and producers. Besides their acting roles, Paul does many commercials, and Ellen has managed actors and produced film projects. Their two children, Tyler and Spencer, are also extremely talented. Tyler composes, sings, plays the piano, and is a regular actor on Disney TV series. He has also done voice-overs for the movies *Wreck-It Ralph* and *Monsters University*. He is a star baseball player who might have a major league career if he doesn't go into performing. Spencer has done many voice-overs for movies, including *Happy Feet*, and was the voice of teenage Elsa in the movie *Frozen*. She started out as the face of Stride Rite shoes and is a talented dancer and piano player.

Years ago, Ellen and Paul lived for a while in Mexico City because they became two of the most popular soap stars in Mexico. Their faces were on billboards all over the country. One day when Paul was leaving the studio after filming, he hailed a taxi that was waiting outside. When he got into the car, a man opened the door and jumped into the back seat with him. The driver locked the doors, and they attempted to kidnap him. As Paul fought back, the man tried to stab him. Fortunately, Paul was wearing a heavy coat, and the blade did not go through to his body. Paul managed to somehow kick out the window, fight off the man, and escape. He and Ellen were so shaken up that they quit their roles and left Mexico. They gave up their star status due to that incident along with the crime wave going on in the city. Today Ellen is a very successful saleswoman for Isagenix and lectures all over the country on nutrition.

A number of our friends' children have turned out to be successful in their own right. Darlene Kleiner's son, Jeremy, moved to Los Angeles to work for Brad Pitt and Brad Grey in their film production company, Plan B Entertainment. In the days when I was meeting Jackie Mason to write comedy, Jeremy would occasionally meet up with us. He was always a very bright young man. He started out in LA reading scripts for Plan B and wound up coproducing movies with Brad Pitt. Jeremy has won two Academy Awards as a producer on the films *Moonlight* and *Twelve Years a Slave*.

Our friends Missy and Jerry Lubliner have a son named Justin, who is in the music business. In 2015, Justin heard a young singer named Billie Eilish and signed her to his company, Darkroom Records. At the Grammy Awards of 2019, she became the first female to win all four major awards. We loved seeing Missy and Jerry proudly walking the red carpet at the Grammys with their son.

Jason Strauss is the son of one of our longtime friends and Lauren's childhood friend. He is a founding partner of the Tao Group, which owns six of the highest-grossing nightclub and restaurant brands in the country, including Marquee, TAO, Avenue, and LAVO. Jason has given our family VIP treatment at all his venues and is an outstanding young man.

Our daughter Lauren's childhood best friend, Graham Reed, worked as Joan Rivers's personal assistant until her tragic death. Another of Lauren's good friends from childhood, Abbe Gluck, attended Dalton and Yale Law School with Lauren. Abbe has had an impressive career and is a professor at Yale Law School. She has too many honors to mention here, but clerking for US Supreme Court justice Ruth Bader Ginsburg was a highlight. Another classmate of Lauren's from Yale Law School, Stacey Abrams, has become a political force in our country. Lauren's close friend and cocaptain of their high school tennis team, Dylan Lauren, has turned out to be a very successful businesswoman. Her Dylan's Candy Bar stores are all over the world. Her parents, Ralph and Ricky Lauren, are lovely people, and they raised a great daughter. Our longtime friends Betty and

Zach Lonstein have a daughter named Shoshanna, who has become an outstanding designer of women's clothing. Shoshanna became well known all over the world when, as a seventeen-year-old high school student, she met thirty-eight-year-old Jerry Seinfeld in Central Park. They dated for four years at the height of his fame, but eventually, they broke up.

We have had wonderful longtime friendships with people involved in the entertainment industry. Jamie deRoy has similar interests to us, and we have spent many hours together at various entertainment venues throughout the city. She is a talented comedian and singer and frequently presents an evening called "Jamie deRoy and Friends," featuring other performers, with Jamie as the host. She has also become a major producer on Broadway, winning seven Tony Awards for her Broadway shows.

Riki Larimer is a pint-size dynamo who has produced many award-winning Broadway and off-Broadway shows. She has been very instrumental in keeping alive our small theater in the Sag Harbor area of the Hamptons.

We have always respected the privacy of people, and I think one of the reasons we have become close to many public figures is that they realize that they can confide in us. Somehow they sense that we are people they can talk to about their problems and personal feelings. This book contains some of our interesting and fun experiences with them and my impressions or personal opinions of people but not gossip about them or secrets they have told us in confidence.

In our second year of marriage, we went to see a popular comedian named London Lee. He was known as "the Poor Little Rich Kid." His comedy routines were based on growing up in a wealthy family. He would joke that his father was so wealthy that he bought a new yacht when the old one got wet. He appeared on *The Ed Sullivan Show* thirty-two times and was a regular on all the talk shows like Johnny Carson's *Tonight Show*. We went to see him perform at a nightclub and spoke with him when he greeted audience members after the show. Somehow he gravitated to us and asked for our phone number. That began a series of many late-night phone calls, sometimes lasting for hours. He poured his heart out to us, describing in detail all his insecurities and thoughts. We hardly knew him, but suddenly, we became his closest friends and confidants. The constant phone calls became overwhelming, and we quickly terminated the relationship.

Another well-known comedian also became attached to us. "Professor" Irwin Corey was a popular personality and frequent guest on Johnny Carson's *Tonight Show* comically billed as "the World's Foremost Authority." For his double-talk comedy style, he dressed in seedy formal wear and sneakers with his hair disheveled. He's been described as "Chaplin's tramp with a college education." For some reason, he took a liking to us and frequently invited us to his unique carriage house on East Thirty-Sixth Street in Tudor City. Over a few years, we had many dinners with him and never knew how much of what he said was brilliant comedy or if he was really a little crazy. We actually had little in common with him, and eventually, our friendship ended.

Eugene Pack is a talented writer, actor, and producer who created a show called *Celebrity Autobiography*. My family and I have attended readings of a number of his plays, but the most unique evenings have been his *Celebrity Autobiography* nights. Entertainers get up on stage and read word-for-word excerpts from other celebrities' autobiographies. It is as much fun as you can have in the theater. The pages, when read out of context, are often foolish, egotistical, or silly. The comically ironic writings by people such as Sylvester Stallone, Justin Bieber, Elizabeth Taylor, Debbie Reynolds, Eddie Fisher, Burt Reynolds, Ivana Trump, Arnold Schwarzenegger, Vanna White, Mr. T, and Madonna, among others, can be hysterical when read aloud word for word. Tony Danza, Susan Lucci, Christie Brinkley, Debbie Harry, Alec Baldwin, Mario Cantone, Kristen Wiig, Jerry O'Connell, Ralph Macchio, and Louis Black are some of the celebrities who have taken part in the readings.

Eugene has put on this show in dozens of places, even on Broadway. One of the venues in NYC was the Triad Theater, which was run by our friend Rick Newman. Rick was the founder of the legendary NYC comedy club called Catch a Rising Star. His club gave a start to many of our famous comedians, such as Jerry Seinfeld, Andy Kaufman, Billy Crystal, Robin Williams, Larry David, Bill Maher, and Chris Rock. We love going out after the *Celebrity Autobiography* shows with Eugene and the cast when friends of ours like Tony Danza appear in the show. There are some great neighborhood bars in the area, and we have had many laughs discussing the autobiographies that were read each night.

Dan Farah has been Tony Danza's manager for many years. Dan is a fun-loving guy, and we have had many good times with him in New York City and when he stayed at our home in Westhampton. Dan is a dynamo when it comes to work, and those of us who know him feel he will one day be the head of a film studio. He recently coproduced a movie with Steven Spielberg called *Ready Player One*, and he is working on a sequel. He also has a number of successful television series that he has produced.

Dina Fanai is a brilliant singer, songwriter, and composer. We first met Dina some years ago when we went with friends to dinner and then to a karaoke bar in Downtown New York. The club had some private rooms where small groups could do their own karaoke singing. We all took turns singing, and when Dina took the mike, she wowed us with her singing ability. Since that time, we have gone to hear Dina sing her original compositions at various venues and love her unique, dramatic style.

Tedd Firth is one of the most sought-after and talented pianists in the country. He has accompanied several of our singer friends, and we have spent time with him before and after many shows. Tedd does not usually hang out after the shows but goes home to his family when he is in the New York City area. We recently flew with him in Michael Feinstein's private plane when we returned to NYC with Michael after a performance in Indiana. As always, Tedd was a delight to be around. He often plays and conducts for one of our favorite NYC cabaret entertainers, Marilyn Maye.

Marilyn is a fantastic singer, and she set the record for the most female singer performances on Johnny Carson's *Tonight Show*, appearing seventy-six times. Marilyn started entertaining regularly in the New York cabaret scene in her late seventies and has become a major star in the clubs here in New York. At ninety-two years of age, she is singing and performing better than ever. On her days off, we often see Marilyn attending other performer's shows. She loves the NYC cabaret scene, and if there is a late show after her performance, she will be there. Marilyn has a warm personality, and we love spending time with her.

Clarke Thorell and Johnny Rodgers were two of the singers who appeared with Liza Minnelli in her Broadway show salute to her godmother, Kay Thompson. We saw a lot of them during the preparation and performance of that show. Clarke has become a popular Broadway actor. Johnny Rodgers is an amazing pianist and singer and has performed at our private parties. He is a great guy, but he lives out west, and we have not seen him in a number of years.

We first met Rob Russell in Palm Beach when he was in charge of the entertainment at the Colony Hotel. Rob is a charming guy and always wants to entertain rather than just introduce the acts. When the Colony Hotel closed its cabaret room, Rob decided to go out on his own as a singer. He has since become a popular entertainer in the Palm Beach area. We have had many fun nights with Rob and always look forward to spending time with him when we are in Palm Beach.

Peter Cincotti is one of the most talented pianists, singers, and composers we know. He is a very close friend of Tony Danza, and we have spent many wonderful Sundays at Tony's apartment with him. To witness Peter playing the piano and hearing Peter and Tony sing together is a treat. One Sunday Liza Minnelli joined us there, and it was a memorable afternoon of music. Peter has also entertained at our private parties.

Clint Holmes is another very talented singer we have known over the years. For many years, Clint had his own showroom in Las Vegas. Besides being a dynamic entertainer, he is a charming and warm person to spend time with. Even though he and his wife, Kelly, live in Las Vegas, we do get a chance to see him perform and spend time with him when he appears in Florida and New York City. He often stays in Palm Beach with our friends Eda and Stephen Sorokoff.

Eda and Stephen have a similar love for the cabaret scene as we do, and many times in NYC and Florida, we all attend the same shows. Stephen writes for BroadwayWorld and Times Square Chronicles, and the entertainers love him. We have become close friends over the years because we are drawn to each other through our mutual love of the entertainment business. Eda was a concert pianist and Stephen is also a terrific pianist. They are two special people.

The actress and singer Michelle Lee is a common friend of the Sorokoffs and us. Now that Michele has moved out of New York City, she stays with Stephen and Eda when she goes to New York City and Florida. Michelle has a lovely home in Los Angeles, and we see her there and whenever she visits New York City. She has a dynamic personality and is great fun to be with.

BarBara Luna is another friend of many years, now living in Los Angeles. BarBara is a wonderful woman and a talented actress. Her most well-known role was in *Star Trek*, and she still regularly greets her fans at the popular *Star Trek* conventions.

We have known Jim Caruso for many years. We first met Jim decades ago when he was performing as part of a comedy singing group called the Wiseguys. We told Liza Minnelli how much we loved them after seeing them perform and suggested they would be a great opening act for her. When the group broke up, Jim did some work with Liza and became good friends with her and us. He appeared in her Broadway show about Kay Thompson as one of the Williams brothers. Jim has been running his popular Cast Party Monday nights at Birdland for many years now and has expanded it into other cities across the country. He also performs with Billy Stritch at Bemelmans Bar in the Carlyle Hotel on Sunday nights. Jim is a great personality, and we love being with him.

We have spent time with Jim's friend Alex Hass over the years. She is a talented singer but doesn't perform anymore. Alex recently joined us at our apartment when we made a small birthday party for Liza Minnelli because she has become a good friend of Liza's.

We also invited another common friend, Lionel Casseroux, to the small birthday party for Liza. He is a charming man who divides his time between NYC and Paris. Lionel is a talented actor, and years ago, he owned a nightclub in the Broadway area. It was at his club where we attended the wedding of Chita Rivera's daughter, Lisa Mordente. Her husband, Donnie Kehr, wrote and sang a lovely song to Lisa at their wedding. Unfortunately, the marriage did not last. Donnie is a fine actor and singer and has had a long career in the theater.

Will and Anthony Nunziata are twin brothers who often perform together. They are fun young guys to spend time with. Anthony recently began performing on his own, singing original songs. Will has been directing shows for various cabaret performers. He recently directed a tribute to Liza Minnelli for one of our friends, Haley Swindal. Will asked if I could arrange for Liza to record a "happy birthday" message to Haley's mother for the show, and I did.

Ron Abel is a friend who is a talented pianist. Ron works as a musical director with Lucie Arnaz and Jamie deRoy, among many others. He is a very nice guy and makes a dramatic appearance at the piano with his long blond ponytail.

Gianni Valenti has been a friend for many years. He owns the fabulous New York nightclub Birdland and has run it successfully for decades. It is one of our favorite nightclubs, and Gianni always takes great care of us. He works very hard to make it a success and has recently expanded a second showroom on the premises called Birdland Theater. He has a home in the Hamptons, and for years, we keep making plans to spend time out there together, but work gets in his way. We always look forward to spending some time with him at Birdland before and after the shows.

For a long time, Gianni dated a lovely girl and terrific singer named Hilary Kole. We liked her a lot and were sorry to see them break up. She also sang at some of our private parties. Hilary went on to marry and have a family and continues to be a marvelous singer.

Erich Bergen is a talented actor and singer. He has an endearing personality and is very witty. He had a starring role in the movie *Jersey Boys* and is also well known for his role as the personal secretary for Téa Leoni in the popular television series *Madam Secretary*. We had not seen the TV show when we met Erich. We have many common friends and have spent a good deal of time with him. When he told us that he was performing at Birdland a few years ago, we wanted to attend and support a friend. Since Gianni always gave us good seats at the club, we figured that it wasn't necessary to make a reservation for the late show on a Sunday night. We walked into the club that night to find a mob scene of women filling every seat in the room. We were not aware of the extent of his popularity from being in a hit TV series. Many in the audience were fans of his TV character. Fortunately, Gianni found two seats for us that night. Erich is not only a terrific singer but a captivating storyteller onstage. He is a very handsome young man, and he is currently developing a project in which he would play the designer Halston, whom he physically resembles. We have had several conversations with him about it because he knows we were very close to Halston. We were able to give him some insight into Halston's life and personality.

Victoria Varela is a dynamic PR lady for many of our friends, such as Barry Manilow, Erich Bergen, Lorna Luft, Randy Rainbow, Countess Luann from *The Real Housewives of NYC*, and Frankie Valli. She is a workaholic, but we have had great fun with her and her clients at their events.

Kelly King is an unbelievably great singer. We used to go regularly to see her entertain at a club where people would yell out a random song, and Kelly would always perform it beautifully. Kelly can sing a Celine Dion song and sound exactly like her. She was enjoyable to spend time with but somehow never had the drive to be a successful singer. I always told her how amazing we thought she was. She has a younger boyfriend, Sean Michael Murray, who is also a gifted performer, and she seemed more interested in managing his career than promoting herself. She is a close friend of the pop singer Ariana Grande (who won a Grammy Award along with many other musical awards) and her brother, Frankie Grande (who became a reality TV star on the show *Big Brother*). Kelly did some backup singing for Ariana, and I always felt that Kelly underestimated her own talent.

Scott Nevins is another talented friend with a fabulous personality. We were introduced to Scott by Lorna Luft and Barry Manilow many years ago. Scott is a television personality and celebrity interviewer who gained national attention on the Bravo TV show *The People's Couch*. He has been the host and MC for hundreds of charity shows featuring wonderful performer friends of his. He is a dynamic person, and we always like being in his company.

Scott Siegel and his wife, Barbara, are two well-known personalities in the NYC cabaret world. Scott organizes and hosts entertainment evenings at various venues. He puts together talented performers for theme nights, and his evenings always sell out. He does a Broadway by the Year series at Town Hall and popular evenings at Feinstein's/54 Below nightclub in New York City. A few years ago, Scott was seriously injured in a bicycle accident, but that did not stop him from hosting his many events. We were happy to see him recently looking back to his old self. They are a cheerful and likable couple.

We met the phenomenal musician Dave Koz many years ago through Ginny Mancini and her twin daughters, Monica and Felice. Dave is one of the nicest people we have known and, for a while, had his own club and restaurant in Beverly Hills. He was kind enough to invite us as his guest several times. Dave was not able to keep the club going because he is on the road, working constantly throughout the year. He is the finest smooth jazz saxophonist in the country. One year Dave opened for Barry Manilow on a tour, and we got a chance to spend time with him after the shows we attended.

Felice Mancini is married to Bob Lefsetz, a music industry analyst and critic. He has a very well-known blog and a newsletter called *The Lefsetz Letter*. We enjoy talking with him when we go to Mancini family gatherings because Bob is a very interesting guy with strong opinions. Felice is a wonderful singer, but she never wanted to perform. She leaves the singing in the family to her twin, Monica. Felice runs the Mr. Holland's Opus Foundation, a charity supplying musical instruments to students who cannot afford them.

Mike Renzi is another wonderful pianist and musical director whom we have come to know over the years. For twenty-five years, he was the musical director and pianist for Mel Tormé and Peggy Lee. He recently has been working with our friend Nicolas King. We get to see a lot of Mike because we try to see Nicolas whenever he performs.

Mike is also close to our good friend Angela Bacari, Nicolas's grandmother and Liza's former vocal coach. Angela also works with the marvelously talented singer and songwriter Billy Gilman. Billy received a lot of notoriety when he finished second in the TV show *The Voice* a few seasons back. Billy is a very sweet guy, and our whole family likes him. We hope he will become a major star because he has the talent and passion. Billy was a child star who lost his voice when it started to change at puberty. When he got older, his voice came back, and he is better than ever. Angela travels with Billy and continues to coach him. Angela is a terrific singer herself, and she has also sung at a number of our parties.

Another person we like and respect is Joe Benincasa. He is the president and CEO of the Actors Fund, an organization that helps everyone in entertainment and performing arts. Joe is one of the finest people we know, and we see him at many entertainment events, always with a happy smile on his face.

Liz Brewer is a world-renowned event organizer and a charming person. She lives in England, and we do not get a chance to see enough of her, but we love her terrific personality. Michele Rella is another event organizer we have known for many decades. Michele arranges many splendid charity events, and we have spent wonderful days and nights with her and her husband, Frank.

Norah Lawlor and Claire Mercuri are two relatively recent friends in the entertainment field and are both impressive and dynamic women. Norah heads the Lawlor Media Group, and she handles PR for many outstanding people we know. We have recently been spending time with her at parties and found her a delight to be with. Claire Mercuri is another dynamic PR person who specializes in celebrity clients. She handles and is very close to Billy Joel, as well as Jimmy Fallon, Christie Brinkley, and Bruce Springsteen. She is another one of those fun, workaholic women, like our friends Joanne Horowitz, Myra Scheer, and Victoria Varela.

We have known Cindy Guyer for many years. She currently owns and runs a small restaurant on the Upper West Side. When we first met Cindy in her younger years, she was the most prolific model on the cover of romance magazines. She was on thousands of covers and had the nickname "Miss Romance." She is a superfriendly person, and we always enjoy her company. Cindy dated a good friend of ours for many years, but that relationship eventually ended.

We have known David Zippel for many years, and he is one of the most likable people in our life. He recently moved into a fabulous house on a small mountain in Palm Springs. David invited us to a party introducing his friends to his new home the last time we were in Palm Springs. David is a marvelous lyricist and has won Tony Awards for his show *City of Angels*. He has been a lyricist and producer for many other shows as well. David graduated from Harvard Law School with Chief Justice John Roberts but did not want to pursue a career in law because his passion was music. We have had many wonderful times with David because he comes to New York City often for projects. We recently had dinner with him and Barry Manilow at Joe Allen Restaurant in New York after they attended the theater together.

Mark Simone is someone we have known for thirty-five years. Mark is a radio and TV personality and currently has the number one, top-rated daily talk show on WOR radio. He was a close friend of Jackie Mason. During the years I was spending time writing comedy with Jackie daily, Mark would often join us at some point in the day. Mark knows everyone in New York City and knows everything going on in town. He has strong opinions on many things and can talk for hours on the radio about any topic. In person, Mark has a reserved demeanor but possesses a very clever mind. He always contributes a lot to the conversation with his knowledge of world events and sharp wit. Jackie has a very strong outgoing personality, so Mark will seem quiet in contrast. Jackie, however, is wise enough to get Mark's opinions on many topics. Mark is very popular as an emcee at NYC events because he is very comfortable at a microphone. We enjoy his company and always come away learning new and interesting information.

Randi Schatz is part of our circle of friends. She is a very sweet young lady and, for a number of years, headed Avenue Magazine

Media Entertainment. Almost every week, Randi would invite us and our friends to various media events, restaurant openings, and cocktail parties. When we first met Randi, she mentioned that her dentist had the same last name as us. It turned out that our son, Marc, was her dentist. We had her add both our son, Marc, and our daughter, Lauren, to her party invitation list.

Katlean De Monchy is a savvy video producer and creative thinker. She has done many interesting media interviews and has invited us to some wonderful events. She is a cordial hostess and has been part of our group for many years. Her husband, David Post, has four major start-up businesses, all very interesting and creative.

We have known Sara Herbert-Galloway for many years. She is an actress and photojournalist and is involved with many charity organizations. She had many acting roles on TV, but her concentration these days is on her humanitarian work for multiple charities. Sara is one of those lovely, sweet people you enjoy spending time with.

We have known Traci Godfrey for thirty-five years. She is a wonderful actress and has been very involved with the Screen Actors Guild for many years. She was a regular on the TV show *Law and Order* and has done many commercials. We met Traci when she first came to New York City and have had many good times with her over the years. We are very proud of the play she wrote based on her life, *Sweet Texas Reckoning*. It has played in many venues and has won many awards.

We met Ernie and David Sabella through Lorna Luft many years ago. They are brothers and talented entertainers. Ernie is best known to the public for his role in *The Lion King* as the voice of Pumbaa. Ernie is one of our favorite people, and we have had delightful times with him over the years. You can imagine the excitement our young grandchildren felt when they walked into our apartment seeing Ernie in our living room one day and were greeted by Ernie belting out "Hakuna Matata." Ernie has starred in many successful TV and Broadway shows, such as *Guys and Dolls*. He met his wife, Cheryl, backstage at the theater in 1996, when he was starring with Nathan Lane in the Broadway musical *A Funny Thing Happened on the Way to the Forum*.

David Sabella won accolades when he played the character Mary Sunshine in the show *Chicago*. It is a very dramatic moment in the show when the female reporter with a high operatic voice turns out to be a man. David's voice has that high range, and he still performs occasionally at various nightclubs. Most of his efforts these days are in teaching voice to aspiring and professional singers in his well-known studio here in New York. We sent our granddaughter, Sydney, to study voice with him. David is a great guy, and we spend time with him whenever Lorna Luft comes to New York to stay with us. Lorna has undergone reconstructive surgery in her chest area due to cancer problems, and David has been extremely helpful in showing her how to get the maximum singing performance from her body. With his help, she is singing great. When Lorna did her show a few years ago at Feinstein's/54 Below in New York City, both David and Ernie joined her onstage for duets.

Mitchell Ivers is another person whom we met many years ago through Lorna and spend time with him whenever Lorna comes to town. Mitchell was the chief managing editor of Random House Books. He is the author of the book *Guide to Good Writing* and was Lorna's editor when she published her best-selling autobiography, *Me and My Shadows*. Lorna's story is about growing up with a superstar mother and sister, Judy Garland and Liza Minnelli, and it became a multiaward-winning TV miniseries.

Kate Johnson is another person we have known for many years. She is close to a number of our friends, including Lorna, Michael Feinstein, and Neil Sedaka. Everyone loves Kate, and she is a delight to be with. Her father was a major film and TV producer, and Kate has the rights to much of his work. She has also been involved in producing movies and theatrical shows. I feel that her biggest mistake was having a personal relationship with Burt Reynolds. Burt did not treat her well in my opinion. She had a beautiful home that Burt persuaded her to sell. No matter how much all her friends warned her about Burt, she seemed blind to his problems, and I believe that he took unfair financial advantage of her. She obviously loved the idea of dating Burt Reynolds but paid the price for it. She is a very special person and deserves to be admired. In all his interviews, Burt never mentioned his relationship with her but only spoke about the famous women he was with, like Sally Field and Loni Anderson.

Raemali King is a Florida resident whom we have known for years. She is a lovely, sweet woman who was married to a dynamic man named Roger King. Roger died at age sixty-three from a stroke. He was an American television and media executive and headed King

World Productions. King World was responsible for launching the careers of Oprah Winfrey, Dr. Phil McGraw, and Alex Trebek, among others. Under Roger's leadership, King World became the leading syndicator of popular television syndicated programming. Roger threw lavish parties, even hiring Elton John for one of his evenings. He was fun to be around but unfortunately had a drinking problem and could be quite loud at times. He was fascinated by Rodney Dangerfield, and every time we were with him at some point in the evening, he did his impression of Rodney.

Brandon Fay is another one of our colorful friends. For years, Brandon was in charge of the food at the popular restaurant in New York Trattoria Dell'Arte. Brandon always dresses very colorfully and has made many appearances on TV, cooking his interesting recipes. He recently went into his own food business and was featured on the popular TV show *Shark Tank*, where he received an investment from the sharks for his new business. We had great times with him at his restaurant and private parties, and I miss not seeing him regularly now that he left the restaurant. He doesn't have a typical athletic build, but every year he runs in the New York City Marathon, dressed colorfully, of course.

Robbie and Stephen Marks had owned the fashion business run by the popular designer Scott Barrie. Scott was one of the premier black American fashion designers. Scott loved Studio 54, and we used to see him there often. He unfortunately died of AIDS at age fifty-two. It was through Robbie and Stephen that we met the entertainment lawyer Allen Grubman, who was dating one of their best friends. When Robbie and Stephen sold their fashion business, they took their two young children out of school, rented a large sailboat, and sailed around the world for one year.

We met Rob Bagshaw through Lorna Luft. He is a charming and talented guy, producing shows for Nickelodeon like *RuPaul's Drag Race*, *Project Runway All Stars*, and *Top Chef Masters*, among many others. A few years ago, he invited us to the TV taping of the *Project Runway* finale, and it was a great experience.

We met Barry Landau during the Studio 54 days when he worked as a press agent. Barry knew everyone, and we spent many nights with him at various events. He became known as a presidential historian, writing books on the subject. He amassed a large collection of presidential memorabilia and had the largest collection of inaugural memorabilia outside the Smithsonian and Presidential Libraries. Unfortunately, Barry and his associate were caught stealing historical documents from libraries and archives over a period. He was sentenced in 2012 to seven years in jail for the thefts. I always wondered how he was able to amass such an invaluable collection, and now that mystery is solved.

We had known Art Garfunkel's girlfriend Laurie Bird in the Studio 54 days but never met him. Many years later, we spent an evening at Birdland at a table with Art Garfunkel at a Monday Cast Party evening. He did not sing that night, but his wife Kim did. Art made a big fuss over her and asked us all to attend a performance of hers at another club the following week. He seemed to be a very doting and loving husband. However, after hearing her sing, Art remains in my mind the singing star of the family.

Sandy Jacobs was a friend of many years, and we fixed him up occasionally with some of our female friends. He is a very nice guy and has invested in many Broadway shows. When Lin-Manuel needed backing for his show *Hamilton*, Sandy and two other partners became the lead producers. *Hamilton* went on to become one of Broadway's great success stories, and I am very happy for Sandy's financial success.

Bobby Zarem was a top publicist for clients like Dustin Hoffman, Cher, Michael Jackson, Diana Ross, Arnold Schwarzenegger, Michael Douglas, Michael Caine, Sophia Loren, Alan Alda, and Ann-Margret. He was also the major publicist for many movies and conceived the "I Love New York" advertising campaign in 1975 when the city was getting a bad reputation. Three weeks after Elaine's Restaurant opened in 1963, Bobby became a regular. He ate there many times a week for forty-seven years, bringing his famous clients with him. He even introduced Mia Farrow to Woody Allen there. Even though he was often stressed from the pressures of his work, he was always extremely friendly and sociable to us. In 2010, he held his farewell party at Elaine's before moving to Savannah, and we do miss his energy and the times spent with him at Elaine's.

One of the unique personalities we met in Elaine's was a flamboyant hairstylist named Sabu. Elaine was extremely obese, and we never observed her with a partner. One night while we were having dinner with Sabu, he told us that he had joined Elaine on a cruise ship for one of her rare vacations. He claimed that she was the most passionate lover he ever had. I must say that we looked at her in a different light from that day on, thinking that you really can't always judge a book by its cover. (I want to apologize to Billy Joel fans if throughout this book you found yourself singing, "They were all impressed with your Halston dress and the people that you knew at Elaine's." For those of you who knew the words to the song but did not know what he was referring to, I think you now have a better understanding of the lyric from his hit song "Big Shot.")

Our friend Karen Lee has been a guest judge on the TV show *America's Next Top Model* and manages the Elite Model town house in New York City. Her excellent eye has enabled her to discover many of the top models in the country. For many years, we have enjoyed going to her town house for wonderful dinners. Our common friend Marilyn usually joins us there, and we all enjoy her unforgettable home-cooked meals. Marilyn is a world-class chef and has worked as a private chef for such notable people as Hugh Jackman, Jann Wenner (the owner of *Rolling Stone* magazine), and the advertising legend and TV star Donny Deutsch.

Robin Cofer, whom I mentioned before, is married to Dominick D'Alleva. He owns several restaurants and clubs in New York, and they also have a fabulous art collection.

Andrea Wernick is a social dynamo and, for years, has been arranging evenings out with many of our common friends. She is the leader of a large group of our friends, always organizing fun times for everyone. She is also a successful real estate agent. Andrea has a website called Fabulous at Any Age, which gives great advice on multiple facets of life.

Dottie Herman is a self-made real estate legend as the CEO of Douglas Elliman. She is a whirlwind of energy, fast talking, and hard to keep up with.

Hank Stampfl is a fun-loving, very entertaining performer. We first met Hank when we brought Liza Minnelli into a restaurant that he was managing. Hank is a big fan of hers and exchanged contact information with us. He has entertained at our parties and now heads a company called Revel Rouge. Hank's company does major party events, and he has a terrific group of performers whom he uses at these functions.

Alan and Diane Lieberman own a number of hotels in the South Beach area of Miami. They join our group of friends in the Hamptons every year and throw a great party every Memorial Day to kick off the summer season.

Debra and Gregg Wasser are another one of the fun couples in our group. They throw some wonderful parties on their boat, at home, and at restaurants. A recent ladies' luncheon thrown by Deb was called Bitches Who Brunch. Hank Stampfl is a good friend of hers, so he usually supplies the entertainment at their parties.

Maribel Lieberman is called "the Empress of Chocolate" and owns the most fabulous chocolate shop, named after her, in the SoHo area of New York City. Born in Honduras near the cocoa fields, she has her chocolates sold all over the world, including Dubai and Japan. Maribel periodically invites our group of friends to cocktails and tastings at her place.

Chau-Giang Thi Nguyen is known to our group as Coco. She currently lives most of the year in Vietnam but, for many years, lived part time in New York City. Coco is a well-known concert pianist who has performed all over the world. She is also a renowned painter and gets together with all of us whenever she returns to NYC from Hanoi.

Lynn White is a former TV newscaster from *Good Day New York*. We still remember when Lynn and her husband, Joel, invited us to a party where she had a psychic do readings in a back room of her apartment. Arlene and I do not believe in psychics, but this person shook us up when she stated facts that no one knew. To this day, we cannot understand how she came up with the things she did. Since that day, we believe that maybe some people may have psychic abilities.

We met Stephen and Louise Kornfeld in London when we traveled there with Liza Minnelli for her concerts twenty years ago. They were at a party with us, and when they moved back to the United States shortly afterward, we became close. Stephen is a very successful builder, and Louise is very active in charity work. We love spending time with them in Florida and New York. They throw wonderful parties at their home and on their boat and are an interesting couple.

We met at the same party in London Dorinda Medley, who is currently one of the stars of the reality TV show *The Real Housewives of NY*. When Dorinda moved to NYC after the death of her husband, we formed a friendship with her and her boyfriend, John Mahdessian. John is the owner of the top luxury specialty dry cleaner in NYC called Madame Paulette. It is the place where celebrities and wealthy people bring their most expensive gowns for cleaning. John and Dorinda were a wild, crazy couple whose relationship was a highlight of the TV show *The Real Housewives of NY*. John had developed a product for the public that removed difficult stains. When he found out about my mouthwash company history, he discussed the possibility of going into business with me to bring to market his product for mass consumption. I liked John a lot, but I did not feel ready to go into business again. He is someone who really likes to have a good time and can be quite flirty. Recently, he and Dorinda broke up due to, I guess, the combination of his partying ways and her fame on the TV show. I notice a change in some people when they feel their self-importance as a TV personality. This can have a damaging effect on their personal lives and their relationships with others.

Marc Bouwer has been a friend and one of Arlene's favorite designers. Julie Budd introduced Arlene to Marc's clothing many years ago. He has designed Arlene's dresses for both of our children's weddings and our grandson's bar mitzvah. He also designed Lauren's dress for her brother's wedding and her son's bar mitzvah. We brought Liza to his studio, and she loved his designs as well. Marc is close to another one of our friends from *The Real Housewives of NY* TV show, Sonja Morgan. We have enjoyed great times with him at parties at her place. Sonja is a free spirit who loves a good time, and we have been with her many times when she has entertained.

Howard Sobel is one of the leading cosmetic dermatologists in New York City and has his own line of products. Arlene is fortunate to have good genes so has never used Botox. (Arlene's father passed away at 102 years of age with no wrinkles at all, and she inherited his great skin.) We suspect that Howard has been a part of our group of friends for professional reasons as well as personal ones because many of them look very youthful for their age.

Paola Bacchini and Arnie Rosenshein are the most social couple we know. Every week they are flying off to some exotic country for a fabulous party. They have developed friendships with people in countries all over the world. Arnie is very successful in real estate, and he recently told me about his involvement in a business that makes products out of horse manure. He joked that his business has actually "gone to s——t." Arnie is very interested in politics and, several years ago, was contemplating running for mayor of New York City. He felt that he had all the right connections to win. He decided against it because he and Paola did not want to miss all the international parties they are invited to during the campaign season. With the state of politics today, it sounds like they made a wise decision. We have been to some great parties at their home in the Hamptons. They have a spinning disco ball in their basement, which is set up as a nightclub.

Arthur Backal has run many successful party venues over the years and owns Backal Hospitality. We had both of our children's weddings at hotels where he was in charge of the special events, and he was terrific. He's a great guy, and we have spent many good times together over the years.

We first met Marcia Levine through our common friends Leba and Neil Sedaka. Marcia is the special projects director of the Marlborough Gallery. She travels all over the world as an expert on art. She is a lovely person and has invited us to many wonderful art events over the years.

Arlene has known Francine LeFrak since her college days. Francine comes from a successful real estate family, and she is a Broadway and film producer as well as a philanthropist for many charities. She and her husband, Rick, are very active in the NY social scene.

Candice and Steven Stark, Michele Walker, Susan Tisch, Paul and Brenda Lane, Nurit and Werner Haase, Marla and Al Helene, Michael Trokel, Lauren Roberts, Joel Koeppel, Matt Adell, Ruth Schwabe, Amy Fitspatrick, Bob and Carole Antler, Paul Arida, David Bram, Eric Whitney, Bob Federman, Murray Fox, Paul and Martha Weinstein, Kevin Bass, Betty and Howard Schwartz, Perin Blank (our family's favorite person in Florence), Bob Mashioff (husband of Arlene's sister, Susan), my nephews Michael Mashioff and Bryan Mashioff, Geraldine Capasso, Andrew Catapano, Margo and John Catsimatidis, Podi Constantiner, Leslie Gelb, Sue and Fred Dweck, Reinhold Gebert, Peter and Penny Glazier, Gerard Haryman, Sara Stephenson, Anne Marie and Stephan Haymes, Marc Hulett, Bismarck Irving, Jennifer and Seth Miller, Jim and Marvin Wein (my financial advisers), Jack and Nancy Katz, Marty Kern, Darlene Kleiner, Kirsten Kief, Debby and Elliott Levy, Mitch Moore, Lynn Pell, Seth Ratner (my daughter Lauren's fiancé), Alisa Roever, Diane Rothman, Amanda Lazare, Maria Elena English-Christiansen, Dr. Sheldon Rosenthal, Andy Stark, Alyse and Gary Ruth, Susanna and Hormoz

Sabet, Vivian Serota, Shirley Weinger, Iris Schwartz, Sandy Borisoff, Vivian and Andy Ganz, Daphne and Michael Schmerin, Terry and Marvin Lerman, Donna and Dick Soloway, Starleigh, Kari Strand, Elia Martinez, MaryAnn Portell, Leon and Linda Teach, Sunny and Lenny Sessa, Nicole Guest, Vanessa Richards, Sydney Wolofsky, Joel Wernick, Harry Cohen, Steven Kornblatt, and Christina Greenfield are some other longtime friends and family members who may not have been mentioned previously but whom we have shared many good times with over the years. There is just not enough room in this book to describe all our experiences together with these wonderful people. They each have many accomplishments, and I am proud to know them all.

My future son-in-law, Seth Ratner, and his two children, Ashley and Dean, have become part of our extended family. He is a terrific guy, and our daughter, Lauren, and Seth make a perfect couple. His parents, Cary and Marian, and sister, Stacey, and her children, Miranda and Robbie, have become part of our extended family. My son, Marc, is currently in a serious relationship with Milda Juzumaite, and they are very happy together. (If my children are happy, then I'm a happy man.)

Arlene and I have had many varied experiences with our relationships with people. Scott Shukat was an entertainment agent at William Morris. He left to form his own personal entertainment management agency. We used to go to dinner regularly with Scott and his girlfriend Marilyn Sokol. Besides dating Marilyn, he was also managing her career. She was starting to get small parts in TV shows and movies. Marilyn is a terrific actress, especially suited for comedic roles.

One day Scott called to inform me that he no longer wanted to go out to dinner with us because he wanted to socialize only with people who could further Marilyn's career. Ironically, the parents of Liza's husband Mark Gero were Broadway and off-Broadway producers. They were mounting a new show, and Marilyn was one of the actresses wanting a major part in that production. Ordinarily, we would have promoted her to Mark's parents, with whom we were very friendly. It would have been easy for us to convince them how talented she was. Since her manager, Scott, wanted us out of her professional life, we minded our own business, and another actress got the part.

Marilyn eventually broke up with Scott and went on to have a terrific career, with major roles in many important films and TV shows. A few years after their breakup, we ran into Marilyn at an event. She expressed how much she missed us and wondered why we stopped calling her. When we explained that Scott did not want to go out with us as a couple because he felt we couldn't help her career, she was shocked. We renewed our friendship with her, and Arlene sees Marilyn regularly at Luigi's dance class to this very day.

Carole and Todd Rome were looked upon years ago by our group of friends as the ideal couple. Todd owned and operated a private airline company called Blue Star Jets, which specialized in renting small luxury planes. They were a beautiful and successful couple and were very popular in our social circle. They had just built a magnificent home in the Hamptons and were driving out to see it completely furnished for the first time. They invited us, their designer, and three other couples to join them for dinner in the new home. During dinner, they did not stop hugging and kissing each other. Arlene remarked to me that they were the most perfectly matched couple she had ever seen. They also had two beautiful young children. Their decorator showed us through all the rooms of this exquisite house. Every time we walked into a room, we would observe Todd and Carole in a passionate embrace.

After dinner, they invited a few other couples to join us on the outside deck area of the house for dessert and drinks. One of our common friends, Jill Zarin, who starred in the first three seasons of *The Real Housewives of New York* TV show, was a close friend of the couple. We were leaving just as Jill and her husband, Bobby, were arriving to see the house.

The next day, we called Jill to share our thoughts on how terrific the house was and what a fabulous couple they were. We were shocked to hear from Jill that, later that evening, Carole and Todd had a terrible fight and were getting a divorce. Apparently, all the passionate demonstrations of affection may have been helped by the alcohol served that evening. Later in the evening, the aftereffects of whatever they drank changed the atmosphere from passionate to argumentative. They put the house up for sale the next day and eventually went through a bitter divorce.

Todd is remarried to a lovely girl named Vanessa, and they both seem very happy together whenever we see them. In 2008, Carole married Charles Crist, who was governor of Florida, and Carole became the first lady of Florida. Charles had strong political ambitions and was considered a possible vice presidential candidate. His political fortunes turned sour along with the marriage, and they divorced in 2017. We learned to never judge a couple on first impressions.

Another couple we knew for many decades also seemed fabulous on the surface. I am changing their real names in this paragraph out of respect for their children. Lydia and Steven were a couple we all looked up to. He was a very successful personal injury lawyer and lived in a magnificent town house he bought for a reported $25 million. They always had wonderful parties with very well-known politicians present. They were one of the most likable couples we had ever met, and most of our common friends put them first on their list when having a dinner party.

About ten years ago, Steven started secretively approaching a number of our common friends, asking them to loan him money. Fortunately, we were one of the few couples he did not ask. He apparently told each couple that he needed money for a few months for a business venture and would repay them quickly. Since he was so very successful and people knew him for many decades as a close friend, they lent him the funds. It was not small amounts but hundreds of thousands of dollars from each couple.

When weeks turned into months and months turned into years, people started to press him for payments. Each person thought they were the only one whom Steven borrowed money from, but soon it slipped out in conversations that there were many people involved. One day Steven was arrested for stealing money from his clients. The accusation claimed that the insurance company paid the personal injury award to Steven, and he would keep the money rather than send it to his clients. Steven's partner had died, and his family claimed that he bilked them out of the life insurance money.

Today Steven is serving a seven-year jail sentence for his crimes, and as far as I know, he has not reimbursed our common friends. One lesson I learned was not to invest or get involved in finances with friends. All of us are in shock about the wonderful, well-respected guy we had known for many decades turning out this way. Another neighbor of ours in Westhampton also went to jail for many years after stealing money from his clients, many of whom were widows. He built a beautiful large home on the water with the funds, but only his wife lives there now while he sits in a jail cell.

In the early years of my marriage, I played in a weekly poker game. One of my best friends in the game was a well-known jeweler named Robert who had a business in the diamond district on West Forty-Seventh Street in NYC. New York City's Diamond District is the world's largest shopping area where one can go for discounted prices on all types of diamonds and jewelry. I went to that area one day to buy Arlene a gold bracelet. After settling on a price with the salesman in one of the stores, I decided to stop and say hello to Robert at his place. When I told him that I had just bought a bracelet for Arlene, he told me that he would speak to the owner and negotiate a better price for me. I explained that I received a fair price and that I did not want him to go out of his way to ask for favors. He insisted, and I felt uncomfortable going back to the store after Robert pressured him to lower his price. When I did go back, the owner informed me that he spoke to Robert and would lower the price fifty dollars. For this relatively small reduction, I vowed never to ask Robert to do me favors in any jewelry purchases in the future.

Over the next number of years, I would buy earrings, pins, watches, cuff links, and other jewelry items in that area because they undersold the regular jewelry stores. Arlene's mother frequented one of the jewelry places there for many years. I went with her one day and saw a pair of earrings that I wanted to buy for Arlene as a birthday gift. I asked the jeweler if he could do me a favor and reduce his asking price. He told me that he would ordinarily be happy to do so, but he had to figure in Robert's cut when quoting me a price. I had no idea what he was talking about. He explained that when one jeweler refers someone to another, they receive a referral fee. When my friend Robert years earlier did me his "favor" and negotiated a fifty-dollar reduction on a bracelet, he actually received a referral fee. Robert then put out the word that Arlene and I were his customers.

From that day on, whenever I bought something at any of the jewelers in the district, he received a cut. So the prices quoted to me were always higher due to the need to put in a fee for him. It was one of my life's lessons on the ethics of so-called friends when it comes to making money. I dropped out of the poker game and ended our friendship, although I never confronted him about it.

One of our interesting lawyer friends is Michael Griffith. He specializes in helping convicted criminals get out of foreign jails. In 1978, there was a very popular movie called *Midnight Express*, about an American named Billy Hayes who was caught smuggling hash out of Istanbul. He was arrested and put in a horrible Turkish prison for thirty years. Prison conditions were unbelievably bad, and the film documented his time there and eventual release. Michael Griffith was the lawyer who flew to Turkey and was able to get him out of jail and bring him back to the United States.

Michael told us about many of his interesting adventures in gaining the release of notorious criminals in different countries. One of his fascinating stories concerned the time he was hired by the mistress of the notorious head of a drug cartel in Colombia who was imprisoned by the government. They wanted Michael to try to secure his release. She paid for Michael's trip and put him up in a hotel near the prison. She was an extremely beautiful and sensual young woman. She picked Michael up at his hotel and drove him to the prison to meet the drug kingpin. Michael would go each day to the prison to gather information for his case and would be driven back and forth from his hotel by this beautiful young woman. The imprisoned drug lord put his mistress up in a beautiful home close to the prison.

Michael is a very handsome man, and on the third day, the young mistress suggested that he come back to her home that night with her rather than sleep in the hotel. The drug lord was to be incarcerated for a long time, and she was lonely for male companionship. Michael was very tempted, but at the last minute on the drive home, he impulsively told her that he needed to go back to his hotel room to prepare papers for the case. When she picked him up at his hotel the next morning, she told Michael that, in the middle of the night, the drug kingpin had managed to bribe his jailers to allow him to leave his cell for a few hours. He made a surprise visit to his home to make love to his mistress. Michael imagined what the scene would have been like if this mobster would have found him in bed with the mistress. Heads of drug cartels are not known to be very kind people. His last-minute decision saved Michael's life. Needless to say, he finished up his work on that case as soon as possible and couldn't wait to fly home. It was literally one of those sudden decisions that was the difference between life and death.

Michael married a former Halston model named Nancy, whom we knew from our days spending time with Halston. They live full time in the Hamptons. Nancy specializes in renting out people's homes for a few days to be used for photographic locations in movies. When a film has a scene taking place in the Hamptons or similar country locations, they go to Nancy to secure the right place.

One of Michael's recent cases concerned someone we have known for many years in Palm Beach named Alex. Alex is an old-fashioned ladies' man, a very smooth operator, and a charming guy. One of the women he was dating in Palm Beach for a long time was someone we knew. He suddenly ended his relationship with her when he met Veronica Atkins, the widow of Robert Atkins, who founded the Atkins diet. Veronica inherited $200 million when her husband died and soon fell under the spell of Alex. Against the advice of some friends, she married Alex. The woman we knew claimed that Alex continued to have sexual relations with her after he was married. Our friend hired Michael Griffin as her lawyer to sue Alex for his behavior toward her.

We were talking with Alex and Veronica at a friend's party in Palm Beach when Michael walked into the party and came over to say hello to us. When I introduced Michael to them, Veronica recognized his name as the lawyer suing Alex. Veronica started yelling at Michael, and it was a very embarrassing scene. Arlene and I were in the middle of this loud exchange at a very elegant formal event. The hostess of the party eventually asked Alex and Veronica to leave because they were creating a disturbance. Michael informed us that his client had all sorts of incriminating material about Alex's extramarital affairs, but Veronica did not want to believe it. Michael described Alex as a sweet-talker who could persuade women to believe anything he said. Michael told us that when he was able to contact Veronica and show her photographs of Alex with other women, she finally got the message and divorced him. I only heard one side of the story, so who knows what the truth was?

Jeff Furman was a great guy who unfortunately passed away too early. He married a Cuban spitfire named Teresa, who looked like a young Ann-Margret. Jeff lived an extravagant lifestyle and was a very big sport. He always gave us the most expensive gifts at any function we invited him to. His business was somewhat of a mystery as he was some sort of middleman who supplied money from one party to another for business financing. One year he threw a large birthday party for Teresa at a summer home he rented upstate. In front of the home, he parked a red Ferrari convertible sports car with a giant ribbon tied around it and a sign saying, "Happy birthday, Teresa." Jeff developed some health issues, and they divorced a year after that party. We had spent many fun times with them as a couple and were sorry to see them break up.

Teresa confided to us that Jeff's life was a lot of smoke and mirrors as far as his finances were concerned. When I jokingly told her that at least she had the red Ferrari from her birthday, she informed me that it was a leased car. Jeff did not buy it for her but put the lease under her name. He paid the first few months' payments, and when they separated, she was stuck with the lease. It was just another of my life's lessons, repeated often in this book, about not judging a book by its cover.

We bought a vacation home in Westhampton Beach after being invited out to spend a weekend by Ron Delsener. His family owned a small home on Dune Road, and we spent a wonderful weekend with him and his sister, Harriette. Ron was already a major entertainment promoter and would soon become the top promoter in the region. He was in charge of all entertainment for venues like Jones Beach and was the major promoter for Madison Square Garden and other large arenas. Harriette worked with him, and she always graciously arranged tickets for us to see top acts. When Live Nation bought Ron's company, Harriette became senior sales director for Live Nation.

Arlene is not a fan of large arenas, but being able to sit in house seats and visit backstage with iconic performers made it enjoyable for her. Arlene passed on seeing some of the very loud entertainers and certain acts, like Bob Dylan, whom I enjoyed but she did not care for. Last year, I went by myself to see Bob Dylan perform at the Beacon Theater in New York City. Ringo Starr and his brother-in-law, Joe Walsh of the Eagles, sat directly in front of me. Ringo Starr recently turned eighty years old, and I could not believe how youthful he looked. If I didn't know that it was Ringo, I would swear that it was a fifty-year-old man sitting there. Dylan drew a crowd with many celebrities. Jerry Seinfeld sat two seats to my right, and a few weeks later, I took the family to see Jerry perform at that same theater.

After the weekend with Ron Delsener and his family in Westhampton, we decided to look for a home in the area. The first home that we looked at was owned by the well-known sportscaster and TV personality Howard Cosell. It was a small home, but it was on the bay, and we liked the location. Howard had a big ego and figured that anybody buying his home would pay a lot because he lived there. The price he set was far too high, and we passed on it. He was not the friendliest person, so we saw little use in trying to reason with him about the price. We bought elsewhere on the water in 1977, and we have been extremely happy with our choice all these years.

One of our favorite New York restaurants is Patsy's, and we love the owner, Sal, and the Scognamillo family, who have run it since 1944. Patsy's was a favorite of Frank Sinatra, who threw many private parties upstairs. When Henry Mancini was alive, we had dinner there many nights with him and his wife, Ginny. We go often with Tony Danza for dinner, and Sal usually gives us jars of his fabulous sauce to take home.

Sal recently threw a big party at the restaurant to celebrate their seventy-fifth anniversary in New York City. We went with Tony Danza and Deana Martin and her husband, John. Deana has followed in the footsteps of her famous father, Dean Martin, and is a popular singer. We have known her and her husband for a long time, and John is quite a character. He loves to fly and unsuccessfully tried years ago to get me to fly with him on a small plane. Deana sang for Sal at Patsy's party. As a gift for Sal, I had Liza Minnelli record a video congratulating Sal on this milestone to show at the party. There are not many New York restaurants left where the owner is there greeting the customers and making them feel welcome.

Soheir Khashoggi is the sister of Adnan Khashoggi and the aunt of our friends Nabila Khashoggi and Dodi Fayed. She is an Egyptian-born Saudi Arabian novelist. For many years, she lived near us in Manhattan, and we would have frequent dinners with her at her home and neighborhood restaurants. We met Soheir through Nabila and found her to be extremely bright and quite a special person. Her father was the physician to the king of Saudi Arabia, and her brother, Adnan, was at one time the richest man in the world and a well-known arms dealer. Her first novel, *Mirage*, was published in nineteen languages in 1999. Other novels include *Nadia's Song* and *Mosaic*. She used her novels to highlight the plight of women in the Arab world.

Soheir told us about her life as a woman growing up in one of the most prominent Saudi Arabian families. Even as a royal, she was not allowed to drive a car or go to school for higher education. Characters in her novel are based on her real life. Women, even in the royal family, are told who they must marry, and they have to totally obey their husbands. She somehow managed to escape Saudi Arabia, divorce her husband, and get to America. It was not easy, and there was a lot of intrigue involved. Many of her personal experiences are described in her fascinating novels. In contrast to her world-famous brother and well-known relatives, such as Dodi Fayed (who dated and died with Princess Diana in a car crash), she is humble and soft spoken.

Georgia Witkin has been a close friend of ours for many decades. Our children played together as babies, and we have observed all of Georgia's numerous successes. She is one of the brightest and accomplished people we know. Her mother, Mildred, was an outstanding therapist, and the famous sex therapist Dr. Ruth was her student. Georgia is a clinical psychologist, an infertility expert, and a director of the stress program at Mount Sinai. She was a regular on NBC TV news and has authored many books on stress. Arlene has attended some of Georgia's informative lectures, which she does all over the country. She has a great sense of style and has thrown many magnificent, entertaining parties. About twelve years ago, she met and married film producer Mike Tadross.

Mike has become one of my closest friends. Arlene and I have had many great times together with him and Georgia, and they have become part of our extended family. Besides heading Paramount Pictures for many years, Mike has been involved in producing movies like *The Devil's Advocate, Rollerball, Thomas Crown Affair, Indecent Proposal, Die Hard 3, Ocean's Eight, Coming to America, Ghost, I Am Legend, Gangster Squad, Hitch,* and *Arthur,* among many others.

We often go with Georgia and Mike to a favorite restaurant in my neighborhood, Campagnola. The manager there for many years, Salvatore, always yearned to be an actor. He was constantly imploring Mike to cast him in one of his movies. One upcoming movie had a scene with a maître d', and Mike offered Sal the opportunity to play that role in the film. However, the shooting schedule coincided with Sal's responsibilities at the restaurant, and Sal was unable to shoot the scene. He was terribly disappointed, and from that day on, Mike and I decided to drive Sal nuts by telling him that Mike cast me instead of him in scenes on his films since Sal was busy at the restaurant. I would arrive on the set of each of Mike's films, and he would have me photographed in a scene. We would then casually take out the picture of me on the film set and show it to Sal when we went to his restaurant.

When Mike made a film in 2013 with Sean Penn, called *Gangster Squad*, he photographed me on the set with Sean Penn. Of course, Mike told Sal how wonderful I was in my scene just to aggravate him. When Mike shot the movie remake of *Arthur* at Grand Central Station in the Cipriani Restaurant, he had me pose as the maître d' seating Arthur, played by Russell Brand. Russell was terrific and a great sport and posed for several pictures that we eventually showed to Sal. Me playing a maître d' in the movie drove the maître d' wannabe actor Sal crazy. Mike gave my granddaughter, Sydney, a real part in another one of his movies, and of course, I took a picture of myself on the set to aggravate Sal.

When Mike finished his film with Will Smith called *I Am Legend*, he invited Arlene and me to the fabulous wrap party. Will entertained the cast and crew by singing some of the rap music he started out doing as a performer. In all of Mike's movies, he puts our common friend Dr. Larry Reed on staff as a medical consultant. Larry is a world-renowned plastic surgeon but loves the movie business. While on the set, he is constantly giving Mike suggestions on how to improve the script; and when we all go out to dinner, Mike teases Larry about that.

When I was a member of the Friars Club in New York City, I brought Mike there often as my guest. He loved it so much that he joined, and he is now an important person on the board of the club. They treat him so well that I no longer saw a need to remain a member, and now I go as his guest.

My granddaughter, Sydney, wants to be an actress. Thanks to Mike giving her small roles in his movies, along with another part she had in a Ben Stiller film, she was able to become a member of the Screen Actors Guild at age sixteen. Sydney is a gifted actress and a marvelous writer, and I expect big things from her in the future. She is attending the LaGuardia High School of Performing Arts in New York City, and we are blessed to have her living with us while she attends. She is also an amazing painter, and people are starting to buy her work. Besides writing two screenplays, she just published a book of her poetry. She also did the drawing and cover design for my book.

Shelley Goldberg was the television parenting reporter for New York 1 TV for twenty-five years. Her TV show was aired multiple times each week, and she is a popular, recognizable personality in New York City. She also does a "where to go" segment on multiple radio stations in the New York and New Jersey areas. She is the author of *Shelley's Learning Adventures*, a guide for parents on where to take their children for family outings. When our friend Julie Budd introduced Shelley to us a decade ago, we bonded immediately. She has since become one of our closest friends, and we speak almost daily. She has put our grandchildren Justin, Devin, and Sydney on her TV show for segment appearances. She was a regular contributor to the Joe Piscopo radio program, giving advice on where to go. Shelley also worked as a consultant with the fabulous chef David Burke. She recently organized a wonderful evening with David at the Friars Club, and Lauren, Arlene, and I had a feast.

Shelley loves the entertainment scene, and we often go with her to see various performers around town. When the NY1 TV host of its *On Stage* program, Frank DiLella, started doing celebrity interview evenings at Birdland, we attended with Shelley. Frank is a great guy, and we enjoy spending time with him at the shows and at other venues. Since Shelley gives where-to-go advice on various media outlets, she often has access to fun events and has taken us and our children and grandchildren. We even went with her to a bull-riding event at Madison Square Garden. (That obviously was a highlight of the year's social schedule for Arlene.) She is constantly being approached by people when we are out to dinner. They recognize her from her constant appearances each week on TV. Her face is so familiar to them that they often think that she is a friend. She has become so close to us and our children that we consider her part of our extended family.

${ \text{CHAPTER} }$

SIXTY-FIVE

Storm Large–More Friends–Luigi

Another person who has become an extended part of our family is someone whom we would never have imagined becoming so close. We consider Storm Large to be possibly the best live performer in the country today. Storm is her real name. She came to the public's attention when she appeared on the CBS TV reality show *Rock Star: Supernova*. She was a finalist in the contest to discover the best new rock star. At that time, Storm was a hard-driving rock 'n' roll performer, and she has since branched out into the theater and cabaret world. She performs with her own band, as well as the world-renowned group Pink Martini. In 2012, she published her autobiography, *Crazy Enough*. The following year, she turned the book into a one-woman show, featuring her original music. She is a well-respected songwriter who has composed some of the finest music of our generation. She is a strikingly attractive six-foot-tall force of nature with a giant tattoo of the word "lover" written across her back.

We first met Storm about ten years ago when Michael Feinstein had her as his guest performer at Carnegie Hall. Michael is a perfectionist and very critical of many performers who he feels are not up to the standards of the Great American Musical Songbook. Michael loves Storm as a performer and often has her as a guest soloist in his shows when she is available. Storm onstage is very dramatic, putting her unique energy and interpretation into the performance of every song. During her show, she will say things that will make a truck driver blush, and she communicates with the audience constantly throughout her performance. She talks about her life openly onstage, and that, combined with her incredible voice and body movements, makes her show an unforgettable experience.

After the first show that we saw Storm do with Michael, we went to his apartment with her and some other people. Hanging out with Storm is always a hoot. She is very open, sensual, raw, and sweet. She had a very rough childhood and grew up with many hardships. She was a wild child and lived a fast life. Through her music, she overcame all her demons and evolved into a fantastic person.

Although a friendship between her and us seemed unlikely, we started to spend time with her whenever she performed in New York City. We also spent evenings with her, Michael Feinstein, and Terrence Flannery in Los Angeles. We hit it off so well that Storm began to stay with us often in New York City and has become a close part of our extended family. Our children and grandchildren love her, and somehow the rough language sounds fine when she converses with us all. We have gone everywhere with her, from a poetry bordello in a Brooklyn club to road trips with her band. We were recently with her while she played her guitar outside the celebrity restaurant Craig's in LA while waiting to meet Michael Feinstein and Terrence Flannery there.

She gets a kick out of the way Arlene bombards her with food, including her famous challah French toast when she stays with us. Storm loves to announce onstage when performing in New York that her New York family is in the audience and ready to feed her after the show. Recently, she appeared on Long Island with her band, and they all stayed at our home in Westhampton for the weekend. We had a lot of laughs, and they each gained a pound or two. We feel that Storm should be recognized as a superstar, but she does not have the desire to go that route. She is just happy writing and performing her music and making people happy at her performances.

One week when Storm was staying with us, Lindsay Wagner flew into New York City from LA for two days. They stayed with us in our guest bedrooms. It turned out that both of them were originally from Oregon, so they bonded wonderfully. Although Storm can be a hard-partying and hard-drinking person, she is basically sweet, kind, and very bright.

When we first saw Storm perform, one of our friends, Marc Cherry, was also in the audience with us. Marc joined us when we all hung out afterward, and he found himself quite taken with her. Marc is an extremely successful TV writer for such shows as *The Golden Girls* but is best known as the creator of the very popular ABC TV show *Desperate Housewives*. Marc is extremely bright and witty and also gay. He kept telling us that Storm was causing problems with his hormones and homosexuality because she was turning him on. He was also fascinated with her as a performer. When she was appearing with Michael Feinstein in New York for two nights, he went both nights. She went on in the second half of the program. Marc asked Michael to leave a chair for him at the end of one of the rows on the second night so that he could catch Storm's performance. Sure enough, he came in, sat down, watched her part of the show, and left when she finished to wait backstage to join us all afterward. Marc never crossed over into the heterosexual world but has remained friends with Storm. Marc is one of the nicest and most knowledgeable people we know and is a very special person. We recently binge-watched Marc's latest TV series for CBS All Access, called *Why Women Kill*. It is amazing and shows his writing genius.

One night we went with Michael Feinstein, Terrence Flannery, Storm, and Marc to Jim Caruso's Monday night Cast Party at Birdland. It's a night when different performers drop by to sing a song with a trio led by Billy Stritch. Storm did one song, and then Marc Cherry volunteered to sing. We were all shocked to witness that Marc was a terrific singer. Jim came over to our table later and offered Marc a regular show at Birdland if he wanted to do an evening there. Marc was too busy working on his new series to take him up on the offer.

When Storm performs in New York, we usually bring groups of our friends to each show and watch their amazement at her performance. Tony Danza joined us at some of her shows, we all had dinner afterward, and they became friends. When Michael Feinstein paid tribute to Liza Minnelli one evening in Pasadena a few years ago, we flew out for the week. He put Storm on the program, and before the show, we introduced her to Liza. They got along splendidly, and both of them performed that night to standing ovations.

When Storm stays with us in New York City, we have had both wonderfully outrageous times and quiet times at home with our family. When the Palm Beach Pops had their formal gala a few years ago, Michael Feinstein conducted the orchestra and featured Storm as one of the guest artists. The elegant, reserved crowd at the gala did not know what hit them when Storm appeared at the back of the theater and made a dramatic entrance singing as she walked through the crowd. The heads of the Kravis Center in Palm Beach were stunned by her performance and invited her back the following year to do her own show there. She unwound after the gala at an after-party at one of the donors' home. It was a very warm night. Storm took off her formal gown and jumped into the pool naked. She then came out, dried herself off, put her gown back on, and charmed the guests.

Another interesting person in our life was the late Martin Richards. Arlene and I were introduced to Martin many years ago by Bob Wachs. Bob told us that he had a friend named Martin who was very active in the Broadway theater world. He explained that Martin was a lovely guy who wanted to be a Broadway producer but was having money problems. Bob said that if I gave Martin $5,000, Martin would invite us to the Broadway parties and introduce us to celebrities. I told Bob it was ridiculous and that I would never pay someone for that. I mentioned that I probably knew more people in the theater world than he did. Bob still introduced us to Martin, and I discovered that he was indeed a very charming and likable man. Even though I never gave Martin any money, we became good friends.

Martin became involved in the production of the original *Chicago* show on Broadway. Even though Martin was gay, he managed to solve his money problems by marrying Mary Lea Johnson, one of the heirs to the Johnson and Johnson fortune. She became his producing partner, using her funds to back his productions. It was a strange marriage, but in his way, Martin actually loved and cared for Mary

Lea. She was considerably older than him and somewhat of a lost soul, but Martin made her happy. She had been married before, and her previous husband was also gay and had an affair with their male chauffeur. When Mary met Martin, the ex-husband hired a hit man to murder them so he could collect her money. The hit man was stopped by security when he tried to break into the home, and Mary Lea and Martin brought charges against her ex, but he was never convicted. When Mary Lea died in 1990, she left $50 million to Martin in her will. The rest of the Johnson and Johnson family sued him for the next dozen years, but he eventually won in court.

When the movie version of *Chicago* was made, Martin owned the rights, and he produced the film along with Harvey Weinstein. He told us that he had constant battles with Weinstein while making the film, but it ended up winning an Oscar for Best Picture in 2003. We became good friends with Martin; his wife, Mary Lea; and the boyfriend Martin kept on the side.

Martin was a great host and had a magnificent home in Southampton. He threw all-day parties every Sunday with hundreds of people in attendance. At the end of one summer filled with weekly parties, we were talking to Martin upstairs in his bedroom while he looked down at all the people gathered around his pool. He confided to us that he felt somewhat saddened by the fact that he didn't know most of the people attending his parties. He remarked that he was reaching a point in his life where he would rather just go out for a quiet dinner with friends like us. He reminded me somewhat of Jay Gatsby, from the book *The Great Gatsby*. He did, however, have many loyal and good friends. When he died, Chita Rivera hosted a wonderful memorial for him at the Edison Ballroom. All the theater marquees were dimmed on the night of November 27, 2012, in honor of his passing.

Doris and Kevin Hurley were a couple whom we spent a lot of time with when they stayed in Westhampton during the summer season. Doris's parents, Reuben and Rose Mattus, were the founders of Häagen-Dazs ice cream. Reuben's family began making ice cream when he was a small child. They came to the USA from Poland in the 1920s. In 1959, Reuben decided to form an ice cream company that made a heavy kind of ice cream. He invented a Dutch-sounding name for his ice cream company in tribute to the way the Dutch helped the Jewish people during the Second World War. Doris worked in the company along with her family and met Kevin, who was the product manager of the company. They sold the company to Pillsbury for $70 million in 1983 and stayed on as consultants until another company bought it from Pillsbury.

When we met them in Westhampton, they were about to launch a new family company named after Doris's father, called Mattus Ice Cream. Their concept was to duplicate the Häagen-Dazs flavors using low-fat ice cream. They stored giant freezers in the basement area of their home and experimented with different flavors. We loved going over with our kids and participating in tasting each new low-fat ice cream flavor. We would leave their home with containers of Mattus ice cream every time we saw them. Ironically, even though the flavors were similar to Häagen-Dazs without the high calories, somehow the public did not go for it. People wanted the high calories and name recognition of Häagen-Dazs so Mattus was not a success.

They had a talented son who was a singer, and we tried to introduce him to as many connections as possible. When they sold their Westhampton home and moved permanently to New Jersey, we lost contact with them. We still have fond memories of the time we spent together, and our family still raves about the low-calorie ice cream.

Denise Rich is another longtime friend whom we hardly see because she moved to Europe. Denise was married to Marc Rich, a billionaire commodities trader. He was indicted in the United States on federal charges of tax evasion and making oil deals with Iran during the Iranian hostage drama. He was in Switzerland at the time of the charges and never returned to the United States. Pres. Bill Clinton pardoned Marc on his last day in office, and it was later revealed that Marc had made large donations to the Democratic Party through his ex-wife, Denise. Marc's tax evasion case, at that time, was the largest in US history.

When they divorced, Marc gave Denise $500 million. She had an amazing apartment on Fifth Avenue in the Sherry-Netherland Hotel that had a wraparound terrace on one floor. One Christmas she had a party and turned her terrace into an ice-skating rink so people could skate around outside her apartment. On another floor of her triplex apartment, she had a recording studio. Denice was a songwriter and collaborated with many well-known singer-songwriters. Some collaborated with her partly because they could have free use of her recording studio. When our daughter, Lauren, got married, Denise teamed up with Neil Sedaka to write and perform an original song for her at the wedding.

Denise, with all her wealth, is a very simple and lovely person. One of her daughters died tragically from leukemia, and every year Denise organizes a huge charity event in New York to raise funds for cancer. She has written songs that were recorded by Sister Sledge, Celine Dion, Natalie Cole, Patti LaBelle, Chaka Khan, Diana Ross, Mary J. Blige, Billy Porter, and Marc Anthony. We have had terrific times with her, including a memorable cruise on a boat she chartered where we enjoyed a great day with Natalie Cole and Patti LaBelle. In 2011, Denise gave up her American citizenship and moved to Europe, so we rarely see her. We caught up with her recently on the phone because Denise wanted us to ask Liza Minnelli about doing a video for her next charity event.

Luigi was an American jazz dancer, teacher, choreographer, and innovator who created the Luigi jazz exercise technique. He is a legend in dance, and numerous famous performers have gone to his New York studio at some time in their career. Liza Minnelli first introduced Arlene to Luigi's studio in New York City many decades ago. Going to his classes daily has been a major part of Arlene's life, and she rarely misses a day. When Liza lived in New York City, Arlene would pick her up every morning in a taxi, and they would attend class together at eleven o'clock. Liza is now living in LA, but Arlene still goes almost every day. Luigi died at age ninety in 2015, but his protégé Francis Roach is following in his footsteps and continues to teach the Luigi jazz technique in NYC today. Francis is an exceptionally talented teacher, devoted to his profession, and is carrying on Luigi's legacy.

Luigi developed techniques, which consist of a series of ballet-based exercises, for his rehabilitation after suffering paralyzing injuries in a car accident at the age of twenty-one. The doctors told him that he would never walk again, and he was in a coma for many months. Conventional therapy could not help him, but he developed a series of stretches and self-therapy that allowed him to not only walk but also dance again. Luigi was the person who invented the phrase "five, six, seven, eight" that every dancer uses as a lead-in to their dance. In 1949, Luigi auditioned for the MGM movie musical *On the Town*. Gene Kelly was so impressed with Luigi's dancing that he hired him for the movie, despite his partial face paralysis and crossed eyes that remained from his accident. Gene also put Luigi in his movie *Singin' in the Rain*. They became lifelong friends, and Gene warmed up using Luigi's techniques and recommended many other dancers to follow the Luigi technique. Soon his reputation as a wonderful dance instructor led him to open his own studio in New York City. Many dance instructors all over the world follow his technique.

Almost every well-known dancer and many Broadway performers have taken classes with Luigi. Arlene has spent enjoyable times with many of Luigi's students, both in and out of class. Ben Vereen, Tony Roberts, Robert Morse, Stefanie Powers, Donna McKechnie, and Valerie Harper are some of those people. When Valerie Harper was diagnosed with inoperable cancer and given only months to live, she went back to regular sessions at Luigi. We spent time with her during and after classes and found her to be a wonderful and charming person. She wound up living for many years, despite the poor prognosis.

After Ben Vereen had his automobile accident, he had trouble with his balance and went back to Luigi for classes. This helped him greatly, and Ben was able to continue his career. We have had shared emotional moments with Ben over the years, and he and Arlene have a special bond from going to classes together.

When Liza Minnelli had trouble walking after a bad attack of encephalitis, Luigi helped restore her movement through his techniques. One year after Luigi worked with her, Liza won a Tony for her singing and dancing on Broadway. Many of the people in Luigi's class, now run by Francis Roach, are not professional dancers. Like Arlene, they enjoy jazz dancing and the exercises. Some, like Tony Roberts and Robert Morse, are actors who just want to learn how to move well on a Broadway stage.

One of the friends Arlene met in class recently is a very well-known novelist named Talia Carner. She is an author, whose recent book on Jewish women sold into sex slavery has become a bestseller. Besides enjoying her exercise and jazz dancing, Arlene has met many very interesting people at her dance class, and it has kept her body limber.

CHAPTER

SIXTY-SIX

Final Thoughts

I am writing this while quarantined with my family at our home in Westhampton Beach during the COVID-19 pandemic. This pandemic has temporarily completely changed our lifestyle. Instead of going out to restaurants, shows, and clubs, we have been staying in with the family. Even though we miss seeing our friends, the quarantine has turned out to be a wonderful family time. We have been living the past five months with all four of our grandchildren, our son, our daughter, and their respective significant others. Family lunches and dinners at the house have been an excellent bonding experience for all of us. It has taught me to count my blessings for having such a fantastic family.

Fortunately, through the telephone and the internet, I have been able to keep in contact with many people mentioned in this book. We speak to Julie Budd, Shelley Goldberg, Tony Danza, Neil Sedaka,

Liza Minnelli, and Lorna Luft weekly. We have frequent conversations with Obba Babatundé about the state of the world and our families. Besides talking regularly to Neil, I get a chance to "see" him because he is doing miniconcerts of his songs every day on his Facebook page. Many of our friends in the entertainment business are not working due to the pandemic. Some are singing at home and posting their performances on Facebook and Instagram. Besides personal text messages, emails, and phone calls, I have been able to enjoy friends like Nicolas King, Billy Stritch, Jim Caruso, Ann Hampton Callaway, Steve Tyrell, Clint Holmes, Storm Large, Lorna Luft, Erich Bergen, Obba Babatundé, Neil Sedaka, Sheryl Lee Ralph, Julie Budd, Barry Manilow, Michael Feinstein, and others as they entertain from home.

There have been many wonderful conversations with Michael Feinstein and his husband, Terrence Flannery, about how much we all miss one another. We speak for hours at a time to Lorna Luft about our respective families. Lorna has a magnetic personality and is one of the best conversationalists that we have known. We have always believed Lorna will be a terrific talk show host. Our phone conversations with her often last for hours. Lorna has experienced health issues, battling cancer for a number of years, but she is doing great. She has become inspirational to many and has been a source of advice for others. When Lauren was going through a divorce, Lorna gave her a gift of a large key on a necklace chain. Lorna told Lauren that she understood what she was going through, having been through a divorce herself, and that she should think positive and that the key was symbolic as a key to her new life.

We keep in regular contact with Sheryl Lee Ralph and Lindsay Wagner, both of whom have helped give career advice to our granddaughter, Sydney, who wants to be an actress and screenwriter. Sheryl is another friend who will be great as a talk show host because she has a very outgoing personality.

Storm Large had been quarantining herself at her home in Portland, Oregon, and giving regular free concerts online. She called to tell us that she was planning on driving from Portland to New York by herself. She wanted to come and spend time with us in Westhampton and, a few weeks ago, arrived at our home. Because of the pandemic, she put a mattress in her large SUV and parked in our driveway. She joined our family for meals outside on our deck and slept comfortably in her car at night so we could social-distance.

She arrived the night our daughter, Lauren, became engaged to Seth Ratner. He is a wonderful, outstanding guy, and they make a fabulous couple. Storm serenaded the newly engaged couple, singing her magnificent original song "Stand up for Me." It is a moving song about love, and she promised to return to sing it again at their wedding. (Lorna's key worked and did open a wonderful door for Lauren.)

Julie Budd's fiancé and our great friend, Dr. John Wagner, is a well-respected and outstanding nephrologist and the head of a hospital in Brooklyn. Because of his daily exposure to hospital patients and personnel, they have not been able to see each other, but we all stay in close contact by phone.

We keep in touch with friends who run clubs and restaurants like Gianni Valenti, who owns Birdland; Jim Caruso, who handles regular entertainment shows there; Michael Feinstein, who has clubs in many cities; Sal at Patsy's; and many others. Their loss of business is hard, and the loss of jobs for the performers is overwhelming. Michael Feinstein and his husband, Terrence Flannery, were due to stay with us this past August when he was scheduled to perform at our local theater in Westhampton. Lorna Luft was planning on staying with us this past June when she was booked at Feinstein's/54 Below nightclub in New York City. Every August for forty-five years, Julie Budd comes to spend a week at our home in Westhampton. For the past two decades, she has been joined by her fiancé, John Wagner. Our friends from Montreal, Bryant and Lillian Shiller, stay with us every August as well. We canceled our plans to see Barry Manilow in Las Vegas. We looked forward to spending time there with him and Garry, but those shows have been canceled as well. Steve Tyrell was coming to our local theater in Westhampton this past July, and that too was canceled. We missed having Tony Danza with us in Westhampton this summer. We love having him cook and play his ukulele on our back deck.

We had to cancel our trip to Italy to see Gina Lollobrigida in September. Gina has spent so much time living with us in New York City that, to this day, her royalty checks from old movies still come to her at our home address. Mike Tadross and Georgia Witkin live near us in the Hamptons, so we are able to see them and social-distance on their back deck. All film production is on hold for now during the pandemic. They are anxiously waiting for it to resume so Mike can return to his movie-producing commitments. Our friend Michele

Lee just lost her husband, but in this time of the COVID-19, there are no regular funerals for people to attend. We speak regularly to Ginny Mancini, who at age ninety-six is still a dynamo. She has been able to experience quality time with her family in Malibu and still loves her Bombay Sapphire cocktails while enjoying good health.

Instead of our Hampton parties this summer, we have been loving our time with the family. Our son, Marc, just texted me today requesting that we keep the Westhampton home open all year round. He wanted to continue gathering the family together here for dinners this fall and winter. That was the best compliment Arlene and I could hear.

We used to spend some winter nights in Westhampton and have working fireplaces in our living room and bedroom. Many years ago, we went with Liza Minnelli to hear a fabulous Brazilian singer. She was terrific, and after her performance, she gave us albums of her music. Her music was very sensual with a haunting rhythm. The following night, we drove out to Westhampton and decided to light our bedroom fireplace, put on this sexy CD, and make love. We had some drinks and began our lovemaking, heightened by the wonderful music. For the first time in my life, I actually heard bells go off while in the throes of passion. I was somewhat amazed at this until I began smelling smoke. It seemed that I had closed rather than opened the fireplace flue, and smoke billowing into our bedroom set off the fire alarm.

As the smoke started to fill up the room, I managed to get a towel and open the flue, letting out the smoke. It ended our evening of passion, and the next week, I had a painter repaint the walls of the bedroom. Our downstairs fireplace had a flue that opened up by pushing it, and I forgot that the upstairs fireplace flue opened by pulling it. We were so traumatized that it was the last time we used the fireplace in our bedroom.

It feels good to know that, with our complex and sometimes frantic lifestyle, we were able to raise such wonderful children and grandchildren in a home filled with love. Last night was a perfect example of our unique lifestyle. We wanted to introduce our grandchildren to the film *Cabaret*, for which Liza Minnelli won her Academy Award. We rented the film on TV, and our children and grandchildren all watched it together. It is a terrific movie, and they all loved it. Even my grandson Hunter, who is more a fan of athletics than movie musicals, was thrilled by the film. When it ended, we picked up the phone and called Liza. Each member of our family got on the phone with her and had a chance to tell her how much they enjoyed it. She told each of us how much our comments meant to her and how happy she was to talk to everyone. We have been best friends with her for forty-seven years, and it was a touching example of our being able to combine our family life with our friendships with amazingly talented people.

As I am writing this last sentence, my grandson Devin just called Arlene and me over to look at his iPhone. He told me that Arlene had thousands of people commenting about her today on Twitter and Instagram. It seems they featured her wearing a very dramatic outfit on last night's episode of *The Real Housewives of New York*. Thousands of viewers wanted to know more about her. Our grandchildren are hysterical that Arlene is trending on Twitter. Some current comments are "That's the NYC legend Arlene Lazare—theater producer & BFF with Liza Minnelli," "I need a spin-off, Arlene and Liza," "Where do you find such a spectacle of an outfit?" "She appears every season—an icon," "Can we get her in more dinner party scenes?" "I don't know Arlene but I want to," "She seems fascinating," "I kept asking my boyfriend, who is that woman!" "Yes! What a fashion statement," "OMG I just posted the same thing—OBSESSED," "I need more Arlene," "She should be a cast member," "Who is this woman?" "I need more information on Arlene," and so on. In response to the thousands of comments was my grandson Devin's tweet "That's my grandma." And everyone thought he was kidding.

Acknowledgments

I cannot properly express in words my appreciation for the help my wife, Arlene, has given me in the preparation of this book. She has spent countless hours checking my grammar, punctuation, and sentence structure. She has been with me for most of my journey in life and has helped me in the remembrances of our shared experiences. Without her input, I would not have been able to properly convey my stories and thoughts. She has been the love of my life and my partner in every aspect of my existence. There is no way that I can thank her enough for her time and efforts. I'm writing during a pandemic, so I certainly can't go shopping for jewelry. These words of praise will have to do for now until the stores reopen.

Another person who was invaluable to me in this project is my grandson Devin Shell. His help with the technical aspects involved in writing this book, including adding photographs, has been fantastic. I cannot thank him enough for actually taking a break from his Xbox games whenever I asked him for his technical help. He is a brilliant young man who has a bright future ahead of him, and I love him very much.

My daughter, Lauren Shell, was an invaluable help in editing this book as well. Her training at Yale Law School in reading complicated documents and her great intelligence allowed her to not only fix typos and grammar mistakes but also pick up the many times I repeated myself throughout the writing of this book (even though I did not always take her advice). Her suggestions were of immense help to me, and had I allowed her more time to reorganize and condense the book so as not to repeat myself as much as she suggested, the book would flow more easily. However, by not doing that, I allowed the reader to see my main fault, my impatience. Once I started writing down my thoughts, I just could not wait to finish the book. I guess when it is safe to go shopping again after the pandemic, my gratitude to Lauren and her mother will help improve the economy.

I also want to thank my extremely talented and creative granddaughter, Sydney Lazare, for her book cover design. She is a marvelous artist, and I love her caricature of Arlene and me.

9 781698 706030